SECOND EDITION

SERVICE MANAGEMENT PRINCIPLES

FOR HOSPITALITY AND TOURISM

Kendall Hunt
publishing company

Jay Kandampully, Ph.D. | David Solnet, Ph.D.
The Ohio State University   The University of Queensland
Australia

BRIEF CONTENTS

Introduction   xv
Acknowledgments   xvii
About the Authors   xix

Chapter 1
Introduction: The Metamorphosis of Service   1

Chapter 2
The Nature of Service   21

Chapter 3
Service Quality   51

Chapter 4
Understanding and Engaging Customers   85

Chapter 5
Service Vision, Service Design and The Service Encounter   113

Chapter 6
Service Marketing: Managing Customer Experiences and Relationships   155

Chapter 7
Service Guarantees, Service Failure and Service Recovery   195

Chapter 8
Managing and Engaging Employees in Service Organizations   223

Chapter 9
Leadership for Service Organizations   249

Chapter 10
Bringing Service Management to Life! Case Studies of Best Practice   283

References   323
Index   343

CONTENTS

Introduction..xv
Acknowledgments...xvii
About the Authors.. xix

1. **Introduction: The Metamorphosis of Service**......................1

   Study Objectives 1
   Outline 1
   Key Words 2

   Introduction... 2
   The service economy 4
   Growth in the service sector 5
   The scope/context of this book....................................... 7
   Global tourism and hospitality 7
      The growing importance of tourism...................... 7
      Changing patterns of tourism............................ 8
      Changing patterns in hospitality 9
      Hospitality and tourism as service industries 9
   Origins of the service management framework 11
   Evolving from product management to service management 12
   Servitization 13
   Interdependency of service provision............................. 14
      Coordinated benefits.................................. 14
      Components of a tourism service....................... 15
      Service interrelationship 15
      Core and peripheral services......................... 16
   Applying service management theory 17

   Summary 18
   Review Questions 19
   Suggested Readings 20

2. **The Nature of Service** **21**

Study Objectives 21
Outline 21
Key Words 22

Introduction 23
Differences between products and service 23
  Intangibility *24*
  Heterogeneity *26*
  Inseparability (of production and consumption) *28*
  Perishability *32*
Management implications for 'IHIP' 35
  Implications with intangibility *36*
  Implications with heterogeneity *39*
  Implications with perishability *40*
  Managing service supply and demand *40*

Summary 48
Review Questions 48
Suggested Readings 49

3. **Service Quality** **51**

Study Objectives 51
Outline 51
Key Words 52

Introduction 53
An historic perspective on quality 54
  The early days of quality control *54*
  Post-war (World War II) developments *54*
Economic impact of quality—Why quality is important 55
  Product differentiation and competitive advantage *56*
  Market share and profitability *56*
  The cost of quality—Is it worth it? *57*
The quality 'gurus' 57
  W. Edwards Deming (1900–1993) *58*
  Joseph M. Juran (1904–2008) *59*
  Philip Crosby (1926–2001) *59*
The core ideas of 'total quaility management' TQM 60

Uniqueness of quality theory for service 61
    Lacking a philosophy or conceptualization of service quality. *61*
    But service is different *61*
    Looking to the customer. *62*
Outcomes of service quality 62
    Customer satisfaction. *62*
    Customer loyalty. *63*
    The relationship between satisfaction and loyalty *64*
    Customer delight *65*
Understanding service quality theory 66
    Comparing expectations and performance *66*
    Confirmation and disconfirmation of expectations *66*
    Meeting or exceeding expectations *67*
    The effect of multiple consumption. *68*
Service quality measurement—No easy task 69
    The 'Nordic' model (technical quality and functional quality) *70*
    Two-dimensional model (process and output quality) *73*
    The 'Gaps' model *76*
SERVQUAL 77
SERVPERF (multi-level models) 80
Electronic (web) service quality 81

Summary 81
Review Questions 82
Suggested Readings 83

4.   Understanding and Engaging Customers **85**

Study Objectives 85
Outline 85
Key Words 86

Introduction. 86
The importance of understanding customers 87
Evolution of the customer centricity concept within the literature. 89
Guestology 90
Categories of customers 91
    External customers. *92*
    Internal customers *106*

Implications for quality. 108
    Employee research *108*
    Inseparability makes employees important *108*
    Management involvement. *109*
    Employees as customer 'advocates'. *109*
    Making it work effectively *110*

Summary 110
Review Questions 111
Suggested Readings 112

5.   Service Vision, Service Design and the Service Encounter. 113

Study Objectives 113
Outline 113
Key Words 115

Introduction. 115
Service vision 119
    What is vision? *119*
    Vision statement vs. mission statement. *119*
    What is a service vision? *120*
    Set apart from the rest *120*
    Ingrained into the fabric. *121*
    Customer-focus. *121*
Service strategy. 123
    What is strategy? *123*
    What is a service strategy?. *123*
    Everyone is involved. *123*
Service process 124
    What is a service process? *124*
    Process as the 'essence' of service. *125*
    Service system. *126*
    Process quality and output quality. *126*
    Ultimately a management responsibility *127*
Alignment: Vision, strategy, process and system 127
Service system design. 128
    Perfecting the service system through design *128*
    What is service design? *129*
    Inbuilt flaws *130*
    Design is a dynamic process *132*
    Creative thinking *133*

Some practical examples 134
   Restaurants.. *135*
   Hotels *136*
   Leisure tourism *137*
The service encounter....................................... 138
   Service encounter triad *139*
   Managing the service encounter *140*
Service blueprinting 146
   Leading to a 'moment of truth'....................... *146*
   The nature of a service blueprint *146*
   A 'snapshot' of a dynamic process.................... *147*
   The 'line of visibility' *147*
   'Fail points' and 'encounter points'................. *149*
   Looking back and looking ahead....................... *149*
   Blueprints within blueprints......................... *150*
   Dreams and reality................................... *150*
   'Moments of truth' remain crucial *152*

Summary 152
Review Questions 153
Suggested Readings 154

6.   **Service Marketing: Managing Customer Experiences** **155**
     and Relationships

Study Objectives 155
Outline... 155
Key Words 157

Introduction... 158
Towards a new marketing paradigm........................... 159
   What does marketing do?.............................. *159*
   How does marketing work? *159*
   A new integrated paradigm of service marketing. *160*
Integrating operations, marketing and human resources 161
   Marketing 'distance' in manufactured goods........... *161*
   Marketing 'experience' in service *162*
   Customer experience *163*
   Impact of pre-, during- and post-consumption of service *163*
   Operations, marketing and human resources. *167*

An extended marketing mix for service 168
    A new formulation required *168*
    Product *170*
    Price *170*
    Promotion *172*
    Place *174*
    People *175*
    Physical evidence *176*
    Process *178*
Building and managing relationships and experiences 180
Delivering the service promise—the critical 'moment of truth' 180
    The 'cascade' in 'moments of truth' *181*
'Internal' marketing 183
    Compete for talent *186*
    Offer a vision *186*
    Prepare people to perform *186*
Relationship and experience marketing 187
    Why are relationships important in service organizations? *187*
    History of relationship marketing *188*
    Service innovation through customer engagement *190*
    All relationships and experiences matter *191*

Summary 192
Review Questions 192
Suggested Readings 193

7.   Service Guarantees, Service Failure and Service Recovery 195

Study Objectives 195
Outline 195
Key Words 196

Introduction 197
Service superiority: the basis for a competitive advantage 198
    Reliability as the core of service quality *198*
    Perceptions of value *198*
    The two-way nature of 'loyalty' *199*
    Empowering employees to 'break the rules' to do the right thing ... *200*
Service failure 201
    Types of service failures *201*
    Recognizing service failures *202*

Strategies for a competitive advantage 203
   Service guarantees *204*
   Service recovery *211*
   Learning from the experience *216*
   The importance of complementary strategies: guarantees,
     empowerment and recovery *217*
Coordinating the strategies for a competitive advantage 218
   Step 1: Identifying 'fail points' *219*
   Step 2: Establishing and guaranteeing service standards *219*
   Step 3: Ensuring employee skills *219*
   Step 4: Developing a recovery strategy *219*
   Step 5: Obtaining feedback *220*

Summary 220
Review Questions 221
Suggested Readings 222

8. **Managing and Engaging Employees in Service Organizations** **223**

Study Objectives 223
Outline 223
Key Words 224

Introduction 224
Setting the benchmark 226
Organizational psychology 227
What is human resource management (HRM)? 227
HRM in a service context 229
Why is HRM important? 230
   Emotional labor *230*
   The internal work environment *231*
Effective HRM practices 235
   Empowerment *235*
Benefits of effective HRM practices 240
   Employee engagement *240*
   Organizational commitment *242*
Links between people, customers and firm performance 243
   Service-profit chain *243*
   Internal service quality *244*

Summary 245
Review Questions 245
Suggested Readings 246

9.   Leadership for Service Organizations **249**

Study Objectives 249
Outline 249
Key Words 250

Introduction. 251
Defining leadership. 252
The leader as more than a manager 253
The leader who serves with style 254
   Situational leadership. *254*
   The transactional leader *255*
   The transformational leader. *256*
   The servant leader *257*
The leader as an emotionally intelligent person 258
   Defining emotional intelligence *258*
   The importance of emotional intelligence *258*
   The history of emotional intelligence. *260*
   The latest understanding of emotional intelligence *261*
   The links between emotional intelligence and leadership *261*
The leader as an authentic person. 263
The leader as a team builder. 265
   Defining teams, team development and team leadership *266*
   Fostering team effectiveness *266*
   Diagnosing a team *267*
   Dysfunctions in a team. *267*
   Team dynamics *268*
   Leading a high-performance team. *268*
   A team charter *268*
The leader as an ethical exemplar and trust builder 269
   Being ethical as a leader *269*
   Being trustworthy as a leader *271*
The leader as a change agent 272
   Leading change *273*
   Being a transformational change agent. *274*
The leader as a strategist and culture builder 275
An integrating model of service leadership 277

Conclusion 278
Final Story 278

Summary 279
Review Questions 280
Suggested Readings 281

10. **Bringing Service Management to Life!** **283**
     Case Studies of Best Practice

Outline 283
Introduction 284
Case studies from Australasia 285
     1. Long Beach Hotel, Mauritius *285*
     2. Cactus Jack's Restaurants, Australia *288*
     3. Emporium Hotel, Australia *291*
     4. Spicers Retreats, Australia *294*
     5. Haidilao, China *296*
     6. Hotel ICON, Hong Kong *299*
     7. Pun Pun Sustainable Living and Learning Centre, Thailand . . . *302*
Case studies from Europe 306
     8. Bio-Hotel Stanglwirt, Austria *306*
     9. Best Western Premier (BWP) Hotel Slon, Slovenia *307*
     10. Strand Spa and Conference Hotel, Estonia *311*
Case studies from North America 313
     11. Starbucks, United States of America *313*
     12. Four Seasons Hotels and Resorts, United States of America . . . *315*
     13. Cameron Mitchell Restaurants, United States of America *317*
     14. The Greenbrier, United States of America *319*

Summary 321
Suggested Readings 322

References 323

Index 343

INTRODUCTION

This is a management textbook about a special and vital kind of management—service management. The content of this book was developed through many years of teaching service management mainly to hospitality and tourism management students.

Our research and teaching interests and, more importantly, our industry experience, has led us to believe that service management theory provides a vital theoretical and conceptual framework that has near perfect applicability in hospitality and tourism. We know of only a precious few resources such as this that provide a framework for applying service management theory to hospitality and tourism.

Our shared philosophy for this textbook is to convey our own journey through service management and the way in which our passion for this subject has developed over the years. Both of us, after many years of industry/management professional experiences, were introduced to service management principles during our doctoral studies. We both realized that there was something special about service management and its applicability to hospitality and tourism. Our mission ever since has been to explore this passion, to continue to learn, and to make sharing this passion a life commitment. This book is one vehicle upon which we share our passion with others.

We realize that there are many business courses in your study program that are also important. Who can manage a business without accounting and financial management skills? Marketing skills? Understanding business law? But in today's business world, dominated by the service sector, the standard management principles of yesterday are simply insufficient. They are *necessary*—but there is a new management fundamental—service management—that any student, particularly with aspirations for working in a service sector such as hospitality and tourism—must fully understand and embrace.

This book introduces you to a range of interrelated topics which are fundamentally critical to success in service enterprises. These principles apply not only to service businesses, as nearly every business today has multiple service components embedded within their offer. Businesses can be primary service providers, or can use service as an important way to add value and gain competitive advantage and differentiation.

You will notice that many of the topics in this book are interrelated. Like Ghandi once said about the human body, "it is all connected . . . you cannot have a problem in one part of the body that does not affect the rest . . ." So bringing the topics of this textbook into the best possible sequence was challenging. We hope readers will find the sequence we have chosen logical. Please let us know your suggestions as we continue to evolve this book.

The title of this book includes the word *'principles'*. This is intentional, as we believe this book provides a sound set of principles of service management. *Why principles?* Many of us remember our science training in school, such as chemistry. To learn chemistry requires some very basic understanding of the basic elements on the 'periodic table of elements'. Similarly, athletes cannot become elite in any sport without first learning the basics. This book is about the principles—the basics—of service management. Without sound knowledge and mastery of these basics, it is not possible to effectively and efficiently manage a service organization.

This book is a journey, surveying many topics covering operations, marketing, and human resources—all of which are capable of being effectively incorporated into any hospitality and tourism organization. Each chapter begins with a helpful framework of the contents of the chapter, and ends with a concise summary, review questions and a selected reading list for that chapter. A full reference bibliography and a comprehensive index complete the book.

Finally—this book will have a web portal. We encourage instructors to use the portal for access to PowerPoints, updated readings and further practice questions.

Thank you for allowing us the opportunity to share our passion with you!

With our warmest regards,

Jay Kandampully and David Solnet

ACKNOWLEDGMENTS

Writing a textbook requires effort and sacrifice from many. Those closest to us, our families, often give up time to support the efforts put forth. Jay acknowledges Ria's continued love and encouragement. David offers his heartfelt thanks to his wife Barbara and daughter Lola for their endless understanding (and tolerance) about the time commitment required for undertaking this task.

This textbook was enormously benefited from some invaluable research support. In particular, we acknowledge two recent graduates from The University of Queensland—Siobhan Freyne from Brisbane, Australia and Maria Golubovskaya from Moscow, Russia. Both of these former service management students became passionate about the topic, and were integral in this significant revision to the first edition, written over twelve years ago. They helped revise references, assisted with the development of new topics, searched for new stories and anecdotes to support the introduction of ideas and theories, helped with the development of the cases, assisted with the flow of each chapter, helped with indexing, tables of contents and performed many other vital tasks.

We also acknowledge and thank Ms. Tingting (Christina Zhang) at The Ohio State University, a PhD candidate. She was a vital contributor of five cases and sourced many other pieces of information. Greg Latemore, a consultant and leadership expert, so kindly assisted in the development and writing one of the new chapters (Chapter 9—"Leadership for Service Organizations").

And finally, we thank our students who inspire us through the way we 'cocreate' excitement for this subject in the classroom, and of course our hundreds of service management academic colleagues who endlessly stoke our knowledge through their research and presentations at conferences.

ABOUT THE AUTHORS

Jay Kandampully Ph.D., is professor of service management and hospitality at The Ohio State University, USA. He is the Editor in Chief of the *Journal of Service Management,* and serves on the editorial advisory board of 12 refereed international journals. Jay also serves as the CTF International Fellow at the University of Karlstad, Sweden, and International Fellow at the University of Namur, Belgium. He holds a PhD in service management, and an MBA, with a specialization in services marketing, both from the University of Exeter, England. Jay is the author of the book "Services Management: The New Paradigm in Hospitality" (translated into Chinese). He is also editor of the following books: "Service Management: The New Paradigm in Retailing" (trans- lated into Chinese); "Service Management in Health & Wellness Services"; "Customer Experience Management: Enhancing Experience and Value through Service Management"; and, the lead editor of the book, "Service Quality Management in Hospitality, Tourism and Leisure" (translated into Chinese, Korean and Arabic). Jay has published over 130 articles. His publications have appeared in journals such as: Journal of Service Management, European Journal of Marketing, Cornell Hospitality Quarterly, The Service Industries Journal, Journal of Services Marketing, Managing Service Quality, Journal of Consumer Behaviour, and The Journal of Product & Brand Management.

David Solnet, Ph.D., is an associate professor of service management and hospitality at The University of Queensland's Business School in Brisbane, Australia. He is also the managing director of Shift Directions, a management consulting firm specializing in business improvement programs, financial analysis, service quality improvement and management development programs. David comes from a restaurant management background, with 18 years of experience including senior management roles in the USA and Australia. His research, teaching and consulting all focus on man- aging and leading service organizations, with particular emphasis on managing the employee-customer interface through various organizational psychology lenses. He has published widely in leading academic journals, book chapters and trade publications in the areas of service management, managing and motivating service employees and organizational service climate.

CHAPTER 1

Introduction:
The Metamorphosis of Service

Study Objectives

Having completed this chapter, readers should be able to:

1. Understand the growing importance of service industries in the modern economy, with particular emphasis on the hospitality and tourism sectors.
2. Have a clear understanding about the complex nature of service and of the concept of service management.
3. Understand the evolution of management from traditional or manufacturing focused management to service management.
4. Be clear about the interconnections among tourism, hospitality and service.
5. Understand the cross-functional nature of services within service provision and the interdependence of service providers in both the hospitality and tourism industries.

Outline

- ► Introduction
- ► The service economy
- ► Growth in the service sector
- ► The scope/context of this book
- ► Global tourism and hospitality
  - ► The growing importance of tourism
  - ► Changing patterns of tourism
  - ► Changing patterns in hospitality
  - ► Hospitality and tourism as service industries
    - ▪ Basic components of hospitality

- ▶ Origins of the service management framework
- ▶ Evolving from product management to service management
- ▶ Servitization
- ▶ Interdependency of service provision
  - ▶ Coordinated benefits
    - ▪ Components of a tourism service
    - ▪ Service interrelationship
    - ▪ Core and peripheral services
- ▶ Applying service management theory
- ▶ Summary
- ▶ Review Questions
- ▶ Suggested Readings

Key Words

Service bundles	Service bundling
Combination of services	Service economy
Commercial hospitality and tourism	Service interrelationship
Core and Peripheral services	Service management
Cross-functional systems	Service marketing
Customer engagement	Service moments
Customer-oriented, service-focused	Service packages
enterprises	Services
Ernest Engel's model	Servitization
Essence of hospitality	Support services
Evolution of Service Management	Technological innovations
Marketing mix 7Ps	Total Experience
Product management	Value cocreation
Service advantage	

Introduction

You may have realized that the world economy is dominated by the service sector. In fact, the service sector permeates the daily existence of every person. Can you think of a job that does not involve working with either a fellow employee or a customer? Can you think of anything you buy which does not have at least some service component to it? Within the past few hours, it is likely that the readers of this book will have listened to the radio, watched television, downloaded / listened to music or apps on iTunes, been to the cinema, taken a trip on a plane, cab or bus, used a mobile or smart phone, consumed a restaurant meal, used a bank, automatic teller machine or online banking for their financial needs, used a gym or observed a sporting event, made an appointment with a doctor or dentist, contacted an insurance agency, had weekly groceries delivered to their home, had contact with their local city council . . . In all of these cases, the ultimate end result for the consumer is a *service or value they received through service.*

What exactly do we mean when we refer to 'service'? Or 'services'? What seems on the surface as such simple words are anything but! Service is often defined as an act or a process (a verb), representing a form of economic exchange (Vargo and Akaka, 2009). Service*s* (with an 's') on the other hand are defined as intangible units of output, or activities (a noun) which in a commercial sense are offered for sale or as part of a sale (for example, restaurant service accompanies the food to form a total experience; both food and service are critical to the value perception of the customer).

We alert readers to the frequent interchanging of the terms service and services. In this text, we adopt the position that it is the managing of 'service' (i.e., managing the delivery of customer value which includes aspects of both tangible and intangible offering) which is the predominant focus for hospitality managers.

Service provision has many parts—including activities, processes and interactions (tangible and intangible aspects) (Kandampully, 2007). Take a hotel as an example. What is a guest buying? Is it a bed? Or is it the temporary use of a bed? Are they buying food? Beverage? The use of a meeting room? Or, are they buying a *total experience* which ideally includes a seamless check-in by friendly, welcoming, knowledgeable staff, a clean, safe and comfortable room and the convenience to eat in a restaurant or have food and beverage delivered to your room? A customer would view the entire offering as a *series of service encounters*. Be clear that the hotel industry is not so much about buildings, beds and food, but rather about service, and about the complexity of creating, selling and managing customer experiences. And as mentioned above, this can apply to a cluster of individual businesses that make up a destination as well.

Important note: This is a book about service *management*. The service literature is generally shared among marketing, operations and human resource management, and most of the concepts in this book can be viewed through either a marketing lens (putting the 'service' out to the customer) or a management lens (what happens inside the organization to make the service as good as it can be). We adopt the position that management is a more holistic term in service, incorporating *all* management functions, *including* marketing. This review will generally use the singular term 'management' throughout the text. Please remember that the applicability of the principles in this book apply perfectly well to either management or a marketing context. This review also makes frequent mention of the term 'customers'. It is important, in the context of tourism, to view 'tourists' or 'visitors' in the exact same context as 'customers' or even 'event attendees'. Therefore these terms are used interchangeably.

The service economy

The service economy plays a significant role in every nation in the world. The national economy of every country depends on its service-based infrastructure—including transportation, communication, education, health care and various government services (law enforcement, utilities, garbage collection).

In the second half of the twentieth century, economically developed nations have undergone extensive social and economic transformation, fueled through industrialization, leading to a significantly increased rate of spending on services. In the twenty-first century, advancement in technology has allowed advancing economies around the world to transform socially and economically, leading to the significant increased rate of spending on services. In the early 1950s, service expenditure accounted for approximately one-third of personal consumption expenditure. It now accounts for about one-half of household expenditure, and is expected to continue to rise. This trend is apparent in both developed and developing countries in the past thirty years. Figure 1.1 provides an illustration of the evaluation of total household expenditure in Australia since 1961. Although this figure shows

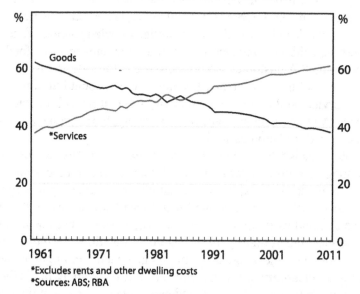

Nominal Expenditure Shares*
Per cent of total expenditure, annual

*Excludes rents and other dwelling costs
*Sources: ABS; RBA

Figure 1.1
Total household expenditure patterns in Australia by goods and services

figures for Australia, we note that the trend line is similar for nearly all developed and developing countries (although the percentages are often slightly different).

Ernest Engel, a German statistician and economist in the 1800s, undertook research that showed that prosperity and an increase in service infrastructure go together. More businesses undertake service-oriented activities—offering services either directly to the final customer, or to other business operations. The majority of the population within a community subsequently becomes employed in service-related activities. Services thus lie at the very hub of the economic activity of society. And we are only just beginning to understand the significance of this change in the way we live and work.

Engel's Seminal Research

Ernst Engel (1857) showed that an increase in family income has the following effects on spending behavior:

- the percentage of income spent on food decreases;
- the percentage of income spent on housing and household operations remains constant; and
- the percentage of income spent on other purchases (for example, education, health care, entertainment, recreation and transportation) increases rapidly.

On the basis of Engel's work it is apparent that, as an economy develops, services become increasingly significant.

Growth in the service sector

The dominance of service industries over the traditional 'primary' and 'secondary' industries (of agriculture, raw materials and manufacturing) has become a global economic phenomenon. Most developed economies have transformed from being farming, mining and manufacturing economies into service economies. The service sector in most of the developed economies (the USA, UK, Canada, Germany, France, Italy and Australia) contributes more than 70% of GDP, and offers employment to more than 75% of the population. According to the World Fact Book published by the Central Intelligence Agency (2011), the service sector currently accounts for over 63% of the world gross domestic product (GDP) and over 76% of the US GDP. Figures 1.2 and 1.3 provide evidence of the growing size and importance of the service sector.

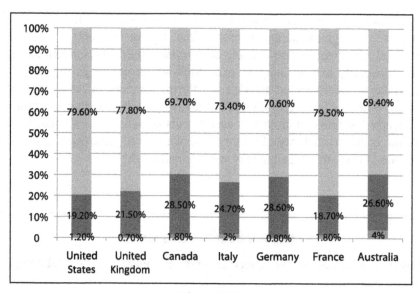

Figure 1.2

GDP composition by sector: Developed countries

SOURCE: developed based on statistics from CIA, 2011, https://www.cia.gov/library/publications/the-world-factbook/fields/2012.html#us

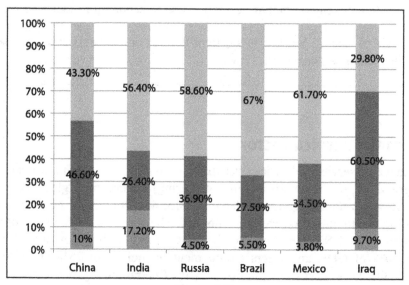

Figure 1.3

GDP composition by sector: Developing countries

SOURCE: developed based on statistics from CIA, 2011, https://www.cia.gov/library/publications/the-world-factbook/fields/2012.html#us

The scope/context of this book

There is a consensus that economic growth, a higher disposable income and technological advances have contributed to the rapid growth in the service sector. Moreover, this growth has not been at the expense of mining, farming or manufacturing. In fact, the service sector has become an enabling factor in assisting these primary and secondary industries to achieve global competitiveness. The internationally competitive market has compelled primary and secondary industries to transform themselves into truly customer-oriented, service-focused enterprises, irrespective of the products that they actually produce and sell. To note, while the service paradigm can be found and studied through various contexts, this textbook has a specific interest in looking at service management within a hospitality and tourism context.

This book is about management—but more specifically about the management of service organizations, drawing knowledge from the fields of *service management and marketing*. If you were studying business or hospitality or tourism even 20–25 years ago, it is not likely that you would have learned about service management because it is a relatively new field of practice and study. One of the aims of this book is to provide an introduction to this subject area because of its logical connection to the hospitality and tourism industries. The theories, frameworks and underpinnings of service management are a perfect fit for the hospitality and tourism industries, yet few other books exist that aim to connect these sectors to the service management framework.

Global tourism and hospitality

The growing importance of tourism

The tourism industry has become a crucial component of national economic development worldwide, with enormous potential to generate local income and employment. More recently, the United Nations World Tourism Organization (UNWTO) has described tourism as a crucial component of worldwide socio-economic development, particularly for developing countries where tourism is the primary export (UNWTO, 2012, p. 3). Government agencies in many countries therefore actively encourage

© Plus ONE/Shutterstock.com

tourism-related entrepreneurial projects, resulting in an increasing number of individuals and organizations venturing into tourism-related services. Tourism has undoubtedly become a major industry worldwide. Forecasts by the World Tourism Organization continue to predict strong growth in global tourism.

As indicated earlier, tourism now stands as one of the world's leading industries, with tourism's contribution to worldwide GDP estimated at around 5%, with total contribution to employment between 6–7%. For smaller and developing countries these figures tend to be much higher (UNWTO, 2012, p. 3).

Changing patterns of tourism

There are many reasons for the growth of tourism in the world economy, and while this issue is beyond the scope of this chapter (book), it is important to have an understanding of why managing service and service organizations are growing in importance. This point was well illustrated at the WTTC's (World Travel and Tourism Council—*http://www.wttc.org/*) 12th Global Summit in 2012. Frits van Paasschen, President and CEO of Starwood Hotels and Resorts Worldwide, noted that 3 billion people will be entering the middle classes over the next 30 years and that another level of travelers—the high end leisure group—are looking for new and exotic destinations.

Dr. Michael Frenzel, Chairman of the Word Travel and Tourism Corporation (WTTC), stated that there are three mega trends affecting the industry: the global shift, the digital shift and the relevance of real experience. The global shift toward developing countries such as India, Russia and China will generate a vast amount of tourists and contribute to the expanding tourism industry. This tourism growth will require a shift in focus to these new markets and their traveling behaviors, patterns and characteristics. The digital shift refers to the digital revolution and social media in particular and the many new opportunities for companies to reach out and build up loyal customers and create new advertising channels getting customers themselves to tell their story and therefore

© OlegD/Shutterstock.com

market to others. Finally, the relevance of customer experiences will always be integral to tourism. As much as we will depend on digital communication, nothing compares to the real thing. For example, there is no crisp, fresh mountain air that comes out of your computer.

Indeed, many changes, sociodemographic, technological, lifestyle, affluence and an active aging population with high spending power, have created a significant change in the social habits of tourists and of people in general. The influence of technology, demographics and lifestyle patterns are expected to continue and accelerate these trends in the present century and for many years to come, and this point is particularly salient in the context of hospitality and tourism.

Changing patterns in hospitality

In parallel with the global transformation of economies and tourism (see above), the hospitality industry has also become a truly global industry. Economic growth in most countries around the world has contributed to this growth in the hospitality industry, with economic prosperity contributing to dramatic changes in social habits.

Socializing outside the family circle has become more common, with the result that gatherings in restaurants, pubs, bars, cafés and so on have become part of everyday life for many people. Going out with friends and family has become a popular form of social entertainment. Changes in work schedules have produced changes in lifestyles. Whereas most people in previous generations lived very close to their workplaces, with their nearby homes providing food and lodging, people today tend to commute longer distances to work, requiring them to eat and seek lodging outside their homes.

© Bikeworldtravel/Shutterstock.com

Many people maintain more than one job to sustain their newly acquired lifestyles. These changes in social and working habits have contributed directly to changes in eating habits, as has the introduction of fast food, convenience foods and international cuisine. In keeping with these developments, rail catering, sea catering and airline catering (although less so on short domestic flights) have adapted to serve changing dietary requirements during travel—both for pleasure and for business. Catering for these changing requirements has spawned global businesses associated with the hospitality industry.

There has thus been an exponential growth in the provision of hospitality-related services in almost every country in the world. In response to this global need, and to take advantage of these changing social phenomena, hospitality firms have expanded nationally and internationally. Firms, customers and employees have all become international and multicultural. Indeed, it is difficult today to name a city that does not have an international hotel or restaurants that do not serve international cuisine.

Hospitality and tourism as service industries

In most circumstances, the growth of the tourism industry has fueled the growth of hospitality, resulting in its development as a global industry. It must be emphasized that the hospitality and tourism businesses are essentially *service* business enterprises. They therefore must be studied within a service industry framework, and service management theory is perfectly suited to understanding and explaining hospitality and tourism management.

Historically, the term hospitality goes back thousands of years. The ancient Romans were known to be obliged to provide hospitality to visitors and passing travelers. The word itself far predates its evolution into an industry. Investigating the meaning of the word hospitality and gaining a broader understanding about the differences between 'serving' and doing so 'hospitably' is important for all hospitality managers. Hospitality is not only about 'service' as a process, but rather about the way guests are meant to be treated, welcomed, entertained, generously greeted and so on. However, the development of the hospitality industry and its growing importance as an economic sector providing jobs and adding to local economies has at times led to a blurring of the boundaries between hospitality as a business

© Harish Marnad/Shutterstock.com

and hospitality as a 'way of being' or an 'essence'. The differentiation between the word 'hospitality' and the 'business' of hospitality is important, and is described in the 'commercial hospitality' literature. Although this book will not discuss these distinctions further, we do adopt a commercial hospitality perspective, in that when we discuss business we refer to 'for profit' enterprises.

Basic components of hospitality

Hospitality as an industry can be seen as comprising three main functional areas—accommodation, food and beverage and entertainment—as illustrated in Figure 1.4.

These three functions within the hospitality sector might be offered separately by individual businesses (for example, motels offering accommodation only, restaurants offering food

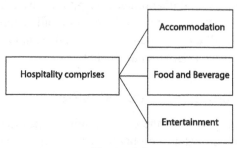

Figure 1.4
The three main functional areas of hospitality

and drinks only, and theatres offering entertainment only). Alternatively, and more commonly, some businesses might offer various combinations of the three elements (for example, hotels offering accommodation, food and beverage and entertainment). The degree of specialization, or the combination of functions that a firm offers, determines the type of clientele it wishes to attract, and the image that the firm wishes to communicate to its customers.

If they are to compete in the marketplace, tourism sector businesses—and in particular commercial hospitality enterprises—must first satisfy their customers. And if they are to tailor their service offerings successfully to meet the expectations of customers, it is essential that hospitality managers understand the perceptions of those customers and also what needs to be done *within an organization* to create a working environment conducive to enhancing customer satisfaction (service culture and service climate, discussed further in Chapter 8). This underlines the importance of the service dimension of the business from a managerial perspective. But in order to gain a better understanding, let us take a step back and look at the origins of the service management framework and define 'service'.

Origins of the service management framework

The term 'service management' was not actually introduced into mainstream scholarship until the early 1980s. One of the earliest, yet still often cited, definitions of service management is that it is

> . . . a total organizational approach that makes quality of service, as perceived by the customer, the primary driving force for the operation of any business. (Albrecht, 1988; p. 20)

This early definition demonstrates the peripheral nature of the concept at that time, yet clearly indicates the underlying theme of today's service management approach—that service management is a comprehensive framework and effective organizations utilize this mindset throughout the entire organization rather than limiting it to parts of an organization.

Ben Schneider (2004, a great advocate of service management from an organizational behavior perspective, defines service management as ". . . a multidisciplinary field of practice and research on service quality that includes services marketing, services operations management, and services human resources management" (p. 144). Both of these definitions emphasize the multidisci-

© Tashaturango/Shutterstock.com

plinary nature of service management, highlighting the point that, while perhaps not a discipline in its own right, it is clearly a vital aspect to success in service organizations.

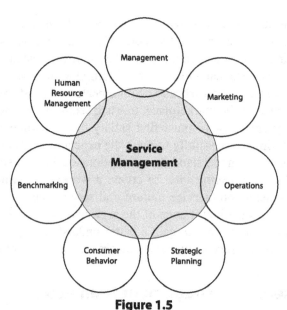

Figure 1.5
The service management overlap

Christian Grönroos similarly proposed that service management is a perspective more than one discipline or one coherent area of its own. He suggests that, in the face of growing competition, firms have to understand and manage service elements in order to gain sustainable competitive advantage, and that these guidelines apply to separate areas, including management, marketing, organizational theory and human resource management (HRM) (Grönroos, 1993).

Figure 1.5 illustrates some of the various academic areas connected to much of the thinking, research and practice in service management. Further discussion and expanded reflection on the evolution of service management will be covered later in this chapter and throughout the book.

Evolving from product management to service management

Why is it important to understanding the evolution of management thought? Let us think metaphorically for a moment. Anthropologists in Ethiopia recently unearthed pieces of bones and other fossilized fragments. This discovery provided a series of new clues in the understanding of the development of mankind. In fact, the skeletons found have now been dated as being 4.4 million years old—and have led to a dramatic rethinking about the development of man and the 'family tree' which distinguishes man from chimp-like animals. This recent discovery has elucidated the history of man's development, and has inspired many scientists to enter or re-enter the discourse about mankind's evolutionary history.

Learning about our history, clarifying old and new thought, inciting enthusiasm amongst scholars and scientists—all of these things are helpful to the research and scholarly communities. These discoveries and the corresponding papers and discourse help us think, criticize, rethink, communicate, test, retest and advance knowledge. Similarly, as we understand the progression of management thinking—its evolution and consequences—we advance our field and improve research, theory and practice in management!

What do we mean when we refer to the evolution of management thought? How is it that the world can evolve, but academic terminology and theory does not, or does so but much more slowly? This is clearly evident in the simple example of the traditional 4 Ps of the 'Marketing Mix' (McCarthy, 1960). These Ps (Product, Price, Place, Promotion) were taken for granted for years as the necessary recipe for successful marketing. When taking an item to market, it was thought, one must consider *what* to sell (Product), *how much* to sell it for (Price), *where* to sell it (Place) and how to *promote* its sale (Promotion).

When service managers and marketers tried to use these 4 Ps for marketing a service (e.g., what you 'buy' at a bank), they found this mix insufficient. Subsequently, researchers sought to expand the marketing mix with a series of proposed additions (see Rafiq and Ahmed, 1995). Of these, the most frequently utilized and accepted mix is the revised 7 Ps (or the 'Extended Marketing Mix') (Booms and Bitner, 1981), which takes into account People (all people who directly or indirectly influence the perceived value of the product or service, including knowledge workers, employees, management and consumers), Processes (procedures, mechanisms and flow of activities which lead to an exchange of value) and Physical Evidence (environment in which the service is delivered and in which the service provider and consumer interact) (see Chapter 6).

Servitization

The development of management thought reflects the fast growth of a service economy which was discussed earlier in the chapter. Indeed, service has become an important value-assessment variable in predicting a firm's success in the marketplace. However, technological innovations have rendered service no longer a choice but a necessity—an inescapable feature of domestic and professional life.

Consider the example of the automobile industry. Twenty or thirty years ago people were able to attend to minor engine problems in their cars—such as adjusting the carburetor. Today's technology has replaced carburetors with fuel injectors, and owners now have to take their cars to mechanics for tuning. Similarly, when buying a washing machine or a dishwasher the concerns of consumers now extend to the various support services provided by the seller in the event of something going wrong. The competitive advantage of service has become increasingly evident—because there is little to differentiate competing products from the customer's perspective. Given that the technical components of products are very similar, the only differentiating factor for products are the service components; the service components are therefore incorporated within the products to support customers. The service component has thus become an integral part of most manufactured products, with the result that various types of industries have recognized the potential development of *service* as one of the few sustainable competitive advantages. This phenomenon is increasingly becoming evident in the tourism and hospitality industries.

Steadily over the past thirty or so years, more corporations have used service as a way to add value to their core 'product' offerings and to enhance and strengthen customer relationships. This is a point which we discuss further below in this chapter in the section about packages or 'bundles'. Bundles are driven by a customer-focused view on how to provide a more holistic and long-term customer engagement. In fact, this shift has seen many companies incorporating more 'service' components within their offers. This concept was coined 'servitization' (Vandermerwe and Rada, 1988) in the late 1980s, and is evident across nearly all industries that at one stage in their lifecycles considered themselves manufacturing or 'product' companies. Examples include the conceptual changes in IBM from a 'computer company' to a 'solution provider', and the way that Lexus created their 'Encore Club' for all buyers of new and used Lexus automobiles in order to overcome competition by adding value to the overall experience of buying and owning a luxury car.

Interdependency of service provision

Coordinated benefits

We introduced the idea of service 'bundles' above in our discussion about servitization. Services are often offered in sequences or in 'bundles', and fall into two general types:

1. a single provider might offer a number of service provisions in sequence to any given customer; or
2. a single customer might receive additional service offerings from other providers before and after the service currently being rendered.

Let us consider, as an example, a tourist or business traveler staying in a hotel. This traveler might have flown in by plane, taken a taxi or a limousine hire service before arriving at the hotel. After leaving the hotel, the traveler might take a taxi or a tour coach to receive the next service. From the customer's perspective, although these services are experienced separately, they are interrelated. The linkage between them is important if the traveler's itinerary is to run smoothly. The needs of customers can thus extend beyond the capabilities of one company's product or service offering.

Although each of these services can be seen as an isolated benefit, they must be compatible, complementary and coordinated.

Service firms cannot and do not exist in isolation. Through partnerships and collaborations with other firms, bundles of services are offered to satisfy the various needs of individual customers. These partners might or might not be involved in serving the customers directly. The entire system, however, is internally organized by an interactive web of relationships in which the customer participates at various stages—in both the production and consumption of the various services.

Components of a tourism service

Tourism services are a composite of many aspects of a visit, and tourists often view a total experience as made up of individual units. This poses a major challenge in maintaining a superior service, particularly at a destination where a visitor will have many experiences. The overall service product is composed of a combination of services which, although fundamentally independent, are consumed by tourists in a continuous chain, one after the other, from the time they leave home, until the time they return.

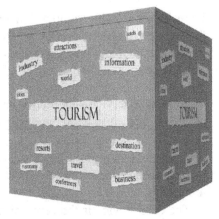

© Keith Bell/Shutterstock.com

Tourism can thus be understood as a system composed of:

- ▶ service received at the tourist's place of origin—for example, travel agents, insurance, advice and so on;
- ▶ service en route—for example, transport and food while traveling; and
- ▶ service at the destination—for example, accommodation, food and attractions at the holiday site.

Thus, the tourism industry is made up of a network of independent, but interrelated, functions operating in a range of service sectors. Poor performance within one sector, or by one service provider, affects the other service providers in the chain. For example, a tourist losing his or her baggage during a flight is likely to perceive every other service negatively, or at least less favorably.

Service interrelationship

This concept of *service interrelationship* is critical to effective service management. It reflects the importance of all of the service provision involved in a relationship. And it must be understood that service interrelationships apply within a single organization, as well as across collaborating organizations.

Within any service organization, almost all service needs are cross-functional in nature. Cross-functional systems are therefore required within an organization—that is, systems capable of fulfilling customer needs in a coordinated fashion. Thus, within any service organization, all departments and functional units must be interdependent and coordinated, with their cross-functionality managed and coordinated effectively.

Essentially this means that, in any service interface, every employee should be capable of going beyond departmental boundaries to assist the customer.

Core and peripheral services

The reality of growing competition among service providers, as well as the interdependency of service provision, is that there is a need to differentiate the nature of service provision, which often encompasses a number of different service offerings.

Most service offerings consist of:

▶ a core service—the major benefit that the consumer is seeking; and

▶ peripheral service—the little things offered as added bonuses.

For example, in a tour package, the core service is the visit to a specific location, whereas the peripheral service is the comfortable bus, the friendly tour guide and the clean toilets at the location.

The core service is the centerpiece of the service offering—the basic reason for being in business. Without the core service, a business enterprise makes no sense. The peripheral service is a naturally compatible set of goods, services and experiences which, when combined with the core service, serve to create an impression of high value in the customer's mind. See Figure 1.6.

The peripheral service should support, complement and add value to the core service. The peripheral service, in most cases, is intended to provide the 'leverage' that helps build the value of the total package in the eyes of customers. Using a hotel as an example, the core service includes a clean, properly equipped room, whereas the peripheral service package includes services additional to accommodation—such as a wake-up call, morning tea, quality of the Wi-Fi connection, coffee, newspaper, laundry service, shoe-shining service, transport to and from the airport and so on.

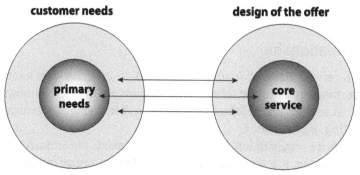

Figure 1.6

Customer needs and the design of the offer

Adapted from Edvardsson and Gustavsson (1992).

Research suggests that the level of satisfaction necessary to create long-term customer loyalty is influenced by elements which include peripherals that surround (or add additional value to) the core service—how the food is served in the restaurant; how the wait staff interact with the customer; how the receptionist assists the customer when a credit card is not accepted and so on.

Companies commonly compete in similar markets and offer comparable core offerings. For example, two 5-star hotels might be located in a city center, with the service and product offered by the two hotels being virtually indistinguishable from one another in the eyes of the consumer. Given these circumstances, often the only way in which either of these hotels can gain a competitive edge is by offering added value.

Thus, from a managerial perspective, the differentiation between core service and peripheral service can be crucial. Once a core service has proved to be effective—that is, able to meet the primary needs of the customer—it is the peripherals of the service package that act as the key factors in a customer's final judgment of the value of the total service product. In many situations, the only possible difference between competitors lies with these peripherals. The strongest company in the marketplace will be the one that offers the best-designed package that includes core (expected) offerings and peripheral (extra) offerings.

Applying service management theory

As noted in the section 'The core philosophy of this book' (page 19), the primary function of a commercial service business should be on providing service, and value, to the customer. Hospitality organizations are not in the business of offering accommodation, food and beverage or entertainment only. In the marketplace, what the customer receives from a hospitality establishment is *service*. What is important to the customer (the point at which the customer determines the value of a purchase) is the *outcome*—that is, the service—not simply the accommodation product, the food and beverage product or the entertainment product. Indeed, the customer pays for the end result (the service) and not for the intermediary (the ostensible product being purchased). Examples of this distinction are well represented by many service firms, such as Starbucks Coffee Company, who proclaim that they are not in the coffee business serving people, they are in the people business serving coffee; and Southwest Airlines, who think of

© rosesmith/Shutterstock.com

themselves as a customer service company that happens to fly airplanes (on schedule, with personality and perks along the way).

This discussion leads to others in this book, notably about 'value cocreation', where value is often formed by a customer during the actual delivery and consumption of the service. This is different from a more traditional perspective on value creation, where value is determined after the purchase and only once the customer starts to 'use' the product.

It is very important that managers understand the thinking behind this concept—that, through their hospitality establishments, they are offering an *experience* which is composed of many service moments. As managers, it is therefore crucial that they understand in depth what they are offering, and how it should be offered, to create the best experience for their customers, tourists, visitors. This perspective necessitates a re-examination and readjustment of ideas, concepts, systems and methods. Fundamentally, this new perspective calls for a better understanding of the real hospitality and tourism product—that is, the nature of a service.

Summary

The emerging global economy, and the competitive forces inherent in globalization, are changing the nature of competition in the international tourism and hospitality industries. Because hotel products are easily replicated by various establishments, traditional competitive strategies based on product features have been rendered inappropriate for sustainable long-term growth. Hospitality and tourism operators have therefore been forced to search for new ways to differentiate themselves from competitors. Education in the hospitality and tourism areas has traditionally been viewed as a distinct subject area that focuses primarily on the technical aspects of hotel and theme park operations—such as knowledge of lodging products and knowledge of food and beverage skills.

In the current and future marketplace, the practical value of this approach is limited by competitive forces and by changes in customers' needs, expectations and perceptions of value. A new managerial perspective that views hospitality and tourism firms as service providers—rather than purely as retailers of accommodation and food and beverage products—is an appropriate strategy to cope with these emerging trends. This represents a major shift in the focus of management—a change in focus that allows managers to form a new basis of competition. And service management principles are essential to success in the modern competitive marketplace. The rest of this book explores these basics in further detail, but before we move there let's emphasize the core philosophy of this book.

The core philosophy of this book

This book is essentially about applying the principles of service management to the hospitality and tourism industry. Three essential principles of this approach are:

1. that hospitality and tourism organizations are business organizations and hence their focus should primarily be on the *customer*;
2. that hospitality and tourism organizations are service organizations and hence their primary orientation should be on *service*;
3. that service in hospitality and tourism organizations is provided by the employees so there must be equally proportional attention on the service *workers*.

These three core principles combine to produce an emphasis on *service* to the *customer*.

Because hospitality and tourism is composed essentially of service business enterprises, they must therefore be studied within a service management framework, and service management theory is required to understand and explain hospitality and tourism management and operations.

This book thus aims to guide hospitality managers away from the traditional management thinking of a departmentalized organization selling physical products to a new perspective which sees hospitality and tourism as essentially service businesses requiring a holistic cross-functional approach to meeting customers' needs within the context of personal relationships and experience.

Review Questions

1. The service economy exploded in the second half of the twentieth century. Explain the underpinning factors behind this growth.

2. Name the core ongoing trends in tourism and hospitality industries. Why it is important for service enterprises to be aware of those?

3. Why do some scholars argue that the service management paradigm offers competitive advantage to a company's operation?

4. Explain how service interrelationship affects total experience as it's perceived by the customer?

5. Explain the difference between core service and peripheral service (give a few examples) and whether service companies should devote more attention to the peripheral services.

6. Explain the 'servitization' concept and how it evolved over the last 25 years.

7. Briefly describe the concept of service bundling. Why is it important, and how might hospitality managers manipulate the different elements of a service package to gain a competitive advantage?

8. Within the context of the service management evolution, explain how the shift in the marketing mix from 4Ps to 7Ps might reflect the progression of management thinking.

9. What is the logic behind value cocreation and explain why it has a great impact on service process and overall customer experience?

Suggested Readings

This is a list of suggested further reading on topics covered in this chapter. For a separate list of full reference citations quoted in the chapter, see 'References', Chapter 1, page 323.

Bitner, M. J., and Brown, S. W. (2006). The evolution and discovery of services science in business schools. *Communications of the ACM*, 49(7), 73–78.

Chesbrough, H., and Spohrer, J. (2006). A research manifesto for services science. *Communications of the ACM*, 49(7), 35–40.

Davis, M. M., and Berdrow, I. (2008). Service science: Catalyst for change in business school curricula. *IBM Systems Journal*, 47(1), 29–39.

Ford, R. C, Sturman, M. C., and Heaton, C. P. (2012). *Managing Quality Service in Hospitality: How Organizations Achieve Excellence in the Guest Experience*. Clifton Park, New York: Delmar Publishing.

Lashley, C., Lynch, P., and Morrison, A. (Eds.). (2007). *Hospitality: A Social Lens*. London: Elsevier.

Meyer, D. (2006). *Setting the Table: The Transforming Power of Hospitality in Business*. New York: Harper Collins.

Ostrom, A. L., Bitner, M. J., Brown, S. W., Burkhard, K. A., Goul, M., Smith-Daniels, V., Demirkan, H., Rabinovich, E. (2010). Moving forward and making a difference: Research priorities for the science of service. *Journal of Service Research*, 13(1), 4–36.

Solnet, D. (2011). Service management in hospitality education: Review and reflection. *Journal of Hospitality Marketing & Management*, 21(2), 184–214.

Vargo, S. L., and Lusch, R. F. (2008). Why 'service'? *Journal of the Academy of Marketing Science*, 36, 25–38.

The Nature of Service

Study Objectives

Having completed this chapter, readers should be able to:

1. Understand the differences between service products and manufactured goods from a management perspective.
2. Understand the distinctive process of service management and the challenges faced by service managers.
3. Apply these understandings in the context of tourism and hospitality management.

Outline

- ▶ Introduction
- ▶ Differences between products and service
  - ▶ Intangibility
    - What is 'intangibility'?
    - The special importance of intangibility
  - ▶ Heterogeneity
    - Heterogeneity at various levels
    - Technology is not always helpful
    - Heterogeneity is not always a negative
  - ▶ Inseparability (of production and consumption)
    - What is 'inseparability'?
    - Inseparable during consumption
    - Inseparable during production
    - Inseparability and marketing

- Inseparability and quality
- Inseparability and 'multiple consumption'
- Inseparability and value 'cocreation'
  - ▶ Perishability
    - What is 'perishability'?
    - Service and economics: A lesson on supply and demand
    - 'Ownership' of a service
  - ▶ Management implications for 'IHIP'
    - ▶ Implications with intangibility
      - Intangibility and the customer's perspective
      - Intangibility and the manager's perspective
    - ▶ Implications with heterogeneity
    - ▶ Implications with perishability
    - ▶ Managing service supply and demand
      - Aspects of demand
        - — Variations in demand
        - — Effect of demand on quality
        - — Waiting and the psychology of waiting
        - — Strategies for managing demand
      - Aspects of supply (capacity)
        - — Capacity and quality
        - — Maximum capacity and optimum capacity
        - — Strategies for managing supply
  - ▶ Summary
  - ▶ Review Questions
  - ▶ Suggested Readings

Key Words

Continuum of intangibility	Optimum capacity
Customer's involvement/input	Part-time marketers
Customization	Perishability
Emotional labor	Personalization
Fluctuating demand	Psychology of waiting
Heterogeneity	Service demand
Inseparability	Service marketing
Intangibility	Service ownership
Managing demand	Service supply
Managing supply	Simultaneous production and
Maximum capacity	consumption
Multiple consumption	Value cocreation

Introduction

This chapter addresses the nature of service, and compares services with the products of manufacturing industries. Service 'products' differ from physical products in their composition, production process, delivery and consumption. The management and marketing of a service therefore requires approaches that are quite different from those traditionally used in the management and marketing of manufactured goods.

These different approaches stem largely from four distinctive features of service: intangibility, heterogeneity (variability), inseparability (of production and consumption) and perishability (otherwise referred to as 'IHIP').

These characteristics lead to different consumer perceptions and behaviors—making it more difficult for service providers to ensure customer satisfaction and to establish a competitive advantage. The distinctive characteristics also present significant challenges in the management of supply and demand, in ensuring consistent service quality and in achieving operational efficiency.

Service managers must understand and cope with these challenges if they are to compete successfully in the complex service environment. This chapter analyzes the nature of service, and identifies some of the implications for service managers.

Differences between products and service

Although the differences between products and service have been well established for many years, many services today are still designed, produced and marketed with little understanding of the true nature of service and the implications for production, consumption, marketing and management. Even though service provision comprises a package of tangible and intangible components (see Chapter 1), many practitioners and academics continue to address service in a traditional management style—a style which is based, predominantly, on knowledge gained from the goods/manufacturing industry.

Such an approach is inappropriate because the service outcome is intangible in nature. The 'product' is essentially an *activity* conducted by people, for people, most often in the presence of people who receive the service. This service is distinctly different from products in the composition, production process, delivery and consumption. The management and marketing of service therefore requires a different approach from that of products.

Several authors have detailed the characteristics that distinguish services from products, and the ramifications of these differences for management and marketing (see for example, Bowen and Ford, 2002). Although service industries are quite heterogeneous (including businesses as different as beauty salons, hotels, adventure tours, hospitals, electrical utilities and so on), they do have distinctive features in common about which it is possible to generalize. Understanding and applying this knowledge is valuable in every aspect of hospitality management.

Four of the most commonly cited characteristics of a service are:

- ► intangibility,
- ► heterogeneity,
- ► inseparability (of production and consumption) and
- ► perishability.

Intangibility

What is 'intangibility'?

During the period of development of the service literature, there has been general agreement that the most distinctive feature of service is its relative *intangibility*. That is, service is a performance, as opposed to an object—it cannot be seen, felt, tasted or touched as goods can be. Although the effects of service might be felt for some time, the service itself essentially goes out of existence at the very moment that it is rendered (more on this below in our discussion about perishability). Although the uniqueness of this and the other characteristics of service have been questioned over recent years (a point which we will discuss later in this chapter), it is still essential to understand these ideas.

Intangibility—the distinctive characteristic of service

Intangibility has been called *the* distinctive characteristic of service. Although there are said to be four distinctive characteristics of services (intangibility, inseparability, heterogeneity and perishability), intangibility is *the* critical difference between service and physical goods. This intangibility is the factor from which all other differences between goods and services emerge.

A service is the result of a deed, a performance, an effort or an encounter in time. Service cannot be displayed, physically demonstrated or illustrated. Service therefore has few of the characteristics technically described as 'search' qualities, 'experience' qualities, and 'credence' qualities—that is, unlike manufactured goods, service cannot be physically examined ('search' qualities), checked ('experience' qualities) or tested ('credence' qualities).

The special importance of intangibility

In 1977, a bank vice president, Lynn Shostack wrote an important article in the *Journal of Marketing*, arguing that marketing the bank product (service) required a mirror opposite view of conventional marketing practices. Her seminal work helped advance the creation of the service management and marketing fields as the argument that marketing a service was quite different to managing goods resonated with academics and practitioners and in many ways opened the floodgates on the service research field. She highlighted the special importance of intangibility as a distinctive characteristic of service—even when the rendering of the service involves some physical good—claiming that when something cannot be held, felt, tasted, resold, etc., that it required new thinking in terms of marketing and management.

© Lisa S./Shutterstock.com

Tangibility exists along a continuum, and all products exhibit some tangible and intangible qualities (see Figure 2.1). For example, in the case of a taxi service, the intangible service (the journey to a desired destination) obviously involves a necessary physical object (the taxi cab itself). But the service remains the primary product offering. Similarly, the service offered at a restaurant involves the combined effect of numerous intangible activities—including the acquisition of supplies, the preparation of meals and the serving of those meals. The tangible components behind all this—the building, the interior decor, the kitchen equipment, the food items and so on—are obviously necessary for the service. However, the intangible service activities make up the key product offering.

Thus, although there are said to be four distinctive characteristics of service, intangibility is perhaps *the* critical difference between service and physical goods. This intangibility is the factor from which all other differences between goods and services emerge.

Rather than striving to 'tangibilize' their offerings, service managers should be selling the intangible benefits—"the most valuable asset in all organizations, whether they are

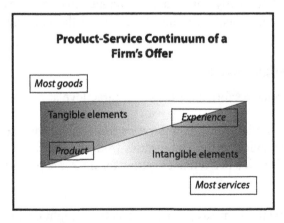

Figure 2.1
Continuum of tangibility and intangibility

non-profit or for-profit, are their intangible brands and what they symbolize" (Vargo and Lusch, 2004, p. 328). It is through the intangible aspects of the offer that firms are able to showcase the value of their offering through customers' experiences. Firms therefore will be able to assess their product—service mix and set a higher experience target to enhance positive customer experience.

Shostack (1977) argued that marketers of intangible offerings do need to develop 'tangible evidence', but she also argued that they actually had more opportunity to do so than managers of tangible offerings because "in product marketing many kinds of evidence are beyond the marketer's control . . ." (pp. 77–79). For example, marketing a television as a service experience may prove challenging. As important, she indicated that the challenge for marketers of tangible offerings is to create an 'intangible image', a potentially more difficult challenge than creating evidence for intangible offerings (Vargo and Lusch, 2004, p. 328).

Heterogeneity

The word heterogeneity or variability implies many or different parts and many or different people. It is derived from the Greek words *heteros* ('different') and *genos* ('part' or 'person'). Service industries differ in the extent to which they are 'people-based' or 'technology-based'. There is a larger human component involved in performing some services (for example, restaurant meals) than there is in others (for example, telecommunication services). The outcomes of people-based service operations tend to be more heterogeneous (that is, more variable) than the outcomes of technology-based operations. Standardized and uniform outcomes are more difficult to ensure.

Heterogeneity in service delivery poses both challenges and opportunities for management in labor-intensive service industries because there is potential for significant variability in the performance of services and this variability can be positive or negative depending on the circumstance. Ultimately, numerous employees over a series of encounters are in contact with any one individual customer, thus raising the potential for inconsistency of behavior.

Heterogeneity at various levels

This variability of service performance occurs at three levels:

1. the quality of service performance varies from one service organization to another;
2. the quality of service performance varies from one service performer to another and
3. the quality of service performance varies for the same performer on different occasions.

For these reasons, what the firm has promised to deliver might be quite different from what is actually received by the service customer. The 'bottom line' is that uniformity of service delivery is difficult to ensure because there is no guarantee of consistent behavior from service persons. Similarly, even the same service delivered at the same time to a group of customers can be perceived very differently between members of the group. For example, one person might really enjoy an outgoing, talkative waitperson, whereas another person might feel that this approach is too overwhelming. So many challenges!

Technology is not always helpful

Although heterogeneity is essentially a 'people problem', the advent of increased technology does not necessarily improve matters. If a service firm attempts to decrease heterogeneity by replacing people with technology, the firm might inadvertently introduce yet another form of heterogeneity in its service delivery. That is, customers might perceive a significant difference between a firm's 'new' service (as delivered via technology) and its 'traditional' service (as delivered by people). In this way, the advent of information technology has, in fact, increased the potential for heterogeneity.

For example, the variation between interaction conducted face-to-face ('high-touch') and interaction via the technology and/or the Internet ('high-tech') can be significant, and service companies that use technology extensively must be aware of this when using this medium. This has implications for customers' perceptions of the firm's quality and image.

This sort of problem is a common complaint from customers in such service industries as banking. Technology might offer the possibility of reducing variability among different service personnel (because every customer receives the same treatment from an impersonal machine or website), but customers might be more concerned about the much starker difference between dealing with a machine and dealing with a person. The introduction of technology might 'fix' heterogeneity at one level, but exacerbate it at another level. This is summed up in the common complaint: "I don't like talking to a machine! I want to talk to *a real* person (and not a web-based 'chat'!)".

Heterogeneity is not always a negative

Having observed that heterogeneity is all but inevitable in service delivery and consumption, it must also be noted that heterogeneity in service is not always a negative thing. As noted above, some customers prefer service from people (even if variable) to service from machines (even if more uniform). Even 'scripted' service (where most of what the provider says is pre-planned) can be seen by some as more appreciated than that from a machine (although others might prefer not to have any human interaction!).

In a similar way, variation can be beneficial in the case of specially customized service. In these cases, variability (at least from customer to customer) is an accepted part of good service.

In addition, heterogeneity exists when customers form personal relationships with particular members of staff. Although there are potential problems in this (if staff members start 'playing favorites' to the disadvantage of others), well-trained staff members should be able to utilize this form of heterogeneity to the advantage of the firm. Customers who receive 'special' treatment feel wanted as individuals. This sort of 'heterogeneity' is not a bad thing. Most customers like the feeling that they received a special treatment and hence consider themselves valued.

Management usually strives for uniformity of service, and therefore usually strives to eliminate heterogeneity. But this is not always a desirable outcome for all customers in all situations. Prahalad and Ramaswamy (2000) note that "it is important to distinguish personalization from customization. Customization assumes that the manufacturer will design a product to suit a customer's needs . . . Personalization, on the other hand, is about the customer becoming a cocreator of the content of their experiences"

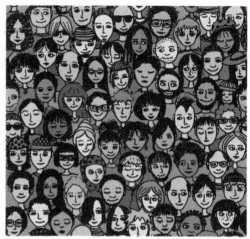

© Franzi/Shutterstock.com

(pp. 83–84). The authors go on to suggest ways in which companies will need to manage personalized experiences—through managing multiple distribution and communication channels, and shaping customers' expectations.

Wind and Rangaswamy (2000) have called for a revolution that they refer to as 'customerization'. Customerization begins with customers and offers them more control in the exchange process. Customerization is driven by a firm's desire to redefine its relationship with customers. In some sense, a firm becomes an agent of the customer—'renting' out to customers pieces of its manufacturing, logistics, and other resources, thus allowing them to find, choose, design, and use what they want (Vargo and Lusch, 2004). Therefore customization takes advantage of the heterogeneous nature of service and allows it to turn into a personalized and unique experience for the customer.

Inseparability (of production and consumption)

What is 'inseparability'?

The inseparability of production and consumption refers to the fact that most service provision is characterized by simultaneous production and consumption. Goods and services are quite different in this respect. Typically goods are first produced, then sold, and then consumed. In contrast, a typical service is first sold, and then produced and consumed simultaneously.

Inseparable during consumption

Simultaneous production and consumption means that the service provider is often physically present when consumption occurs. A hotel receptionist has to be present before a guest is able to check-in; or in the case of technology-enabled check-in (e.g., smartphone, self-

© Kzenon/Shutterstock.com

service kiosk), the service is still produced during consumption, but by a machine rather than a service employee; a barman has to prepare and serve drinks for guests at the bar; a dentist is present when examining a patient; an airline flight attendant is present when serving an in-flight drink and so on. In contrast, a physical good, such as a washing machine, might be manufactured in Germany, stored in London and used in Scotland. This means that the employees of the manufacturing firm have no opportunity to interact with the customer and impress customers with their knowledge, expertise or willingness to help.

Inseparable during production

Simultaneous production and consumption also implies the presence of the customer during the production of a service. A diner is present during restaurant service; a customer is in the chair for a haircut; a patient is physically examined during a medical consultation; a child experiences the thrill of a roller coaster ride at a theme park.

Inseparability thus forces the buyer into intimate contact with both the process of production and the process of delivery. And, in most cases, there is no time lapse between production and consumption. But service providers are human, and client–provider interaction is spontaneous and simultaneous—whether it is face to face or via a telephone. Control of service output thus becomes a difficult and complex issue.

Inseparability and marketing

As we have seen, the production and consumption of service occur virtually simultaneously. The same could be said of *marketing*. For example, when a receptionist offers assistance to a customer, the information is certainly being consumed at the same time and in the same place as it is being produced. But the service is also being *marketed* at the same time. The receptionist is effectively 'selling' the service (convincing the customer of its value) at the very same time as the service is being produced and consumed. The three elements— production, marketing and consumption (and value creation)—are inseparable.

Produced, then sold, then consumed? Not with service!

Typically goods are first produced, then sold and then consumed. This seems logical enough. But it does not apply to service. A typical service is first sold, and then produced and consumed simultaneously. For example, you first buy a football game ticket and then experience the game while it is being played. The idea of the 'inseparability' of service thus changes the way we think about the apparently logical progression from production to sale to consumption.

And it does not stop there! The 'inseparability' of service also means that traditional ideas of marketing and quality require radical reappraisal. As the service is being delivered to the customer, the product is effectively being marketed, consumed and judged. The traditionally separate management functions such as production, consumption, marketing and quality control are *inseparable* in the provision of service.

The presence of both service provider and service customer during the production and consumption of the service critically alters the traditional concepts of production and marketing as they have been applied to goods. In the marketing of goods, great emphasis is placed on distributing goods where and when customers desire them—that is, the key to goods marketing is to get goods to the *right place* at the *right time*. However, in the case of service, the emphasis shifts from attempting to ensure the *right place* and the *right time* to attempting to ensure that service is produced and delivered (that is, distributed) in the *right way*. A service customer's main concern is not so much about *what* is being offered but *how* it is being offered. The way in which a waiter, a mechanic, a physician, a lawyer, a teacher, a bank teller *behaves* in the presence of the customer influences decisions on future patronage. The simple fact is that service firms win or lose during the direct moments of contact ('moments of truth') between the firm (employee or technology) and customer. This point will be expanded when we turn our discussions to the employee-customer interface (or the service encounter, in Chapters 4 and 8).

Inseparability and quality

In a service that relies on personal contact and interaction between service deliverer and customer, quality is determined by service delivery. Service providers are therefore simultaneously involved in production, marketing and quality control.

The concept of 'inseparability' also has implications for the involvement of the consumer in quality control. Service customers participate in a more or less active fashion, cooperating in the process of production and delivery, and therefore participating in determining the quality of the service received. For example, in a restaurant a customer selects food and drink, engages with the waitstaff, and might even partially cook his or her own meal (in the case of a fondue, or the Chinese hot pot, for example). The input from the recipient of the service is crucial to the quality of the service.

The degree of customer involvement varies from service to service. For example, the role played by a customer in a fine-dining restaurant is very different from that played in a quick-service restaurant. In the fine-dining restaurant, the customer is deeply involved in determining how the service works. In a quick-service outlet, the consumer is much more of a passive recipient, although there are more and more quick service and fast casual restaurants that ask the customer to personalize every order (think Chipotle or Subway). In a service where customer input is crucial, the customer's involvement effectively dictates the final quality of the service rendered. In a classroom, the degree to which students become actively involved in the lecture process often determines the quality perceptions of the learning. So it is in the provider's best interests to facilitate and encourage customer (student) involvement because this shared participation can enhance the experience for all parties.

© Smart Design/Shutterstock.com

This has implications for the overall question of quality control in service—a subject considered in more detail in Chapter 3. The involvement of customers in the service-production process significantly affects a service firm's managerial control over its own service quality.

Inseparability and 'multiple consumption'

Finally, in considering the inseparability of production and consumption in many service interfaces, it should be noted that many services are delivered in a setting of 'multiple consumption'—that is, the service is consumed by more than one person simultaneously. A typical example is a music concert, in which each member of the audience enjoys the music in the presence of others, but without having to 'share' the service with others.

However, although the music is not 'shared' (in the sense of any one consumer not receiving all of the 'product' or experience), the presence of others *does* influence the perception of the quality of the service. In such cases, the perception of quality is influenced by two types of interaction—the interaction between the customer and the service provider, and the interactions among customers. At a football stadium or at a music concert the positive experience shared by participants often flows across to others.

Inseparability and value 'cocreation'

There have been a number of interrelated concepts developed over recent years all linked to inseparability. One of the most discussed concepts in recent years in the service literature is the concept of 'cocreation' of value. Cocreation implies that not only are service production and consumption tied closely together, but also that *value* is created at the same time and is a process whereby the organization, employee and customer are 'coresponsible' for its creation.

Prahalad and Ramaswamy (2000) advanced this thinking when they argued that the shared production leads to shared creation of value. They stated that customers are 'code-velopers' of experiences and that firms and customers have shared roles to play in creating a service (they are cocreators of value). These authors suggest that, given the input of skills and knowledge by customers and the way they actively engage in dialogue, customers have become a new source of competence for the corporation. And such competence can be a source of competitive advantage.

Cocreation of value not only benefits the customer, but also the firm. Shah et al. (2006) argued that the essence of a customer centricity paradigm lies not so much with how to sell a product or service but rather how *to create value for the customer and firm*, or what they coined as the process of dual value creation (Shah et al., 2006).

Rather than focusing on the active customer who cocreates value from the producer's perspective, Heinonen et al. (2010) argue that we should be emphasizing the customer's perspective—that what needs to be addressed is how value emerges for customers and how they make sense of the experience and formulate a perception of value. These researchers argue for a more holistic understanding of the customer's practices and experiences, in which service becomes naturally and inevitably embedded.

The interrelationships inherent in value cocreation are debated in the literature (with the marketing literature focused on the customer role, and the HRM and management literature more focused on the firm and employee aspects). There is, however, a general agreement that value is formed by the customer, through the support of a firm's offering which enables the customer to gain something useful to them and the firm to gain financial value—that "reciprocal value" creation is the basis of all service businesses (Grönroos, 2011).

Perishability

What is 'perishability'?

Perishability, closely related to intangibility, means that a service cannot be stored, and therefore it is produced only when needed by the customer. Service production is thus dictated by demand at any given time.

Examples of perishable items are a room in a hotel, a seat in a restaurant, an appointment at the doctor, a seat at a concert. If not used at the time, the opportunity for sale is lost. Similarly, if an aircraft takes off without its seats being filled, the revenue from the empty seats constitutes a non-recoverable loss. Even if, due to a sudden surge in demand, all subsequent flights are full, lost revenue from the previous flight can never be recovered. In general, capacity not profitably utilized in service production represents a non-recoverable loss.

Service and economics: A lesson on supply and demand

Unlike most goods, service is highly perishable and cannot be stored for future sale. Demand thus plays an especially significant role in the production and delivery of service. Supply refers to the total amount of a specific good or service that is available to consumers. This means the total number of seats on an airliner, total number of available rooms in a hotel, or seats in a restaurant. Demand refers to the quantity of a product or service which would be bought at a given price and at a given time.

A car producer who is unable to sell a company's total output during one period of sale can carry the stock forward to sell during a subsequent period. A service supplier, however, does not have that 'luxury'. In contrast to manufactured goods, service must be produced at the exact time and place demanded by the customer. For example, food is needed when the customer is hungry. The fact that food was available in the restaurant a few hours previously is of no consolation to a hungry customer now. Similarly, a fire brigade service is required when there is a fire—not at any other time. Immediate access is thus crucial in most service businesses. This is understandable in many respects. Consider the importance of the reliability and timing of service delivery in the examples given in the box below.

Reliability and timing are important in service

Reliability and timing are important issues for services consumers. Consider the following scenarios:

- A hotel room must be available exactly when the traveler wants it. A vacant hotel room tomorrow is useless to a traveler who wants accommodation in a fully booked hotel tonight.
- A restaurant seat must be empty when the customer wants it, and the food must be served when the customer is hungry. It is no use telling a hungry customer that he or she might like to come back and eat in several hours' time.
- An airline seat on a suitable flight must be available when the customer wants to fly. An empty seat tomorrow is no use to a traveler who needs to be in a particular city tonight.

The perishability of service does not pose a problem when demand is steady. In such circumstances, it is relatively easy to predict requirements and arrange for the services to be adequately staffed. But when demand fluctuates, service firms encounter problems. The breakfast rush in a hotel restaurant is an example of fluctuation in demand on a daily basis, or the lines of a theme park during peak vacation periods. The high seasonality of some resorts is an example of fluctuation over a longer time period. Some of these fluctuations are relatively predictable. Others are more difficult to manage.

Perishability, ownership and control

Perishability of service is a characteristic closely related to intangibility. Unlike physical goods, service cannot be 'possessed'. It cannot be stored, taken away or used at a later time. Service 'disappears' as quickly as it is delivered.

Perishability thus forces service managers to reappraise the ideas of *ownership* and *control* of their products. This sort of reappraisal has significant implications for two fundamental management tasks:

▶ the management of supply and demand and
▶ the management of patents, rights and risks.

It is difficult to own and control products that 'disappear' as quickly as they are delivered.

'Ownership' of a service

The perishability and intangibility of service renders 'ownership' impossible—by either the producer or the customer. Essentially, there is no 'ownership' of a service.

When purchasing physical goods, buyers acquire a title to the goods. However, when a service is performed, there is no corresponding transfer of ownership. Buyers of a service are buying only the *right* to a service—and then only at a designated time. Consumers do not buy the service itself to take away and use as they see fit at a time of their choosing. For example, a dinner ticket for a New Year gala function, a theatre ticket for a particular performance or an appointment for a specified portion of an accountant's time are all instances of the consumer securing the right to enjoy a service at a designated time. The consumer never 'owns' the service in any real sense (they might own a replica, a recording, a photo, but not the actual service).

The fact that perishability and intangibility prevent 'ownership' in any meaningful sense has implications for both suppliers and customers. For suppliers, there is a problem with patenting. Service cannot be 'owned' and patented in the way that physical goods can be, and there is always a possibility that services can be copied by competitors.

For consumers, the lack of 'ownership' increases the perception of 'risk' in purchasing a service. At the end of the transaction, the consumer does not actually 'possess' anything. In marketing a service, managers must be aware of this heightened perception of risk among their customers.

The perishability and intangibility of service makes 'ownership' impossible. Further hospitality examples include the room you sleep in at a hotel. You are essentially only 'borrowing' that space for a period of time. Some researchers have used the terms 'rental' to help explain the ownership of product vs. service challenge, whereby a customer never 'owns' a service, but rather rents it for a period of time and receives the value from it (transport, medical support) on a short-term basis.

It is important not to confuse perishability with lost value. Service researchers argue that the customer should be the focal point of service management and marketing activities, and that value creation is only possible when a good or service is consumed. That means that value is created at the point of consumption. What service managers aspire to is for customers to purchase and therefore consume a service—value is always coproduced with the customer—and, once consumed (or not), the service has perished. So a positive perspective on perishability is for the service firm to sell a service before it perishes.

(Note: Later in this book, we will discuss a number of strategies, such as service guarantees, designed to mitigate the risk inherent in purchasing a service).

Management implications for 'IHIP'

This is a text about managing service organizations. So it is one thing to understand the generally accepted characteristics of service—intangibility, inseparability, heterogeneity and perishability—but it is critical for managers to understand the implications for these challenges on managing their service firms. Some of the more important challenges and solutions are explored in greater detail in the rest of this chapter. There are other noteworthy management implications and strategies to manage the relationship between employees and customers as coproducers. For example, service producers (employees) are faced with challenges related to 'emotional labor' (service employees are expected not only to do work, but to act in a way which may contradict how they really feel). One solution to offer includes careful selection processes of employees who have the ability to control their emotions. Further, service employees are expected to work as 'part-time marketers' (selling future service while providing a service). This is made more possible when customer contact employees are enthused about their product and service offering, which helps integrate marketing with human resource management, ensuring that these employees are both aware of the firm's offerings and enthusiastic about them. For example, a visit to a local quick service sandwich shop encounters a cashier who clearly loves the product and company they work for—thus rendering the experience for the customer more enjoyable and informative ("I just love the way we do our fries with sweet potato—what a great recipe our owners came up with!"). The next section provides specific implications for the four service challenges discussed above.

Implications with intangibility

Intangibility and the customer's perspective

From the customer's perspective, the intangibility of service is an especially significant challenge, and managers must be sensitive to this. Intangibility in this context means that:

1. customers have difficulty in discriminating between one service offering and another;
2. customers perceive the service purchase as involving high levels of risk; and
3. customers seek personal information regarding the reliability of service.

Each of these is discussed below.

1.   Difficulty in discriminating between one service offering and another

Because customers have difficulty in discriminating between one service offering and another, management needs to develop a means of offering 'clues' (see Berry, Wall, and Carbone, 2006) with which customers are able to associate the additional benefits. This does not alleviate all problems associated with intangibility, but it does provide reinforcement of the organization's commitment to fulfilling the needs of the customer.

This approach can be effectively communicated to the customer using various types of package deals. For example, a hotel can offer special packages to a business traveler inclusive of air travel, taxi service and various business-related services such as printing, Wi-Fi access and photocopying. These recognizable benefits assist the customer to evaluate the service benefit before consumption, thus providing a means of assessing the service on the basis of individual need.

2.   Perceiving the service purchase as involving high levels of risk

Reducing the customer's perceived risk is the most effective way in which an organization can market its service. This is particularly pertinent in the case of a new service, or if customers are availing themselves of an organization's services for the first time. Research has shown that explicit service guarantees reduce the perceived risk. This practice has been adopted by many leading service organizations. For more on this subject, see 'Service guarantees', Chapter 7.

Detailed information about the service and the benefits that customers are entitled to receive also reduces the perceived risk. Those responsible for advertising information (in all its forms) should bear this in mind. Customers are able to foresee and evaluate the service outcome by referring to such information. They also do this by recalling their previous experiences of a similar nature.

3. Seeking personal information regarding the reliability of service

Because service is an intangible experience that cannot be picked up and taken away for examination by customers, word-of-mouth recommendation among consumers is necessarily one of the most common means of comparing and judging services. The fact that potential customers rely on word-of-mouth (directly and on various social media outlets) opinion more than any other form of message means that this form of 'advertising' must be acknowledged and addressed as a significant management tool.

Service managers thus need to design systems and approaches to enhance word-of-mouth advertising opportunities by customers who have already used the service. Offering incentive sales to existing customers is a useful means of enhancing word-of-mouth recommendation (see further discussion on word-of-mouth in Chapter 6). For example, a holiday resort might offer accommodation for a free second holiday to customers able to recommend and substantiate five further bookings. Moreover, the recommended guests might receive a 10% discount on their accommodation bill. Similar systems, in varying combinations, are very successfully used by many service organizations. It is commonplace now for businesses to incentivize participation in social media forums, such as being put into a prize draw for 'liking' or endorsing a social media page.

Intangibility and the manager's perspective

Just as the intangibility of service can be a significant issue from the customers' perspective, intangibility also has implications from a management perspective. For the manager, intangibility of service means that:

1. customers take an active role in the production process and, essentially, coproduce the service;
2. other customers coconsume the service and affect the perceived outcome; and
3. the service is often provided only at specified locations.

Each of these is discussed below.

1. Customers taking an active role in the production process

The fact that consumers take an active role in the service-production process is an excellent opportunity for staff members to develop personal relationships with their customers. Systems can be devised, and service personnel can be trained, with a view to providing customers with opportunities to make immediate changes or requests—thereby enhancing the perceived quality of service. Of course technology has also provided greater opportunities for customers to be involved in the production process of the intangible service. There are now endless examples of how a service is coproduced with active participation of a customer. Think about ordering a product online and all of the questions that the online provider asks during the process (Which size monitor? Do you wish to have it gift wrapped? Would you like that express delivered? And so on).

In addition, the way customers have been empowered to engage in communication about organizations with which they do business has been radically changed by technology over the past few years. Fisk (2009) noted that the Internet and mobile smartphones have enabled greater communication and collaboration between customers (e.g., through social media, YouTube, Facebook, Twitter, etc.), arguing that customer behavior will never be the same. "Customers who have never physically met are now interacting with each other. Customers are raising their voices in unison (Surowiecki, 2005) and customer communities are forming (Tapscott and Williams, 2006). Employees are collaborating too. This is the future of co-creation!" (Fisk, 2009, p. 139). Fisk calls this trend customer liberation and a paradigm changer in the realm of customer-firm relations.

2.   Other customers coconsuming and affecting the perceived outcome

Management has to make every effort to plan both the production process and the 'multiple consumption' stage if the desired effect is to be achieved.

Consider, for example, how a hotel might manage this aspect of service consumption in its nightclub, as compared with its formal restaurant. In the nightclub situation, the service should be designed and offered in a way that facilitates customer-to-customer interaction and generates a lively, crowded atmosphere. It is this atmosphere that, from a customer's perspective, actually constitutes the service. In contrast, in a formal restaurant, the emphasis is on balancing one customer's need for social interaction with another's need for privacy.

Coconsumption of service is the shared experience that has enormous capacity to influence customer perceptions, and it must be managed effectively and creatively to the enjoyment of the customer and to the advantage of the service firm.

3.   Providing the service at specified locations

Many types of service offerings (such as a restaurant meal) can be received by a customer only at a specific location. This effectively limits the number of customers served at a specific time. The limit is the capacity of the restaurant. However, management might be able to offer selective components of the service away from the main location—such as take-away food from a specific outlet. Similarly, a hotel or restaurant might offer a dinner banquet at a customer's preferred location. In this case, the food is prepared at the hotel or restaurant, but the service is provided at another location. Also, some TV shows are now streaming real-time Twitter feeds during their program—an example of how technology has enabled coconsumption across vast distances. Customers can be physically removed from each other, but can still influence others' consumption through their feedback and perspectives given during the shared experience.

The service-delivery system can thus be designed in a way that allows numerous services to be offered, at least in part, at different locations.

According to Bowen and Ford (2002), the setting in which the service experience is simultaneously produced and consumed is an important part of the service. The coproduction requirement means that not only the location is important but also the appearance and design of the location are important. What the customer senses (smells, sees, feels) influences the perception of the service and has a significant effect on quality and value perceptions. The term often used to convey the location of the service is the 'servicescape', which provides tangible cues and helps the customers navigate the service process. Further discussion about this physical aspect of service design and delivery appears throughout this book, and in particular in the discussion about service quality (see Chapter 3).

Implications with heterogeneity

Two management challenges particularly associated with heterogeneity are:

1. customers experience the same service differently, according to the time, day and service producer; and
2. variability can pose problems in maintaining brand standards at different service locations.

Each of these is discussed below.

1. Variability according to the time, day and service producer

In a service business, many employees are required to perform a similar service in a similar manner. For example, receptionists at a hotel are expected to conduct their service in a broadly similar style. However, customers commonly perceive differences in the service provided by different employees.

Management needs to establish training that facilitates consistency in the service offering and that supports the delivery process. In addition to such specific training of employees, service procedures and systems can be streamlined to reduce variability in task performance; however, providing employees the flexibility to meet specific requirements of individual customers is imperative. Customers value consistency in terms of reliability; however, the value is often associated with meeting the individual needs of the customer in different situations.

Therefore, in some situations, variability can present opportunities for personalized service. This is particularly pertinent in professional services where professionals from different disciplines are involved to meet a customer's various needs. In these cases, variability constitutes an asset to the organization.

2. Variability in brand standards at different locations

In large service organizations, in which service is offered from a number of outlets, maintaining a comparable service at all outlets is an ongoing management concern. The delivery of service is so dependent on individual personalities and attitudes that consistency in service interactions at different sites is extremely difficult to maintain.

Creating a company-wide culture to maintain standards has been successfully adopted by many leading service organizations. Examples include Marriott, Hyatt, Four Seasons and Ritz-Carlton. This requires a carefully constructed company policy by which all staff members are not only aware of the 'customer-centric' philosophy of the firm, but also trained and empowered to implement it (we will discuss these ideas further throughout the book, for example empowerment and service culture in Chapter 8).

Implications with perishability

The perishability of service is one of the most obvious management concerns. The problem with perishability is not an inability to offer the service at all, but an inability to offer the service when required by the customer. The problem is essentially the inability to store services and offer them when needed.

Because a service cannot be stored, the focus must be on managing demand—as opposed to managing supply. In fact, the successful management of demand must be the guiding principle in the design of any system or process in the service industry.

Strategies that can be utilized to manage demand fluctuations are discussed further below.

Managing service supply and demand

Balancing supply and demand presents a real challenge for most service firms; and hence success or failure in managing supply and demand determines the overall fate of the organization. The crucial issue is the degree to which available capacity is effectively utilized. When demand is low, productive capacity is wasted; but when demand is high, potential business is

© Pavel L Photo and Video/Shutterstock.com

lost due to the inability to supply the services in accordance with that demand. This constitutes an irrecoverable revenue loss.

Aspects of demand

Although capacity and demand must be coordinated and considered in an integrated manner, it is conceptually useful to consider them separately in attempting to clarify the important issues involved. After the issues have been clarified in isolation, management is in a better position to consider integrated and coordinated strategies.

In searching for strategies to coordinate demand and capacity in services, let us first consider the 'demand side' of the equation. The following aspects of demand are worthy of note:

1. variations in demand;
2. effect of demand on quality;
3. waiting and the psychology of waiting; and
4. strategies for managing demand.

Each of these is considered below.

1. Variations in demand

The search for strategies to manage demand should start with an understanding of the factors that govern the demand for a specific service at a given point in time. Some of the questions a service manager needs to ask to understand these governing factors are:

1. Does the level of demand for the service follow a regular predictable cycle?
2. If so, what are the underlying causes of these predictable variations?
3. Or are changes in the level of demand largely random in nature?
4. If so, what are the underlying causes of these random variations?

When demand for a service fluctuates widely in the short term, but follows a predictable pattern over a known cycle, it might be economically worthwhile to develop strategies designed to smooth out major fluctuations over time. Regular fluctuations in demand—such as seasonal cycles—can be influenced, to a large extent, by creative marketing. However, no strategy is likely to succeed unless it is based on an understanding of why customers seek to use the service when they do.

In contrast, marketing efforts can do little to smooth out random fluctuations in demand over time because these are usually the result of factors outside human control. Examples include natural calamities, political events, economic crises, personal illness, family disruptions, and so on.

2. Effect of demand on quality

Demand significantly affects quality in service organizations. Customers expect a firm's quality of service to be consistent—whatever the level of demand. When demand for a service is low it not only is a loss for the firm but more importantly the customers perceive the experience as less enjoyable and possibly of lower quality because few others are patronizing the business. Interestingly, employees can have lower perceptions about the firm when the demand for their service is below the optimum capacity. If this continues, employees' motivation and moral will be affected. On the other hand, if the demand exceeds maximum capacity, it is a clear loss for the firm. In this case, customers who did not receive the service might not give the firm a second chance and hence the opportunities to impress those customers are lost forever. At the same time, those who are receiving service will feel the pressure of the overcrowded service environment and experience reduced quality because of the reduced personalized attention by the service employees. If this continues for a longer period of time, employees will not be able to cope with the pressure and may even leave. Similarly, customers continue to see the reduction in quality and may not use the service in the future. Figure 2.2 provides a visual representation showing the impact of demand fluctuation on customers, firm and employees. To gain customer confidence, maintain image and engender customer loyalty, quality must be delivered consistently. It is imperative that service managers design strategies that assist them to manage demand and quality simultaneously.

In general (but not invariably), increased demand tends to decrease quality. Personal service is less likely to be as attentive and comfortable if there is a crowd of people to be looked after. This can be likened to maintaining an appropriate balance on a see-saw, as illustrated in Figure 2.3. However, if a firm has adequate quality-improvement programs in place, the drop-off in quality in these circumstances can be minimized.

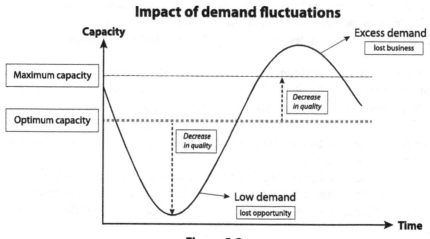

Figure 2.2
Impact of demand fluctuation

Figure 2.3
The supply/demand/quality challenge

There are circumstances in which increased demand actually improves quality as perceived by consumers. For example, a crowded dance floor in a nightclub might engender a desirable 'party atmosphere', and a sporting contest with a large crowd cheering enthusiastically might be experienced as a more exciting and stimulating event. Despite these exceptions, it is generally the case that increased demand threatens quality.

3. Waiting and the psychology of waiting

One useful way to approach customer waiting is to think about it as the organization is 'charging' their customers in 'time' currency. So saving a customer's time is one of the quickest ways to increase the value of the service experience! (Fisk, 2009). Shemwell and Cronin (1994) state that the challenge is to make the wait less painful.

©Photo courtesy of David Solnet

Waiting for a service often causes a misperception of the amount of time a person was waiting. This concept is called the 'psychology of waiting' (Maister, 1985), and there are many different conditions that affect a person's perception of wait times. Some of these include:

1. Unoccupied time feels longer than occupied time.
2. Anxious, sad and angry waits feel longer than relaxed ones.
3. Waits of uncertain length feel longer than certain ones.
4. Unexplained waits feel longer than explained ones.
5. Uncomfortable waits feel longer than comfortable ones.
6. Unfair waits feel longer than fair ones.

It is important for service managers to understand the psychological impact that waiting has on customers. These conditions, if integrated into management thought and action, can reduce the negative impact of waiting perceptions. In fact, many successful service firms now take advantage of technology in order to reduce the wait or wait perception. For example, the virtual-queue concept eliminates physical waiting by allowing customers to register their place in line and then spend that time doing other activities. Restaurants hand out buzzers so that customers can leave the immediate area and return to the restaurant when paged, while some use short messaging services (SMS) to contact customers. Disney World invented a concept known as FASTPASS which allows customers to leave a line and return at a predetermined time when they would not have to wait. Even McDonald's now have a system where food is ordered at one place and collected at another, with a monitor displaying the assigned number corresponding to each order. There are many other examples now where technology is being used to reduce the need for customers to wait.

4.   Strategies for managing demand

The service literature contains many different strategies for managing demand and readers are encouraged to consult the references given at the end of this chapter for more detail. Some of these strategies are summarized in Table 2.1 below.

Table 2.1   Strategies for Managing Demand

Strategy	Description / Management Benefit	Example
Differential pricing schemes	An incentive offered through price variations by the service organization to shift customer demand from peak to non-peak periods.	'Happy hours' at bars, 'early bird' prices for concert tickets and special hotel room rates at particular times of the week or year.
Product variation	Different versions of the same service can be offered simultaneously—in response to variations in customer preference and ability to pay.	First-class, business-class and tourist-class services on airlines, or the range of room and service categories in hotels.
Product packaging	Services packaged in such a way that they are presented to customers as a variety of product offerings, resulting in services being used by different customer groups during slack periods.	Sunday 'brunch' attracts many customers who, having skipped breakfast, welcome the option of an early lunch in late morning—a slack period of demand at most restaurants.
Developing complementary services	Additional services offered to either attract consumers away from 'bottleneck' operations at peak times or provide them with an alternative service while queuing for operations restricted by limited capacity.	Hotels might offer a poolside breakfast to reduce breakfast congestion in the restaurant during holiday periods, or restaurants might seat patrons in a lounge with cocktails while they wait for a table on busy nights.
Developing non-peak demand by promotions	Using promotions to increase volume during periods of low demand. While this can provide significant benefit, it is important that caution be exercised when developing plans to increase demand for under-used periods.	A hotel might introduce a 'one-off' promotion that is successful, but adversely affects the experience of regular patrons to the extent that they cease to patronize the establishment, leaving the hotel with a loss of its usual 'baseline income' from regular off-peak patronage.

Other strategies for managing demand include focusing on different market segments that use the product differently. For example, a seaside resort hotel may focus on corporate meetings and training during the low season or a business hotel can offer special events for filling empty weekend rooms (Bowen and Ford, 2002).

A vast array of online service providers and websites, such as LastMinute.com and Wotif.com, allow service providers to sell hotel rooms and flights at a discounted price that might not have sold otherwise. This is called third-party distribution marketing and many hoteliers use some kind of discounted distribution to clear their inventory of unsold rooms in addition to using these channels to broaden the scope of their marketing efforts. Similarly, companies such as Expedia.com and Travelocity are commonly used by customers to access the lowest possible rates in many travel-related sectors by giving customers access to wide varieties and choices in one place. Many firms use these companies to help (a) fill unused capacity and also (b) to capture a wider range of potential customers.

Aspects of supply (capacity)

In searching for strategies to coordinate demand and capacity in services, let us now consider the 'supply side' of the equation. The following aspects of capacity are worthy of note:

1. capacity and quality;
2. maximum capacity and optimum capacity; and
3. strategies for managing supply.

© Malcolm Chapman/Shutterstock.com

Each of these is considered below.

1. Capacity and quality

If the fluctuation of demand is rapid and unpredictable (for example, as occurs on a stock exchange), it is extremely difficult for managers to forecast requirements, and to develop contingency plans in terms of altering capacity to meet demand.

However, simply increasing capacity can be a rather blunt response. Excess capacity not only results in a loss of profit, but also can actually decrease the quality of the service experience. For example, although many patrons might say that they like a relatively uncrowded restaurant, a restaurant that has only one table occupied has such an excess of capacity that it fails to offer the desired social ambiance to its patrons.

Nevertheless, a chronic inability to meet service demand does constitute a serious quality and revenue problem for many service businesses. A demand far in excess of capacity usually leads to dissatisfaction regarding quality among those who are served, and no service at all for those who cannot be accommodated! Taken together this represents a significant loss (both potential and permanent) for the business—hotels and restaurants potentially lose the customers they do have, and can never recover the business missed completely during the peak season.

Having said that, it must be noted that there is a subtle distinction between optimum capacity and maximum capac-

© Radu Bercan/Shutterstock.com

ity. In assessing capacity and quality, a distinction must be made between these two concepts of capacity.

2.   Maximum capacity and optimum capacity

There is a difference between maximum capacity and optimum capacity. At any given point in time, a service organization is faced with one of four conditions (Lovelock, Patterson and Walker, 2001):

1. demand exceeds maximum available capacity and potential business can be lost; or
2. demand exceeds the optimum capacity level; no one is turned away, but all customers are likely to perceive deterioration in the quality of service delivered; or
3. demand and supply are well balanced at the level of optimum capacity; or
4. demand is below optimum capacity, productive resources are underutilized and, in some instances, customers might find the experience disappointing or have doubts about the viability of the service.

In this context, it is important to understand the distinction between maximum capacity and optimum capacity. Maximum capacity represents the upper limit that the organization can possibly achieve, whereas optimum capacity is the desirable level achievable. When demand exceeds maximum

© Photo courtesy of David Solnet

capacity, potential customers can be disappointed when they are turned away, and their business might be lost forever. When demand is operating between optimum and maximum capacity, there is a risk that all customers being served at that time might receive inferior service, and consequently decide not to return in the future. The optimum level of capacity is likely to vary from one service business to another, and even from one market segment to another.

Occasionally optimum and maximum capacities are the same—for example, as previously noted, a crowded nightclub or bar is often regarded as both desirable and necessary to create the atmosphere of excitement and participation that enhances the service experience. In contrast, a restaurant's customers might feel that they receive a markedly superior service if the restaurant operates below full capacity. Similarly, airline passengers nearly always feel more comfortable if the seat adjacent to them is empty.

In most service businesses, however, a full-capacity operation frequently results in a reduced service quality, and therefore represents a concern for service managers, employees and customers alike.

© Air Images/Shutterstock.com

3.   Strategies for managing supply

Generally speaking, service managers are able to exert a more direct influence on the supply side of capacity planning than they are able to apply to the demand side. There are several measures that a service manager can adopt to adjust capacity to fluctuating demand, some of which are summarized in Table 2.2 below.

Table 2.2   Strategies for Managing Supply

Strategy	Description / Management Benefit	Example
Using part-time employees	Maintain a base of full-time employees who operate the facility during non-rush periods, and augment these staff members with part-time assistance during peak periods.	Some peaks occur during the hours of the day (such as in restaurants), others vary across the days of the week (such as in city hotels, which are busy during weekdays, but not as busy at weekends), and still others differ according to the months of the year (such as in summer and winter resort hotels).
Maximizing efficiency	Managers examine peak-time tasks to discover if certain skills are lacking or are inefficiently used. If these skills can be made more productive, the effective capacity of the system can be increased.	Many restaurants combine buffet service and table service during the peak periods of lunch and dinner, thereby enhancing the efficiency of the supply system.
Sharing capacity	Sharing expensive equipment and specialist labor skills with another business during non-peak times.	Two or more hotels in close proximity often share complementary airport shuttle services.

Summary

The main objective of service management is to provide guests with *a superior experience*. It is thus imperative that managers understand the nature of their service offerings and be able to ensure customer satisfaction with the service provision, rather than with the *technical features* of various products.

The four basic differences between service products and manufactured goods—intangibility, inseparability, heterogeneity and perishability—are well established in the literature. The four characteristics are well described, but the *ramifications* of these characteristics have not been as well explored. The fact is that the management and marketing of service products have been significantly influenced by theories from the manufacturing sector and/ or by the intuitive judgments of individual service managers. But this is not good enough! Theory from the manufactured goods sector is inappropriate for services marketing. Thus, a reliance on such theory can significantly decrease customer satisfaction with a firm's services, and thereby affect that firm's overall business performance.

The ramifications of the distinctive characteristics of service products present significant challenges to service firms. However, service providers who can meet these challenges will significantly improve customer satisfaction, maintain the firm's competitive advantage and lift its overall profit performance.

It is therefore important that service managers understand these distinctive characteristics of services, and the implications that flow from them—not only from a managerial perspective but also from the customers' point of view.

Managers must be able to design and implement appropriate strategies to overcome the challenges and thus maximize the potential for competitive advantage.

Review Questions

1. Briefly describe the four distinctive characteristics of service. Which of them is considered to be the most critical distinctive feature?

2. Briefly describe the challenges and managerial implications of each of the characteristics described in the previous question.

3. What is value cocreation and what are the implications for service managers? Think of the examples of services where a customer has a critical and a minimal involvement. In which case do you think it is easier for the service provider to deliver a superior service—when a customer is being a passive or an active recipient?

4. While technology innovations allow a firm to soften some of the negative effects of heterogeneity, can you think of other advantages from using technology from the customer's point of view? Is there any potential downside in a 'high-tech' approach as opposed to a 'high touch' approach?

5. Compare the usual order of production-selling-consumption for tangible goods vs. service provision.

6. Think about a situation you have been in where supply and demand seemed to be imbalanced. How did it affect you as a customer?

7. Explain the relationship between service demand, supply and quality. Explain where the 'sweet spot' for demand should be in relation to capacity in order to ensure the best service quality.

8. Name any three conditions of the 'psychology of waiting' concept and discuss possible ways to address a negative impact of each of those waiting perceptions.

9. Based on the four unique characteristics of service, compare the hospitality industry with other service sectors (for example, airlines, health services and so on). Can you think of any special features that characterize the hotel business that are not found in other service businesses? For example, whereas airlines can adjust their schedules, allocate their aircraft to other routes and hire additional aircraft in response to demand, hotels cannot change their locations or rent additional rooms to meet seasonal demand. As a result hotels generally have less flexibility than airlines in managing their capacity, which makes it more difficult for hotel managers to adjust their supply according to the demand. Can you think of other special features affecting the hotel industry?

Suggested Readings

This is a list of suggested further reading on topics covered in this chapter. For a separate list of full reference citations quoted in the chapter, see 'References', Chapter 2, page 324.

Bendapudi, N., and Leone, R. P. (2003). Psychological implications of customer participation in co-production. *Journal of Marketing*, 67(1), 14–28.

Buell, R. W., and Norton, M. I. (2011). Think customers hate waiting? Not so fast . . . *Harvard Business Review*, 89(5), 34.

Dickson, D., Ford, R. C., and Laval, B. (2005). Managing real and virtual waits in hospitality and service organizations. *Hotel and Restaurant Administration Quarterly*, 46(1), 52–68.

Ford, R. C., and Bowen, D. E. (2008). A service-dominant logic for management education: It's time. *Academy of Management Learning and Education*, 7(2), 224–243.

Grönroos, C. (2008). Service logic revisited: who creates value? And who co-creates? *European Business Review, 20*(4), 298–314.

Lusch, R. F., Vargo, S. L., and O'Brien, M. (2007). Competing through service: Insights from service-dominant logic. *Journal of Retailing*, 83(1), 5–18.

Noone, B. M., and Coulter, R. C. (2012). Applying modern robotics technologies to demand predication and production management in the quick-service restaurant sector. *Cornell Hospitality Quarterly*, 53(2), 122–133.

Payne, A. F., Storbacka, K., and Frow, P. (2008). Managing the co-creating of value. *Journal of the Academy of Marketing Science*, 36, 83–96.

Sasser, W. E. (1976). Match supply and demand in service industries. *Harvard Business Review*, November–December, 133–140.

Shah, D., Rust, R. T., Parasuraman, A., Staelin, R., and Day, G. S. (2006). The path to customer centricity. *Journal of Service Research*, 9(2), 113–124.

Shaw, G., Bailey, A., and Williams, A. (2011). Aspects of service-dominant logic and its implications for tourism management: Examples from the hotel industry. *Tourism Management*, 32, 207–214.

Taylor, S. (1994). Waiting for service: The relationship between delays and evaluations of service. *Journal of Marketing, 58*(2), 56–69.

Vargo, S. L., and Akaka, M. A. (2009). Service-dominant logic as a foundation for service science: Clarifications. *Service Science,* 1(1), 32–41.

Vargo, S. L., and Lusch, R. F. (2004). Evolving to a new dominant logic for marketing. *Journal of Marketing*, 68(1), 1–17.

Xie, C., Bagozzi, R. P., and Troye, S. V. (2008). Trying to prosume: Toward a theory of consumers as co-creators of value. *Journal of the Academy of Marketing Science,* 36, 109–122.

CHAPTER 3

Service Quality

Study Objectives

Having completed this chapter, readers should be able to:

1. Understand the differences between service quality management and the traditional (goods) quality management from a management perspective;
2. Understand the distinctive process of service management, and the challenges faced by service managers;
3. Understand the outcomes and importance of service quality management for companies; and
4. Have a thorough understanding of the various service quality models and their application in the service-related industries.

Outline

- ► Introduction
- ► An historic perspective on quality
  - ► The early days of quality control
  - ► Post-war (World War II) developments
- ► Economic impact of quality—Why quality is important
  - ► Product differentiation and competitive advantage
  - ► Market share and profitability
  - ► The cost of quality—Is it worth it?
- ► The quality 'gurus'
  - ► W. Edwards Deming (1900–1993)
  - ► Joseph M. Juran (1904–2008)

- ► Philip Crosby (1926–2001)
- ► The core ideas of 'total quality management' (TQM)
- ► Uniqueness of quality theory for service
  - ► Lacking a philosophy or conceptualization of service quality
  - ► But service is different
  - ► Looking to the customer
- ► Outcomes of service quality
  - ► Customer satisfaction
  - ► Customer loyalty
  - ► The relationship between satisfaction and loyalty
  - ► Customer delight
- ► Understanding service quality theory
  - ► Comparing expectations and performance
  - ► Confirmation and disconfirmation of expectations
  - ► Meeting or exceeding expectations
  - ► The effect of multiple consumption
- ► Service quality measurement—No easy task
  - ► The 'Nordic' model (technical quality and functional quality)
  - ► Two-dimensional model (process and output quality)
    - ▪ Process quality
    - ▪ Output quality
    - ▪ Two types of output
  - ► The 'Gaps' model
  - ► SERVQUAL
    - ▪ Zone of tolerance
  - ► SERVPERF (multi-level models)
  - ► Electronic (web) service quality
- ► Summary
- ► Review Questions
- ► Suggested Readings

Key Words

Assurances	Customer satisfaction
Competitive advantage	Disconfirmation of expectations
Confirmation of expectations	Electronic service quality
Consumer behavior	Empathy
Consumer expectations	Gap model
Cost of quality	Joseph Juran
Customer delight	Market and profit share
Customer loyalty	Multiple consumption

Nordic model
Output quality
Philip Crosby
Process quality
Product differentiation
Quality control
Quality cost
Quality gurus
Quality management
Reliability
Responsiveness
Service quality management
Service quality measurement
Service quality model
SERVPERF model
SERVQUAL model
Statistical quality control
Tangibles
Total quality control
TQM (total quality management)
Two-dimensional model
W. Edwards Deming
Zone of tolerance

Introduction

In all industries, quality has long been recognized as essential to business survival. This chapter begins with an outline of the history and development of quality management and the contribution of quality 'gurus' to the formation and promotion of quality control principles.

Although these general principles of quality management in manufacturing do have relevance to service industries, it must be recognized that service industries have characteristics not generally found in manufacturing (see Chapter 2). Service quality is therefore not the same as product quality, and the management of service quality is not the same as the management of goods quality.

© Stuart Miles/Shutterstock.com

© FuzzBones/Shutterstock.com

Service quality is difficult to define and difficult to control, and various measures of service quality have been proposed. However, in the final analysis, the expectations and perceptions of customers are what matters in any assessment of service quality. Ultimately, the needs and expectations of customers guide the design of quality strategies in services.

As service academics have recognized a need to define service quality accurately, and as service practitioners have felt the need to manage it effectively with a view to a sustainable competitive advantage, various ways of defining and measuring service quality have been introduced. This chapter presents some of the most significant service quality management theories, together with their implications for hospitality and tourism managers.

An historic perspective on quality

The early days of quality control

Quality control was first developed in manufacturing by engineers and statisticians during the 1920s, with control focusing on the physical production of goods and internal measurements of the production processes. Quality control was originally seen as a means of ensuring consistency among the parts produced by different sections of a single company, so that parts could be interchanged with confidence. At first this was achieved by inspecting 100% of all outputs.

A breakthrough occurred with the introduction of the concept of statistical quality control—the idea that only a random sample of output warranted inspection to ensure an acceptable quality level. Modern quality control began in the 1930s when Walter Shewhart, a physicist employed at Bell Labs, invented process control, using control charts and the 'Plan–Do–Check–Act' cycle of continuous improvement. During arms manufacturing in World War II, American industry used a combination of Shewhart's process control and the statistical sampling methods of an American statistician and government consultant, Dr. W. Edwards Deming, who had become an early disciple of Shewhart. The combination became known as statistical process control.

Post-war (World War II) developments

In 1951, another significant development in the story of quality management came with the publication of the first edition of Joseph Juran's *Quality Control Handbook*—a publication that became the 'bible' of the quality-control movement. Also in 1951, Armand V. Feigenbaum took Juran's ideas a step further by proposing a concept of 'total quality control' (TQC). Feigenbaum's ideas were based on his observation that all new products moved through three stages of activity—design control, incoming material control and product (or shop floor) control—and that TQC required quality control at all stages.

While these new concepts were slowly gaining acceptance in Western countries, crucial changes were taking place in Japan following World War II. These changes resulted in Japan playing a vital role in the historic development of the quality movement. At the end of World War II, Japan's economic recovery was dependent on its only plentiful resource—people—and on their ability to export manufactured goods produced from imported raw materials and energy. Japan's likelihood of success at that time seemed remote. It had a largely unskilled and illiterate labor force and its industries had been devastated by war. At that time, Japan had a universal reputation as a producer of cheap and unreliable goods.

In July 1950, the Union of Japanese Scientists and Engineers (JUSE) invited Deming to Japan. Deming held a series of lectures during which he taught the basic principles of statistical quality control to Japanese executives, managers and engineers. This was followed by a meeting with the presidents of twenty-one major Japanese companies, including the present-day world giants Sony, Nissan, Mitsubishi and Toyota. His teachings made a deep impression and provided great impetus to the implementation of quality control in Japan. In appreciation, JUSE created a prize in 1950 to commemorate Deming's contribution, and to promote the continued development of quality control in Japan. Annual awards of the Deming Prize are still given each year.

More than six decades following the award of the first Deming Prize in Japan, the concept of quality management has become the recognized guiding strategy for almost all firms around the world. Quality ultimately gives firms a competitive advantage. This emphasis has been felt across all lines of business, whether profit making or non-profit making, in both the manufacturing and service industries.

Economic impact of quality—Why quality is important

Product differentiation and competitive advantage

Conventional theory recognizes two generic strategic alternatives for developing a sustainable competitive advantage. The first is *product differentiation*, and the second is *overall cost leadership* (Porter, 1985). Quality control is a crucial element of the first of these. Although product differentiation can take many forms, superior quality is the most common basis of differentiation (Crosby, 1979, 1984; Deming, 1982; Kiechel, 1981). If customers see a clear-cut quality advantage, they usually favor that product, without trying to weigh all other factors.

A preoccupation with quality on the part of customers has become increasingly recognized, and quality has become the key to gaining competitive advantage. Firms today know that they cannot afford to ignore quality. Japanese domination of the market in the second half of the twentieth century, through the manufacture of exceptional quality products, had a significant effect on the balance of payments in Western Europe and the USA. It became crucial, therefore, for manufacturers to lift competitiveness in Europe and North America to meet the quality of the reliable products offered by Japanese competitors.

This became even more apparent with the rapid development of 'globalization'. In a competitive global market, with its fragmented and deregulated markets, it soon became apparent to management that companies could not survive without quality. Profitability and long-term sustainability depended on it.

Market share and profitability

This apparent link between quality and profitability has been confirmed by numerous studies over the years, and depending on which market segment you are in, quality perceptions generally drive loyalty. Quality soon became established as the means by which firms sustained their position among competing firms over time, and the means by which they therefore maintained market and profit share.

Many past studies have confirmed the strong positive association between quality and market share. Similarly, subsequent studies of profit impact of market share (PIMS) indicated that improved quality increased the market share of firms five or six times faster than those which declined in quality. The link between quality of product (or service) and market share was confirmed in subsequent studies by service researchers, who also found a positive association between quality and profitability.

Although there are wide variations in research studies, there is a predominance of evidence showing positive correlations between customer variables (satisfaction, repurchase intention, perceived quality, perceived value and loyalty) and financial outcomes. We discuss the relationships among satisfaction, quality and loyalty later in this chapter.

The cost of quality—Is it worth it?

The concept of the 'cost of quality' is a relatively new phenomenon in the business world. Quality costs. It costs money to achieve quality. But, more significantly, it costs money *not* to achieve quality.

The cost of poor quality is well recognized. Grönroos (1991) noted that it is not too much quality that really costs, but too much *low* quality—a point that had been made earlier by Crosby (1979) who coined the startling phrase 'quality is free' to emphasize the general point that the presence of poor quality is the real drain on resources, rather than the costs of attempting to fix the lack of quality.

Indeed, according to the literature on operations management, quality and costs have been proven to be inversely related. That is, quality saves more than it costs. Or, to put it another way, the costs of improving quality are less than the resulting savings that would have otherwise been lost in rework, scrap and warranty expenses. This is a view widely held among Japanese manufacturers, and explains much of their dedication to the goal of 'continuous improvement'. Of course this general truism must be tempered by circumstance. For example, the degree of quality offered will vary depending on the service 'concept' of a firm. If a coffee shop decides to provide 'high quality' five star service to its customers, the outcomes would not be beneficial.

Product quality is synonymous with the absence of defects, and the costs in question are quality costs. These quality costs include:

- ▶ prevention costs;
- ▶ appraisal costs;
- ▶ internal failure costs;
- ▶ external failure costs;
- ▶ the cost of exceeding customer requirements; and
- ▶ the cost of lost opportunities.

Crosby (1979) argued that, taken together, these various costs can drain a company of 20–30% of its revenue or turnover. In service industries, this total cost can be as high as 40–45% of revenue or turnover.

The quality 'gurus'

The historic evolution of the quality movement has been led by three American experts on quality who have become known as the quality 'gurus'—W. Edwards Deming, Joseph Juran and Philip Crosby. Their emergence was predominantly a response to changes in American and Japanese markets, and the need to adapt to survive. The contributions of the 'gurus' extend from the mere theory of overall management philosophy to the development of the practical tools of quality management.

W. Edwards Deming (1900–1993)

Dr. W. Edwards Deming was the first of the American quality 'gurus' to arrive in Japan and is generally considered to have been the 'father' of the Japanese quality revolution. Deming's message to the Japanese was really quite simple. It was encapsulated in the so called 'chain reaction' (Figure 3.1).

Although Deming did not introduce the Japanese to statistical quality control (these concepts and their importance having been well known in Japan long before he went there), his contribution was to help his hosts cut through the academic theory, such that the essential ideas were presented in a simple way that was meaningful—right down to the level of production workers.

Once the Japanese accepted his new approach, Deming concentrated on showing them how to improve quality by the use of statistical control of the process. The main thrust of Deming's philosophy was the *planned reduction of variation*. He demonstrated how productivity improves as variability decreases and, since all things vary, the need to use statistical methods to control work processes. According to Deming, statistical control did not imply absence of defective items; rather it was a state of random variation, in which the limits of variation were predictable.

© tkemot/Shutterstock.com

Although he was primarily a statistician, Deming was clearly involved in more than the mere teaching of statistics in his fourteen points. He was, in fact, proclaiming a whole management philosophy. However, at that time (and, sadly, even today), Deming's approach represented the complete antithesis of conventional management thinking. As a result of Deming's influence in the early 1950s, various quality-control

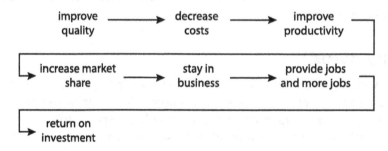

Figure 3.1
Deming's chain reaction
Source: Adapted from Deming (1982)

methods were developed, and many good results were achieved. However, three major shortcomings in these methods remained:

- ▶ over reliance on statistical methods;
- ▶ over reliance on promotion of standardization; and
- ▶ top management lagging behind in the progress towards effective quality control.

Joseph M. Juran (1904–2008)

W. Edwards Deming was not the sole instigator of the Japanese 'conversion', and nor was he the only 'prophet' on quality in the immediate post-war period. Another American, Dr. Joseph M. Juran, visited Japan in 1954. He emphasized that quality control should be conducted as an integral part of overall management control. Although a statistician himself, he did not limit his work to statistical analysis. Juran pointed out that companies could have a comprehensive knowledge of the technical aspects of quality, such as statistical process control, but that this did not help them to *manage* quality. He was the first of the 'gurus' to emphasize that achieving quality was all about communication, management and people. His message was clear—quality did not happen by accident; it had to be planned and executed by enlightened management. Juran believed that the majority of quality problems were the fault of poor management, rather than poor workmanship on the shop floor.

Philip Crosby (1926–2001)

Philip Crosby has probably done more to alert Western management to the need for quality improvement, and management's responsibility for it, than all the other 'gurus' and experts combined. Beginning with *Quality is Free* (1979), his books, speeches and broadcasts have influenced thousands of executives to change their behavior and commit themselves to quality. Crosby's best-known ideas have been the exhortation to achieve 'zero defects' and the concept of 'do it right first time'. Crosby's thoughts, expressed in his book *Quality Without Fears* (1984), exerted a major influence on management in the early 1980s and initiated a growing body of research and literature in the field.

Crosby believed that, since most companies allow a certain deviation from specifications, manufacturing companies spend approximately 20% of their revenue doing things wrong, and then having to correct the errors. According to Crosby, for service companies this cost could amount to 35% of revenue. He did not believe that workers should take prime responsibility for poor quality; the reality, he said, was that management had to be improved.

Crosby argued that effective quality management required:

1. a definition of quality that can be readily understood by all; that is, the beginning of a common language that will aid communication;
2. a system by which to manage quality;

3. a performance standard that leaves no room for doubt or fudging by any employee; and

4. a method of measurement that focuses attention on the progress of quality improvement.

These points provided the premise for Crosby's 'four absolutes' for managing quality, as outlined below. These steps have proved successful in many companies and therefore demand careful examination.

Like other 'gurus', Crosby listed his core philosophy in a series of memorable points. He expressed these 'four absolutes' for managing quality as follows:

1. Quality is defined as conformance to requirements, not as 'goodness' or 'elegance'.
2. The system for producing quality is prevention, not appraisal.
3. The performance standard must be zero defects, not that which is close enough.
4. The measurement of quality is the price of non-conformance, not indices.

The core ideas of 'total quality management' (TQM)

From the above discussion, it is apparent that there is no single entity called 'total quality management' (TQM). TQM is an overall management philosophy that has been influenced by numerous academics and practitioners since the term 'total quality control' was first introduced by Armand Feigenbaum in a 1956 issue of the *Harvard Business Review*.

Because this movement has had input from many people over several decades, and because the idea is difficult to define with any precision, there is little consensus in the literature regarding the core ideas of TQM. Everyone seems to have a different set of essential principles.

Whichever words are chosen by different authors, and whichever points are emphasized, there are certain recurring themes. In terms of these *general recurring themes* of TQM, we note that TQM:

© moomsabuy/Shutterstock.com

▶ is focused on the customer and efficiency;

▶ has a conscious philosophy of continual systemic improvement;

▶ requires empowered employees involved in collaborative action; and

▶ requires committed management showing inspiring leadership.

Uniqueness of quality theory for service

Lacking a philosophy or conceptualization of service quality

Most of the above discussion on the historical development of quality control has centered on goods-manufacturing industries. In virtually all industries, the combination of globalization, deregulation and more demanding consumers has increased competition and pushed quality to the forefront of management concerns. The service sector has certainly not been immune to these developments. Indeed, delivering high quality service has been recognized as the most effective means by which a service company's offerings can be made to stand out from a crowd of look-alike competitive offerings. Research studies have repeatedly demonstrated the strategic advantage of superior quality in contributing to market share and profits. For example, Gupta, McLaughlin and Gomez (2007) studied a national restaurant chain and linked customer satisfaction, repeat-purchase intentions (customer loyalty) and restaurant performance (increased sales), all connected to the service-profit chain (see Chapter 8).

As we have seen, the 'quality movement' in goods manufacturing gained enormous impetus in the decades immediately after World War II. But the service sector lagged behind in coming to grips with these ideas, and 'quality' was not really introduced into the service literature until the beginning of the 1980s.

When service quality did start to become an issue, it was, to a large degree, influenced by traditional goods marketing, and it tended to follow a similar historical pattern. That is, initially, there was minimal reference to an overall *philosophy* of quality; little was said about *concepts* of quality, or *management models* of quality. Rather, service quality was more or less treated as a given variable. Variations in quality were seen as an unavoidable fact of life. Indeed, this is a situation that still unfortunately applies in many aspects of the service businesses.

But service is different

As they attempted to develop an appropriate philosophy of service quality, service managers recognized that the characteristics of service did not fit the characteristics of physical goods. Although the rendering of a given service might involve some physical goods, the service 'products' themselves were clearly different. Whereas goods quality could be measured objectively by such indicators as durability and the number of defects, there were no objective measures to assess the quality of intangible services.

Because most published works on quality focused on manufactured goods, the clear differentiation of products from services (see Chapter 2) became an important issue. It was clear that many of the quality strategies available to manufacturers were inappropriate for service firms. Researchers and practitioners alike realized that available knowledge about goods quality was insufficient for a proper understanding of service quality.

Looking to the customer

Because of these historical and conceptual factors, ideas of service quality had to be developed very much 'from scratch'. Instead of using quality concepts from the manufactured goods industry, service management researchers developed their own concepts of service quality. In drawing up these 'service-specific' models, they turned from an emphasis on manufacturing design to an emphasis on *consumer behavior, expectations and satisfaction.*

The consumer became central in these deliberations because, as many authors have noted, people evaluate services in a fundamentally different way from that in which they evaluate goods. A service is often a *performance*, usually conducted in the presence of the customer, and service quality is therefore very much a function of *subjective perception* of an experience, rather than objective examination of a physical object.

The service quality literature has thus been firmly based on the notion that service quality is defined by the *customer*—as opposed to the situation in manufactured goods where quality tends to be defined by designers or operations managers.

Outcomes of service quality

Before we progress with a review of the way service quality has been conceptualized and measured, we first turn our attention to some of the reasons why we even care about service quality—the 'hard' business outcomes that businesses aspire for—satisfaction, repeat purchase, loyalty, word-of-mouth behaviors, etc. We will look at these ideas in different places in this text (also see Chapter 6), but we offer a basic overview here to help the reader understand the 'outcome' of effective service quality management.

Customer satisfaction

Whenever discussions about service quality take place, there is inevitably overlap or even confusion about the differences between the concepts of quality and satisfaction. Our aim here is not to go too deeply into a detailed description of the conceptual differences between these two terms, except to provide a few points of difference and to make the case that there are definite similarities and differences. The concepts explained in this chapter are focused mainly on service quality, not satisfaction.

© Minerva Studio/Shutterstock.com

Satisfaction is often defined as the degree of consumption-related fulfillment provided by a product, service or experience (see the Richard Oliver (1980) reference in the References list for this chapter). That is, the "customer senses that consumption fulfills some need, desire, goal or so forth and that this fulfillment is pleasurable—and it is always related to a transaction. Thus, satisfaction is the customer's sense that consumption provides outcomes against a standard of pleasure versus displeasure" (Oliver, 1999, p. 34).

If satisfaction is related to 'consumption', quality is more 'observational'/'attitudinal' or 'process' driven. Satisfaction (with a firm) requires frequent and consistent positive experiences, whereas quality is often evaluated on a transaction basis (meaning when the service interaction occurs). There is research evidence showing that high service quality perceptions do not necessarily lead to satisfaction, and that low quality perceptions can lead to satisfaction. Service quality is only one driver of overall satisfaction. For example, in a restaurant setting, factors that influence satisfaction with the dining experience include "waiting time, quality of service, responsiveness of front-line employees, menu variety, food prices, food quality, food quality consistency, ambiance of the facilities, and convenience" (Gupta, McLaughlin and Gomez, 2007, p. 285). So while satisfaction and quality are related concepts, there are important distinctions. And while it would appear on the surface that satisfaction is an outcome of quality, it is not always the case. Nevertheless, there is strong evidence to suggest that the right service provided at the right level of quality for the customer segment leads to higher levels of satisfaction, which in turn leads to customer loyalty. Like many concepts covered in this book, there is rarely a 'black and white' answer in terms of how much of something is needed. Circumstances and context matter!

Customer loyalty

Another important consideration of any business is customer loyalty; that is, the degree to which customers repeatedly do business with the firm. Customer loyalty has been described as the feeling of attachment to or affection for a company's people, product or service (Jones and Sasser, 1995). Crotts and Ford (2008) define loyalty in terms of "high return frequency, high likelihood to recommend, and high overall satisfaction" (p. 233). Oliver (1999), in a seminal paper on the subject, defines loyalty as "a deeply held commitment to rebuy or patronize a preferred product/service consistently in the future, thereby causing repetitive same-brand or same brand-set purchasing, *despite* situational influences and marketing efforts having the potential to cause switching behavior" (p. 34). Loyalty is said to be either attitudinal (a person feels or says they are loyal to

© donskarpo/Shutterstock.com

a firm) or behavioral (when this attitude of loyalty is converted into repeat patronage and even word-of-mouth advertising).

A basic business principle related to loyalty is called customer lifetime value (CLV), where a firm seeks to maximize profitability over the lifetime of a customer (Crotts and Ford, 2008). Oliver (1999) argues that 'ultimate loyalty' emerges from a combination of "product superiority, personal fortitude, social bonding and their synergistic effects" (p. 33). Similarly, Parasuraman, Berry and Zeithaml (1991) promote the need for businesses to become a 'customer franchise'—with *unwavering* customer loyalty which comes from exceeding customer expectations continually.

The relationship between satisfaction and loyalty

One might intuitively think that as satisfaction rises, so does loyalty. However this 'linear relationship' does not generally hold up to scrutiny. Although satisfaction is a necessary step in the formation of loyalty, there are many factors that influence loyalty. According to Jones and Sasser (1995), seemingly loyal customers can still defect to the competition. In a competitive environment, they argue, organizations must strive for extremely high levels of satisfaction to avoid customer defection (rather than merely satisfied). They argue that, except in a few rare instances, complete customer satisfaction is the key to securing customers. Their research provides evidence that there is a significant loyalty gap between merely satisfied and completely satisfied customers. Figure 3.2 shows how the relationship between satisfaction and loyalty can change depending on circumstances. Note that in markets with little competition, customers can be very dissatisfied, but still remain loyal (as they have few choices to switch to the competition). However, in highly competitive markets, even moderate levels of satisfaction do not equate with commensurate levels of loyalty.

Figure 3.2
The non-linear relationship between satisfaction and loyalty
Source: Adapted from Jones and Sasser (1995)

Knowing and understanding the drivers of customer satisfaction and loyalty is critical. Studies regarding restaurants have shown strong links between satisfaction and loyalty (repeat-purchase intentions); however, the importance of one aspect of the offering can vary by type of restaurant and the customer circumstance. For instance, food quality is the critical attribute influencing repeat-purchase intentions in full-service restaurants, while speed and efficiency are more important attributes in quick-service and fast casual restaurants (Gupta, McLaughlin and Gomez, 2007).

© donskarpo/Shutterstock.com

Therefore, managers must realize that achieving satisfaction is not a 'one size fits all' situation and needs to be framed by the particular context of the service.

Customer delight

Another stream of related research proposes the term 'customer delight', meaning a profoundly positive emotional state generally resulting from having one's expectations exceeded to a surprisingly large degree (Rust and Oliver, 2000). This approach is one that is followed by Ritz-Carlton Hotels, highlighted by their "fulfilling even the unexpressed wishes of our guests" commitment. However, this type of approach is a contentious strategy because at some point it becomes unsustainable to exceed expectations of a customer who regularly patronizes a business. Other research (Dixon, Freeman, and Toman, 2010) suggests that in many service settings, such as phone-based and self-service interactions, loyalty is driven not by how dazzling the service experience might be, but

© Gromovataya/Shutterstock.com

rather by how well the company can deliver on the very basic service promise. They found (through a very large study) that delighting customers does not by itself build loyalty; rather, reducing the required effort of the customer and solving problems quickly does.

One pattern developing in this discussion about service quality and the outcomes of service quality is that it is important to understand customers in order to plan the type of service and the degree of quality. Chapter 4 will explore the issue of understanding customers and their expectations.

Understanding service quality theory

Service quality has become a great differentiator among service providers. Indeed, it is the most powerful competitive weapon that many leading service organizations possess. Business survival and success are dependent on the delivery of superior service quality. However, even though it is well accepted that service quality is a crucial element in the success of any service organization, there are no clear-cut definitions of service quality.

Service quality is an abstract and elusive concept because of the well-known features—intangibility, perishability, heterogeneity, and inseparability of production and consumption (see Chapter 2). Because of these features, definitions of quality can vary from person to person, and from situation to situation.

In developing an understanding of service quality, it is therefore important to understand what *customers* are looking for, and what *they* deem to be quality in services. According to Grönroos (1982b), such an understanding requires two distinct elements:

1. a clear conception of service quality—a conception that describes how customers perceive the quality of a service; and
2. an understanding of how such service quality is influenced, and which resources and activities affect service quality—that is, how service quality can be managed.

Comparing expectations and performance

How do consumers choose among various service offerings, and how do they evaluate the quality of the service offerings they receive?

When purchasing physical goods, consumers employ various tangible cues to ascertain quality. These include style, color, hardness, feel, package, brand name, price and so on. In contrast, when purchasing a service, consumers are forced to rely on a smaller number of available cues. In many cases, tangible evidence is limited to the service provider's physical facilities, equipment and personnel. In a service where personal experience of quality is a high priority, consumers who are attempting to evaluate service before purchase seek and rely on information from personal (such as word-of-mouth or social media) sources rather than from non-personal sources (such as advertisements).

Confirmation and disconfirmation of expectations

Having made a choice, how do consumers assess the quality of the service they have received? According to theories of consumer behavior, the subjective evaluation of various experiences associated with consumption is based on what is technically called a 'confirmation/disconfirmation paradigm'—that is, consumers compare their *prior expectations* of performance with the *actual performance*.

Several studies have been conducted in an effort to clarify how customers' expectations and preconceptions of performance affect the subsequent level of customer satisfaction or dissatisfaction with actual performance. In these studies, after using the product or service, the consumer compares the perceived or actual performance with the expected performance. In the jargon of the 'confirmation/disconfirmation paradigm', we can say that:

- ▶ *confirmation* results when the two performances match; but
- ▶ *disconfirmation* results when the two performances do not match; this can be of two types—*positive disconfirmation* when the perceived performance exceeds expectations, and *negative disconfirmation* when the perceived performance falls below expectations.

Because service experiences are inherently *personal* experiences, this confirmation or disconfirmation (as defined above) leads to an emotional reaction—referred to as 'arousal'. That is, if a product or service appears to be performing above or below expectations, the customer experiences an emotional reaction of significance (a sense of growing pleasure or a sense of growing concern). This arousal is then followed by a final assessment of satisfaction or dissatisfaction. In experiencing these changing emotions, the consumer is comparing prior expectations with actual experience.

But what did they expect? What is an 'expectation'? The term 'expectations', as used in the literature on consumer satisfaction, differs from the term as used in the literature on service quality. In the consumer satisfaction literature, expectations are viewed as predictions made by the customer about what is likely to happen during an impending transaction.

In contrast, in the service quality literature, expectations are viewed as what the customer desires, or wants, or thinks should happen. The crucial difference is between what consumers expect a service provider *will* offer and what they think the provider *should* offer. This subject will be discussed in more detail below.

Meeting or exceeding expectations

Service organizations can achieve a strong reputation for quality service only when they consistently meet or exceed customer service expectations. As we have seen, service quality is a measure of how well the service (as received) positively matches with expectations (as preconceived). These expectations might be expressed in terms of what is *likely* to happen or in terms of what *should* happen. Firms that satisfy what is *likely* to happen will do well. Firms that satisfy what *should* happen will do even better. Truly successful firms are those that consistently exceed customer expectations.

The issue of meeting and exceeding expectations (similar to the question of satisfaction vs. delight) has been debated in the literature. For example, Johnston (2004) argues that "exceeding expectations implies that organizations have continually to do more in order to deliver excellent service and delight their customers . . . this definition of excellent service is inappropriate, unachievable in the long term and difficult to operationalize" (p. 129). Exceeding expectations may be unnecessarily costly and "as delivered service quality increases so might customers' expectations of subsequent service. As a result, what might previously have been regarded as excellent service becomes simply adequate (expected) service, unless the organization continues investing in this spiral of increasing quality and expectations in order to continually exceed expectations" (Johnston, 2004, p. 130).

© iQoncept/Shutterstock.com

Exceeding Expectations—Ritz-Carlton Hotels

Carter Donovan was the concierge of the firm's Buckhead property in Atlanta. Donovan was informed a little girl had lost her teddy bear in the hotel. Although she managed to track it down, the bear went missing again on the day the family came for it. With the typical forethought displayed by all good Ritz-Carlton staff, Donovan realized that admitting to the little girl her bear was lost would break her heart. Instead, she ran to the gift-shop, bought a huge new bear and put it in the back of the hotel limousine. Taking the girl's hand, she opened the limousine door and said "Look how big you've gotten while staying at the Ritz-Carlton!" It worked."

Source: "Delighted, returning customers: Service the Ritz-Carlton way: Gold star advice from the leaders in service excellence." Republished with permission of Emerald Group Publishing Ltd, from *Strategic Direction*, 20(11), 7–9, Emerald Group Publishing Ltd, 2004; permission conveyed through Copyright Clearance Center, Inc.

The effect of multiple consumption

In many service situations, other customers can affect positively or negatively the quality perceived by any given individual. For example, a customer in a bar interacts with another customer and creates an enjoyable conversation while the two jointly enjoy the live music at the bar. Although the live music is good, it is the interaction with the other customer that makes the experience lively and memorable. The effect of other customers on the perception of service quality has been well explained by Grove and Fisk (1982) through a series of research projects involving real-life 'dramatic' events. In their framework, using the idea of a drama being enacted in a theatre, they considered that a number of people being served simultaneously was an 'audience', and that the service personnel were like 'actors' performing roles in a drama. In such situations, the audience influences the performance, and some members of the audience affect other members of the audience. The audience component clearly becomes important in an environment in which consumers are required to share the same service facility.

The concept of *multiple consumption* is an important related idea. Unlike tangible goods, many service products can be enjoyed by more than one consumer simultaneously—but without having to share the product. Musical concerts, educational lectures and cinema screenings are good examples. However, although the consumers do not share the actual product, the intimacy that links production and consumption of these services means that consumers are influenced either positively or negatively by their coconsumers.

Furthermore, the size of the 'audience' can have an effect (positive or negative) on the service experience. In the case of a crowded dance floor in a nightclub, a large group adds to the atmosphere of the experience. However, in the case of a crowded flight or grocery shop, a large number of customers can have a negative effect on the service experience.

Service managers have difficulty controlling such customer-generated effects. However, being aware of what cannot be controlled at operational stages encourages managers to assess overall design modification. Assessment of these variables when designing (or redesigning) the service process is an important aspect of quality management.

Service quality measurement—No easy task

So, how do customers assess service quality? What parameters matter in their assessment? How can service quality be analyzed in conceptual terms? There have been various models proposed by different researchers in the field. Some of these proposed models have certain similarities to one another. Others are quite different in their ideas and arrangements of factors. The variety of conceptions in the service literature demonstrates the difficulty in developing a single acceptable model that adequately describes all aspects of service quality. This is to be expected. After all, it is not easy to find a single model which takes into account every aspect of something as complex as how human beings make a subjective assessment of a personal experience. And this is what service quality is essentially all about—the subjective assessment of a complex human experience. This is certainly not an easy concept to analyze and model in simple terms!

In this next section we offer a number of the more well-cited service quality conceptualizations in order to provide a flavor of the thinking which has gone into the development of service quality.

One of the earliest models was that proposed by Sasser, Olsen and Wyckoff (1978), which introduced three different dimensions of service performance—*materials*, *facilities* and *personnel*. Thus, service performance (or service quality) was conceived to be affected by:

▶ the quality of the *materials* that form part of the service offering (for example, food in a restaurant);

▶ the quality of the *facilities* that complement the core offering (for example, comfortable seating in an aircraft); and

▶ the quality of the *personnel* (for example, a friendly and pleasant hotel receptionist).

All have the potential to influence service quality. The important point to appreciate in this trichotomy is the notion that service quality involves more than the outcome quality—that is, the methods and manner by which the service is delivered are of vital importance.

Developments and variations of this view of service quality have been offered by many researchers (see for example Grönroos (1982a); Lehtinen and Lehtinen (1983); Parasuraman, Zeithaml, and Berry (1985; 1988); Rust and Oliver (1994); Dabholkar, Thorpe, and Rentz (1996) and Brady and Cronin (2001) among others). They differ in their approaches, but what they have in common is recognition that service quality is multifactorial, complex and variable in origin. Space does not permit a full exploration of each of them here, but all have important contributions to make. The rest of this chapter provides a summarizing overview of these various models (see Table 3.1). Readers who are interested in particular models are invited to review the various contributions of researchers by noting the reference citations given in this text. We stress the point that there is no 'one best way' established in the literature—however, understanding the different ways that service quality has been conceptualized over the years helps in gaining a greater understanding about the central issues surrounding service quality challenges and opportunities.

The 'Nordic' model (technical quality and functional quality)

Grönroos (1982a) identified two dimensions in service quality. He argued that service quality is a combination of *technical* quality and *functional* quality (see Figure 3.3).

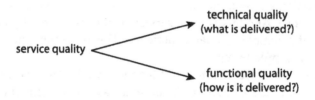

Figure 3.3
The Nordic model: "technical quality and functional quality"

Table 3.1

Service Quality Models

Service Quality Model	Researcher(s)	Description of Model	Conceptual Uniqueness of the Model
The 'Nordic' Model	Grönroos, 1982	Technical / functional (what / how)—service quality is a combination of what the customer bought and how it was delivered to them.	The 'how' is more important. Focus on functional quality to achieve organizational success.
Two-Dimensional Quality (Process-Output)	Lehtinen, 1983	Process / output—service quality is a combination of the customer's assessments both during and after the service experience.	By controlling the process quality, output quality can also be controlled.
The 'Gaps' Model	Oliver, 1980 or Parasuraman, Zeithaml and Berry, 1985	Confirmation / disconfirmation—service quality is determined when customers evaluate the experience based on their expectations and perceptions.	Customer judgments occur across multiple encounters involving service design, communication, management and delivery.
SERVQUAL	Parasuraman, Zeithaml and Berry, 1985, 1988	A multi-item scale designed to measure customer expectations and perceptions according to five (originally 10) service quality dimensions. An extension of the Gaps model.	Using the 'Gaps' model with five specific service dimensions developed over many years of scale development.
SERVPERF	Cronin and Taylor, 1992	A multi-item scale derived from the SERVQUAL scale.	Does not measure expectations, only measures performance.

In discussing *technical* quality, Grönroos argued that, although service is basically intangible, and although production and consumption are virtually simultaneous, the material content in the buyer–seller interaction is still important in the customer's assessment of perceived service quality. Examples of this technical quality include:

▶ food in the restaurant service;
▶ the room and bed in a hotel;
▶ computerized systems in a bank;
▶ machines used in a car-repair service center;
▶ the ski-lift machine at a ski resort; and
▶ an employee's technical skills and ability in serving a firm's customers.

In short, *technical quality* relates to *what* the customer receives in material terms. Technical quality represents the core component of the service, and the primary need of the customer. In discussing *functional* quality, Grönroos pointed out that, because a service is often a subjective experience of the customer (for example, the experience of a meal in a restaurant), and because these experiences are produced through close interaction with the employees of the service firm, the technical quality dimension alone cannot account for the customer's perception of the total quality they have received. Customers will be influenced by *the way in which the technical quality is transferred to them*. Examples of this functional quality include:

► the friendliness of a hotel receptionist;
► the behavior of a restaurant waiter;
► the helpfulness of a train conductor;
► the attitude of a consultant; and
► the accessibility of a teller machine (in the context of technology-supported services).

In short, *functional quality* relates to *how* the customer receives a service.

What Grönroos sees as *technical quality* relates to what Sasser, Olsen and Wyckoff (1978) identified to be the first two dimensions of service performance—the *materials* and the *facilities*. Accordingly, Grönroos' *functional quality* equates to Sasser, Olsen and Wyckoff's (1978) third service performance dimension—*personnel*.

Of these two elements—technical quality ('what') and functional quality ('how')—the former can often be quantitatively measured (as an objective phenomenon), whereas the latter is difficult to evaluate (because it constitutes a subjective perception). Despite the fact that technical quality is easier to measure, it is often of lesser importance in the perception of service quality by the customer. How the service is rendered (that is, the functional quality of a service) is, in most cases, much more important than the material means by which it is rendered (that is, the technical quality of the service).

There are exceptions to this, like in nearly any case of satisfaction and quality. For example, if you pay a company to come to your home and wash your car, and the technician is the nicest, most helpful and friendly person (functional quality), but he does an awful job on the actual cleaning (technical quality), then it is unlikely that you would see this as a quality experience. In that case, technical quality wins out over functional quality. Technical quality, however, relates to the core service (see Chapter 1 about the difference between core and peripheral services) and hence customers will not compromise on any shortcomings in technical quality.

Functional quality commonly constitutes the key to an organization's success. From the perspective of the customer, while technical quality is essential, any deficiencies in technical quality can be compensated by superior functional quality. However, the opposite is not true. It is the functional quality that provides the perfect context for customer experience that nurtures the all-important customer-firm relationship. Crotts and Ford (2008) agree that the organization that is able to create a guest experience that keeps customers coming back will have a competitive advantage. Similarly Pine and Gilmore (1998) would also agree, as they see the *how* (i.e., the experience) as being of greater importance than the *what*. Pine and Gilmore argue that the world has entered a fourth economy—the experience economy—where "experiences have emerged as the next step in what we call the *progression of economic value* . . . From now on, leading-edge companies—whether they sell to consumers or businesses—will find that the next competitive battleground lies in staging experiences" (see Chapter 6, p. 97).

In addition to this basic idea (that service quality involves both technical quality and functional quality), Grönroos also incorporated the concept of 'corporate image', arguing that the customer-perceived image of a firm is of the utmost importance to most service organizations, since this determines the way in which consumers perceive the firm. The most important part of a firm, as seen and perceived by its customers, is its service. Combining this with his idea of technical and functional quality, he argued that corporate image is derived mainly from a combination of a firm's technical quality and its functional quality. He went on to suggest that corporate image often influences customer expectation, and helps to reinforce the organization's advertising, marketing and public relations activities.

An example of the power of image is that of Apple products. Many customers all around the world buy Apple products simply because they have strong brand recognition, and are known for reliable, easy-to-use and attractive technology items such as phones, computers, iPods and tablets (iPads). In a case of such strong and positive brand recognition, customer perceptions of service quality can often be significantly influenced not by the item or the service itself, but rather, or partly, by the image of the firm. *Service organizations that can create strong brand image can significantly increase value and quality perceptions.*

Two-dimensional model (process and output quality)

Another way of conceptualizing service quality was proposed by Lehtinen (1983) who also identified two sets of quality dimensions. He called his dimensions 'process quality' and 'output quality'. These, he said, are inherent in all services, and combine to form service quality (see Figure 3.4 on next page).

Process quality

Customer participation is integral to the experience of process quality. The intimacy of the service-production process means that the customer experiences the production process through interaction and participation. The customer therefore judges every component of the service process and assesses its quality during the service (the 'process quality'). Given that customers are unable to judge the outcome until the service is completed, their only option is to judge the process they go through during the production process. Thus judging the process allows them to stipulate whether the outcome they are going to receive will match their expectation/requirement. This would mean that customers simultaneously judge

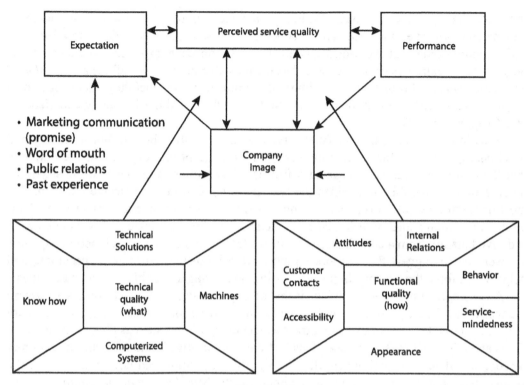

Figure 3.4
The expanded 'Nordic' model

the service provider's ability to interact with them and to make them feel comfortable. For example, a bartender may chat and joke with a customer who is sitting alone at the bar, so as to provide a feeling that he/she is with friends. The interactive quality is judged by the customer according to how his or her expectations are met during the service-production process and, more pertinently, how the customer's participation style is understood by the contact persons (representatives of the service provider) and the degree to which these persons can adapt their service styles accordingly.

The customer's judgment is essentially subjective—how the customer sees and assesses the production process. For example, in delivering hairdressing services, the stylist's conversation with the customer while cutting the customer's hair contributes to the experience of making the long hairdressing process appear short and entertaining to the customer. Of course, the stylist's demonstration of technical skill in cutting the hair is important, but process quality is what makes the experience memorable. Process quality therefore is the customer's judgment of the experience of the 'moments of truth' (service encounters). Process quality therefore is the core of the firm's ability to showcase how those technical services are delivered.

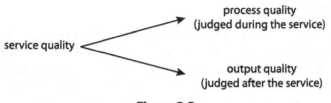

Figure 3.5
Service quality—process and output quality

Parallels can be drawn between Lehtinen's 'processes quality' and Grönroos' 'functional quality'. Both dimensions relate to the delivery process—the 'how'. The difference lies in Lehtinen's emphasis on the role played by the customer in cocreating the service experience and how this can affect the service quality.

Customer participation is present in almost every consumer and professional service production, and is thus integral to the assessment of process quality. In some services, in which customer participation is especially direct and active, such as in the case of the entertainment business, including music concerts, magic shows, comedy shows, football games and so on—customer participation positively influences the customer's perception of process quality, and simultaneously positively influences the provider of the service, bringing out the best in the performance.

Output quality

According to Lehtinen (1983), output quality is the consumer's evaluation of the service following completion of the service production process. For example, output quality depends on evaluation of the appearance of a finished haircut. In addition, in some service situations, output quality is not always evaluated by the customer alone, but is also evaluated by others. For example, a haircut is often evaluated by friends and colleagues of the customer. When customers value the judgment of friends and colleagues, this aspect of output quality becomes crucially important.

However, Lehtinen (1983) asserted that the customer is the only one to judge the *process* quality (as opposed to *output* quality). A classic example of this can be found in education. If a degree obtained by a student from a famous university is considered by the student's friends and family to be of a high quality (an assessment of output quality), the student's personal sense of status and prestige is enhanced. However, the educational services that he or she received throughout the period of academic study at the university were experienced only by the student, and thus only the student is capable of judging the *process quality* of the educational services. *Process quality* represents the 'moments of truth' in a service organization and hence it represents the experience from the customer's perspective. Often it is the service process that creates the experience that offers the memory. In a service context, memory of a customer's positive experience is one of the most important assets of a firm.

Two types of output

Lehtinen also drew attention to two types of output in service production, which he termed 'tangible' (or physical) and 'intangible'. Both a car wash and a haircut constitute typical tangible outputs, since both can be evaluated by outsiders who have not participated in the production process. In contrast, the output in tourism services is intangible—because it reflects a feeling or an experience, and can thus be judged only by the customer. Thus, according to Lehtinen, the output of any service production process is created during the entire period of the transaction. As a result, by controlling the process and process quality, output quality can also be controlled.

The 'Gaps' model

As noted previously (page 66), the quality perceived in a service can be determined as a function of the gap between consumers' expectations of a service and their perception of the actual service delivered. In other words, customers assess service quality by comparing the service they *receive* (perceptions of 'what I get') with the service they *desire* (expectations of 'what I want'). See Figure 3.6, below.

This gap is actually made up of several other gaps—all of which are potential breaks in the links of the relationship. Research has identified four intermediate gaps which, taken together, lead to the overall gap between expected quality and the overall perceived quality of service as received.

In developing this idea of four intermediate gaps (and a resulting overall fifth gap, being the total of the other gaps), the researchers looked beyond a single transaction and devel-

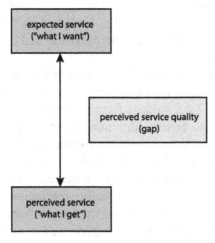

Figure 3.6
Perceived service quality gap

oped a model of service quality representing customer judgments across multiple interme-diate encounters involving service design, communication, management and delivery.

Gap 1 is the difference between consumer expectations and management perceptions of consumer. Gap 2 is the difference between management perceptions of consumer expecta-tions and the means by which these expectations might be met. Gap 3 is the difference between the specifications for the service and the actual delivery of the service. It can be referred to as the 'service performance gap'—that is, the extent to which service providers do not perform at the level expected by management. The service performance gap occurs when employees are unable or unwilling to perform the service at the desired level. Gap 4 is the 'communication gap', the difference between service delivery and external commu-nications (such as media messages which might exaggerate or falsely convey the offering). Gap 5 is the overall difference between expected service and perceived service. It is made up of the sum total of the preceding four gaps, and is thus determined by the nature of the gaps associated with the overall design, marketing and delivery of a service.

SERVQUAL

This model is the most commonly used and cited of all of the service quality models (and it is also subject of frequent criticism!). In developing their SERVQUAL model of measur-ing service quality Parasuraman, Zeithaml and Berry (1985) embarked on an extended, multi-staged research project designed to identify dimensions that accurately capture a mea-sure of service quality. Early stages of their research netted ten items (see Table 3.2), which were later statistically tested and reduced to five service dimensions (and 22 total items used to measure these five dimensions) that are considered highly by customers when assessing the quality of service (see Figure 3.7).

Table 3.2
The original ten service quality factors from Parasuraman et al. (1985)

1. **Reliability**—consistency of performance and dependability.
2. **Responsiveness**—willingness or readiness of employees to provide service.
3. **Competence**—possession of the required skills and knowledge to perform the service.
4. **Access**—approachability and ease of contact.
5. **Courtesy**—politeness, respect, consideration and friendliness of contact personnel.
6. **Communication**—keeping customers informed in language they can understand.
7. **Credibility**—trustworthiness, believability and honesty.
8. **Security**—freedom from danger, risk or doubt.
9. **Understanding / knowing the customer**—making the effort to understand the customer's needs.
10. **Tangibles**—physical evidence of the service.

The five 'final' dimensions were reliability, responsiveness, empathy, assurances and tangibles.

1. *Reliability* represents the service provider's ability to perform service dependably and accurately; this includes such qualities as dependability, consistency, accuracy, 'right the first time', and so on.
2. *Responsiveness* represents the willingness to help customers and provide prompt service in a timely manner; this includes helpfulness, friendliness, warmth, willingness, openness, and so on.
3. *Empathy* involves the caring personal attention which the firm offers its customers; this includes ease of approach and contact, jargon-free, understandable communication, an understanding of the customer's needs and so on;
4. *Assurances* reflect the knowledge and courtesy of employees and their ability to inspire trust and confidence in the customer; this includes competence, experience, qualifications, skills, courtesy, politeness, credibility, trustworthiness, honesty and security of all types (physical, financial, confidentiality, and so on).
5. *Tangibles* consist of the appearance of physical facilities, equipment, personnel and communication materials used.

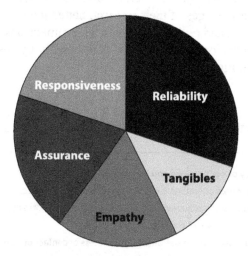

Figure 3.7
Relative importance of service dimensions in meeting expectations

Zone of tolerance

In subsequent work, these authors further examined variances and nuances of customer expectations and argued that the five dimensions could be further broken down into process dimensions (similar to the prior discussion about process), being responsiveness, empathy, assurance and tangibles, and one outcome dimension, reliability. These authors conceptualized a 'zone of tolerance' for customer expectations (see Figure 3.8) for process and outcome dimensions. They concluded that even though reliability is the most important element in *meeting* expectations, it is also the most difficult service quality dimension in which to *exceed* expectations (because customers expect reliability and have minimal tolerance for this expectation not being met). On the other hand, the process dimensions (especially responsiveness, empathy and assurances) are the key to *exceeding* expectations. With the process dimensions, the opportunity is present to surprise customers with uncommon swiftness, grace, courtesy, competence, commitment or understanding, and go beyond what is expected (Parasuraman, Berry and Zeithaml, 1991).

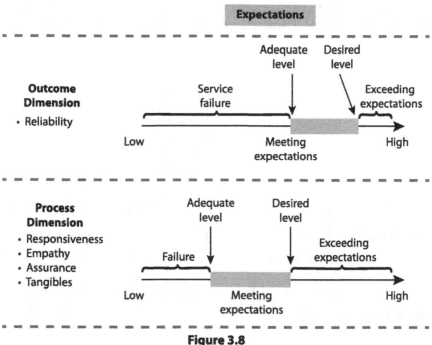

Figure 3.8
ZOT's for Outcome and Process Dimensions
Source: Adapted from Parasuraman, Berry and Zeithaml (1991)

SERVPERF (multi-level models)

The complexity of human reactions to a service experience has led some researchers to propose that perceptions of service quality are not only multidimensional (as noted above), but also occur at various levels.

Brady and Cronin (2001) proposed a hierarchical model to conceptualize perceived service quality. Their model suggested three primary levels of service quality—interaction quality, physical environment quality and outcome quality. In turn, each of these were conceived to have three sub-dimensions (see Figure 3.9). Thus:

- ▶ *interaction quality* was understood to be made up of the three sub-dimensions of attitude, behavior and experience;
- ▶ *physical environment quality* was made up of the sub-dimensions of ambient conditions, design and social factors and
- ▶ *outcome quality* was conceived as being made up of the sub-dimensions of waiting time, tangibles and valence (variable personal factors that affect experience).

Their studies found that customers aggregate their evaluations of the sub-dimensions to form their overall perceptions of an organization's performance in each of the three primary dimensions. These perceptions, it was argued, lead to customers' overall service quality perception.

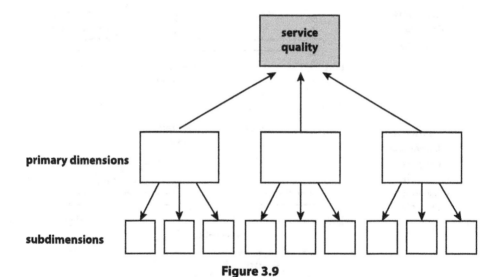

Figure 3.9
A hierarchical model of perceived service quality
Adapted from Brady and Cronin (2001)

Electronic (web) service quality

The early conceptualizations of service quality occurred in the 1970s and 1980s—before the advent of the Internet and the explosion of online retailing. Some of the original researchers involved in the development of service quality measures turned their attention to how customers would evaluate service in an online platform. E-service quality was therefore defined broadly to encompass all phases of a customer's interactions with a Web site: the extent to which Web site facilities enabled efficient and effective shopping, purchasing and delivery (Parasuraman, Zeithaml, and Malhotra, 2005). Through another complex research process a measure of E-service quality was developed, called "E-S-QUAL" (for electronic service quality). The items proposed to measure online service were:

1. Efficiency: The ease and speed of accessing and using the site.
2. Fulfillment: The extent to which the site's promises about order delivery and item availability are fulfilled.
3. System availability: The correct technical functioning of the site.
4. Privacy: The degree to which the site is safe and protects customer information.

Summary

To remain in business, sellers in the modern marketplace must be able to offer quality to increasingly demanding customers. This applies equally to those offering manufactured goods and those offering services. Failure to maintain consistent quality standards jeopardizes a firm's reputation and its ultimate profitability.

Quality has thus become essential to business performance. Although the importance of product quality has long been recognized in the manufacturing industry—in which various quality management concepts and strategies have been developed and implemented over the years—the services sector has been less aware of the importance of these matters. However, the increasing economic importance of the service sector and the emergence of service marketing in recent years have highlighted the need for management to gain an understanding of quality strategies that are specifically appropriate for service firms.

In today's economy, service is crucial to customer satisfaction and business success in every industry. For a service firm, the ability to provide quality service is, in fact, the most effective means of differentiating itself from competitors. But the distinctive nature of services and service provision predetermines and requires different approaches and tools from those that are used in the manufacturing industry. The quality of service is not only different but also more difficult to define, measure and control. In addition, a firm's service quality is significantly affected by the subjective judgment of its customers.

From a marketing perspective, service quality is the most important determinant of customer satisfaction. It is therefore imperative that hospitality and tourism managers understand the factors that influence a customer's perceptions, expectations and satisfaction with service—and design their strategies accordingly.

This chapter has offered an overall understanding of quality concepts in general, as well as specific information pertaining to quality management in a service context. It should thus prove of assistance to service managers, as service providers, to focus their efforts and resources effectively on improving their firm's market position through quality service and customer satisfaction.

Review Questions

1. Analyze the importance of quality management in terms of costs and benefits.

2. Briefly describe various quality principles proposed by W. Edwards Deming, Joseph M. Juran and Philip Crosby.

3. Briefly describe the general recurring themes of 'total quality management' (TQM).

4. What is your understanding of service quality? How is service quality different from goods quality?

5. What are the outcomes of effective service quality management? Explain the 'customer franchise' concept.

6. How would you define customer satisfaction, customer loyalty and customer delight? Is there any interdependence between them?

7. This chapter described the relationship between customer loyalty and satisfaction relevant for highly competitive industries. Now think about and describe how the relationship between satisfaction and loyalty would look like for monopolies. Give examples of such service industries.

8. Explain the idea of multiple consumption and think of the challenges it might create for quality management.

9. What is the similarity between the 'Nordic' model and the two-dimensional model?

10. Which dimensions of the SERVQUAL model should the service manager leverage in order to pursue customer loyalty? Which dimension on the ZOT would this relate to?

Suggested Readings

This is a list of suggested further reading on topics covered in this chapter. For a separate list of full reference citations quoted in the chapter, see 'References', Chapter 3, page 324.

Bank, J. (2001). *The Essence of Total Quality Management*. New York: Prentice Hall.

Berry, L. L., Zeithaml, V. A., and Parasuraman, A. (1990). Five imperatives for improving service quality. *Sloan Management Review*, Summer, 29–38.

Bodet, G. (2008). Customer satisfaction and loyalty in service: Two concepts, four constructs, several relationships. *Journal of Retailing and Consumer Services*, 15, 156–162.

Brady, M. K., and Cronin Jr., J. J. (2001). Some new thoughts on conceptualizing perceived service quality: A hierarchical approach. *Journal of Marketing*, 65(3), 34–49.

Dixon, M., Freeman, K., and Toman, N. (2010). Stop trying to delight your customers. *Harvard Business Review*, July–August, 116–122.

Gracia, E., Bakker, A. B., and Grau, R. M. (2011). Positive emotions: The connection between customer quality evaluations and loyalty. *Cornell Hospitality Quarterly*, 52(4), 458–465.

Hyun, S. S. (2010). Predictors of relationship quality and loyalty in the chain restaurant industry. *Cornell Hospitality Quarterly*, 51(2), 251–267.

Kimes, S. E. (2001). How product quality drives profitability: The experience at Holiday Inn. *Cornell Hotel and Restaurant Administration Quarterly*, June, 25–8.

Magnini, V. P., Crotts, J. C., and Zehrer, A. (2011). Understanding customer delight: An application of travel blog analysis. *Journal of Travel Research*, 50(5), 535–545.

Parasuraman, A., Berry, L. L., and Zeithaml, V. A. (1991). Understanding customer expectations of service. *Sloan Management Review*, Spring, 39–48.

Yu, Y-T., and Dean, A. (2001). The contribution of emotional satisfaction to consumer loyalty. *International Journal of Service Industry Management*, 12(3), 234–250.

Understanding and Engaging Customers

Study Objectives

Having completed this chapter, readers should be able to:

1. Understand the notion of the 'customer' from a managerial perspective;
2. Understand the importance of internal marketing for successful external marketing;
3. Understand the importance for a firm to be knowledgeable about its customers' expectations and
4. Be familiar with various techniques of collecting and using customer information and feedback.

Outline

- ▶ Introduction
- ▶ The importance of understanding customers
- ▶ Evolution of the customer centricity concept within the literature
- ▶ Guestology
- ▶ Categories of customers
  - ▶ External customers
    - ▪ The importance of customer information
    - ▪ Customer-perception research
      - — In-depth interviews with individual customers
      - — Focus groups
      - — Market surveys
      - — In-house customer satisfaction surveys
      - — Critical-incident / complaint analysis

- — Mystery shoppers
- — Customer-to-customer communication (social media, Web 2.0)
  - ▶ Internal customers
    - ▪ Internal service
- ▶ Implications for quality
  - ▶ Employee research
  - ▶ Inseparability makes employees important
  - ▶ Management involvement
  - ▶ Employees as customer 'advocates'
  - ▶ Making it work effectively
- ▶ Summary
- ▶ Review Questions
- ▶ Suggested Readings

Key Words

Complaint analysis
Critical-incident analysis
Customer advocates
Customer centricity
Customer Experience Evaluation program
Customer perception research
Customer-centric focus
Customer-to-customer communication
Employee research
External customers
Face-to-face research
Guest communications

Guestology
In-depth interviews
In-house customer satisfaction surveys
Internal customers
Internal marketing
Internal service
Listening posts
Market surveys
Mystery shoppers
Partial customers
Social media

Introduction

If a commercial organization is to remain in business, it must understand, engage and satisfy its customers. Meeting and exceeding the expectations of customers is the essence of service quality and customer satisfaction, both of which are important in creating a loyal customer (see Chapter 3). Having explored the concepts of quality, satisfaction and loyalty in Chapter 3, we now move on in the present chapter to further understand our customers—how to stay attuned to them, in touch with them and in a constant state of listening and engagement with them. Great service organizations create a genuine 'customer listening' organizational culture (we will discuss culture further in Chapter 8).

From a managerial perspective, the term 'customer' encompasses more than those from whom an organization earns revenue. This chapter explores the idea that a service firm really has *multiple* groups of customers in two broad categories—'internal customers' and 'external customers'.

The very nature of service emphasizes the role of human beings in producing service products and delivering service experiences to other human beings. To offer quality service to *external* customers (those who ultimately pay for the final service offering), service firms must first realize the importance of the *internal* customers (the staff personnel who render the various services that make up the final service offering to the external customer). It might seem strange to describe staff personnel as 'internal customers', but these people actually give and receive service from one another as part of an internal chain of staff interactions preceding the final delivery of service to the external customer. These internal customers must give and receive satisfactory service to and from one another if the final external customer is also to receive satisfactory service. This concept is explored in greater detail later in this chapter.

© Artkwin/Shutterstock.com

To fulfill customers' expectations and perceptions of service quality, service firms must continuously collect customer information and measure customer perceptions and satisfaction as a basis on which to assess performance. This chapter presents various methods of acquiring and using customer information, and explores the role of service employees in gathering and providing management with customer feedback.

The next section of this chapter examines two very important themes—the idea of internal and external customers.

The importance of understanding customers

Chapter 1 provided an introduction to the concept of core and peripheral service. What we now understand is that the 'core' (e.g., accommodation, food, skiing, touring, seat on bus, etc.) will not be sufficient to fulfill customer needs nor exceed their expectations (see the Zone of Tolerance discussion in Chapter 3). Additionally, supporting service and experiences must therefore be offered by firms today as they seek to fulfill both the primary and secondary needs of customers. These needs are mainly service-oriented, and a hospitality or tourism firm's competitive advantage will thus be primarily dependent on the service components of its offerings, rather than the product components.

It is the service component of the offering that is often the deciding factor in determining customer loyalty. Firms have traditionally associated customers with sales and revenue, but the concept of the loyal customer has assumed a strategic significance that goes beyond mere revenues. The concept of 'customer' has thus become

© Ivelin Radkov/Shutterstock.com

an icon that focuses and orients the direction of the entire firm. A customer-centered and service-oriented focus has thus emerged as the prerequisite for gaining market dominance. A service-oriented focus must be aligned with a customer-centric focus.

Competitive advantage is derived through service excellence and differentiation. Competing service firms might look alike, but how they provide the service makes them feel different to the customer. The quality of service can be the centerpiece that demonstrates a firm's commitment to its customers—thus elevating the firm's image in the mind of its customers. Customers' perceptions of the firm's service quality, and its perceived value, offer firms the most sustainable basis of differentiation and their most powerful competitive weapon.

Research studies have repeatedly confirmed the strategic advantage of adopting a customer-orientation if firms wish to improve market share and profits. In both research and

practice, there has been a gradual but definite shift of focus from the supplier (or the firm) to the customer. Focus on the firm itself (rather than the customer) tended to restrict management's concern to questions of production and internal administration, whereas a focus on the customer compels management to recognize that the firm's primary responsibility is to serve the customer. This focus on the customer has stimulated numerous studies of customer-related issues within a business context, including

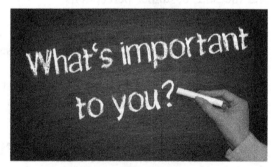

© docstockmedia/Shutterstock.com

those on customer satisfaction, customer care, customer expectations, customer loyalty, customer value, customer relationships, customer engagement, customer centricity and many others (some of which we will review).

Evolution of the customer centricity concept within the literature

This interest and the importance of the customer was well summed up by the management thinker Peter Drucker (1973), who observed that "to satisfy the customer is the mission and purpose of every business" (p. 79). In fact the whole idea of customer centricity is not a new one. In 1954, Drucker proposed that it is customers who ultimately define what a business is, what it actually produces and whether or not it will prosper. Such a customer focus implies a re-orientation to a service focus. However, firms have realized that serving the needs of customers is not as simple as it sounds. It requires a whole new approach to the internal activities of a firm as the firm reappraises how it undertakes its business.

The service literature offers a significant shift to a customer view of the world. This might seem a logical idea, but businesses for many years often made decisions based on internal motivations—such as cost savings, ease of distribution or convenience for employees (see Chapters 1 and 2). Customer centricity, or even obsession, must be central to a service management paradigm.

Customer centricity differs from previous product-centric models on a number of dimensions. The product-centric approach is drawn from the early years of marketing where scholars and industry directed their attention towards the exchange of goods, and where the prime function of marketing was to find ways to bring its products to the market. Customer centricity should be at the heart of the strategy of any service business, and because of the high customer contact nature of most service businesses, must predominate in the culture of service (and therefore the hospitality and tourism businesses).

Levitt (1981) proposed that firms should not focus on selling products but rather on fulfilling customer needs. Still, the importance of customer centricity has only recently been embraced by the business community. It sounds simple enough to become a fully customer centric firm, but

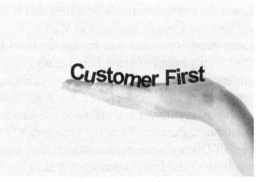

© Ai825/Shutterstock.com

it is apparently much more difficult to practice than meets the eye (Shah, Rust, Parasuraman, Staelin, and Day, 2006). Although the concept has been in the management vocabulary for many years (see the Drucker quotes above), firms typically struggled to fully align themselves to the customer-centric paradigm. Shah et al. (2006) identified four fundamental issues and challenges that typically deter a firm from becoming customer-centric being related to organizational culture, structure, process and financial metrics. They propose changes starting with leadership commitment, organizational realignment, changes in systems and process support and more appropriate customer centered financial metrics.

So how can we become customer centered and stay in touch with our customers? Service quality is defined as the extent to which a service meets (and exceeds) the expectations of customers (see Chapter 3). *The first challenge of management is to identify just what those expectations are.*

Firms typically invest considerable resources (time, talent and money) in attempting to understand the needs, wants and expectations of customers. However, in the case of service (as opposed to physical goods), identifying and agreeing upon easily understood criteria by which the subjective expectations of service quality can be assessed and communicated has been challenging.

The benefits of understanding and measuring service quality are now widely recognized, with poor understanding and connection to customers two major causes of poor performance by service organizations. Many firms are eager to provide good service, but fall short—simply because they do not understand exactly what customers expect from the service offer and how these needs change over time.

Guestology

Putting customer centricity into practice requires a range of strategic and practical steps. Exemplary service organizations build customer listening into the fabric of their operations. Disney is a prime example of a firm that is driven by the wants, desires and behaviors of its customers. A senior manager at Walt Disney, Bruce Laval, coined the term 'guestology' to focus everyone's attention on the study of guest behavior. Although Disney is known for their family entertainment, they are also renowned for their never-ending quest to know and understand customers. Guestology challenges traditional management thinking, placing emphasis not on organizational design, managerial hierarchy and production systems to maximize organizational efficiency, but rather, forcing the firm to look systematically at the customer experience from the customer's (or guest's) point of view. There are many examples of Disney's use of guestology. For example, the value that Disney accords its young customers (children) is demonstrated in the design features of their hotel room doors: there are two peepholes—one at the usual height, and one at a child's level. In response to the importance Disney's customers have placed on cleanliness, rubbish bins are placed at 27-foot intervals around the parks, the calculated distance a person would walk before dropping garbage on the ground. (We encourage readers to learn more about Disney through various means, including books, e.g., *The Disney Way*, as well as through their Web site, blogs and professional development courses.)

Disney (n.d., online) collects customer feedback through a variety of listening posts, including:

1. *Face-to-face research:* Directly asking guests where they are visiting from, or what they thought of a specific ride or event. This allows for immediate feedback and the opportunity to make short-term adjustments quickly and, if necessary, invoke immediate service recovery.
2. *Guest communications:* Vigilantly listening to all letters, e-mails and phone calls. Every complaint is viewed as an opportunity to improve.
3. *Web sites and social media:* Because what happens on the local level has global impact, it is vital to know what customers are saying online. Online monitoring allows the observing of trends as they occur in real time.
4. *Talk to your employees:* Front-line employees know and understand customers better than anyone! Disney views their 'cast members' as honest about the areas where Disney could do better. Many of their service experience enhancements come directly from cast member suggestions.

Categories of customers

Before we review some of the ways that a service firm can become more customer centric, it is important to categorize customers, as this might not be quite as straightforward as you would have thought. Customers can be categorized into five broad groups:

1. *internal customers*—employees and managers of the firm;
2. *current external customers*—a firm's current customers;
3. *competitors' customers*—those whom the firm would like to attract and make its own;
4. *ex-customers*—customers who have chosen to leave, and now use a competing firm's services; and
5. *potential future customers*—customers who are likely to be customers in the future (e.g., university students).

Although all of the above are vital for a full understanding of customers, this chapter focuses predominantly on the second category—*external customers*. We will review the concept of the 'internal customer' in this chapter, but we will spend more time examining this issue in more detail in Chapter 8 when we introduce the concepts of service culture, service climate and service orientation.

External customers

The importance of customer information

The most important component of any business endeavor is the customer (or tourist, visitor, attendee, passenger etc.). Organizations conduct various forms of research to obtain information about the needs, expectations and perceptions of their present and prospective customers. These expectations and perceptions are constantly changing, as is the nature of the service offered by competing organizations. It is therefore important that research into these matters is administered on a continuous basis—so that any changes can be picked up quickly, and acted upon as appropriate.

Research about customers might establish answers to the following sorts of questions:

▶   Why did a customer buy (or not buy) a particular product or service?

▶   Is the customer satisfied or not with the product or service?

▶   Will the customer return?

▶   What were the customer's expectations about the product or service before purchase and consumption?

▶   How do customers experience and perceive the different components of a given service?

▶   What are the trends in customer preferences over time?

▶   Would the customer recommend the product or service to someone else?

▶   What types of things do customers in a particular market segment like?

▶   And many others!

Reichheld (2003) argues that you can substitute all the questions that typically appear on a customer satisfaction survey for one single question—about a customer's willingness to recommend a product or service to someone else. This 'would recommend' question is shown to be highly effective in determining loyalty and predicting growth. The point is that if someone is willing to recommend, to give their word, that they must feel strongly about it. When a customer is so faithful as to recommend the product to others, they in effect become the most effective firm marketers!

The way in which the information is utilized is of the utmost importance. It is the responsibility of management to collect, analyze and interpret information accurately, and to communicate the findings to employees. Such information—gathered from the customers and fed back to the employees—is a powerful tool in effecting changes in both the 'controllable' aspects of service (service system, methods and process) and the 'uncontrollable' aspects of services (the quality of the service encounter as perceived by the customer).

Customer-perception research

Customer-perception research usually employs a combination of qualitative and quantitative methods. Many hospitality establishments employ such studies to develop future management and marketing strategies. The aim is to gain a better understanding of how customers view the establishment to help management see its establishment as guests see it.

- ► *Quantitative research* involves the collection of statistical data on various *measurable aspects* of customer behavior.
- ► *Qualitative research* involves researchers identifying *attitudes* of current (and potential) clients, as well as those of the wider community. This might involve eliciting information from journalists, intermediaries and even competitors.

The objective of customer-perception research is the identification of the characteristics of the service product that are most critical to the customer, and thus to isolate characteristics that can form the basis for successful differentiation of the organization's service product from others in a competitive market. In the past, the most commonly used methods for learning about customers' perceptions were:

- ► in-depth interviews with individual customers;
- ► focus-group interviews with selected groups of customers;
- ► statistical customer surveys of representative customer populations;
- ► critical-incident technique (complaint analysis);
- ► mystery shoppers (customer experience evaluations); and
- ► employee opinion / attitude surveys.

Of course today, firms make use of social media and various other web-based communications in order to get a regular 'pulse' of customer moods, trends, interests. We will review some of these approaches later in this chapter; however, we offer a word of caution in that web and online communities based feedback offers many challenges in terms of accuracy of information. The methods above, while being somewhat overtaken by technology-based methods, remain solid and appropriate methods by which a firm can learn about their customers.

Many readers of this text will be 'digital natives', very familiar with the use and application of social media. Defined, social media refers to a collection of online services that supports social interactions among users and allows them to cocreate, find, share and evaluate the online information repository. It is a group of applications that build on the ideological foundations of Web 2.0, and allow the creation and exchange of user-generated content (Kaplan and Haenlein, 2012).

Starbucks and MyStarbucksIdea

Starbucks is an example of a firm that has been quick to recognize the importance of customer engagement and the role played by social media in achieving this. They have created a process of involving customers in product development, incorporating customer comments from the Web site "MyStarbucksIdea" to create coffee recipes and drinks, and also to notify customers about promotions. This process of bringing the customer and the firm closer is a way to engage and innovate with minimal cost, and the mutual benefit is that customers feel valued by having their ideas considered, discussed or even implemented.

Starbucks—like many companies these days—has web facilitators (made up of current and past coffee makers—baristas), thereby enabling the company to engage customer social media traffic promptly. In addition, most companies now use Facebook and other similar social media platforms to all but replace e-mail and websites for many young people. With senior managers in an older generation, it is vital that service firms turn to their younger workers to engage the younger customer segments.

With all these methods, it is important to select carefully the people from whom the information is to be collected. They should constitute a reasonably representative sample of the customer population being studied. Ideally, the sample should include people who have never bought the service, as well as those who have. It is also helpful to collect information from people who prefer the services of a competitor—because disgruntled customers can provide information that is as valuable as that from happy customers.

It is important to understand that rarely if ever will a firm employ all of the approaches discussed here. However, as a service manager, it is vital that you have familiarity with a range of ways to get closer to your customers, to engage with them and to keep the channels open and welcoming. The list below, while not exhaustive, is designed to help service managers be more aware of the options available. Effective managers learn how to choose the right combination depending on circumstance (and budget). The list below represents a reasonable sample of the approaches that a service manager should be aware of.

1. In-depth interviews with individual customers

Perhaps a dying art but certainly still effective is that in-depth interview where an interviewer asks numerous questions about all aspects of the service product. This might involve half-an-hour or more with a single customer. Because of the time and expense involved, this type of interview is the least frequently used; however, it often proves to be very effective—

because it provides the most pertinent and current information in an in-depth way. The aim of the interviewer is to uncover the key attributes of the service that customers deem to be important and desirable, and the attitudes of customers towards these attributes.

For example, in researching the service offered by a restaurant, the interviewer first wants to know why customers choose to go to a restaurant at all—rather than eating at home, or having a meal in some other way. What attributes of a restaurant meal induce a decision to go to a restaurant in the first place? Then inquiries can be made about price, meal times, preferred locations, favorite restaurants, favorite types of food, whether customers usually go out for a meal with friends, whether they ever go alone and so on.

In-depth interviewers 'actively listen'—to detect 'cues' that reveal aspects of the experience about which customers seem to feel strongly. The effectiveness of the interview lies in discovering more about customers' feelings, needs and expectations regarding particular aspects of the service, and knowing which aspects to explore in greater detail. The interviewer needs skill in knowing which 'cues' to follow.

Following a series of interviews, the interviewer will frequently detect that a certain pattern of response is developing. At this point, nothing new seems to be forthcoming, and the interviewer can assume that it is reasonably safe to stop interviewing and compile the results. An analysis usually identifies recurring themes in the customers' statements regarding aspects of the service and its delivery. From this, the researcher might be able to draw up a list of attributes that defines the total service experience, as perceived by this customer.

(For a more detailed discussion on interviews and other qualitative research methods, readers are referred to any number of excellent books such as Denzin and Lincoln, 2008.)

2. Focus groups

Focus groups involve organized discussions with a selected group of individuals to gain information about their views and experiences of a topic. One of the major benefits of a focus group is to gain insights into people's shared understandings and perceptions of the particular topic of interest. Focus groups have been utilized for many purposes including market research and product evaluation.

Identifying appropriate participants for a focus group can be problematic. If a group is too heterogeneous (e.g., in terms of gender or class, or in terms of professional or 'lay' perspectives) the differences between participants can inhibit their contributions. Alternatively, if a group is too homogeneous on specific characteristics, diverse opinions and experiences may not emerge. Nevertheless, participants need to feel comfortable with each other. Meeting with others who are perceived to possess similar characteristics or levels of understanding about a given topic will be more appealing than meeting with those who are perceived to be different. Skillful moderation is required to ensure that discussion remains focused on the topic of interest and to generate useful outcomes.

Once the types of participant have been decided, locating them is the next challenge. It is likely that people with specific interests will have to be recruited by word-of-mouth, through the use of key informants, by advertising or poster campaigns or through existing social networks. Incentives, such as payment, gift vouchers or presents, will usually need to be offered. Groups usually involve six to ten participants and sessions typically last from one to two hours.

Although focus group research has many advantages, there are limitations. Some can be overcome by careful planning and moderating, but others are unavoidable and peculiar to this approach. For example, the moderator/researcher has less control over the data produced than in other data collection methods. The moderator has to allow participants to talk to each other, ask questions and express doubts and opinions, while having very little control over the interaction other than generally keeping participants focused on the topic. By its nature, focus group research is open-ended and cannot be entirely predetermined. It should not be assumed that the individuals in a focus group are expressing their own definitive individual view. They are speaking in a specific context, and it is difficult at times to clearly identify an individual message.

3. Market surveys

Large-scale market surveys are often used if customer-perception information is required from a relatively large number of people. Individual interviews and focus-group interviews (as described above) might not involve a large enough sample to make statistically valid judgments about the customer base. Wider surveys are required for such statistically valid judgments. However, in-depth interviews and focus-group interviews are relevant to surveys in that they serve a crucial role in determining the questions to be asked in surveys. In other words, the interview process involving a small number of people provides the basis of a research model for questionnaires aimed at a bigger population.

A research model involves the selection of the desired demographic group to be surveyed, and a list of key topics about which information is desired—opinions or preferences about the key attributes of the service being offered. This information can be processed statistically to develop a profile of the service preferences of the customers and their attitudes towards the organization and competing organizations. All of this information can be expressed as a demographic breakdown of preferences in terms of age, gender, educational level and income level.

Such surveys are nearly predominately administered electronically now, with software packages (such as SurveyMonkey, Survey Gizmo, Qualtrics, FreeOnlineSurveys.com and others) that are simple and easy to use, and they compile basic statistical responses for little effort and investment. Because capturing data and analyzing it in a meaningful way presents a range of challenges, it is important not to just assume that the right questions and the right analysis will occur using a basic 'market ready' software program. If an organization aims to do research using simple web-based software, it is important to seek out professional advice on the way to ask questions, how to measure certain variables of interest and the types of analysis which will provide the most relevant, accurate and informative information.

4.   In-house customer satisfaction surveys

The use of customer satisfaction surveys has become increasingly common in service industries, with many organizations now realizing the importance of accessing direct feedback from guests. Many businesses leave guest questionnaires or comment cards in bedrooms, lobbies and restaurants. Such surveys usually ask customers to relate positive and negative features of the service experience, as well as suggestions for improving the services. Other channels through which the surveys may be deployed include the use of an automated SMS (short messaging service) to a customer after checkout, asking them to answer a few short questions about their visit, or an e-mail from the company referring the customer to a link to fill in a short survey (there are a number of options

© Bloomua/Shutterstock.com

for firms to use now, even a self-created SurveyMonkey or similar survey, referral to the company Facebook site and many others). We encourage readers to refer to the current literature on online customer feedback mechanisms, as they change and innovate nearly every day.

Another frequently used method to collect customer feedback is for companies to use their point of sale systems (for example, the computer ordering hardware/software system used by many restaurants and hotels) to generate random notes on guests checks (bills), inviting the customer to call a phone number or visit a website and complete a generally short survey about their experience. The benefit of this approach is that guests are chosen at random which allows for a more statistically appropriate sampling of patrons. Customers are often encouraged to participate with a small gift of some kind (e.g., a small discount or to be put into a drawing for a larger gift).

Regardless of the method used, it is vitally important to have a mechanism whereby any urgent customer feedback is considered and acted upon by management immediately.

However, this is often far from the truth in the vast majority of organizations. If such surveys are to be beneficial to management, customers and employees, planning and management of the questionnaire feedback system is essential. Questionnaires should have a definite purpose, and the survey should deal with a limited number of issues at any one time. Moreover, a definite time period should be designated for the gathering of information, and for subsequent action on any identified issue. In some cases (see Figure 4.1), the survey can be very short and provide high traffic feedback due to its convenience and ease of use (in this case in an airport bathroom in Singapore!).

© Dusit/Shutterstock.com

Once the data is collected—it is to be interpreted. One of the challenges which firms often face is an overabundance of data, and the management concern about how to store and appropriately interpret the data. It is one thing to read some feedback on a written survey left at the front desk, but the sheer amount of information now collected provides major challenges to organizations about how to use the data effectively and how to respond to important concerns in a timely way. The term 'big data' is now used to explain any collection of data large and complex enough that it becomes difficult to process using existing management tools or resources.

Figure 4.1
One-question satisfaction surveys even for rating bathrooms!

A final note here about too much customer feedback. With the ever-increasing interest in learning about customers, there is evidence of customer feedback saturation, where customers become impatient when asked to complete even a short questionnaire (this is one of the reasons for the growth of very short questionnaires, like the 'NPS' or Net Promoter Score which only asks the single question about how likely the person would be to recommend the product or service to someone).

Photo courtesy of David Solnet

5. Critical-incident / complaint analysis

Incident-based measurement or critical-incident technique (CIT) is based on the principle that long-term total customer satisfaction can be achieved only by identifying a list of all the problems that customers experience when using a service. Management needs to know what worries customers. A related phenomenon is that observed in many surveys—when it is often the case that the 'additional comments' made by customers at the end of the survey prove to be the most valuable of all the information elicited from surveys. A survey might be carefully constructed and might seem to ask all the right questions. But then researchers discover that the most important information is contained in an 'additional comment' about a subject that had not even occurred to researchers!

The fundamental idea of all incident-oriented measurement thus hinges around efforts to express the quality experiences of customers as precisely as possible through evaluation *of their own accounts* of these experiences. CIT focuses on the active and systematic investigation of customer experiences of critical incidents. In general terms, for an incident to be defined as 'critical', it must deviate significantly from what is expected—either positively or negatively—and it must be possible to describe it in detail.

In formal terms, the CIT process has been defined as a systematic effort to gather and analyze information about incidents of employee behavior with respect to a designed activity. The aim of this method is therefore to compile and evaluate 'critical incidents' in a systematic and planned manner.

CIT can assist management to identify problems in service delivery, and can also help management to redesign the service-delivery system. The important point is that any such redesigned system is firmly based on the most important quality attributes *as perceived in practice by the customers*—not as perceived in theory by management.

6. Mystery shoppers

Known by a number of similar names (Phantom Guest, Mystery Shopper, Secret Shopper), mystery shopping is a means of auditing the standard of service offered. The main focus is to assess the capacity of service personnel to offer service at the established standards. Regular checks on the levels of service performance are essential for any service organization if it is to maintain a consistent quality of service. Indeed, eliminating or reducing variability is one of the major tasks of service managers. The service performance 'gap' (the variation from the established standard of service) might be due to a number of causes—such as defective systems or procedures, inability of the employee, unwillingness of the employee and many others. The function of mystery shopper surveys is to monitor the extent to which specified quality standards are actually being met.

Having a formalized process of proactively evaluating the service experience is important because a service experience to a 'regular' customer is often only a fading memory after it has occurred. So it is particularly difficult to measure the effectiveness of service and the adherence to service standards (Ford, Latham, and Lennox, 2011) without some kind of proactive program. In manufacturing, quality and evaluation is based on a process of continued inspection (see Chapter 3), but service organizations must find other ways to understand how a customer perceives the organization, the service and the actions, attitudes and behaviors of the employees.

The aim of such a program can be either to assess predetermined service standards against standards or to provide general feedback on the experience. Done well, a mystery shopper program puts pressure on the organization to design and clarify the exact expectations for service—a template of the 'perfect customer experience'.

This questionnaire then serves the dual purpose of being an assessment tool and a training tool, making it clear to all employees what the company aspires to give its customers.

Such programs are often embedded into wider programs of assessment, such as 'Balanced Scorecards' (discussed in Chapter 8). In such cases, the mystery shopper program would often be seen as part of a wider program of assessment of management performance.

One of the authors of this book owns a management consulting firm and regularly implements such programs into hospitality organizations, so it is with this experience, combined with the academic literature, that this section is written. Rather than using the term 'mystery shopper', this consulting firm uses the term 'Customer Experience Evaluation' (CEE), because

© Brian A Jackson/Shutterstock.com

many service workers viewed the term 'mystery shopper' in a derogatory way—something designed to 'catch people' doing things wrong. So the term Customer Experience Evaluators seems to provide a softer terminology for what is in essence a mystery shopper program. Figure 4.2 illustrates a small sample of a 55-question

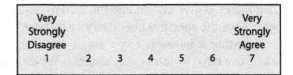

| | Very Strongly Disagree 1 | 2 | 3 | 4 | 5 | 6 | Very Strongly Agree 7 |

	would be the waitperson for the evening. If applicable thy explained any current specials or offers (e.g. happy hour from 5–7pm; Chilli Tuesday's; Why No Wednesdays)... If Not applicable, write 'NA'		
24.	The food waitperson appeared knowledgeable about the menu (be careful as to how you make this determination—avoid 'scripted' types of questions).		
25.	Our food order was taken within a 'reasonable' amount of time. (You decide what is reasonable to your circumstance—i.e. did the staff sense your needs appropriately?). In the comments section, please indicate the number of minutes between being seated and order being taken.		
26.	The food waitperson did an appropriate job suggesting starters and add-ons (such as Cactus Rolls, Dips, etc.) without appearing too pushy, robotic ("do you want fries with that?"), or 'revenue' focused.		
27.	The food waitperson seemed genuinely friendly and welcoming.		
28.	All waitstaff are required to repeat back all orders for all items ordered and make eye contact with each guest. Rate the level to which this standard was achieved during your visit.		
29.	Was the appropriate cutlery placed to the right hand side of each customer for each course served, and finger bowls placed nearby as appropriate? Please comment. (disregard if 4 or more people seated in a booth—leave blank in this case).		
30.	Rate the level of follow up given for <u>each meal</u> served (should happen during each course).		
31.	Entrees arrived in a reasonable amount of time *(**start timing after waiter leaves table**)*. Feel free to comment in the 'comments' column. Use the following scale as an indicator More than 25 mins 1 — 2 — 20 mins 3 — 4 — 15 mins 5 — 6 — 10 mins 7		
32.	The food waitperson seemed to have the right amount of time to provide reasonable levels of service (e.g., it did not seem as though their sections were unreasonably large, nor were they seemingly without any work to do).		

Figure 4.2
Sample from a restaurant mystery shopper questionnaire

CEE report to give insight into the kind of detail requested in the case of this restaurant company. Note the specifics about service standards which should inform employee behavior.

Whether a business has a single location or multiple locations, such evaluation programs can have wide-ranging benefits. When a small company grows, in particular, and the company standards can potentially become watered down, such a program, where the questions and evaluation are identical across multiple units, allows management to evaluate standards in a unit and across many units.

A mystery shopper program should be set up to give feedback to the organization and its employees. Employees, like all human beings, crave feedback (think about how anxious students are to get results back from an exam or assignment!). A well-designed, well-run mystery shopper program can be an excellent feedback and training process (Ford, et al., 2011). Some of the many benefits of a well-considered CEE program include:

▶ Forces an organization to create and communicate clear standards and expectations.
▶ Provides regular and ongoing feedback to staff and management about customer experiences.
▶ Helps pinpoint areas where continual problems or shortcomings in standards exist.
▶ Offers an opportunity to talk to staff about results and praise excellent performance.
▶ Displays trends that may give rise to the possibility of revising standards when it becomes clear that something may not be achievable or reasonable.
▶ Keeps everyone on their toes—never knowing when there might be an evaluation.

In addition, there are a number of important considerations in designing and implementing a CEE program. These include, but are not limited to:

▶ The program must be well thought through and well communicated.
▶ It should be designed to facilitate constructive feedback and evaluation.
▶ It must be independent (usually administered by an outside company), objective, honest, consistent and fair.
▶ Positive behaviors of staff must receive equal focus as negative ones.
▶ Evaluators must be trained and their performance as evaluators monitored regularly.
▶ Anonymity is vital, so remaining 'unspotted' is a crucial part of being an evaluator.
▶ Results should be broadcast regularly (with positives celebrated); but names of employees negatively evaluated should not generally be posted publicly ('praise in public, reprimand in private' is a good policy).
▶ Additional 'open-ended' questions should be added to any structured questionnaire, allowing evaluators to write in other comments (see Figure 4.3 below).
▶ Like with any human activity, it is possible that errors or misinterpretations can be made. All parties must be aware of this and be committed to the long-term benefits derived from such a program.

► Most importantly, the purpose of such a program should be clearly stated to all involved, and should never be used as a negative but rather as a tool for training, coaching and evaluation of service standards.

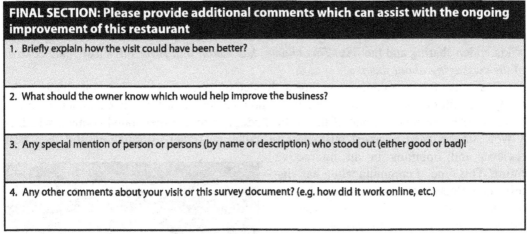

FINAL SECTION: Please provide additional comments which can assist with the ongoing improvement of this restaurant

1. Briefly explain how the visit could have been better?

2. What should the owner know which would help improve the business?

3. Any special mention of person or persons (by name or description) who stood out (either good or bad)!

4. Any other comments about your visit or this survey document? (e.g. how did it work online, etc.)

Figure 4.3
Open-ended questions on a mystery shopper questionnaire

Like any customer research method, there are some issues and challenges in using mystery shopper programs effectively. Firstly, because the service sector is heterogeneous, there is a lot of subjectivity involved in these types of evaluations. The best mystery shopper programs use trained evaluators and ensure that as much of the margin for error as possible is minimized. Also, random evaluations might not provide a clearly generalizable review of actual customer experiences, particularly as the frequency of visits is usually fairly low (say every week or two). Other issues include the variations in interpretation of quality and satisfaction, asking the right questions and ensuring that evaluators remain anonymous.

These evaluations should be part of a program that the organization is committed to, and evaluations should occur as frequently as possible (minimum of two visits per month). Frequency increases the reliability of results, but must be balanced against the cost as evaluators generally would have their meal costs reimbursed (which means that the actual cost to the business would be whatever the cost of goods is rather than the 'retail' cost—so a $100 reimbursement for a dinner for two might only have a 'real' cost of $30 on a 30% cost of goods).

7. Customer-to-customer communication (Social Media, Web 2.0)

The purpose of this part of this chapter is to promote the importance of service firms staying as closely connected to the customer as possible. We are not attempting to be a 'handbook' of all of the mechanisms for such connection, but rather we hope to provide a range of ideas from current practice, which are connected to the theoretical principles of customer orientation, customer centricity and customer engagement.

With the advent of Web 2.0, where users are able to interact and collaborate with each other in dialogue in a virtual community (as opposed to Web sites where people are limited to the passive viewing of information), an explosion of opportunities to engage with customers has occurred. These 'user-generated' platforms include social networking, blogs, wikis, video sharing and the like. *This change has meant that firms have lost some control of the messaging about them.*

Customers are now communicating with each other en masse, often completely separately from sites created by firms. One well-known example of the way customers communicate is TripAdvisor.com, one of the earliest adopters of user-generated content, which is a Web site designed to assist customers in gathering travel information, and then post reviews and opinions in an interactive forum. This type of communication has significant influence on customer purchasing decisions, and there is significant evidence that shows that many customers use various social media and interactive review forums to inform their decision-making.

When we used to talk of word-of-mouth (WOM), we referred to customers literally 'talking' to each other. This advent of user-generated web platforms means that customer-to-customer interactions (C2C) now rule the airwaves about how customers

© Cienpies Design/Shutterstock.com

communicate to each other. But this has implications for firms wishing to (a) obtain 'real' feedback from customers and also (b) respond to comments. While we caution anyone who believes that user-generated conversations represent statistically and methodologically valid customer research, most firms today monitor this 'traffic' and learn about trends and general perceptions about customer experiences in their businesses. There are a vast array of challenges to consider as well, mainly about the veracity (truthfulness) of the reviews, and the degree to which customers and competition can sabotage these communications or start a thread of negativity that can spread and in many ways distort the messaging. Nonetheless, service firms today **must**:

1. be aware of these communications;
2. engage in conversations where it would be beneficial to respond to concerns or fallacies; and
3. decide to which degree they will allocate resources to this.

Many firms today actively encourage customers to 'like' their sites and pages and often offer incentives for customers to do so. Such open and easy access to customer communication has led to changes in the fundamental relationships of firms with their customers. We all know that it is more likely that we will ask not only friends and relatives about a possible purchase (restaurant visit, hotel stay, online product, travel destination), but we are equally as likely to consult online guides and social media sites. The failure to keep up with technological change is often cited as one of the main influences on financial failure of independent restaurants (Camilo, Connolly, and Woo, 2008).

Unfortunately, smaller, independent businesses often do not have the strategic foresight nor the resources (financial and expert) to undertake a full assessment of the way in which they operate in social media and online platforms. However, it is becoming evident that nearly all businesses are subject to online conversations and therefore must be willing and able to enter this domain. There are web-based tools (e.g., ReviewAnalyst and many others) that allow organizations to monitor social media and their online reputations. Other smaller businesses often source a young technology-savvy employee and engage this person to assist, or 'reverse mentor', the owners of the business who might be less familiar with how to engage. Regardless of the approach, how management monitors and responds to social media and various electronic guides can go a long way towards the destruction or longevity of a hospitality business (Pantelidis, 2010). Not only can hospitality operators gain a better understanding of what their customers want and how they perceive the business, but also recognition and awareness of such comments can protect their brand.

It is also important to be aware that different methods of communication are more effective for different age groups. With the 'baby-boomers' heading into retirement and making up a very large percentage of hospitality and tourism customers, it is important not to forget this group and to cater for different market segments (Dev, Buschman and Bowen, 2010).

Here we provide a brief description of some common terms related to technology-based communication (as of mid-2014):

- *Social media*—websites and applications that enable users to create and share content or to participate in social networking.
- *Blog*—a personal website or web page on which an individual records opinions, links to other sites, etc. on a regular basis.
- *Chat rooms*—an area on the Internet or other computer network where users can communicate, typically limiting communication to a particular topic.
- *Online communities*—an online community whose members enable its existence through taking part in membership and frequent communication and sharing of information.
- *Mobile app*—a computer program designed to run on smartphones, tablet computers and other mobile devices.

The darkside of social media

Of course social media has a darkside too! Without strong proactive management and policies, it is very easy for thousands or even millions of people to hear about a bad customer service experience (even if they are not telling the truth!). One such experience is known in the folklore of the airline industry as "United Breaks Guitars". This is a song that was posted on YouTube and iTunes by Canadian musician Dave Carroll and his band, Sons of Maxwell. The song was written as the result of a real-life experience of how fellow passengers saw baggage handlers throwing guitars on and off the airplane. When he arrived at his destination, he discovered that his $3,500 guitar was severely damaged. What made the situation worse was the attitude of the staff he tried to talk to. He filed a claim but was denied as it was outside the stipulated 24-hour timeframe required to make such claims. The story ends somewhat better, as the airline received permission to use the video in customer service training. The song became an immediate YouTube and iTunes hit upon its release in July 2009 and a public relations embarrassment for the airline.

Internal customers

The customers of first concern to a firm should be its internal customers—its own service personnel. Management's primary task is to 'sell' its service concept to the firm's employees, before attempting to sell it to external customers. And the most important of these employees in this context are those who actually deliver the service to the external customers. Management thus needs to develop trust and strong relationships with its own internal customers—a philosophy of 'internal marketing'.

© zimmytws/Shutterstock.com

The concept of internal marketing is relevant to virtually all organizations. It is particularly important, however, for labor-intensive service organizations. The concept of the internal customer should be viewed as a managerial philosophy which has strategic and tactical implications throughout the company and its various business functions.

In any service organization, employees are both receivers and providers of service. Hence, services offered and received by internal customers inside the organization invariably affect the service offered by the firm to its external customers. Given the relationship between employee performance and the delivery of service quality, service-oriented organizations should treat front-line employees as 'partial customers'—that is, as individuals deserving treatment similar to that which management wants its customers to receive. This concept is further discussed later in this chapter and in further detail in Chapter 8.

Internal Service

Because a single isolated service is of limited use to the customer in the absence of various supporting services, customer demands on most service organizations are 'cross functional' in nature. Services are *interdependent* in nature, and rarely can exist or function inde-

© Dusit/Shutterstock.com

pendently. It is therefore essential that the various departments and personnel work collaboratively to offer service commensurate with the customer's requirements.

Within most service organizations, there are numerous departments and personnel performing various tasks, functions and services. These can be fundamentally different—for example, in a hotel, the revenue manager might be working on room demand and pricing, while a chef is preparing the guest's meals. In other cases, the different functions are more closely linked—for example, a chef preparing a meal and a waiter serving it. However, whether the functions are closely allied or not, the provision of a full hotel service requires all functions to be interlinked and coordinated. This is particularly true in larger hospitality and tourism organizations because many of the 'back of house' employees, those not coming into direct contact with the customer, still do influence the customer, directly or indirectly. For example, the revenue manager might have to work on the front desk during a peak period or to cover an absent employee. So the revenue manager can set the tone for the front desk staff, depending on what kind of mood they are in, even though the revenue manager usually works 'behind' the scenes. The same is true for a theme park, where all of the activities that the tourist/visitor experiences are supported by a literal army of back-of-house employees keeping the park functioning, clean, stocked and safe.

Therefore, it can be argued that all personnel in a service organization receive or offer service from other members of the organization. In this sense, everyone in a service firm *is* a customer, and *has* customers. For example, the waiter receives a service from the chef (the provision of a meal), and provides a service to the guest (the serving of that meal). Or a front office employee discusses with the rooms division manager before re-allocating the room to a customer. Essentially, this is the idea expressed by the concept of the 'internal customer'—it indicates the interdependency of every function within a service organization.

The success of every service organization is dependent on collaboration between the internal customers (the employees) of every department. No service firm can give its external customers the quality they want and expect without the active participation of all of its employees. J. W. Marriott (Jr.), president of the Marriott Corporation, famously summed up the idea in these words: *"We must do all we can to ensure that our organization's systems, methods, and policies serve the people who serve the customers" Marriott, 1988.*

Unless employees receive good service from the other employees with whom they interact, they will be unable to serve their customers well. For example, it is difficult for a hotel receptionist to settle the accounts of a guest quickly if the accounting personnel have not entered charges in the customer's account in an appropriate fashion. It is equally difficult for a waiter to 'sell' the service quality of a meal to a diner if the waiter is dissatisfied with the service that he or she has received from the chef.

Quality internal service and satisfied internal customers are essential if an organization is to establish an effective customer-oriented service culture. This point is expanded further in Chapters 6 and 8.

Implications for quality

Tracing these internal links from contact with the firm's external customer, and then backwards through the chain of internal customers, is a useful method of assessing quality. It is apparent that it is just as important to deliver high-quality products and services to the internal customers as it is to deliver high-quality products and services to the external customers. Ultimately, quality represents a satisfied external customer—the road to which is paved by satisfied internal customers. Chapter 8 will provide a more detailed review of intraorganizational practices that lead to and create positive service experiences for customers.

Employee research

If internal marketing is an important concept, then we must go one step further to better understand the employees' needs and changing expectations. In a service business, *everyone* is responsible for managing service, and front-line customer-contact employees represent one of the most valuable means for gathering information about customers. By eliciting information about customers, these employees are ideally placed to help senior management know their customers better. They are, in reality, 'listening posts' (Heskett, Sasser and Schlesinger, 1997). And a service firm probably has more such 'listening posts' than management commonly believes—virtually every employee can function as a valuable 'data-collection center' and on-the-spot 'market researcher'. Service personnel are, in fact, in a better position to evaluate the customer's experience than anyone else in the organization (Dietz, Pugh, and Wiley, 2004).

Inseparability makes employees important

As previously noted on several occasions, one of the distinctive features of service is 'inseparability'—that is, service is produced and consumed simultaneously, and therefore differs from physical goods in that there are no channels of distribution to isolate the producer from the consumer. Service personnel meet and communicate personally with the customer each time a service is rendered. Service personnel are thus the direct 'face' (or 'marketer') of the organization, and are the most important link in a service organization's communication with its customers. One good way to think about the relationship between employees and customers is that the boundaries between them are either nonexistent or permeable—hence whatever is occurring inside the organization usually can easily spread to the customer through the employees who serve them, and vice versa (Schneider, Macey, Lee, and Young, 2009).

Management involvement

Such communication is one of the critical factors in the success of any service organization. In the words of Deming (1982), effective *two-way* communication can 'drive out fear'. But the emphasis must be on effective two-way communication. Unless management makes itself easily accessible and approachable, upward communication will not take place. Top management must emphasize a company philosophy in which the focus is on the customer, and must demonstrate its support of those employees who actively live this out by really serving customers.

Management must recognize the importance of feedback from employees, and actively encourage it. If information regarding customers' expectations and perceptions, as obtained by customer-contact employees, is passed onto top management, management's understanding of their customers *must* be enhanced. Indeed, in most companies, management's understanding of their customers largely depends on such communication as received from customer-contact personnel. However, large organizations often have an organizational structure consisting of many levels, and usually communicate through fixed and formal systems. Such formal communication systems can prevent the full benefit of feedback information—which might otherwise be more readily available from employees in less-formal arrangements.

Managers must encourage and support employees in their service endeavors, and senior managers must make themselves available to receive feedback. They must be active in personally seeking feedback from employees, and transparent in their willingness to act upon it.

Employees as customer 'advocates'

Employees should be encouraged to become 'advocates' for the customer. Indeed, many employees have a natural tendency to do so.

In many service-interface situations, employees take customers 'under their wings' to see that their needs and wants are met, and that their problems are solved. By doing so, a door is opened to important information about the buyer of the service. If employees begin to function as customer advocates, a new sense of responsibility for knowing those customers 'inside-out' will develop.

A customer advocate goes beyond providing a service or product to the customer. In many service situations, a personal relationship with the customer becomes established (as is evident in the case of many professional services, such as legal services, medical services and so on). The same sort of relationship can be encouraged in a service organization such as a hotel. Although the relationship is clearly not as intimate as, say, a medical consultation, the same general principles apply. As customers become known on a more intimate basis, their trust grows, and their willingness to express their concerns, wishes and preferences increases.

Indeed, relationships can develop to an extent where front-line employees prove to be more loyal to their customers than to management. This is consistent with the Japanese management approach, whereby employees are constantly informed that their loyalty *should* be with the customers because, ultimately, the customers are paying their wages. This sort of strong commitment to customer orientation is to be encouraged. It can ensure a service firm's survival, in even the most turbulent market conditions.

Making it work effectively

Employees can and should become directly involved in the process of collecting customer feedback for the following reasons:

- ▶ to create an opportunity to extend appreciation to customers for their business; and
- ▶ to establish communication back to customers, to reassure them that they are being listened to.

It might be desirable to implement service quality 'circles' as a deliberate formal mechanism for gathering customer feedback. Many service settings provide the opportunity for joint problem-solving activity, involving both the customer and the contact person. Through such active communication, employees who provide services can identify the customer's needs and find a configuration of the service that best satisfies those needs.

This encourages employees to participate actively in problem solving and decision-making. This improves morale in the workplace, and fosters a positive customer-oriented culture.

Regular feedback communication systems ensure a continuous flow of information from employees to management, and back again. This communication system should have formal and informal channels to capture the full spectrum of available knowledge, and thus to provide maximum benefit in tailoring effective quality service.

Summary

In the present competitive marketplace, business firms must adopt a customer-oriented managerial approach to attract and retain their customers. As discussed in previous chapters, the distinctive nature of service products forces service organizations to place even more emphasis on *customers* in the design, development and delivery of their service offerings. It is thus imperative that the firms understand customer expectations and perceptions, as well as the factors that influence their evaluation and satisfaction with the service provision.

Market-oriented firms must be up to date with new market trends in customer needs, perceptions and expectations. And service providers who are able to anticipate customer needs and desires before they become apparent in the marketplace will be advantaged in gaining a winning market position. To gather, analyze and act on market information effectively is thus of paramount importance to service providers who wish to stay ahead in the marketplace.

Within the service sector, hospitality and tourism industries offer services that entail prolonged and intensive customer contact. This presents a great opportunity for the firm to solicit and gather valuable information and feedback from the customer. While quality interaction with customers is essential to ensure quality service and guest satisfaction, management should not restrict its efforts and resources to traditional forms of market research.

This chapter offers a vast number of available tools which allow firms to better understand the needs and desires of service customers from different perspectives—those of the customer, managers and employees (or 'internal customers'). These methods, which can be used independently or in conjunction, can assist service managers in understanding the behaviors and characteristics of customers / tourists, and in improving their managerial effectiveness, market insights and overall business performance.

Review Questions

1. Thinking from the managerial perspective, explain why it is important to get a regular 'pulse' of customer moods, trends, interests.
2. Why is the customer centricity concept vital for tourism and hospitality businesses? How is this concept translated in practice by Disney?
3. What are the five categories of customers presented in the chapter? Briefly describe each of them.
4. List two examples of tourism-destination-related interview questions, one that would be best explored through quantitative study, and one that would be best explored through qualitative study.

5. Briefly describe any three techniques for gathering customer information, as presented in this chapter.
6. Explain the concept of internal marketing.
7. Explain how internal customer service can affect the quality of external customer service. Give examples of how a hotel manager might serve his or her internal customers.
8. Explain which challenges customer-to-customer communication creates for businesses. What are the potential ways to address those?
9. Explain the idea of employees being customers' 'advocates'. Think of the possible benefits for the customers and for the organization itself.

Suggested Readings

This is a list of suggested further reading on topics covered in this chapter. For a separate list of full reference citations quoted in the chapter, see 'References', Chapter 4, page 326.

Bolten, R. N., et al. (2013). Understanding Generation Y and their use of social media: a review and research agenda. *Journal of Service Management*, 24(3), 245–267.

Ford, R. C., and Heaton, C. P. (2001). Lessons from hospitality that can serve anyone. *Organizational Dynamics*, 30(1), 30–47.

Kandampully, J. (2006). The new customer-centred business model for the hospitality industry. *International Journal of Contemporary Hospitality Management*, 18(3), 173–187.

Kumar, V., Lemon, K. N., and Parasuraman, A. (2006). Managing customers for value: An overview and research agenda. *Journal of Service Research*, 9(2), 87–94.

Libai, B., et al. (2010). Customer-to-customer interactions: Broadening the scope of word of mouth research, *Journal of Service Research*, 13(3), 267–282.

Meyer, C. and Schwager, A. (2007). Understanding customer experience, *Harvard Business Review*, February, 117–126.

Solnet, D., Kralj, A., and Kandampully, J. (2012). Generation Y Employees: An examination of work attitude differences. *The Journal of Applied Management and Entrepreneurship*, 17(3), 35–52.

Verma, R., Plaschka, G., and Louviere, J. J. (2002). Understanding customer choices: A key to successful management of hospitality services. *Cornell Hotel and Restaurant Administration Quarterly*, 43, 15–24.

Verma, R., Stock, D., and McCarthy, L. (2012). Customer preferences for online, social media, and mobile innovations in the hospitality industry. *Cornell Hospitality Quarterly*, 53(3), 183–186.

CHAPTER 5

Service Vision, Service Design and the Service Encounter

Study Objectives

Having completed this chapter, readers should be able to:

1. Appreciate the importance of a service vision and service strategy to an organization's long-term success;
2. Understand the importance of a well-designed service system;
3. Understand the implications of service networks in building a firm's competitive advantage; and
4. Understand some of the practical techniques for managing service operations.

Outline

- ▶ Introduction
- ▶ Service vision
  - ▶ What is vision?
  - ▶ Vision statement vs. mission statement
  - ▶ What is a service vision?
  - ▶ Set apart from the rest
  - ▶ Ingrained into the fabric
  - ▶ Customer-focus
- ▶ Service strategy
  - ▶ What is strategy?
  - ▶ What is a service strategy?
  - ▶ Everyone is involved

- ▶ Service process
  - ▶ What is a service process?
  - ▶ Process as the 'essence' of service
  - ▶ Service system
  - ▶ Process quality and output quality
  - ▶ Ultimately a management responsibility
- ▶ Alignment: Vision, strategy, process and system
- ▶ Service system design
  - ▶ Perfecting the service system through design
  - ▶ What is service design?
  - ▶ Inbuilt flaws
  - ▶ Design is a dynamic process
  - ▶ Creative thinking
- ▶ Some practical examples
  - ▶ Restaurants
    - ▪ McDonald's
    - ▪ Cactus Jack's
    - ▪ The Fat Duck
  - ▶ Hotels
    - ▪ Pod Hotels
    - ▪ Holiday Inn
    - ▪ Ritz-Carlton
  - ▶ Leisure tourism
    - ▪ Dreamworld
- ▶ The service encounter
  - ▶ Service encounter triad
  - ▶ Managing the service encounter
    - ▪ Customer as 'coproducer'
    - ▪ Challenges and stressors
    - ▪ Managerial actions and solutions
- ▶ Service blueprinting
  - ▶ Leading to a 'moment of truth'
  - ▶ The nature of a service blueprint
  - ▶ A 'snapshot' of a dynamic process
  - ▶ The 'line of visibility'
  - ▶ 'Fail points' and 'encounter points'
  - ▶ Looking back and looking ahead
  - ▶ Blueprints within blueprints
  - ▶ Dreams and reality
  - ▶ 'Moments of truth' remain crucial
- ▶ Summary
- ▶ Review Questions
- ▶ Suggested Readings

Key Words

Alignment

Back stage

Blueprinting

Boundary spanners

Co-producer

Customer deviance

Duchenne smiles

Dyadic interaction

Emotional contagion

Emotional labor

Employee deviance

Employee stress

Encounter points

Fail points

Failure-prone points

Front stage

Front-liners

Gatekeepers

Image-makers

Impression management

Jay customer

Line of visibility

Moment-of-truth

Output quality

Process quality

Scripting

Service design

Service encounter

Service encounter triad

Service image

Service mission

Service offer

Service process

Service strategy

Service system

Service vision

Introduction

Having discussed the needs of customers in Chapter 4, we now proceed in the present chapter to discuss how a service firm might organize its internal arrangements to ensure that these needs are met. Steven Covey (2004), author of the famous book *The Seven Habits of Highly Effective People* suggests in his second habit that successful people start each day with conviction about how they want their day to end ("Begin with the End in Mind"). He says that whatever you do on a particular day should not violate the criteria you have decided are important to you. In many ways, this advice holds true for business as well. Managers need to be clear about what it is that the business stands for and then organize every aspect of the business so that there is a perfect alignment between the big picture and each of the small steps taken throughout the day. Indeed, successful service organizations know who they are and what they are good at, and ensure that all aspects of the organization stay true to this clear message.

Successful service organizations pursue visions of service excellence that clearly indicate to customers and employees the objectives of the firm's service vision and its position in the marketplace. Please note that in some firms this may be different from the firm's mission and vision in terms of its purpose. This distinction is important for us to understand since some firms' visions may not necessarily be focused entirely on 'service' only. For example, while a hotel provides service to its customers, given that it is a commercial enterprise its owner/shareholder's vision is to maintain a high return on investment. Therefore, while the hotel maintains an overall vision of high return on investment, it will also maintain a service vision knowing that it is the service excellence that provides them with the unique advantage in the marketplace. Thus, this *service vision* provides the foundation upon which the firm designs its service offerings such that they are always consistent with the overall image which the organization has attempted to create in the minds of customers. Related to the service *vision* is the service *concept* which is a theoretical expression of exactly what the service company proposes to do. Figure 5.1 shows the interrelationships between the service concept, strategy, process and systems and should be referred to as we describe each component below.

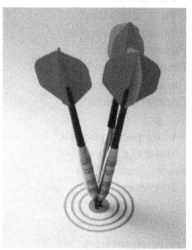

The service vision is the practical expression of the service concept! The service concept aims to fulfill customer needs within the firm's expertise. In this book and this chapter, you will see the words concept and vision used often, sometimes interchangeably. However, the nuances of service vision and a service concept are less important than the simple fact that a service organization must be clear about who they are and what their service offer (concept) is and ensure that all activities are centered around and informed by them.

An example of a service concept is Jimmy John's Gourmet Sandwiches (a US-based quick service restaurant which now has over 1900 restaurants). Their service concept is clear.

© John Smith Design/Shutterstock.com

Jimmy John's Gourmet Sandwiches

Jimmy John's makes sandwiches, but works very hard to be different from other similar types of quick service sandwich businesses. They strive to have unique and delicious bread, service and speed-focused systems in place, and employees and leaders who are trained to take responsibility. Their shared commitment is to be efficient, quick, and dependable. From their stores to their corporate office, they have a 'right now' attitude where excuses are not acceptable. A visit to a Jimmy John's restaurant usually finds employees who may be no different than those in other similar businesses, but who seem to be uncharacteristically committed to and engage in the extraordinary behaviors centered around the service concept and striving to be the best. Indeed, Jimmy Johns has a clear service concept and it permeates through the whole organization and is palpable to anyone who walks in their front door.

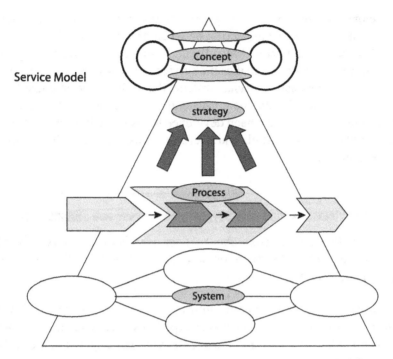

Figure 5.1
The service model—Connecting service concept to strategy, process and system

For this company, their service concept is 'honest, fast and value'. It is not fine dining. All employees of Jimmy John's know this before they put on the uniform—and the grace and mechanical synchronicity shown by staff during a busy shift is testament to their single mindedness and shared purpose.

Remember too that one of the characteristics of service organizations is the frequent employee-customer interactions and the intense reliance on the employees in building relationships—great ideas in the 'boardroom' have to be translated and actioned on the 'shop floor' by the workforce. So clarity of purpose and then outstanding execution are paramount. It is at these interactions where

© Orla/Shutterstock.com

strategies developed in the boardroom get translated into customer experience—where the rubber meets the road. This connection between broad vision to the actual delivery is the nature of this chapter and critical to fully understanding service management.

The nature of service products makes the service delivery process especially important. It is imperative that firms design service systems that effectively organize the firm's processes to produce the desired outcome consistently every time. To this end, various techniques, such as 'blueprinting', have been developed to visualize interrelationships of service processes, to identify common pitfalls and to enable firms to channel their efforts efficiently to achieve maximum benefits.

Service vision, service strategy, service process and service system

The first part of this chapter talks about (i) service vision, (ii) service strategy and (iii) service process. These terms are obviously interrelated, but they do have distinct meanings and applications.

▶ *A service vision* is an overall philosophy of a firm's service orientation and position—a sense of self-awareness (perhaps even a sense of 'self-destiny') which explains to staff and customers what the organization stands for and what it aims to offer.

▶ *A service strategy* is a distinctive formula for delivering the above service vision—a plan of action which energizes an organization and effectively defines the practical meaning of the word 'service' for that firm.

▶ *A service process* is the actual delivery of the service—a series of acts or performances which make up the very *essence* of a service. "Not what is done—but how it is done" a step-by-step outline of how the service is delivered. Process requires an implication of various tools, techniques and people.

▶ *A service system* consists of management systems, departments, delivery system of products or information, organizational structure and technology.

This chapter addresses the above issues from a managerial perspective to provide readers with a broader awareness of a more strategic level of service management, and to provide readers with an understanding of the more important *techniques* in service operations management.

Service vision

What is vision?

A vision, from a business point of view, is simply a picture of what success will be at a particular time in the future. It answers an array of questions such as, "What do we want to be known for?", "How are we different?", "Why did the business start?". These are issues which should not change frequently. A well-put-together vision inspires people—it gets people excited to come to work! It must be real, achievable and strategically possible.

Most companies have a vision statement—a declaration of goals for the mid-term or long-term future. This can range from one line to several paragraphs, and lay out the most important primary goals for a company—not the plan to get there. An inspiring vision statement for a small business should have two key characteristics. First, it needs to state where the company wants to be in the near future, and second, it must have a level of excitement and motivation to it.

Vision statement vs. mission statement

A vision statement should not be confused with a *mission statement*. The terms are often used interchangeably, but mission statements are present-based statements designed to convey a sense of why the company exists to both members of the company and the external community. Vision statements are future-based and are meant to inspire and give directions to the employees of the company, not anyone outside the company. A mission statement answers the question, "Why does my business exist?" while a vision statement answers the question, "Where do I see my business going?"

Vision statements are dynamic and can change over time. As a company grows, its objectives and goals may change. Vision statements need to be revised as needed to reflect the change as goals are met, but they should be written to last for at least a few years.

According to Collins and Porras (1996), a vision articulates the firm's core ideology (values and purpose) and their envisioned future (a vividly described 10–30 year goal). They argue that the broad ideology remains fixed, but strategies and practices need to be fluid and evolve in order to achieve the envisioned future—what they refer to as "the dynamic of preserving the core while stimulating progress" (p. 65).

Figure 5.2 provides a visual depiction of how the company vision should be positioned at the organization's core, and that mission, strategy, processes and systems are subsequently built around, yet always remain grounded by, the vision.

© ml/Shutterstock.com

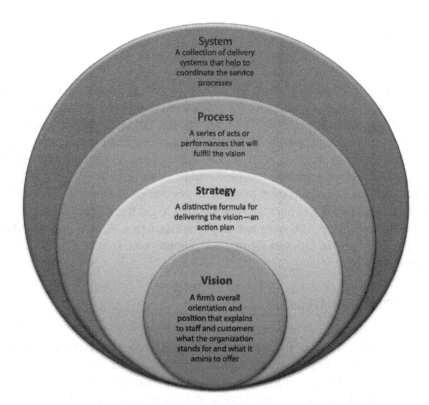

Figure 5.2
The role of the company's vision

What is a service vision?

Now that we have reviewed the general concept of vision, we continue the discussion with a particular focus on service organizations that are tasked with not only a broad vision for the firm but also a vision for the service promise. Similar to the general conceptualization of company vision, a service vision represents all that a service organization stands for—the image of the organization as the customers see it. From a theoretical point of view, it is this concept which explains to both employees and customers what the organization stands for—focused on the service promise—and what it aims to offer. *The service vision is the expression of the planned service offer, including the delivery systems and procedures required to achieve this objective.*

Set apart from the rest

All outstanding service firms have a compelling vision of their own position of leadership in the marketplace (in many ways the service 'promise'). This sense of self-awareness (perhaps even a sense of 'self-destiny') provides outstanding firms with a direction that differentiates them from other companies. In a sense, firms with such a vision of superior service do not have to compete—because they always stand apart from other firms. Their vision represents quality, superiority and value to the customer, and this vision nurtures, motivates and binds every member of the organization in pursuit of a common goal. While it is often more common for large multi-national companies to have a clear service vision, it is no less important for smaller, privately held businesses to do the same. Big or small, the company and service vision informs everything else in a business—and smaller, regional, family-owned businesses can benefit equally from understanding and utilizing these principles.

As they work towards this compelling vision of superior service, successful service organizations meticulously orchestrate every employee, every individual process and every system. In turn, this uncompromising vision of superior service captures the attention of customers, provides value to those customers and gains the loyalty of those customers.

Ingrained into the fabric

Because the service outcome is intangible and closely connected to the employee-customer interface, it is imperative that all service personnel from the boardroom to the shop floor know and understand the service vision. The vision must be nurtured, promoted and 'sold' to all personnel in the organization until it becomes ingrained in the fabric and thinking of the organization (the way that employees perceive the service vision is discussed further in Chapter 8 in the section about organizational culture and climate, and in particular, the discussion around employees 'living the brand').

The service vision of an organization should provide employees with clear information as to:

▶ the offerings of the organization; and
▶ the specific needs and wants of the customer that the organization is offering to fulfill.

That is, every person in the organization needs to have a clear vision of *what* the firm is trying to do for its customers, and *why* it is trying to do these things. Once these basic goals are established, the service vision moves on to the more practical questions of designing a structure and putting that structure into effect.

Customer-focus

The service vision is thus an umbrella concept covering the whole service offering of a firm. But, in talking of how a firm proposes to operate, the service vision should never lose sight of the fact that the *customer* is the focus and purpose of the whole concept. In discussing the *firm* in detail, and how the firm proposes to behave, it is easy to lose sight of the fact that the whole purpose of the service vision is to serve the *customer*—not the firm (and equally, the employees of the service firm are tasked to be the agents assigned to convey this vision via the many customer contact moments, a point covered further in Chapters 4 and 8).

The service vision should therefore state the core service that the firm proposes to offer to the customer, the facilitating and supporting services it proposes to offer to the customer, how the basic package is to be made accessible to the customer, how customer interactions are to be developed and how customers are to participate in the process.

The service vision is thus not ultimately defined in terms of products or service. Rather, it is defined in terms of *the results produced for customers*.

The components of a service vision

The service vision is defined in terms of the *results produced for customers*. The service vision of a firm should therefore state:

1. the core service (or services) it proposes to offer to the customer;
2. the facilitating and supporting services it proposes to offer to the customer;
3. how the basic package is to be made accessible to the customer;
4. how customer interactions are to be developed; and
5. how customers are to participate in the process.

Although the focus of a service vision is on the *customer,* and hence on the service attributes that best express benefit to the customer, an effective service vision must nevertheless be mindful of the realities of the marketplace in which the organization wishes to operate. The service vision must take into account a realistic assessment of the organization's position in that marketplace, and must develop a clear idea of a service offer that matches this position. For example, a café located near a busy public beach is more likely to require speed, efficiency and the ability to provide items to take away as opposed to a similar café in a dining precinct where customers are more likely to want to sit down and enjoy their experience.

In making such a market assessment and the appropriate service offer to match that assessment, the service vision must therefore provide direction for:

▶ *market segments*—the specific market segments that have been identified;
▶ *service processes*—how the proposed service is produced, distributed and consumed in the marketplace;
▶ *organization of the service offer*—how the interface with the customer is to be organized in the marketplace; and
▶ *service image*—how to maintain the desired marketplace image to present to potential customers.

Service strategy

What is strategy?

Strategy represents an integrated set of plans for building and maintaining a sustainable competitive advantage. In its original sense, strategy is derived from the Greek word, *strategos,* a military term used to describe a General's plan for arraying and maneuvering forces with the goal of defeating an enemy army. In business, a strategy is a plan for controlling and utilizing resources (human, physical and financial) with the goal of promoting and securing their vital interests (Harvard Business School Press, 2005).

Strategy is about shaping the future, about determining how to achieve your vision. You move between where you want to go (ends) and what you need to do to get there (means). Great strategy is the quickest route from means to ends to shape your future.

Michael Porter, one of the world's most acclaimed scholars in the area of strategy, argues that strategy is about being different, about choosing a different set of activities to deliver a unique mix of value in achieving a vision. A strategy focuses on what you do (and importantly, what you do not do), what you want to become and how you plan to get there.

What is a service strategy?

A service strategy flows from the general definition of strategy above. If a *service vision* or concept is an overall focus of a firm's service orientation and position, a *service strategy* can be defined as a distinctive formula for *delivering* that service vision.

An overall strategy can be made up of smaller strategies related to specific benefits or promises that are valuable to customers. By developing specific strategies, rather than vague 'wishes', management has an opportunity to reassess and reorganize its options in its attempts to establish and maintain an effective competitive position.

Such service-focused strategies are incorporated into the overall service vision that delivers a powerful corporate statement to the internal and external markets. An effective service strategy energizes the organization—effectively defining the practical meaning of the word 'service' for that firm (Berry, 1995).

Everyone is involved

A service strategy is thus an organizing principle that allows everyone in a service organization to focus his or her efforts within the overall plan of action. The value of each individual employee's offerings is enhanced if they are conducted in such an integrated service system.

A service-oriented strategy that percolates effectively through the entire organization strengthens the service culture (refer to Chapter 8) from the inside and thereby strengthens the image of the organization as perceived from the outside. It clearly communicates to every member of the organization what the business and vision are all about, the key operational priorities and the things that they should all try to accomplish. If comprehensively explained to all employees, it establishes itself as the firm's corporate strategy, and as the personal strategy of every individual employee.

What a *service* strategy does

A service strategy determines every aspect of a service offering—including its development, its distribution and its promotion.

To be effective, a good service strategy should thus provide detailed guidance for:

1. bringing together every aspect of the organization to focus on the service offering;
2. the delivery of that service offering; and
3. the marketing, advertising and promotion of that service offering.

Southwest Airlines

Southwest Airlines exemplifies the correlation between a plan of service strategy and follow-through. Their mission highlights their quest to give each customer friendly service. Their people exude a sense of personal pride and company commitment, which they believe sets them apart from others. Their shared vision and mission reinforces commitment to their employees by ensuring a work environment that encourages new ideas and offers avenues for new opportunities. Staff are treated in the same way the company expects them to treat the customers—with care, respect and courtesy. Southwest Airlines has had the same philosophy since 1988. It has been a central part of all marketing campaigns since that time.

Service process

What is a service process?

Having described the *service vision* or service concept (the overall service philosophy and focus of a firm), and the *service strategy* (the distinctive formula to bring together every aspect of the organization to focus on delivering that service vision), we now turn to the actual service delivery. The first step in planning service delivery is to identify *service processes* that are essential to ensure that the delivery of the service will meet customer expectations and will match with both the service concept and service strategy. Service steps or processes are the necessary series of acts or performances that are undertaken in a logical sequence so as to ensure that customers receive a positive experience.

Service is an act or performance that is often carried out in a series of steps. Such a series of steps makes up a service process. As previously noted, such service processes have certain features that distinguish them from physical goods (see 'Differences between product and service,' Chapter 2, p. 23). These include the fact that services are produced and consumed almost simultaneously, and that customers participate with the service organization in the process of production and consumption.

Analyzing a service process

Compared with the theory involved in analyzing a 'service vision' and a 'service strategy', the idea of a 'service process' sounds simple enough—the actual practical delivery of a service. But a service process is more complex than it seems. It really involves three distinct parts, and all three must be analyzed and assessed if the service process is to be effective.

1. First, there are the steps, tasks and activities necessary for the rendering of the service—the list of activities involved in the actual service process itself.
2. Secondly, there are the means by which the tasks are executed—the combination of people and goods that make up the surrounding 'infrastructure' of the service-delivery process.
3. Finally, there is the role and personal experience of the consumer—what Shostack (1990) calls the evidence presented to the consumer.

In summary, to understand a service process properly, we have to: (i) analyze what has to be done, (ii) work out how it is to be done (and by whom) and (iii) assess how the customer responds to it.

Process as the 'essence' of service

Production and consumption of service, and consumer involvement in these, all occur at about the same time. Simultaneously, the quality of service is judged by the consumer. The design of a service process—the mapping out of how a service is to be rendered—is thus of vital importance in maintaining the quality of service. Process is so important that many service scholars describe process as being the very *essence* of a service.

Similarly, Susan Segal-Horn (2003) argues that the most important part of a service strategy is the implementation of that strategy by the front-line staff of the organization. These are the 'moments of truth' which define the organization. Front-line staff are therefore critical to the strategy implementation and, hence, the service experience for customers. In a service business, bridging this interface between strategy and operations is critical!

According to Shostack (1990a) the actual delivery of a service is part of an overall integrated service system that can be broken down into three distinct parts. Each of these must be analyzed and assessed if service delivery is to be effective.

▶ First, there are the steps, tasks and activities necessary for the rendering of the service—this is the list of activities involved in the actual service process itself.
▶ Secondly, there are the means by which the tasks are executed—the combination of people and goods that encompass the surrounding 'infrastructure' of the service-delivery process.
▶ Finally, there is the role and experience of the customer—what Shostack calls the 'evidence' presented to the customer.

All service delivery systems can be understood in their entirety by understanding the above three elements.

Service system

The service system helps to coordinate various service processes for consistency. It ensures that all processes follow a pre-designed pattern so that the service outcome will consistently fulfill what was promised through the firm's service vision or concept. The service system therefore may consist of management systems, information flows, organizational structure and technology.

Process quality and output quality

When considering service quality concepts in Chapter 3, the service quality dimensions proposed by Lehtinen (1983) were noted. It will be recalled that Lehtinen identified two sets of quality dimensions—*process quality* and *output quality*.

In appreciating the significance of service quality, it is therefore important to recognize that service is experienced by customers as both an *outcome* and as a *process*. Both are significant in the assessment of quality.

1. The *outcome* is the culmination of having a service need met—a customer *does* wish to obtain a loan, *does* wish to have a car properly repaired and *does* wish to enjoy a delicious meal. Service outcome is the core service and hence customers expect the outcome to be good; if not they would not have chosen this firm. Therefore, quality of the service outcome will not provide the firm a competitive advantage.

2. But the *process* is perhaps more important to the customer since he/she participates in the entire process until the delivery of the service outcome. In obtaining these outcomes, the customer *does* wish to have simple paperwork at the bank, *does* wish to experience a short wait time at the car repairer and *does* wish to receive the ordered food and drinks served by a courteous waiter. Therefore, a service firm's competitive advantage is often attributed to the service process. User-friendly service process provides a unique attraction to the customer, for example, Amazon and Google.

Dissatisfaction with a service is often attributed to the service process and not necessarily the outcome. It is important to note that, although the customer may be satisfied with the outcome, he/she may not consider using the service again if they were dissatisfied with the process.

According to this view, the output of any service 'takes form' during the whole transaction, and is being judged by the customer during that transaction. By controlling the process (and the quality of that process), the output quality can also be controlled.

Remember too that process quality has been shown to be the driver of increased levels of customer satisfaction, whereas output or outcome quality is generally related to reliability (refer to Chapter 3). Parasuraman and his colleagues (1991) suggested that the outcome (reliability) can satisfy a customer—but the process dimensions of service quality (in SERVQUAL, these are assurance, tangibles, empathy and responsiveness) are those most likely to *exceed* expectations.

Ultimately a management responsibility

As noted in Chapter 3, one of Deming's great contributions is his insight into process design as being a management responsibility. In goods manufacturing, management alone has total control over the resources needed for goods production (Deming, 1982). Similarly, in the service sector, it is management's responsibility (often in collaboration with those employees involved in service delivery) to set up appropriate service processes.

The key to a comprehensive service quality program is thus achieved through management taking responsibility for the philosophy, strategies and processes involved in the delivery of service. To achieve this, service managers in tandem with those involved in service delivery need to analyze each of the processes in the overall service offering, and must ensure that they are coordinated and effective as an integrated system.

Alignment: Vision, strategy, process and system

It is important that a service organization's vision, strategy, processes and systems are clearly communicated in order to strengthen the service firm both inside (employees and culture) and outside (image and perception of customers and other external stakeholders). To ensure that it is, Crotts, Dickson and Ford (2005) propose an audit that organizations should conduct to align their practices, policies and procedures with their overarching goals. The authors state that alignment is the idea of developing and making consistent the various practices, actions, policies and procedures that managers should use to communicate to employees what is important, what has value to the organization, what they should do and what they should not do. Ultimately, the point is made that misalignment causes confusion, while alignment can lead to organizational success because employees 'get' the message. This work on alignment serves as an appropriate justification for the importance of service organizations being clear about who they are, what they aspire to do and having mechanisms in place—including feedback and measurement—can ensure that this occurs from start to finish.

This chapter now proceeds to examine some of the principles and techniques that can be used to perfect the service system.

Service system design

Perfecting the service system through design

Changes to strategy or personnel, altering pricing and improving general 'know-how' of the firm will not improve the final result if the overall service delivery system is defective.

In survey after survey of customer dissatisfaction, mediocre service consistently tops the list. Legendary service organizations—such as Marriott (in the hotel business), Disney (entertainment, tourism), Federal Express (transport) and Nordstrom (retail)—seldom feature in such surveys of dissatisfaction. Competing organizations find it difficult to duplicate the superior service of these firms in their various fields because the service systems of the opposition are inferior.

We often wonder why so many of the service systems that we encounter in our daily lives are so ineffective in meeting our needs as customers. This does not result from someone deliberately developing a system that is capable of providing only mediocre service. Rather than being deliberately designed, such a system is likely to have *evolved*. But if an organizational system is allowed to evolve on its own, it is certain to evolve in the direction of the self-convenience of the people inside the organization, rather than for the benefit of the people whom they are supposed to be serving

Allowing a service system to evolve is insufficient. It is imperative that service delivery be systematically designed if the organization is to offer reliable superior service. The goal of systematic design is to eradicate or minimize any policies or 'rules' that stand between the service and the customer.

The basis of a well-planned and executed service system in any line of business is:

- ▶ keep the service itself simple and uncomplicated;
- ▶ make the service truly customer-friendly; and
- ▶ add value for the customer.

What is service design?

Service design is the activity of planning and organizing people, infrastructure, communication and material components of a service in order to improve its quality and the interaction between service provider and customers. It literately refers to an operationalized version of the service vision. There are a wide variety of forms in which the design can be visually presented. This sort of tangible representation clarifies what the service includes and how the service production is to be performed.

Those who design a service system need to hold two perspectives in mind at the same time:

1. the *external* aspects—those factors that will directly affect customer satisfaction; and
2. the *internal* aspects—the supporting systems and processes that are coordinated to fulfill customer needs.

There are four major steps involved in designing services and their delivery systems (Shostack, 1984a):

1. Identify the processes that constitute the service. It might be necessary to break the organization down into detailed parts to develop the appropriate flow throughout the entire organization. Project programming and computer-aided devices can assist in identifying the appropriate flows. These procedures allow managers to visualize the process, and to define and manipulate it at arm's length. However, what they miss is the consumer's interaction with the service—that is, they make no provision for people-rendered services that require judgment and a less mechanical approach.
2. Anticipate problems with service delivery in the service encounter, consider contingency approaches and incorporate plans for reaction to problems.
3. Establish an overall timeframe for execution of the service plan through various stages—including paperwork and the various service-handling steps that will be required.
4. Finally, analyze the proposed layout in terms of (a) the expected satisfaction of the customer and (b) the expected profitability of the firm as a consequence. In other words, the designer should develop an expected *customer satisfaction* cost (the positive or negative cost of goodwill). It might be necessary to compare alternative plans to determine which design offers the best trade-offs of satisfaction and dissatisfaction in terms of the expected sales and profits for each proposed plan. See, for example, the discussion in Chapter 4 about mystery shoppers and the importance of using these, not only to evaluate the service but also as a tool to systematically design the 'perfect' customer. When approaching service design, it is important to focus on the human interactions that underlie the service encounter. Researchers (see for example Cook et al., 2002 and Chase, 2004) have suggested approaching service

design using behavioral science principles. To do so, managers must understand the factors that shape customers' feelings, rather than simply what customers felt about the experience. Such an approach will allow service managers to focus on these key factors in their design of the service system, thereby providing greater depth to the encounter and enhancing the customer's experience and recollection of it.

Similarly, Frei (2008) proposed four key elements that should be considered when designing a service. These are:

1. *The offering.* Focus on the experience rather than characteristics.
2. *The funding mechanism.* How will the service be paid for? A number of considerations are suggested, including fair charging, creating a win-win between costs and value, understanding the importance of investing in customers and the up-front costs and, finally, wherever possible, have customer engagement in the process.
3. *The employee management system.* Consider what makes employees *able* and *motivated* to achieve service excellence, then translate these into policies and programs.
4. *The customer management system.* How will the customer engage with the firm? Will the customer participate in the service? How will the firm manage the interaction? Examples include self-service check in, self-service payment and pumping your own fuel.

Although it is important to note that there is no one perfect combination of elements, appropriate service design usually depends on the right blend of these four. The decisions you make in one dimension should be supported by those you have made in the others. And most importantly, service design should not be left to chance!

Inbuilt flaws

Many errors in service delivery have their root cause in the design of systems—especially those dealing with internal service encounters. These service faults then crop up in one form or another at the service encounter with the customer—producing negative experiences at the crucial 'moments of truth'.

Since such errors are often caused by inappropriate design of systems, they tend to be repetitive. Once a fault is built into a system, its users are faced with quality problems on a daily basis. For example, in a hotel setting, there might be a recurrent problem in allocating the wrong room to guests. This might not be due to carelessness on the part of the receptionists. It might be due to a systemic flaw in the system. For example, many hotels and restaurants now have booking systems which incorporate information not only on their own websites but also via third-party websites (e.g., Wotif for accommodation, Tripadvisor for tourist attractions and UrbanSpoon for restaurants). If there is a flaw in the way these systems communicate with each other, or there is a problem with real-time alignment between them, then issues could occur such as over-booking or bookings not getting recorded properly. Clearly, the integration of technology into the booking phase of the service design has on the one hand revolutionized the industry through speed and convenience, but also created another possible area of system breakdown. There are many stories about how customers have shown up to a restaurant certain that they have made a reservation on an online booking system only to find out there is no reservation. How would you handle this as a service manager?

The fault can therefore often be in the system, not the service personnel, and the fault causes recurrent lapses in service quality. In a large, complex organization such as a hotel there are innumerable possibilities for systemic flaws of this sort.

According to the 'Pareto principle'—an idea established by Italian economist Vilfredo Pareto (1848–1923), who found that a large share of national wealth was owned by relatively few people—most effects come from relatively few causes. For example, in considering the problem of check-out delays at hotel reception, 80% of such delays are due to the same three or four causes (See Figure 5.3).

By applying the Pareto principle, it is thus possible for management to identify the causes of virtually any problem in service delivery because it is likely that management will not face a huge number of causes for any given problem. Indeed, it is likely that the number of significant causes will be found to be rather small. Remedial action can then be assessed and prioritized. This sort of analysis is especially valuable in investigating any problems encountered in the critical 'moments of truth'—the actual moment of delivery of service, and the customer's simultaneous experience and assessment of that service.

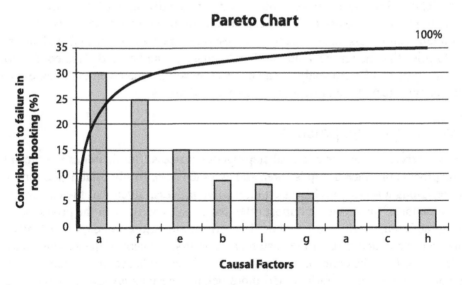

Figure 5.3
A Pareto chart of causes of failure in hotel room booking

Hotel Fishbone Diagram

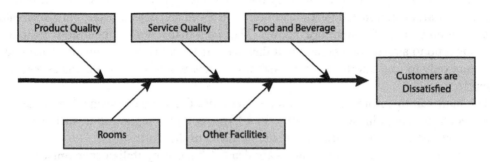

Figure 5.4
A fishbone diagram of causes of failure in hotel management

Professor Kaoru Ishikawa (1915–1989) of the University of Tokyo believed that any attempt to improve service delivery was doomed to failure unless management was prepared to engage in ongoing and continuous research designed to obtain information about exactly what constitutes the service delivery process. As a result of his studies, Ishikawa developed a diagram in the shape of a fishbone to show/explain how various factors could be related to cause and outcome (or cause and effect). This diagram is often referred to as the 'Ishikawa diagram' or the 'fishbone diagram' (Figure 5.4). This cause and effect diagram can be effectively used to represent the relationship between an effect and all the possible causes that influence failure or poor performance. The first step is to identify the problem (delay in breakfast service), followed by an identification of the various resources that are required for breakfast service (personnel, equipment, materials, procedure and others). Problem causes associated with each resource are then identified and prioritized. Finally, to prioritize the remedial action, Pareto analysis can be used. This combination of fishbone analysis and Pareto analysis can be used by service management to assess and fix virtually any problem at the critical level of service delivery.

Design is a dynamic process

Designing a service system is a logical step-by-step process. But this does not mean that it is a static process in which a step is taken and assumed to be firmly established for all time. Rather, designing a service system is an interactive process, given that the customer is not only the initiator of the service but most often participates actively in the production of the service. In addition, service design should be organic in nature to adapt constantly to the changing needs and demands of the customers. The first concept of the service leads to an initial design sketch. The concept may undergo modification based on the needs of the customers and hence is then modified, and more detailed designs are made as required. The process is continued as the service concept alters and the service design changes with it.

The customer plays a crucial role in this interactive process. As previously noted, in all service situations the customer is a cocreator of the experience and hence contributes value to the service. This contribution must be clarified, assessed and acted upon throughout the design process.

Flexibility is required to receive such customer feedback and promote an effective interactive environment during service design. Service designs cannot be inflexible and prescriptive. There must be a balance between programmed behavior and personal initiative. Within this framework, service employees are required to act in accordance with their own judgment, note customer reaction and thus provide valuable interactive feedback to the design process through a variety of available communication methods as described in Chapter 4.

For example, the service plan might state that a customer at check-in *must* receive the room previously allocated by the reservations department. At the time of designing the service plan, this might have seemed to be a sensible measure to avoid confusion and double-booking. But the on-duty receptionist might become aware of unexpected special requirements—such as adjoining rooms for two guests, or some other reasonable request. The receptionist must be able to show initiative and make changes to ensure customer satisfaction. And the overall design of the system must then be adjusted to allow for such sensible last-minute changes by receptionists. This might require a rethinking of the overall system to allow for reasonable flexibility.

Creative thinking

Designing a service system does not mean that the service design becomes prescriptive and inflexible. Experience and feedback can produce sensible and effective changes to the service design. In a similar spirit of flexibility, service designers should always be prepared to think creatively about services—especially services that seem to be so routine and mundane that they are taken for granted. Consider hotel cleaning services as an example.

Cleaning service is often one of the last matters to be considered in an integrated hotel service system. Consider the following sorts of questions.

Q: When is cleaning done?

A: When a room is not wanted for any other activity.

Q: What routine is used?

A: Whatever routine is needed for the cleaning of the particular room's shape and size.

Q: What chemicals and processes are used?

A: Whatever chemicals and processes are required for the furnishings, fabrics and materials already built into the room.

When we look at the answers to the questions above, we notice that cleaning 'comes last'. It is reactive. That is, cleaning tends to be relegated to certain times and certain methods that are largely beyond the control of those responsible for cleaning services. Cleaning is 'added-on' later. It is not built into an integrated service system.

In contrast, in a properly developed service system, this service could be taken into account from the very beginning when a room is being designed. Materials, furniture, room shape and so on could be designed in such a way as to make cleaning efficient and effective. Everyone knows that it is inevitable that a cleaning service is going to be required and that a clean room is a core product of hotels. Rather than 'adding it on' later, a service designer can plan ahead and embed this essential service into the design of the service system.

As another example of creativity in designing a cleaning service, an insightful service designer will be aware that, in hotels, cleanliness is not just a matter of health and safety. Cleanliness is also a crucial marketing tool. This is obviously the case in guest rooms and public areas—cleanliness in these areas is essential if customers are to be attracted and retained. But what about 'back-of-house' areas? Many successful restaurants have recognized the marketing potential of demonstrating the cleanliness of their kitchen areas by installing glass walls between the public areas of the restaurant and the kitchen. Customers can then see how the food is prepared and the cleanliness of the food-preparation environment. This effectively becomes a marketing tool. Firms can thus showcase that part of the organization that is not normally visible to the customer—in effect, the 'service factory' becomes a showroom.

Some practical examples

All successful service firms—hospitality, tourism and many other service firms—have developed and implemented effective service visions, strategies, processes and designs. Indeed, they are successful precisely because they have thought through each of these elements and ensured that all aspects of the organization work in conformity. Some well-known successful organizations are briefly considered below. The first three examples are from the food service / restaurant segment of the hospitality industry, the second three examples are from the accommodation segment and the last example is from the leisure tourism segment. In each segment of the hospitality and tourism industries, there are in fact many different categories. For instance, the food service / restaurant segment includes quick service (also known as fast-food), fast casual, casual theme, buffet and fine dining. The important point to remember is that the service vision, strategy, processes and system will all vary depending on the segment or category you are in, so it is vital to be crystal clear about these elements before proceeding to set up or alter the way the service delivery is designed. The following examples illustrate the variations within the same segment across different categories.

Restaurants

McDonald's

McDonald's has been the world leader in the fast-food market for more than fifty years. They place the customer experience at the core of all they do, making it clear that customers are the reason for their existence. This is demonstrated through high-quality food, fast and efficient service in a clean, welcoming environment, and great value. Their goals are simple: quality, service, cleanliness and value, or "QSC&V" for each and every customer, each and every time.

Every feature of McDonald's is aligned with this service vision, including the decor, systems, machinery and management style. The company spends a great deal of its resources in testing new food products before introducing them, and in refining the already efficient service delivery system.

McDonald's goes beyond a minimal interpretation of a franchise contractual role to ensure full adherence to its concept strategy among all franchisees. All of McDonald's franchisees worldwide maintain the same corporate strategy (the so-called 'McDonald's promise'). The food is prepared in the same high-quality manner worldwide. The service level rarely varies from one outlet to another, or from one country to another. The low-key decor and friendly atmosphere of all outlets remain constant.

Cactus Jack's

Another category in food service is the casual theme restaurant—which offers full service, yet still casual dining. Cactus Jack's restaurant group is a regional dining company based in North Queensland, Australia. They serve fresh, high-quality food in a uniquely designed atmosphere, with friendly, fun, energetic and informal service. Although a full service restaurant company, they never take reservations on groups under eight people (thus keeping the dining area full for longer and reducing unused space during peak time), keep their prices and portions such that customers have high value perceptions, focus on families and allow people to pay with separate checks—even encourage it! Their décor appears to be from old items found in a shed or storage area and just nailed onto the walls, creating a 'rustic' yet comfortable atmosphere. Every employee at Cactus Jack's knows the story of the company and the values and vision of the family who own it, and are expected to act and behave directly in line with the values of the company.

The Fat Duck

World-famous chef Heston Blumenthal's three-Michelin-starred restaurant in Bray, Berkshire, UK is called The Fat Duck. It is rated among the world's top restaurants, is a multi-award winner and has received a perfect score (10/10) by the UK *Good Food Guide*, every year since 2007. This restaurant is known for its unusual and complex dishes and uses principles of 'molecular gastronomy' in the creation of its menu. The food production is so complex that it takes nearly one chef for every customer who can dine in the restaurant at one time—a far smaller ratio than almost any other kind of restaurant.

Table 5.1
Examples of Three Categories in the Restaurant Industry

	McDonald's (*Economy*)	**Cactus Jack's** (*Mid-Market*)	**The Fat Duck** (*Luxury*)
Service Vision	McDonald's strives to be the chosen place for people to go when they are hungry and thirsty.	"To serve inexpensive high-quality food in a uniquely designed atmosphere."	To bring a multitude of perceptions to the customer's dining experience
Strategy	—Global expansion/presence —Consistent experience and quality across all outlets —Low prices / 'value for money' —Fast and convenient	—Cooked fresh to order —Keep prices as low as possible —All casual and fun	—Awaken all the senses (taste, sight, touch, smell, sound, sensory perception) —Create a unique and memorable dining experience
Processes and Design	—Multiple ways to eat to suit different customers (i.e., dine-in, take-away, drive-through, or McCafé) —Standardized processes (preparation, cooking, serving) to ensure a consistent experience	—'Eclectic' design of the restaurant with themed items and bright colors —Systems designed for speed and personal service (e.g., allowing separate bills)	—Menu items are original and the names contribute to the 'theatrical' dining experience (e.g., there is a dish called the 'Mad Hatter's Tea Party') —Website is interactive / multisensory

Hotels

Pod Hotels

At the lowest end of the accommodation continuum are 'pod' or 'capsule' hotels. This type of hotel, developed in Japan, features extremely small 'capsules' (rooms) intended to provide cheap and basic overnight accommodation for guests not requiring many of the peripheral offerings of more conventional hotels. These hotel rooms are often not even big enough to stand in. There are many variations within this segment, including a more luxury version with high quality bedding but shared services such as lounges, cafés, work areas, etc. Although many of these hotels are located in airports, aimed at travelers with long layovers, there are many in cities around the world, including Tokyo, Singapore and New York. This is a fast-growing segment, offering hip, convenient and personalized accommodation for the spend-thrifty traveler. One such example is The Pod Hotel in New York City, located in the heart of Manhattan. They offer individually climate-controlled rooms equipped with efficient, stylish furniture that is designed to maximize comfort and living space.

Holiday Inn

Holiday Inn hotels provide convenience at a median price for travelers. Many of their hotels are found near a busy area. The rooms are clean and comfortable, with special facilities for those who want them. Holiday Inn hotels are a preferred choice for many travelers due to their commitment to service, consistency, and value. Holiday Inn wants to make your stay feel like you never left home, no matter where you are.

Ritz-Carlton

Ritz-Carlton is a name associated with quality at the luxury end of the accommodation market. To help employees remain engaged and committed to the vision of the company, staff carry the company's 'Gold Standards' with them in the form of 'Credo Cards'. The Credo Cards have three well-defined and easily remembered phrases or the Ritz-Carlton's definitions of an 'ultimate guest experience'.

There are three points that the Ritz-Carlton wants to keep foremost in employees' minds: that their guests and their guests' needs are the focus; that their commitment is quality for guests, who should enjoy a comfortable yet special atmosphere; and that the Ritz-Carlton guests have a stay that invigorates and relaxes them, as well as makes every wish they have come true.

These credos are more than reminders—they convey the ideology of their service culture and of the service vision of the company. Although we may not advocate that every service firm have cards for its employees, some easy-to-remember phrases which define the company's core values and brand promises, and some way to continue to instill these so that they are literately 'under the skin' of all employees, are good ideas.

Table 5.2 presents a comparison of these organizations' service systems and demonstrates the way exemplar service firms not only create a service vision and strategy, but also how to align these ideals through the organization.

Leisure tourism

Dreamworld

Dreamworld is Australia's largest theme park, situated on the Gold Coast in Queensland, with over 40 rides and attractions. The theme park is made up of a variety of individually themed 'worlds', including the Dreamworld Corroboree, Wiggles World, Tiger Island, Ocean Parade, DreamWorks Experience and Gold Rush Country, and is home to 'The Big 8 Thrill Rides'. Visitors are offered an exciting, unique and unforgettable experience through the collection of themed rides and attractions, wildlife experiences, live shows, dining and shopping. Dreamworld's promise is that it will provide exceptional service and each guest will leave with wonderful memories of the vacation. Its success as a tourist attraction has been shown by the many awards that the park has received (see Table 5.3).

Table 5.2

Examples of Three Categories in the Hotel Industry

	Pod Hotels (*Economy*)	**Holiday Inn** (*Mid-Market*)	**The Ritz-Carlton** (*Luxury*)
Service Vision	Affordable hotels with thoughtful design and attention to detail	Excellent value for both business and family travelers at the comfort level close to their own home	Genuine hospitality and the finest service provided in a warm and relaxed atmosphere
Strategy	—Focus on particular market segments (i.e., travelers in transit and young travelers with small budgets) —Match location of properties to suit market segments (i.e., airports and big cities that are popular tourist attractions) —Cost efficient and convenient	—Consideration of both physical comfort and emotional comfort —Keep up-to-date with innovations to remain relevant to guests' lifestyles	—Well-defined HRM strategy to ensure the right 'ladies and gentlemen' are hired —Focus on providing exceptional service to create a competitive advantage
Processes and Design	—Small room size and providing few amenities allows prices to be kept low —Incorporating stylish furniture into room design appeals to younger generation of travelers —Automated self check-in available	—Providing 'creature comforts' such as high speed Internet, restaurants, fitness centers and lounges creates a 'home away from home' —Consistency across properties creates familiarity for return guests —Allowing kids to eat and stay free makes families feel welcome	—Employee training and empowerment (allowed to spend up to $2,000 to make a guest happy) —Clear service standards and expectations, e.g.: Three Steps of Service: 1. A warm and sincere greeting. Use the guest's name. 2. Anticipation and fulfillment of each guest's needs. 3. Fond farewell. Give a warm good-bye and use the guest's name.

The service encounter

Central to the concept of service design is the way in which the service organization plans and manages the multitude of interactions between itself (and its employees) and its customers. This interaction has come to be known as the 'service encounter'.

The service encounter has been defined as the dyadic interaction between customer and service provider, or that period of time or moment(s) when a firm and customer interact. Such contact is not necessarily limited to interactions between people, as technology is becoming an increasingly vital component of the firm-customer interface.

This concept is critical to know and understand in relation to both operating and managing service organizations effectively. The majority of accepted measures of service qual-

Table 5.3
Example from the Leisure Tourism

	Dreamworld
Service Vision	—Vision: To be the favorite theme park in Australia.
	—Mission: To provide exceptional service and give each guest wonderful memories of their visit.
Strategy	—Cater to various market segments including families, school groups and the MICE (meetings, incentives, conferences and exhibitions) market
	—HR strategy that includes hiring staff who are bilingual and providing in-house cultural and tour guide training
	—Leverage affiliations with national and international brands and entertainment
	—Partner with local attractions and accommodation providers on the Gold Coast and offer a 'World Pass' that gives unlimited entry to Dreamworld for specified periods, in order to extend visitors' stays and improve their overall experience
Processes and Design	—Unique theming for the individual 'worlds', including themed food outlets and merchandise
	—Q4U: Dreamworld's virtual ride queuing system available as a mobile app (Q-Mobile) or on a portable unit available for rent (Q-Bot)
	—Providing peak and off-peak itineraries to help visitors maximize their experiences

ity and satisfaction (see Chapter 3) give significant consideration to these 'encounters'. The following sections of this chapter provide an introduction to the service encounter concept and its theoretical base, and then offer a range of challenges and practical solutions to managing these critical service encounters.

Service encounter triad

Figure 5.5 illustrates the 'service-encounter triad'. In nearly all interactions between a customer and a firm, there are at least three main parties involved—the customer, the service employee and the service organization. Each is critical to the overall outcome of the service encounter. In a perfect scenario, there is a collaborative, harmonious relationship between each of the three parties, with engaged employees, fully supported by their organization, serving customers who are loyal. But such harmony is not very common; it is rare indeed! Only in the best service organizations is such harmony part of the firm's service vision. Great service organizations realize the importance of this harmony, trying to limit tensions between the organization and its employees (such as labor disputes); tensions between employees and customers (such as customers coming in after hours or being overly needy); and tensions between customers and organizations (such as reduced seating space on aircraft to increase capacity on planes at the expense of guest comfort).

The employees in service organizations who take up (or are tasked with) the vitally important job of providing face-to-face service (or sometimes via telephone/Internet) are often referred to as front-line employees (they also have been labeled as 'front-liners' /

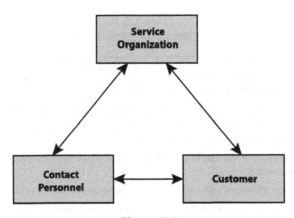

Figure 5.5
The service encounter triad

'boundary spanners' / 'gatekeepers' / 'image-makers'). Front-liners, a metaphor to the battle-field, refers to the simple fact that these employees are the ones who will have that first inter-action with a customer when they enter the organization. In a hotel this could be the bellman, doorman, front desk clerk etc. In a tourist destination it can be the ticket salesman, the secu-rity guard etc. In a restaurant it might be the host/hostess. There is a particular irony here that there is actually an inverse relationship between the vital importance of this role and the pay levels given to these 'front-liners' (usually some of the lowest in a service organization!).

Jan Carlzon's (1987) famous book, *Moments-of-Truth*, (MsOT) is about the dramatic turnaround of Scandinavian Airlines in the early 1980s and brought the importance of the service encounter to light, reminding his employees that their company had 50,000 MsOT every day and that it was the culmination of these moments which led customers to forming an image about the organization.

Managing the service encounter

In a sense, the prior discussions in the chapter about vision, strategy, process and system were preliminary to the *real* issue—the management of the 'critical encounters' or 'moments of truth', when the customers personally experience the service. In many ways, this is the end-point of all management strategies for service industries. This is what it is all about!

Cook et al. (2002) suggest three concepts that are critical to understanding the service encounter, these are:

- ▶ the flow of the service experience (what's happening);
- ▶ the flow of time (how long it seems to take); and
- ▶ counterfactual reasoning in judging the encounter performance (what you thought about it later).

Customer as 'coproducer'

Customers, intentionally or not, are often involved in the production of a service, and can influence the outcome of their service or that of other customers. For example, a person paying for their meal at a fast casual restaurant who takes a very long time to find their money, or whose credit card does not work properly, or who just likes to talk a lot, can impact the overall service, irrespective of all of the great planning of the service organization.

In reality, it is important for a service organization to know and understand if and when customers play a crucial part in the service process. Many service organizations have learned to 'train the customer'. For example, customers at a national chain of bagel shops (Einstein Bros. Bagels) know exactly how to order their bagels efficiently, with staff coaching customers to work through the menu quickly and move from ordering to paying efficiently. Of course sometimes it is the other customers who 'coach' a new customer by pushing them along and assisting them to ensure a seamless and fast service process. Firms can view customers as 'partial employees', knowing that without good 'employee' behavior, service can be negatively impacted. Indeed, when a service firm has to rely on the customer for the service process to be efficient and satisfactory it places a whole new level of challenges on the service organization!

The degree of customer participation in a service can be one of either:

▶ *Low participation* (employees do nearly all of the work, such as dropping clothes at the dry cleaner);
▶ *Moderate participation* (requires a customer to provide information so that the service provider can do their job more effectively. Examples include having a hair cut or visiting the dentist); or
▶ *High participation* (when the customer's participation is vital to the service, such as exercise class, marriage counseling, visiting the gym or even university study!).

Challenges and stressors

Planning and managing the service encounter is far easier said than done! Yet the great service organizations seem to get these 'moments of truth' right, more often than not. In addition to the issues raised above, there are many other challenges and 'stressors' facing service managers with respect to managing the service encounter. These are listed below:

1. *Employee stress.* There is much evidence about the stress that service workers often feel. Job or role 'burnout' can then occur—a state of emotional, mental and physical exhaustion caused by excessive and prolonged stress, caused by a drain of a person's emotional resources, which may manifest in indifferent and distant attitudes towards work and a lack of satisfaction. In addition, 'role conflict' and 'role ambiguity', where the specific responsibilities for a worker are unclear, or 'role creep' where a person's job subtly changes over time, can increase the stress and strain on

a worker. Role conflict refers to the degree of incompatibility of expectations associated with a role (House and Rizzo, 1972). Hence, role conflict occurs when two different members of an organization (e.g., managers and customers) have conflicting demands. Role ambiguity, in contrast, refers to a lack of clarity about one's role. When the actions and behaviors of a front-line worker are so important, it is easy to see how stress, burnout and role ambiguity can impact their effectiveness (see more in Chapter 8).

2. *Emotions and moods ('emotional labor').* Here we refer to moods and emotions of employees, the customers and owners / managers. The concept of 'emotional labor', discussed further in Chapter 8, is a clear challenge to service managers. Emotional labor is the kind of exertion—not physical or mental—that a service employee must provide over and over again each day. This means acting or showing emotions (sincerity, empathy, friendliness) that the worker may not genuinely feel. So the service employee often must display an emotion counter to their actual emotion. Exerting emotional labor continually can be difficult and causes stress.

3. *Customer variability.* As discussed in Chapter 2, one of the many challenges in service organizations is dealing with heterogeneity—both from an employee and a customer perspective. Determining exactly what each customer wants can be very challenging, especially for young, inexperienced 'front-line' workers. Customer variability can be the result of many circumstances—from varying moods from one day to the next, to differences in culture, demography and generational backgrounds. How then can a front-line service worker know how to deal with so much variability?

4. *Other customers.* Providing excellent service on a consistent basis is difficult enough, but service firms must also accept that other customers can impact the service experience. For example, a loud passenger on a plane can impact the quality of the flight for other passengers. Similarly, a table of loud customers at a restaurant could interfere with another group hoping to have a quiet business meeting or a romantic dinner. These customers may not be unintentionally disruptive; however, since their actions may be impacting on other customers' experiences, service managers need strategies to manage them.

5. *Customer and employee deviance.* When a customer or employee is intentionally disruptive, or tries to negatively impact the service encounter, it is known as 'deviance' or 'sabotage'. Service sabotage is when a customer deliberately causes poor service. As Fisk et al. (2010) report, the promotional display of the smiling, happy worker cheerfully serving equally smiling, contented customers is in fact often somewhat divorced from reality. Customers and employees frequently act like enemy combatants, practically competing with each other. Harris and Reynolds define customer deviance as "actions by customers who intentionally or unintentionally, overtly or covertly, act in a manner that, in some way, disrupts otherwise functional service encounters" (Harris and Reynolds, 2003, p. 145). Similarly, some

have used the term 'jay customer' to define those customers who deliberately act in a thoughtless, harmful or abusive manner, often intentionally disregarding common sense etiquette and consideration.

6. *Balancing service quality and financial performance.* As important as service excellence is, and even for those firms which fully embrace service as central to their success, there are competing dynamics in any organization where there are financial expectations. Many service firms have to strike a balance between service quality and profit. It is not uncommon for financial pressures to put a strain on resources and impact service. Many of the best service firms live by a philosophy which preaches "balancing service and profit", which is in many ways the greatest challenge for service managers—but also knowing, depending on their service concept, how much service is needed for the situation. The degree to which customer service is provided at a very busy coffee shop in a train station will be very different than a coffee shop in a residential area where customers are more likely to return and stay longer. Balance and clarity about customer expectations are vital.

Managerial actions and solutions

Great service organizations employ many strategies and actions to proactively combat the challenges above. Like a professional athlete who spends hours in the gym preparing their body for their sport, great service organizations work hard 'behind the scenes' to create a culture which is grounded on a service vision that may conflict with the immediate financial goal. In the long run, however, it nurtures a working environment which facilitates excellent and consistent employee-customer interactions.

The list below, although not exhaustive, offers a glimpse into some of the ways that great service organizations overcome the service encounter challenges highlighted above. Above all, remember that consistent, high-level service does not happen by accident. Great service organizations continually use training and a culture of excellence and continuous improvement to underpin their competitive advantage. *It never just happens!*

1. *Understand service and hospitality.* Top-performing service organizations understand and practice service management principles. They know that the first step in creating a loyal customer is to understand that service is central to customer perceptions and satisfaction, and that the best 'product' in and of itself does not lead to long-term customer loyalty. Consciously or not, great service organizations intuitively know and understand that they are in service settings. A client of one of the authors of this book once remarked, "it's nice to have a label now for all of the philosophies our company has lived by over the years—indeed, we are a service organization and we have known that for 50 years—but the service management principles you have taught us put the perfect frame around our business model and philosophy". As highlighted in Chapter 1, the hospitality and tourism industries fit within the service sector. In particular, hospitality is a special kind

of service industry—one which requires a deep understanding about the essence of hospitality—of caring, generosity and thoughtfulness about the needs of a customer. Great service organizations know that they are in the service industry and create a culture and mindset to match (Grönroos, 1993; Meyer, 2006).

2. *Smiling and impression management.* Impression management is the process whereby a firm strategically works on creating a positive impression by having staff who are both competent and likeable. By now, readers of this text would realize that great service and customer satisfaction require far more than just happy, smiling staff. However, in many service circumstances, smiling and positive emotions are very important. And in great service organizations, the employees seem to be happy! Few would argue the power of an authentic human smile—in fact emotional 'contagion' suggests that strong emotions felt and displayed by one person easily rub off on others. Although some research suggests that a displayed smile is enough, other research has proposed that inauthentic smiles undermine any benefits. Genuinely felt smiles, also known as 'Duchenne' smiles, which are characterized by the activation of certain muscle groups around the eye as well as by the symmetry and duration of the smile, make an enormous difference to the way people feel. It is the 'felt' smile that is authentic. So 'making' an employee smile might be achievable, but influencing the authenticity and quality of the smile is more difficult to enforce. Great service organizations spend time and resources facilitating authentic smiles! (Grandey et al., 2005; Kim and Yoon, 2012).

3. *Human resource management practices.* Great service organizations find a way to attract and retain high-performing, service-oriented employees. This does not happen by accident! Because service organizations have 'flimsy and permeable boundaries between organization and customer', having the right people in the right jobs who are motivated to try hard and are committed to the firm is critical. The top-performing service organizations put extraordinary effort into the human resource management function. The types of activities involved in HRM include manpower planning (predicting staffing needs in advance), effective and innovative attraction techniques, strong 'employer brand' presence in the marketplace (e.g., through best place to work type of recognition), clever and effective interview skills and techniques, effective reference checking and ongoing commitment to 'human' resources. There are many examples of the way leading service organizations apply time and effort to improving the HRM function. Chapter 8 provides further details about the connection between human resource management practices and service organization success.

4. *Optimism.* People are all different. One of the many 'intrinsic' differences between people is the degree to which they are generally optimistic about life. Optimism can be defined as a tendency to expect the best possible outcome or dwell on the most hopeful aspects of a situation. Individuals differ in their ability to cope with stress—with optimists generally dealing with stress in a more positive way. In a stressful

service environment (e.g., busy restaurant, long lines to check-in at a hotel), it is ideal that the front-facing (boundary-spanning) employees are optimistic, because coping has a lot to do with a person's general level of optimism vs. pessimism. Pessimism is the tendency to stress the negative or unfavorable, or to take the gloomiest possible view. Research has shown that optimists are "psychologically and physically better adjusted than their pessimistic counterparts" (Chang 1998, p. 1109). Great service organizations consider personality in their recruitment and selection process. Many use employment tests or even evaluations by potential coworkers to help determine the generally positive attitude of the prospective recruit. In addition, it is also possible to nurture and develop optimism in the workforce. Previous research suggests that managers can enhance optimism through individualized support, modeling behavior and reward and recognition. In addition, cognitive training can be used as an effective method for nurturing optimism in boundary-spanning employees. Cognitive training methods aim to change the 'internal voice' of individuals into positively focused thought processes. Optimism (or pessimism) tends to spread through an organization (emotional contagion). Great service organizations tend to have a more optimistic culture through recruitment and ongoing skills training. No accident! (Crosno, et al, 2009)

5. *Listening skills.* Setting the stage for high-quality customer service involves more than selecting the right employees and training them. Service managers must develop a strong service culture by focusing on what happens inside the organization, thereby paying great attention to nurturing the right work environment. One of the elements of such a working environment is creating effective listening skills, or what Brownell (2008) calls a 'listening environment'. In order to serve customers well, employees must know and understand their needs. We saw earlier (Chapter 3) that one of the ways we conceptualize service quality is the variance between expectations and performance. So knowing customer expectations is vital—and listening enhances this. Similarly, within the organization, the way that employees serve each other influences organizational effectiveness. Great service organizations teach listening skills—focused on listening to customers and listening to each other. Brownell (2008) argues that listening skills improve accuracy of communications, increase frequency of employee information sharing, reduce misunderstandings, improve problem solving, increase customer satisfaction and loyalty and improve employee commitment and morale (see also McKechnie, Grant, and Bagaria, 2007).

6. *Service 'scripting'.* Many service firms systemize the employee-customer interaction with scripts. Scripts are used to help ensure a more consistent process. A service script creates a guide for front-line employees—including a predetermined set of words, phrases, gestures and other expectations—to be used during each step of a service process. Scripts can vary. Tight scripts leave little room for the employee to improvise, whereas loose scripts provide a broad framework of expectations.

Some research suggests that heavily scripted service encounters are seen negatively by customers—particularly in less-standard service encounters. For example, checking into a hotel requires many steps, so some tight scripting can be of value in order for each of the important questions to be asked (upgrades, Wi-Fi access, smoking etc.). As highlighted in Chapter 4, many service organizations ensure that all customer-facing staff have a clear understanding about the 'perfect customer experience'—some of which requires specific questions and processes, while other aspects require only that the customer feels cared for (Victorino, Verma, and Wardell, 2008).

There are many other organizational practices for overcoming the service encounter challenges, including creating an organizational culture and climate that are strategically focused on service (see Chapter 8) and service 'blueprinting' (see section below).

Service managers can utilize various quality-management techniques to examine performance during the service encounter. Of these techniques, blueprinting is especially useful. This analytical technique not only allows managers to identify service problems and solutions, but also assists managers to prioritize their responses to identified problems.

Service blueprinting

Leading to a 'moment of truth'

The quality experienced by the customer is created at the 'moments of truth', when the service provider and the client meet in a face-to-face interaction. The most perfectly designed and engineered service-delivery system will fail if the customer's needs are not fulfilled during this 'moment of truth' at the service encounter. One of the most promising tools in designing an effective service system that meets the needs of the 'moments of truth' is service 'blueprinting'.

The nature of a service blueprint

© ml/Shutterstock.com

Lynn Shostack was an early advocate for systematic service design and she pioneered the concept of service blueprinting. In a series of articles (1981; 1983; 1984a; 1984b; 1985; 1987; 1990a; 1990b), she convincingly argued the case for the undoubted benefits to be obtained from using a service blueprint as a tool for depicting and analyzing all the processes involved in the production and delivery

---

What is a service blueprint?

A service blueprint is essentially a detailed planning and diagnostic document that depicts the service events and processes as a flowchart—a 'map' of intersecting paths.

In essence, a blueprint represents, in diagrammatic form, the various processes that constitute the entire service system, and the interrelationships among these individual processes.

The service blueprint thus allows management and employees to visualize, organize and manipulate the entire service system.

---

of services. Such a service blueprint is essentially a detailed planning and diagnostic document that depicts the service events and processes as a flowchart—a 'map' of intersecting paths.

Blueprinting rests on the notion that the 'moment of truth' in rendering a service is the final act in a series of service processes. Blueprinting can be used to represent, in diagrammatic form, the various processes that constitute the entire service system, and the interrelationships among these individual processes. The service blueprint thus allows management and employees to visualize, organize and manipulate the entire service system.

A 'snapshot' of a dynamic process

A service blueprint thus serves as a unique management tool that provides a 'snapshot' view of what is actually a dynamic, living phenomenon.

Because it is reflecting a dynamic process, a blueprint is not frozen in time. A service blueprint also depicts the chronology and pattern of performances that make up a service (Kingman-Brundage, 1989). Thus a service system blueprint provides explicit answers to both the *structural* question (What are the various components of the service?) and the *functional* question (How is it offered?). It can therefore be used effectively to identify 'encounter points' and 'fail points' (or failure-prone areas) in any service system. This assists management to install preventive measures, and also to organize backup support services.

A service blueprint of this type gives meaning and structure to an otherwise intangible abstraction. As a management tool, it provides an opportunity to view, in a graphical presentation, the full range of customer needs, and the way in which the organization is structured in time and place to respond to these needs.

The 'line of visibility'

As has been noted previously, a service business can be understood as a system composed of two parts—those parts responsible for the *production* of the service offer, and those parts responsible for the actual *delivery* of the service offer (Lovelock, 1996; Lovelock, Patterson and Walker, 2001). In a typical service business, only part of the system is apparent to customers. The majority of the production processes are invisible to the customer, with only the final outcome being experienced.

In the hospitality industry, these two parts of the organization are typically referred to as 'back-of-house' functions and 'front-of-house' functions. Customers commonly do not know, or do not want to know, of the activities in the back of the house.

In keeping with this division of functions, a service blueprint can be divided into two major parts—'front-stage' ('front-of-house' in hotel operations) and 'back-stage' ('back-of-house' in hotel operations). These are separated by a 'line of visibility' (see Figure 5.6, below).

The visible front-of-house functions are supported by all the unseen back-of-house functions. These, in turn, are typically a combination of many cross-functional activities involving a whole range of people and skills. For example, the food served to a customer by a waiter in the visible service interaction has been first ordered, purchased, received, stored, prepared, cooked, arranged and so forth.

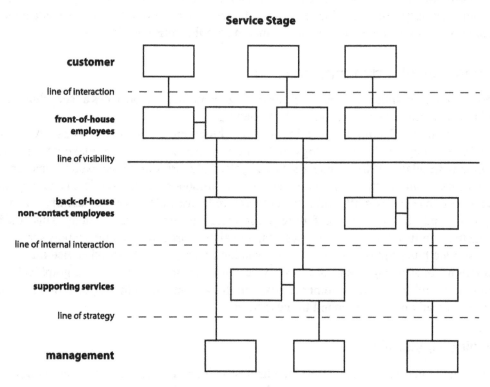

Figure 5.6
The line of visibility in a service blueprint

Careful attention must be paid to designing quality into these service processes that are not visible to the customer. The proportion of the blueprint above the line of visibility varies according to each service, but the majority of the blueprint frequently remains hidden below the line of visibility. Shostack, who has done much of the pioneering work on blueprinting of services, likened what lies above the line of visibility to the tip of an iceberg. She believed that particular attention must be paid to the processes *below* the line, even though customers are often totally unaware of them. Activities below the line ultimately determine success or failure in the visible process, and therefore ultimately determine output quality.

'Fail points' and 'encounter points'

It is apparent that the blueprint is a very useful tool for systematically evaluating a service. As such it can be used to identify potential problems that might ordinarily escape detection. Shostack described certain points in any service system as service 'fail points'. By this, she meant points in the service system where deficiencies are known to have occurred in similar systems in the past, or points in the system where it might reasonably be predicted that problems could occur in future. These 'fail points' are, therefore, the points in the system that require very close managerial attention (Senior and Akehurst, 1990).

Service blueprints also identify other places in the service process that are especially vulnerable to breakdown. We have already discussed the importance of the concept of the 'moment of truth'—the interpersonal interaction when the service is actually delivered and experienced. In service blueprints, these are known as 'encounter points'. Where 'fail points' and 'encounter points' coexist, there is maximum potential for problems with service quality.

Identifying 'fail points' and 'encounter points' in a service blueprint can guide the attention of managers to the need for preventive action or remedial action—special training, additional support, the establishment of recovery processes or even the redesigning of the whole system.

Looking back and looking ahead

A service blueprint can thus act as a 'problem solver' in fixing problems quickly as they occur. More usefully, it can also act in a preventive fashion as a 'change influencer' before problems actually become apparent (Hosick, 1989). Reducing vulnerability in a service system is one of the most important objectives of service managers. In effect, a service blueprint can assist managers to 'pre-test' the service concept on paper, and to identify the most effective methods to ensure failure-proof service delivery. It can be utilized in this way for various management tasks:

- ▶ the design of new services;
- ▶ the evaluation of existing services; and
- ▶ the identification of the cause of recurrent service problems.

Blueprints within blueprints

The very act of creating a service blueprint provides management with a rich insight into every aspect of the production, consumption and quality of the overall service. Even if there are no apparent problems, managers gain a better perspective of their overall service system, and a useful insight into how various functions fit together.

Moreover, any particular component of the blueprint can be further expanded into a detailed blueprint if needed. A 'blueprint within a blueprint' gives management helpful guidance in the setting of standards for individual components within the system. It also enables particular problem areas to be examined in detail. For example, if it is learned that delay during check-out at reception is unacceptable to customers, that particular step can be blueprinted in detail to identify and rectify the problem.

Dreams and reality

A blueprint should represent reality—not dreams. That is, a blueprint examines how the system *really* works, as opposed to some ideal version of how it is *supposed* to work.

If it is to reflect the reality of the service, the blueprint must be developed in consultation with the people who are directly involved with the process in question. Managers might believe that they have an excellent overall strategic understanding of the system. But this is mere abstract theory unless it is informed by close consultation with the people who *actually know* how the system works.

Consider the blueprinting of serving breakfast to a hotel room. A blueprint could be drawn up in theory, but this might not reflect the reality of the service as it is actually practiced. For example, where does the breakfast service process actually begin? A guest might telephone through to room service in the morning. Another guest might leave an order card on the room door the night before. In this case, there are *two* process pathways that can be described in the blueprint. Should the blueprint start from the point at which room service receives a call from the guest, or from the point when the customer chooses the items on the card that the guest has discovered in the room? The two processes are clearly different, and they contain quite different potential 'fail points' and different 'encounter points'.

In this case, *two* blueprints might well be necessary to ensure that the blueprinting exercise actually reflects the chain of service processes as they are conducted in reality. Input from those who actually conduct the service is required to assist management in understanding the two service pathways, and in sorting out answers to such questions as which service pathway is more frequently used, which service pathway fails more often and which service pathway offers better quality outcomes for customers.

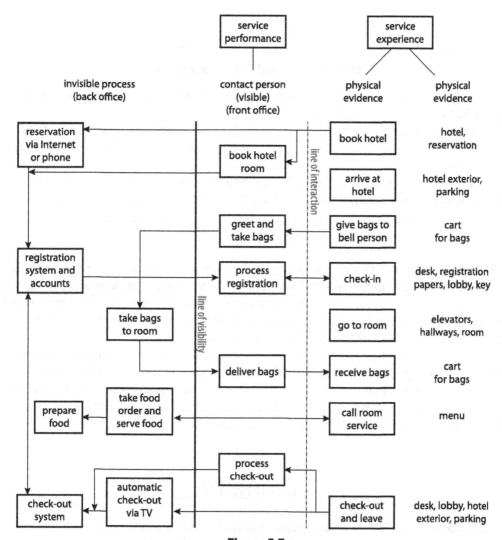

Figure 5.7
Service blueprint of overnight hotel stay

'Moments of truth' remain crucial

A 'beautiful blueprint'—but does it work?

It is very important that designers of service blueprints never lose sight of the practical purpose of the blueprinting exercise.

The aim is not to produce a 'beautiful' theoretical service system that satisfies management. The aim is to produce a quality practical service outcome that satisfies the customer.

A service blueprint must always be customer-oriented and therefore is fluid—not fixed. It will take different forms and shapes based on customer requirements.

In drawing up service blueprints, it is easy to become preoccupied with a comprehensive overall scheme, and consequently to lose sight of the vital importance of the 'moments of truth' in service delivery. Designers must always be aware that the most important task in drawing up any blueprint is to identify the vital customer 'encounter points' to ensure a positive outcome from each and every service interaction.

In this context, identifying possible service bottlenecks or failure-prone areas is crucial—for example, checking-in and checking-out procedures. Identified failure-prone points in the blueprints should then be complemented by support services—for example, assistance from food and beverage staff at reception during check-in and check-out times. Pre-designed recovery mechanisms can also be included.

Summary

As discussed in Chapter 4, business organizations must adopt a customer-oriented managerial approach to compete successfully in today's marketplace. To satisfy the needs of customers, it is important for managers to improve the firm's internal efficiency on an ongoing basis both in terms of strategic management and in terms of operational delivery of services.

Thus, at the macro level, the main task of management is to establish an organizational philosophy that drives the entire firm towards the achievement of its goals and objectives. Moreover, it is essential that this philosophy is effectively communicated to employees at all levels, and is clearly understood by them. It must also be understood by the customers. Thereafter, the firm needs to design and implement service systems and processes that support, substantiate and reinforce the organizational philosophy.

By establishing and communicating its service concept and service strategy, a firm positions itself in the marketplace and communicates its market position to its employees, customers and competitors. This also assists managers to focus the firm's efforts and resources effectively on appropriate areas to improve its services and competitive position.

At the operational level, the ability to design, deliver, improve and tailor services to meet the needs of customers is of paramount importance to success. This chapter highlights the particular importance of well-designed service systems which represent the internal arrangements and allow firms to achieve service excellence and customer satisfaction. Both an effective management of service encounters or 'moments of truth' and the blueprinting technique allow firms to identify their potential service pitfalls and ensure consistency in the firm-customer interface.

This chapter has provided service managers with a holistic perspective that enables businesses to improve their competitive power at all levels of the organization. This approach creates a 'win-win' situation in which customers benefit from improved services while the service organizations enhance their operational efficiency and business performance.

Review Questions

1. What is the relationship between service vision and service mission?
   a. Why it is important for the staff to have a clear understanding of both?
   b. Think of any well-known vision and mission statements for any tourism or hospitality business: can you see any reflection in the company's performance?
2. What are the interrelationships among service vision, process, strategy and system? Briefly define them and allocate their roles from a managerial perspective.
3. What does it mean to 'align' service vision, strategy, process and system?
4. What are the benefits for the firm to have a well-planned and executed service system?
5. What is service design and what are the four key steps in designing a service system?
6. Due to the complex nature of service firms' operations, there are a lot of opportunities for possible errors in service systems and service delivery. Explain whether you agree or disagree with this statement, and describe the available tools or techniques for managing service operations.
7. Define a service encounter, and explain the concept of the service encounter triad.
   a. Who are the 'gatekeepers' and what is their role?
   b. Why is a customer seen as a 'coproducer'?
8. Name any three 'stressors' for managing the service encounter.
9. Name three methods to overcome the service encounter challenges you have mentioned in the question above.

10. What is a service blueprint?
    a. What role does a service blueprint play in designing a service system?
    b. Explain the difference between the front-of-house and back-of-house in regards to a blueprint. Explain using an example of serving food in a restaurant.
11. What are the roles of 'fail points' and 'encounter points' in a service blueprint?

Suggested Readings

This is a list of suggested further reading on topics covered in this chapter. For a separate list of full reference citations quoted in the chapter, see 'References', Chapter 5, page 327.

Ford, R. C., and Heaton, C. P. (2001). Managing your guest as a quasi-employee. *Cornell Hotel and Restaurant Administration Quarterly*, 42(2), 46–55.

Harris, L. C., and Reynolds, K. L. (2004). Jay customer behavior: An exploration of types and motives in the hospitality industry. *Journal of Services Marketing*, 18(5), 339–357.

Harrison, J. S. (2003). Strategic analysis for the hospitality industry. *Cornell Hotel and Restaurant Administration Quarterly*, April, 139–152.

Kumar, V., Lemon, K. N., and Parasuraman, A. (2006). Managing customers for value: An overview and research agenda. *Journal of Service Research*, 9(2), 87–94.

Mckeown, M. (2013). *The Strategy Book: How to Think and Act Strategically to Deliver Outstanding Results*, Pearson: UK.

Patricio, L., Fisk, R. P., and e Cunha, J. F. (2008). Designing multi-interface service experiences: The service experience blueprint. *Journal of Service Research*, 10(4), 318–334.

Ramaswamy, V., and Gouillart, F. (2010). Building the co-creative enterprise. *Harvard Business Review*, 88(10), 100–109.

Ramdas, K., Teisberg, E., and Tucker, A. L., (2012). 4 ways to reinvent service delivery. *Harvard Business Review*, 98–106.

Rayport, J. F., and Jaworski, B. J. (2004). Best face forward. *Harvard Business Review*, December, 47–58.

Solnet, D., Kralj, A., and Baum, T. (2014). 360 degrees of pressure: The changing role of the HR professional in the hospitality industry. *Journal of Hospitality & Tourism Research, in press*.

Testa, M. R., and Sipe, L. (2006). A systems approach to service quality: Tools for hospitality leaders. *Cornell Hotel and Restaurant Administration Quarterly*, 47(1), 36–48.

Victorino, L. and Bolinger, A. R. (2012). Scripting employees: An exploratory analysis of customer perceptions. *Cornell Hospitality Quarterly*, 53(3), 196–206.

Service Marketing: Managing Customer Experience and Relationships

Study Objectives

Having completed this chapter, readers should be able to:

1. Understand the limitations of the traditional '4Ps' model of marketing and the importance of three new Ps in the modern service management context;
2. Understand external service implications and the role of service marketing when compared to traditional marketing functions;
3. Understand the significance of other marketing concepts, such as internal marketing, 'moments of truth' and relationship marketing, and be able to apply them in a hospitality and tourism context; and
4. Recognize a complex and interdependent relationship among operations, human resources and marketing concepts (and associated service encounter, internal processes and marketing, loyalty, customer engagement and customer experiences concepts) which to a degree are also covered in other chapters of this book.

Outline

- ► Introduction
- ► Towards a new marketing paradigm
  - ► What does marketing do?
  - ► How does marketing work?
  - ► A new integrated paradigm of service marketing

- ▶ Integrating operations, marketing and human resources
  - ▶ Marketing 'distance' in manufactured goods
  - ▶ Marketing 'experience' in service
  - ▶ Customer experience
  - ▶ Impact of pre-, during- and post-consumption of service
    - ■ 'Pre-consumption marketing' becomes less important
    - ■ 'During-consumption marketing' becomes most important
    - ■ 'Post-consumption marketing'—the unique role of promotion
  - ▶ Operations, marketing and human resources
- ▶ An extended marketing mix for service
  - ▶ A new formulation required
  - ▶ Product
    - ■ What is a service product?
    - ■ A process, not a physical object
  - ▶ Price
    - ■ Pinning a price tag on the tangible
    - ■ Price must reflect value
    - ■ Price discrimination important in services
    - ■ Putting a price on knowledge
  - ▶ Promotion
    - ■ Traditional role of promotion
    - ■ Promotion of production skills in service
    - ■ Promotion of image
  - ▶ Place
    - ■ Accessibility important in service
    - ■ Timing and speed important in service
  - ▶ People
    - ■ People intrinsic to service
    - ■ Taking cues from employees
    - ■ Taking cues from other customers
  - ▶ Physical evidence
    - ■ No service is truly intangible
    - ■ The importance of servicescape
    - ■ Other physical evidence
    - ■ Coordinating the physical evidence
  - ▶ Process
    - ■ The significance of process
    - ■ Customer-centric processes
    - ■ Customized service processes

- ▶ Building and managing relationships and experiences
- ▶ Delivering the service promise—the critical 'moment of truth'
  - ▶ The 'cascade' in 'moments of truth'
- ▶ 'Internal' marketing
  - ▶ Compete for talent
  - ▶ Offer a vision
  - ▶ Prepare people to perform
- ▶ Relationship and experience marketing
  - ▶ Why are relationships important in service organizations?
  - ▶ History of relationship marketing
  - ▶ Service innovation through customer engagement
  - ▶ All relationships and experiences matter
- ▶ Summary
- ▶ Review Questions
- ▶ Suggested Readings

Key Words

Co-innovation communities
Customer as an ambassador
Customer engagement
Customer experience
Customer loyalty
Customer-centric processes
Customized service processes
During-consumption marketing
Experience marketing
External marketing
Holistic relationship
Human element
Interactive marketing
Internal customer
Internal marketing
Marketing experience
Marketing mix
'Moments of truth'
Part-time marketer
People
Perception of value

Physical evidence
Place
Post-consumption marketing
Pre-consumption marketing
Price
Price discrimination
Process
Process description
Product
Promotion
Relationship marketing
Service factory
Service innovation
Service interrelationships
Service marketing
Service promise
Servicescape
Social media
Talent wars
Word-of-mouth

Introduction

Marketing as we know it was built on a product-focused and typically manufacturing-based perspective grounded on the notion of economic exchange conceived during the time of industrial revolution. As we have seen, service organizations have features that are different from manufacturers of products, and the marketing of service is consequently different from that of product marketing. This chapter focuses on how the distinctive qualities of service affect the marketing of the service interface. The following chapter looks at the internal structures and strategies that are required to make this work.

Because they were primarily designed for goods marketing, the traditional '4Ps' of the marketing mix *(product, price, place* and *promotion)* have proved inadequate for service marketing. It is essential that goods marketing focus on sales, since the role of goods marketing is external to the firm, meaning that it has limited involvement in the production process. On the other hand, in most service contexts the true impact of marketing happens inside the firm where customers interact with almost every element of the organization, particularly those employees who are closely involved in all aspects of production and consumption. Moreover, given that most service outcomes are produced by people for people, the primary focus of service marketing is on value enhancement through relationship building during the production and consumption of service. To address this new perspective of service marketing three additional 'Ps' have thus been introduced as service marketers have attempted to create more appropriate marketing models for the service industry. This chapter addresses these various aspects of service marketing.

In a similar vein, to address the needs of the service industry, new marketing concepts—such as: customer experience; customer engagement; customer communities; employee engagement; employee participation; internal marketing; relationship marketing; service encounter; and

© kentoh/Shutterstock.com

the 'moments of truth'—have been identified as being specifically related to customers' perceptions and satisfaction in a service situation. These newer concepts are also discussed in this and in the following chapters.

It is vital that service managers understand and manage the challenges posed by the marketing of service at the interface with customers. This chapter addresses these challenges at the point of contact with the customer—the external service implications of service marketing. The next two chapters will follow this up by examining the internal mindset, structures and strategies that are required to facilitate effective external service marketing.

Towards a new marketing paradigm

What does marketing do?

The primary function of marketing is to bring buyers and sellers together with the intention of exchanging products and services to create mutual value. The exchange essentially involves the obtaining of a desired product or service from another party by giving something in return. During this process of interaction and exchange, value is cocreated by both customers and the employees of the firm. To render this possible, the primary role of marketing is communication, where the firm communicates to its potential customers about the benefits of its products and service while at the same time finding out from the customers their expectations, preferences and changing needs.

To effect successful exchanges (or transactions), the marketing department analyzes what each party can be expected to give and receive. A full understanding of marketing therefore requires product and service development to be planned in response to the changing needs and wants of customers. Marketing essentially constitutes a 'knowledge bridge' between the customer and producer—effectively informing the producer of what must be offered if its products and service are to meet the expectations and demands of customers, and at the same time to find out as much as possible from the customer about their needs, expectations and perceptions.

How does marketing work?

Marketing includes many interrelated and interdependent activities. In product marketing, the term 'marketing mix' describes how management attempts to utilize these variables creatively.

The marketing mix has many facets, but the four basic variables are known as the '4Ps':

- product;
- place;
- price; and
- promotion.

These are also described as the *controllable* variables of marketing—because they are capable of being controlled and manipulated by the firm (marketer). However, in a service context, given the unique nature of service, three additional variables play an important role in service. These three additional service marketing variables are: *people, process and physical evidence.* These are recognized as the three 'Ps' of service marketing first introduced by Booms and Bitner (1981).

A new integrated paradigm of service marketing

Previous chapters have indicated some of the differences between firms that produce manufactured goods as opposed to service (refer to Chapter 2). In a similar vein, the literature insists that service marketing requires different approaches and strategies from those used in product marketing if the specific characteristics of service are to be addressed. In particular, the nature of service means that marketing is not an independent function of the service organization, but an *interrelated holistic concept encompassing every activity within the organization with particular focus on people, value enhancement and relationship development.*

From a basic business perspective, every business enterprise strives to achieve two basic objectives to stay in business (see Figure 6.1):

- ▶ to satisfy the customer; and
- ▶ to make a return on investment (ROI).

To achieve the second (a satisfactory ROI), the first is essential (the satisfaction of the customer). No organization will be able to achieve its ultimate objective in terms of ROI without first successfully attaining its primary goal of satisfying its customers. This is particularly important in service firms as customers cocreate value by participating and interacting with the production process. Therefore they are highly critical of the service and the value they receive.

Return on investment (ROI) is thus totally dependent on customer satisfaction, but the reverse is not true. A focus on a high ROI will not guarantee customer satisfaction. In keeping with this, the primary focus of successful service firms is now squarely on the customer first, rather than the profit of the firm. In turn, this change in focus has produced numerous changes in the way that service businesses are managed, and how they compete in the marketplace.

In the past twenty years or so, this quantum shift in management focus has caused leading service organizations to concentrate their energies on improving the total experience of the customer. Moving away from a departmentalized approach, successful service providers *unify* their efforts through cross-functional strategies that bring together marketing, operations and human resources as a collaborative function created to satisfy, indeed exceed, customer expectations. Such an integrated approach to marketing, operations and

Figure 6.1
The two basic objectives of a business enterprise

A paradigm shift in thinking

The primary focus of successful service firms is now squarely on the customer first, and the profit of the firm second. Profit comes from customer satisfaction. This is a quantum shift in management focus.

Leading service organizations now concentrate their energies on improving the total experience of the customer and employees (as internal customers) through integrated strategies that satisfy, or exceed, customer expectations and gain their commitment to engage and serve as brand ambassadors.

Such an integrated approach also requires that operations, human resources and marketing collectively aim to develop exceptional service, so as to propel the firm to the forefront of service leadership and success.

---

human resources has enabled some organizations to develop exceptional service and propel themselves to the forefront of service leadership and success. Although the quality of service is defined by the customer, the experience and the relationship is 'created' by the employees of the firm. It can be argued that the employees therefore not only take ownership to create quality and experience, but also that it is the 'human factor' within the organization that holds the ultimate balance of quality, satisfaction, experience and relationship. Service personnel not only create and deliver the service but are often seen as synonymous to the firm in the eyes of the customer (see Chapter 8 for a full review of managing the service employees).

Integrating operations, marketing and human resources

Service firms have realized that they have to address marketing from a different perspective, since relationship building both inside and outside the organization is of primary importance. They have realized the key role of employees of the firm, who play a significant part in nurturing and maintaining relationships with the customer. Hence, service marketing is not seen as an independent function; rather, it holds a relationship-building role to bring together traditional functions of operations, marketing and human resources. Additionally, due to the distinctive features of service, as discussed in Chapter 2 (IHIP), marketing in service organizations differs significantly from marketing in traditional goods manufacturing.

Marketing 'distance' in manufactured goods

As practiced in the goods-manufacturing industry, marketing is distant, both physically and conceptually, from the production process. Marketing in manufactured goods can be said to exist primarily to connect production and consumption (see Figure 6.2). For example, a

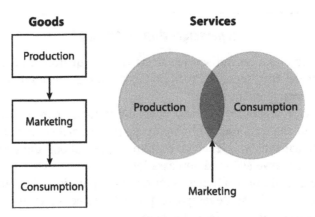

Figure 6.2

Production, consumption and marketing in goods- vs. in service-manufacturing

product might be manufactured in one country and used by customers in another country. In this case, production and consumption are physically distant, and the consumer has no direct interest or influence in the manufacture of the product. Therefore, marketing is often the only way in which the manufacturing firm communicates with its customer for the purpose of sales and also for gaining information from customers to understand their needs, wants and changing expectations, so as to guide production.

This separation of function not only separates the customer from manufacturer, but also, within the firm itself, there is a separation of production from marketing. This separation of production and marketing makes it more difficult for each of these vital functions to influence one another effectively and constructively. In contrast, in the case of service offerings, marketing, operations and human resources are inextricably linked.

Marketing 'experience' in service

In the case of service firms, as we have previously noted, production and consumption occur simultaneously, as opposed to the goods-manufacturing companies. In addition, customers are often required to be physically present, to interact closely with employees and all other aspects of the production process (for example, technology, systems etc.), and to influence the production and consumption of service (see discussion of this in Chapter 2).

From the customer's point of view, production, marketing and human resources are inextricably intertwined, and the personal interaction with the employees during the production and consumption process itself thus constitutes an important marketing instrument, since it is during this interface that the all-important experience and the relationship between the firm and the customer is created. In contrast, marketing in manufactured goods can be said to exist primarily to connect production and consumption which can occur with a gap in time (goods can be stored before the customer will buy them) and distance (manufactured in one country and consumed in another) (see Figure 6.2).

Customer experience

Offering a positive customer experience has been identified as one of the most important success-driving factors in the hospitality and tourism industries. Both researchers and managers agree that creating positive customer experiences can provide economic value for firms (Pine and Gilmore, 1999). Some of the useful definitions of customer experience include:

▶ The internal and subjective response customers have to any direct or indirect contact with a company (Meyer and Schwager, 2007).

▶ It encompasses all aspects of the production, delivery and creation of value considered from the customer's perspective (Ostrom et al., 2010).

▶ It originates from a set of interactions between a customer and a product, a company or part of its organization, which provoke a reaction. The experience is strictly personal (Gentile et al., 2007).

Based on the above understandings, it is clear that hospitality and tourism organizations must ensure that customer experiences are positive both within offline and online contexts. Therefore service firms have to enhance customer experience at every 'moment of truth'. It is only through positive experiences that firms will have the opportunity to engage customers to become their brand ambassadors. In this connected society, many firms have realized that customers are their best advocates (which is reciprocal to the role of employees as customers' advocates, discussed in Chapter 4), and are far more effective than any other form of marketing. Moreover, customer-induced product and service innovations not only create customer engagement but more importantly provide a powerful resource for the firm (this is discussed further in the service innovation section of this chapter). It is therefore imperative for hospitality and tourism firms to think 'outside the box' and create experiences beyond the traditional ideas of accommodation, food, beverage, entertainment, tours etc. Leading hospitality and tourism firms ensure that they create and manage customer experience throughout the entire service consumption stages, namely: pre-, during and post-consumption stages.

Impact of pre-, during- and post-consumption of service

Customer experience is not confined to that which is created when customers enter the firm, but in fact customers often experience the firm's service before they visit the firm physically or online. Similarly, customer experience in most cases extends far beyond the context of service delivery. In fact, service firms seek ways by which they can maintain lasting relationships with the customer and gain their continued engagement. Successfully providing positive customer experience through the entire chain of customer experiences requires both internal and external collaboration and coordination. In the service industry, operations, marketing and human resources are so closely interrelated that each has the capacity to influence the other, and therefore every employee within a service organization has to possess marketing, production and in people skills. For example, a restaurant waiter not only serves food and beverages to customers, but also, during this process, markets his or her personal waiting skills communicated through his or her people skills. It is these functional skills that serve as the icing on the cake to help influence the restaurant's overall service rating and memory in the customer's mind. The waiter is thus a *'part-time marketer'* using his people skills more than any other to create a lasting, positive impression on the customer, leading to a long-term relationship with the restaurant. As another example, a receptionist providing advice and assistance to a guest is simultaneously *producing* and *marketing* that service; however, it is the people skills of the receptionist that creates the true marketing impact on the customer. Since the service 'factory' is at the point of interaction between the employees and the customer, it is imperative that service employees receive appropriate encouragement, incentives and training to help them market their own services effectively to customers, whether in person, via telephone or online. Therefore in service organizations marketing, operations and people skills are an integral part of their service role.

'Pre-consumption marketing' becomes less important

The intangible nature of service makes it difficult for customers to assess the benefit of a service before consumption. For example, an airline customer cannot assess an in-flight experience until the service is actually being consumed. Most traditional approaches to marketing and advertising are therefore ineffective in most service contexts. Customers' expectations therefore depend heavily on 'word-of-mouth' (WOM) information from others who have already experienced the service. Apart from such word-of-mouth advice, customers seek cues (such as the cleanliness of a restaurant) to gain an indication of the likely quality of the service outcome. Moreover, at the pre-consumption stage of service there is very limited interaction between the firm and the customer, making it difficult for the firm to convince the customer of the quality of the experience they will receive. Therefore, the role of marketing at the pre-consumption stage is more on attraction rather than on retention. Given that service cannot be pre-tested before consumption, customers therefore rely on word-of-mouth and various cues before making a service purchase decision. Marketing of service is therefore more effective if directed towards the consumption and post-consumption phases of service delivery.

'During-consumption marketing' becomes most important

During the consumption stage, the firm is able to showcase its competency to provide superior service through its employees. It is through personalized, superior service that employees create the all-important relationship with the customers. Thus in most service contexts the most important task of marketing happens during the consumption stage when relationships are created and maintained by employees. This also implies that marketing is most effective during the consumption stage, representing the 'moments of truth', to convince the customers of the firm's service superiority. For example, a housekeeper going out of her way to locate a child's bed (cot) for a family with a young child who arrived late at night.

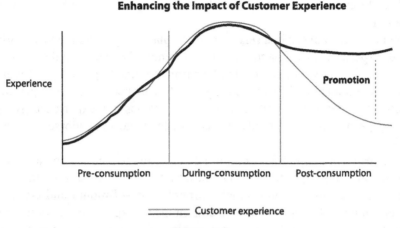

Enhancing the Impact of Customer Experience

Experience

Promotion

Pre-consumption   During-consumption   Post-consumption

═══════ Customer experience

Figure 6.3
Customer experience effectiveness before, during and
after consumption—the new role of promotion

Thus the housekeeper utilized the 'moments of truth' to create a trustful relationship with the customer. Positive customer experience is far more reliable and impactful than a glossy marketing brochure customers receive prior to arrival. This is in contrast to the situation in the goods-manufacturing industry in which customers are able to assess products *before* purchase, and in which the marketing process therefore predominantly focuses on the pre-consumption stage.

The traditional role of promotion has very limited influence in service organizations at the pre-consumption stage. In turn, the effectiveness of marketing in a service firm during the consumption stage is even more superior. Service delivery requires customers to interact closely with various aspects of the firm. It is imperative that the firm convince the customer of its superiority through exceptional service, and by providing customers with a memorable positive experience—the all-important 'moments of truth'. Creating positive customer experiences is pivotal for hospitality firms as value is set in the experience of the customer rather than embedded in goods or services. If this opportunity is missed, very rarely will customers give the firm a second chance. All marketing efforts will prove worthless if the firm has not utilized the opportunity to impress customers at the during-consumption stage (see Figure 6.3).

'Post-consumption marketing'—the unique role of promotion

Promotion has a different role in service marketing. Promotion often takes up the role of engaging customers after providing them with superior service. The role of promotion in this context serves to remind customers of the superior service they received and to entice them to take up the role of firms' ambassadors. Service firms cannot afford to offer superior service and let the customers walk away without contributing to their brand through positive word-of-mouth.

Customers and employees in a service context play a key role in the cocreation of value and customer experience (see Chapter 2), thus subsequently leading to the enhanced perception of quality and loyalty. This understanding from a marketing standpoint is important so as to allocate both human and financial resources to enhance customer experience. Promotion therefore should aim to extend the memory of the positive experience (see Figure 6.4) but also to engage customers as brand ambassadors to create and endorse the firm's message to the public.

As can be seen from Figure 6.4, traditional marketing techniques for service prove least effective at the pre-consumption stage. The best that can be done at this stage is to create a mechanism to gain customer endorsement through word-of-mouth and e-word-of-mouth. Research has demonstrated that customers communicate experiences to others in many different ways, for example: word-of-mouth, blogging, customer references, testimonials and social media. Positive endorsements from other customers are an outcome of superior service which customers value highly. Unlike paid advertisements, customers trust and often act positively based on other customers' reviews. Consumers regard the opinions of other users as important and reliable sources of information, as opposed to the information provided by firms or other marketing sources. Word-of-mouth, however, is not something that happens following every service delivery, service managers have to plan and create circumstances that provide customers with a unique story to tell their friends. In today's digital world, both positive and negative word-of-mouth have considerable impact via Internet and social media.

Studies of consumer behavior indicate that word-of-mouth communication is of special significance in the marketing of service industries. This is due primarily to the 'high risk' of many service purchases—in that services cannot be pre-tested, returned or reworked if they do not meet the expectations of customers. In an effort to minimize this perceived risk, customers seek out recommendations from others before deciding to purchase a service. In this way, satisfied customers often serve as *'ambassadors'* of service organizations, providing service firms with an inexpensive, but very effective, form of advertising. Conversely, dissatisfied customers can ruin even the best attempts at promotion.

Technology-mediated connectedness between customers and its widespread use to share experiences has given rise to a new form of customer voice, primarily intended for other customers. User-generated content (UGC) and shared experiences communicated through social media websites such as blogs, virtual communities, wikis and social networks, along with collaborative tagging and media files on sites such as Facebook or YouTube, have gained substantial popularity, leading to consumers' increasing use and reliance on other customer-generated information (see further discussion in Chapter 4 and in the 'service innovations' section of the current chapter). Consumers today rely heavily on consumer-generated reviews; therefore, firms actively seek to encourage their customers to influence potential consumers' purchase decisions and loyalty.

Disney and the customer experience

The success of many leading organizations in the tourism industry can be attributed to the effective blend of their products and services to meet and exceed customer expectations. What Walt Disney invented in 1955 was not just the concept of a theme park, but also a near-perfect package of product and service that produced a distinctive experience of sight, sound and touch. Disney's advantage over other theme parks is not merely the number of attractions, but also the unique mix of these attractions in a package that offers customers a unique experience unlike any other. In order to do this better than anyone else, the entire theme park focuses entirely on customer experience. The ability of Disney's management is to bring together the expertise of their entire organization to focus on creating an unforgettable customer experience that captures the imagination of young and old at all hours of the day and night. When Disney's managers design an attraction for their parks, they 'imagineer' the entire experience. Their focus is not on how the ride operates mechanically, but on the entire sensory experience it creates for the customers—the things they see, hear and interact with. Management could design the rides to run faster (and thus shorter) with a view to increasing productivity. But they do not do this. Rather, they allow sufficient time for their customers to look around, talk with fellow travelers, scream out with excitement and become generally immersed in the surroundings. Every participant is given the time and opportunity to engage in an imaginary world. In the theme-park industry, Disney has redefined what can be done for the customer. It is this meticulous focus on customer experience that has made Disney consistently superior to its competition in the theme park industry that it created.

Operations, marketing and human resources

In goods manufacturing, the departments of operations, marketing and human resources are separate entities with separate functions. In contrast, in the service sector, these functions can never be separated.

The human element plays such a significant role in *every* aspect of service that it is impossible to separate out these traditionally distinct functions in any meaningful way. Production, consumption and marketing are all dependent on the personality of employees, and the way in which they interact with customers.

The human resources department in most organizations is traditionally responsible for such personnel matters as selection, training, empowerment, discipline and so on. In the case of service organizations, these matters become intertwined with production, consumption and marketing in a way that simply does not occur in goods manufacturing. Although it is true that the functions of production, marketing and human resources can be conceived and examined independently *as a matter of theory,* effective service delivery *in practice* requires an ongoing coordination and integration of all three departments.

In the hospitality and tourism sectors, if a hotel or other service sees itself as a truly integrated service within a destination, all employees must be selected, trained and empowered with a view to their aptitude in both production *and* marketing for both the business and the destination. The apparently separate functions of production, marketing and human resources must thus become integrated and coordinated in effective service.

An extended marketing mix for service

A new formulation required

From the above discussion, it should be apparent that the traditional '4Ps' of the marketing mix in goods marketing—product, place, price and promotion—are insufficient for the needs of modern integrated service organizations. There are two major reasons for this:

- ▶ the distinctive characteristics of service; and
- ▶ the interrelationship of marketing, operations and human resources in service (further discussed in this chapter).

The combination of these two factors means that a new formulation is required. As a result, an extended marketing mix of '7Ps' has been proposed for service products (Bitner and Zeithaml, 1987; Booms and Bitner, 1981). This extended service marketing mix consists of the traditional four 'Ps', together with three new 'Ps'. It therefore consists of '7Ps', as follows:

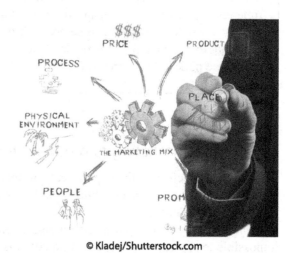

© Kladej/Shutterstock.com

- ▶ product;
- ▶ place;
- ▶ price;
- ▶ promotion;
- ▶ people;
- ▶ physical evidence; and
- ▶ process.

See Figure 6.4 for a pictorial representation of this extended service marketing mix. Each of these seven elements is examined in more detail.

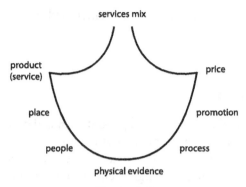

Figure 6.4
Extended marketing mix in service

Keeping up with service enhancements

A recent service-enhancement initiative at a major airline, marketed via a targeted e-mail campaign, permitted customers to check-in 'virtually' and get their boarding pass as a QR code via their mobile phones.

Upon arrival at the airport, the customer was to report directly to the boarding gate, bypassing the front ticket counter and boarding area check-in counter. At the boarding gate, the customer was supposed to be asked only for the SMS received on his or her mobile phone and personal identification. Convenience and speed were promised.

Attempting to use this service more than a week after the announcement, I found that the boarding attendant had no idea what I was doing. Indeed, he had never heard of this new process! As a result, I had to get back in the queue at the check-in counter, go through the full routine and get a standard hardcopy paper boarding pass.

This experience was repeated at three other airports across the USA. Clearly, a highly trumpeted new service enhancement had became an embarrassment.

I contacted the airline and described my experience. The airline replied that its biggest problem with the new system was in properly educating the thousands of gate employees.

When I asked the gate employees about this, they indicated that they were overwhelmed with information and had missed the enhancement training.

So much for improving service ...

The case in the box above indicates the importance of integrating production, marketing and human resources in services industries. The people who deliver the service are also 'selling' the service. These people must be trained, encouraged and empowered to see their role as an integrated function aimed at serving the customer, and thus marketing themselves and their firm effectively.

Product

What is a service product?

A service product, as defined here, is anything—either in isolation or in combination—that an organization offers to potential customers to satisfy their needs. The service product constitutes the foundation of an organization's existence. Accommodation in a hotel room, food in a restaurant, a conference function, a sightseeing trip, a taxi ride, an airline flight, secretarial assistance and an insurance policy are all examples of service products.

A process, not a physical object

In service, the product is a process. The decisions on product mix (see discussion on service bundles and packages in Chapter 1) faced by a service manager are therefore very different from those faced by managers who deal in goods. Most fundamentally, service in most cases can be described only in terms of *process descriptions,* not as tangible descriptions or outcomes.

In addition, overall quality and value perceptions represent an especially key element in defining the service product. Other elements of the traditional product description—such as design, reliability, brand image and product range—are less important in service. The key issue therefore is the customer's *personal experience* of service delivery.

Price

Pinning a price tag on the intangible

The intangible character of service (see Chapter 2) causes many difficulties in pricing a service. Customers cannot see it, examine it or assess it in the way that they can with physical goods. It is difficult for the firm to convince the customers that the price tag is justified on something that does not 'exist' from the customer's perspective!

In the absence of available cues, customers often use price as an indicator of the quality of a service they might reasonably expect. Thus the price of a service offering can influence, in advance, perceptions of quality, satisfaction and value. Customers often relate high-priced service to high quality and, consequently, *expect* high quality. On the other hand, if the service is priced too low, customers might doubt whether this organization is likely to deliver quality.

Pricing in service organizations is thus less influenced by cost than it is by the customer's *perception of value or worth.* The actual pricing of a service is often determined by matching the customer's perception of value.

Price must reflect value

Matching the customer's perception of value and achieving the right price mix involves a host of strategic and tactical decisions regarding such matters as:

- ▶ the average price to be charged;
- ▶ discount structures to be offered;
- ▶ terms of payment to be made available; and
- ▶ the degree of price discrimination to be allowed among different groups of customers.

In short, successful proactive pricing depends on recognizing the value that a customer places on a service, and pricing it accordingly.

Price discrimination important in services

The personal and non-transferable nature of service presents opportunities and challenges for *price discrimination* within service markets—opportunities and challenges that are less apparent in most goods markets. That is, in pricing service, there is much greater scope for significant price cutting in certain circumstances (and for price rises in other circumstances).

Price discrimination can be more readily used in service than in goods because the purchaser does not actually end up 'possessing' the service in the way that a purchaser of goods takes possession of the product. Because the vendor is not actually 'losing' the service to the ownership of the buyer, price cutting can be practiced more readily. The vendor does 'lose' time and effort, but these can be offered again. In contrast, a goods manufacturer actually 'loses' a physical object which might be difficult to replace. For these reasons, a service vendor might feel more comfortable about selling its product at a lower price at a certain time of the day (for example, happy hour in bars). Indeed, this is often the only way for a firm to convince customers to use its service during that time period.

The lack of transferability of ownership is not the only factor to be considered in price discrimination involving a service product. Perishability of service is also an important factor. Because service is characterized by variable capacity over time, such factors as operational efficiency, productivity, resource utilization and profitability depend on astute management of demand—that is, by shifting the peaks to accommodate the troughs (see discussion in Chapter 2).

Lastminute.com and similar sites that offer cheap hotel rooms or airline seats are examples of this sort of cut-price offering. Prices can be extremely low at certain times—not only because the room or the seat are not actually 'lost' by the vendor in any physical or permanent sense (as previously noted), but also because the service product will 'perish' immediately if it is not sold. Vendors of service often cannot afford *not to sell*. In certain circumstances, it suits the vendor to 'give it away for a song' (as the saying goes). Goods retailers can rarely do this.

Conversely, service firms can actively discourage demand at peak periods by raising prices—thus diminishing the strain on limited resources. In a sense, a service firm sometimes does not want to sell more product (de-market its service). Goods suppliers are not often in this situation.

This issue of controlling demand and supply in service is further discussed in Chapter 2 (page 40).

Putting a price on knowledge

Another difference in pricing policy between goods and services is the problem faced by service vendors in putting a price on experience, accumulated knowledge and practiced skills. Some service products, such as a consultant's knowledge, might not involve any obvious additional cost at the point of production of the service. However, the extra cost is determined by the days, months or years already spent in acquiring that knowledge.

The pricing of the intellectual component of a consulting service, and/or the pricing of practiced skills acquired over many years, is a very difficult problem for service vendors—a problem not faced by most goods vendors.

Promotion

Traditional role of promotion

Traditional promotion employs a variety of methods—including advertising, sales promotion, public relations and personal selling—to attract the attention of existing and potential customers, and to inform them of the products, service and special offers made available by the firm. Market communication performs three basic roles in marketing—to inform, to persuade and to remind. However, due to the intangible nature of service, some of the traditional methods can prove to be inappropriate if applied to service. Nevertheless, with certain modifications, most of these traditional methods can be utilized to promote service effectively. Promoting service through word-of-mouth is considered most effective and impactful, as discussed earlier.

Promotion of production skills in service

The fact that production and consumption are simultaneous affords an organization an opportunity to showcase their service, the service process and environment where service is carried out, their personnel and their skills to customers. This is particularly evident within the hotel and restaurant industry. For example, an open kitchen, or tortillas being baked to order at the front of a restaurant, are commonly utilized as marketing tools. As a development from this, it has become increasingly common in restaurants for the presentation of personnel and skills to be extended to a visually exposed kitchen and cooking process. Many restaurants are setting up glass walls that allow customers to observe the food-preparation process in action. There are few goods-manufacturing factories where the production process is actually promoted as a selling point! Such is the distinctive nature of service marketing.

Promotion of image

Image is crucially important for any organization—both goods providers and service providers—because it markedly influences customers' perceptions of the goods and services offered. The intangible nature of service poses special challenges for service marketers in developing and maintaining a desirable corporate image; but it also presents significant opportunities. The image of a service organization is built up in the customer's mind through repeated delivery of a superior service experience and word-of-mouth. However, advertising, public relations and physical image have limited influence on the customer's perception of the firm. Theory suggests that an employee's service mindedness and thoughtful action enhances customer perception and therefore leads to a favorable image.

Image can be an extraordinarily powerful weapon. A positive corporate image often serves as an unwritten service 'guarantee' in the minds of first-time customers, providing comfort and reassurance even when there is no explicit written guarantee. This extends to the engendering of customer 'loyalty'. Indeed, a positive image that is sincerely believed by customers has been shown to engender a sense of 'loyalty'—even among customers who have not personally tried the service! In general, research suggests that customers are loyal to the firm provided the firm consistently offers superior customer experience.

A positive image can, in certain circumstances, serve as a buffer when unexpected service failure occurs. On the other hand, it must also be noted that high expectations of a service firm can cause a minor service failure to be viewed less tolerably by some customers. That is, a very positive image 'can lift the bar' for the organization, provoke high expectations among customers, and make minor errors seem important. However, in general, this is not a significant problem, and a favorable image is better than a negative one! Certainly, if consumers have an unfavorable image of an organization, they are more likely to become extremely challenging and unhappy when things do go wrong.

An often overlooked aspect of image in a service organization is its effect on the firm's internal customers (see Chapter 8). It is important to recognize that the image of an organization reflects on internal relationships, as well as external relationships. A favorable image will attract desirable employees, suppliers and distributors to the organization—because these employees, suppliers and distributors prefer to deal with firms which appeal to them personally and which appear to have a better chance of success in the marketplace. In turn, having superior employees and products assists in gaining customer satisfaction. In this way, a good image leads to satisfied customers who, in turn, reinforce an organization's image and elevate it to a still higher level. Moreover, a good image might even induce customers, employees and suppliers to become shareholders in the firm, thus developing a vested interest in the success of the organization. *Image thus reinforces itself.* Once this attitude has become established within the internal and external community of the organization it becomes self-fulfilling (see Figure 6.5).

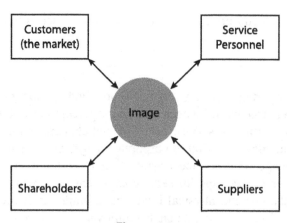

Figure 6.5
Service interrelationships

Image is thus a management tool of great potential. Its ability to be self-reinforcing can exert a considerable 'snowball effect'. The image that a service company creates in the minds of its own staff and in its wider environment is largely determined by the nature of its service, its organization, its culture and the market segment it serves. Hospitality managers, therefore, have to develop long-term service-oriented strategies that will help to orchestrate the firm and its employees to focus on the customer. It is the firm's intense customer focus that helps them to become service oriented and that will enhance the firm's image in the customer's mind.

Place

Accessibility important in service

Place constitutes an important factor in the marketing of service. In service, the customer physically enters the 'service factory' to receive a service (for example, restaurant, hairdressing salon). It is thus imperative that the physical location where the service is being offered is accessible, appealing and customer-friendly. If customers are obliged to travel to avail themselves of the services on offer, as is the case with a restaurant or a retail shop, the accessibility of the location to the customer is clearly important. For example, the availability of car parking at a restaurant or retail shop might make the difference between a customer using or not using the service. In the case of a hotel service, the location and accessibility of the hotel is obviously a very important marketing factor.

Timing and speed important in service

In certain other services—such as fire services, plumbing services, pizza home delivery and so on—the service center is taken to the customer. In these cases, it is the speed with which the service reaches the customer that determines its value. The arrival of an ambulance an hour after it is needed constitutes no service at all. In this and many other service situations, the proximity of the service to the community becomes an extremely important consideration for the service provider.

People

People intrinsic to service

Customers of service organizations are very much aware of the emotions and attitudes of contact employees. From a customer's perspective, the behavior of contact employees represents more than the service product; in a very real sense the behavior of contact employees represents the organization itself.

This obviously affects the marketing of service products. People are more than usually important when it comes to consideration of a marketing mix for service. For example, a friendly barman might well prove to be more of an attraction to a customer than the drinks that he serves. Indeed, for many services—such as consulting service, medical service, educational service and other professional services—the provider is the service. Although this one-to-one correspondence (between provider and service) is not as marked in the hospitality or tourism industries, it is still true to say that the quality of personnel is absolutely crucial to the perception of service quality.

Taking cues from employees

The employees of a service firm involved in service delivery provide cues to the customer regarding the nature of the service itself. The grooming, personal attitudes and behavior of employees all influence customers' perceptions of the service. A waiter who appears dirty or unkempt in an otherwise attractive environment might cause customers to avoid that restaurant. Similarly, a beautifully clean and new tour bus can be negated by a bus driver who is ungroomed and in a wrinkled, unclean uniform with dirty shoes.

Taking cues from other customers

Other customers in the service environment also provide such cues. The way in which a receptionist interacts with other customers influences a customer's perception of the receptionist's service, and the customer's perception of the organization as a whole. Customers thus observe interactions between service personnel and other customers, and draw certain conclusions about the nature of the service.

However, interaction occurs not only between customers and the firm's personnel, but also among customers who are in the service environment at the same time. These customer-to-customer interactions also affect perceptions of the service. Before purchase, a person might make use of other customers as a cue to the type of service being offered and the market segment being targeted. For example, before entering a restaurant a potential customer might peer through the window to ascertain whether he or she 'fits in' with the customers already in the restaurant. The decision to enter is then partially determined by other customers and the evidence they provide regarding the type of restaurant and the market segment being serviced.

Furthermore, customers frequently have to share services and experiences (e.g., in classrooms, hospitals, retail stores, airlines, restaurants, hotels), where the behavior of one customer influences the experience of others. Sometimes the needs of one customer might conflict with the needs of another—for example, smokers and non-smokers in a restaurant, or a long queue for a restaurant or airline service. In other cases, the simultaneous consumption of service might be made more enjoyable by a crowd—as for example in the case of a busy dance floor in a nightclub (adding to the excitement of the experience) or the case of a crowded bar (providing a sociable, cheerful ambiance).

Physical evidence

No service is truly intangible

It can be argued that no service is truly intangible because services are almost always accompanied by products. For example, the seats of an auditorium are part of the service of a music concert; the computer or books of an accountant are part of the accountancy service; the operating instruments of a surgeon are essential to the surgical service and the aircraft is certainly essential for an airline flight! Although these physical objects cannot be categorized as true product elements (in that they are not 'sold' to the customer in any meaningful sense), they play a vital role in the service delivery process (see more details in Chapter 2). In most cases, these product elements serve as cues to the customers during their assessment process.

The importance of servicescape

These objects, as cues or pieces of evidence, play a critical role in making an intangible service somewhat tangible to the customer. For example, a theatre ticket or a flight ticket provides confirmation of the service requested and expected; this is something that the customer can actually hold in his or her hand as tangible 'evidence' of the promised service.

Customers desire the security of evaluating something tangible in this way, and do so by analyzing the physical evidence available to them. For example, patients evaluate the attractiveness of a physician's waiting room, passengers consider the comfort of a tour bus and hotel guests assess the grandeur of a hotel foyer. This service setting or *'servicescape'* defines the built environment or man-made, physical surroundings of the service. This provides a setting for the service, and conveys the values of the organization and the ideals it aspires to achieve.

Such tangible cues are an indication of the quality and nature of the service to be performed, especially in those cases in which consumers have little or no previous experience of the service offering. When consumers have little on which to judge the actual quality of service, they rely on the tangible physical cues, just as they rely on the cues provided by other people.

Other physical evidence

As noted above, a simple piece of physical evidence might be one of the few pieces of tangible evidence that a customer can actually 'possess'—and with the digital age, such evidence is rapidly declining! Other tangible representations of the service might include items such as advertising brochures, billing statements, letters, business cards and written service guarantees. This sort of physical evidence provides excellent opportunities for a service firm to send clear and consistent marketing messages regarding the firm's purpose, the intended market segments and the nature of the service. However, it is important to note that with the rapidly developing era of the Internet, physical evidence is fading away and being overtaken by digital media, online websites and e-commerce. For example, creating e-flyers and upgrading websites may seem a more current and attractive marketing perspective than investing in printed brochures. The importance of marketing through physical evidence remains; however, its usage is decreasing.

Coordinating the physical evidence

Successful service firms are aware of the importance of coordinating these various pieces of physical evidence into a coherent marketing message. Airlines, for example, are careful to coordinate all tangible evidence—such as uniforms, aircraft decor, tickets and all manner of advertising material. Although all airlines provide the same essential service, the differences that do exist are contrasting 'packages' of evidence.

In a similar way, an integrated hotel service ensures that its physical cues are coordinated and coherent in sending the same marketing message. Staff uniforms, the hotel foyer and all hotel literature and written material work together to produce the desired image in the mind of the customer. The hotel's ultimate product—its service experience—might be intangible, but the physical evidence surrounding this intangible product is most certainly 'real', and is very important in giving customers something definite on which to base a marketing impression.

Physical evidence thus serves to reinforce customer perception of the firm's *image*—especially with respect to such qualities as capability, competence, trust and safety. This can be quite subtle, and left 'unsaid'. Compare, for example, a Holiday Inn Hotel and a Ritz-Carlton Hotel. A Holiday Inn Hotel conveys an image of modest, clean and reliable accommodation. On the other hand, a Ritz-Carlton Hotel suggests luxurious comfort, social status and so on. The service provider does not have to state this overtly for the customer to become aware of such an image. Visible evidence of a service must be designed as carefully as the service offering itself to ensure that it represents quality, value and the desired image to the customer (see further discussion on service design in Chapter 5).

Process

The significance of process

Unlike goods, service is made up of *processes*. Service therefore is the end result of deeds, acts, performances and activities performed by the firms' employees alone or in conjunction with various equipment, machinery, facilities and so on. These deeds are carried out in sequences that can be termed 'service processes'.

In almost all services, the customer participates in the production process. Some service operations (financial service, medical service, legal service and so on) are very complex and require the customer to follow a complicated series of actions to complete the process. Others (for example, hotel reservation and guest check-in) are less complex. From a customer's perspective, the service process provides vital evidence of both the quality of the service and the range of services offered. Marketing of service must take this into account.

Customer-centric processes

As noted above, the customers actively participate in most service processes. Indeed, they are often *essential* to the process—for example, in the reservation and checking-in processes customers provide essential information about the preferred kind of room, the time at which they are expected to arrive, special requirements and so on. In a very real sense, the customer has no choice but to participate because the service simply cannot take place without his or her active involvement. This must be taken into account in marketing service. Because customers have no choice but to be involved, the ease and friendliness of the service process is crucial to their assessment of the quality of the service.

Customers are thus impressed by a service process that is deliberately designed to make it easier for them to participate in the production process. Good service managers are aware of this, and consciously use this opportunity to arrange the process to appeal to the customer. This is the rationale behind such service processes as drive-through restaurants, drive-through banks, fondue food and flambé food preparation in front of the customer. In all of these, the service is clearly designed to involve the customer in a very overt way. But the principle of designing customer-centric services to facilitate the involvement of the customer also applies to many other services in a more subtle way. For example, an astute reservations clerk can greet a customer by name, know the likes and dislikes of that customer and generally facilitate the check-in process by being familiar with the guest's details *before* arrival—thus avoiding the need for a whole lot of unnecessary questions and filling-in of forms at the time of arrival. This reservations clerk is effectively marketing the hotel by facilitating the enforced involvement of the customer in the service process. Service process is thus an essential element of service marketing in a way that does not apply to goods marketing (see further discussion on service process in Chapter 5).

The importance of process in service

From the perspective of the customer, service is intrinsically made up of processes. Customers do not perceive goods in this way. The service process is thus of the greatest importance in marketing service.

The following important points must be remembered.

▶ In almost any service, the customer participates in the production process.

▶ Hence customers cocreate value which can be mutually beneficial.

▶ Customers are thus impressed by a service process that is deliberately *designed to make it easier* for them to participate in the production process.

▶ In marketing service, management must be aware that efficiency is not everything. *Personalized* and *customized* service processes are crucial to service marketing.

▶ Successful marketing in any field of business demands foresight and planning. In the case of service, such planning must include careful assessment of process—in advance, and in detail.

Customized service processes

In assessing process, customers evaluate whether the service follows a 'production-line' approach or whether the process is a customized one in which the customer is given personalized attention and the employees are allowed to alter their tasks to meet customers' specific needs. For example, in the airline industry, it has been shown that flight delays are the single most important factor in producing customer dissatisfaction. The problem here is not so much the delay in itself—people will accept that delays occur in any complex service such as air transport service. What really irks them is an impression that they do not matter as individuals. Similar comments apply to check-out delays in hotels, when customers can easily feel like herded cattle, rather than valued persons.

Designing the service process in advance allows management to foresee the flow of the interaction, and to anticipate the association of people and materials at various stages. This offers management the opportunity to prevent mistakes or to isolate the cause of recurrent problems, take corrective action and influence the quality of the service outcome. Successful marketing in any field of business demands foresight and planning. In the case of services, such planning must include careful assessment of *process*—in advance, and in detail (e.g., blueprinting method, discussed in Chapter 5). In summary, the process characteristics of a service are thus another important form of evidence used by customers to judge quality. Process characteristics are therefore of the greatest importance in marketing a service.

Building and managing relationships and experiences

Service research indicates that, in almost all circumstances, customers wish to develop relationships with their service providers. These relationships are important—whether interaction with the firm is frequent or intermittent. For example, a customer might visit a local retail outlet once a week, a hairdressing salon once a month, a dental clinic every six months and a travel agent once a year. Whatever the frequency of visits, customers will choose to go back to the service provider with whom they have formed a good relationship.

Customers' perceptions of a firm are based on such factors as whether they have had positive experiences with the firm, whether they believed the employees were friendly and helpful, whether they were satisfied with the service received and whether they considered the goods and service to be of good value. In almost all cases, employees' interactions have a profound effect on customers' perceptions of the quality of the service experience. All these aspects of service allow for the development of a personal relationship, which is the key to successful marketing strategies developed for a service.

Delivering the service promise—the critical 'moment of truth'

The term 'moments of truth' was introduced into the management literature by Normann (1984) and has subsequently been successfully used to illustrate service encounters in a variety of service organizations. The 'moments of truth' are critical individual interactions that have the potential to determine a customer's attitude towards the overall service offering. These are numerous such episodes that illustrate, to the customer, the *true value* of the organization—at least as the customer perceives it. Such 'moments of truth' can 'make or break' a service experience.

Although the firm offers the service promise to its customers, it is indeed the employees who have the opportunity, ability and willingness to fulfill the promise and often go beyond their call of duty to provide customers a superior experience. The challenge of managing customer experiences is thus vital for the successful marketing of any service organization. But, although it is generally recognized that the consistent quality of encounters is vital to the success of service operations (see further discussion on service encounters in Chapter 5), many organizations leave much of the process to chance. Every service interface can be broken down into its critical 'moments of truth'. To manage service effectively, it is imperative to identify, analyze and manage these individual episodes of interpersonal interaction to ensure positive experiences, desirable customer reactions and effective marketing of the entire service organization.

These critical 'moments of truth' vary, depending upon the nature of the business, the nature of the product and the nature of the service provided to the customer. But one thing is common in all cases—the critical 'moments of truth', if left unmanaged, invariably lead to loss of customer confidence. And once a firm loses the confidence of its customers, loss of loyalty and loss of repeat business follow soon after. However, the only person who, in fact, is capable of ensuring that the customer will receive positive 'moments of truth' and experiences is the service employee.

In assessing the importance of customer experience, it must be recognized that the service provider who is the 'face' of the organization is typically the very last link in the chain of production, and is quite often the least-valued member of the service organization in terms of status and pay. In goods manufacturing this might not be a critical matter. The last person in the production line of physical goods is important, but not nearly as important as the last person in the production line of a service. This is because production and delivery are virtually simultaneous in service. The last person in the production line of a service is also the customer-contact person, and this contact person is invested with enormous responsibility for conveying the 'personality' of the service organization. In the eyes of the customer, at the point of service encounter, these contact employees *epitomize* the company. In a very real sense, service quality and service experience are *created* by employees, but *judged* and *defined* by customers. The fact that customer-contact employees are often underpaid and undertrained can result in low levels of motivation, job dissatisfaction, high turnover—and, ultimately, in dissatisfied customers and unsuccessful marketing.

Effective management of the service experience involves an empathic understanding of the motivation and behavior of such employees—behavior that can make the difference between a highly satisfactory service experience and an unsatisfactory one. Effective management therefore involves training, motivating and rewarding employees to exhibit the preferred behavior consistently (see further discussion in Chapter 8). In short, effective marketing of service involves a real appreciation of the importance of the people at the 'coalface', and a real commitment to their recruitment, training, motivation and welfare. As we have noted before, the management of a truly integrated service organization cannot separate operation, marketing and human resources.

The 'cascade' in 'moments of truth'

Each of us has a personal storehouse of memories of the 'moments of truth' in our own experience. As customers, we have experienced awful moments when it seemed that people or systems (or both) went out of their way to be difficult or unhelpful. And we have also had shining moments—when we felt appreciated, cared for and genuinely valued as persons. As customers, as receivers of the service, each of us experiences the 'moment of truth' as an intensely personal matter.

In this context, service interactions that occur in the first stages of an overall service experience are particularly critical. A failure at an early point in the relationship results in a greater risk of dissatisfaction at each ensuing stage because we tend to take things personally, and interpret each successive failure as further evidence of the personal 'insult' that we initially received. Conversely, a cascade of goodwill can occur. If the first interactions are positive and affirming we tend to look positively on each ensuing interaction, anticipating

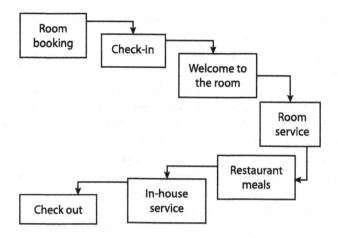

Figure 6.6
The 'cascade' in 'moments of truth' in a hotel

goodwill and 'looking for' satisfaction. This phenomenon, both positive and negative, is known as the 'cascade' in 'moments of truth' (see Figure 6.6).

This 'cascade' has real practical implications. For example, the Disney Corporation estimates that each of its amusement park customers experience about 74 service encounters and over 100,000 'moments of truth' during each visit. This is a huge number, and the cascade phenomenon becomes very important when it is realized that a negative experience in any one of these experiences, especially early ones, increases the risk of the next encounter being negatively interpreted. In turn, this substantially increases the risk of a negative evaluation of the overall service experience. Conversely, each positive experience reinforces the likelihood of the next encounter being viewed positively, and of the overall experience being perceived as enjoyable.

Jan Carlzon and Scandinavian Airlines

As an example of the importance of 'moments of truth', consider the case of Scandinavian Airlines System (SAS). This is an old but still very relevant story about how the 'moments of truth' concept can be used to literally turn an entire company from near bankruptcy to profitability and represents a perfect case in excellence in service management and marketing.

Jan Carlzon, former president of SAS, used the phrase 'moments of truth' to rally the employees of his airline at a time when the organization was in dire economic straits. Carlzon convinced his staff members that every contact between a customer and employee of the airline constituted a 'moment of truth', and that these 'moments of truth' had a cascading effect. In these brief encounters, Carlzon argued, the customer made up his or her mind about the overall quality of service offered by SAS.

Carlzon (1987) told his employees that we are not in the business of flying airplanes, but rather in serving the travel needs of the public. Carlzon estimated that, taken overall, the whole SAS workforce managed 50,000 'moments of truth' every hour of every day. This is a huge number of critical episodes—each one of them having the potential to wreak considerable damage on the overall organization.

Service management is thus about focusing all the energies of the organization—including all the various functions and individuals of which the organization is composed. In focusing the energy of the organization in this way, service management can be likened to a laser. A laser, in itself, is a weak source of energy. It takes a few kilowatts of energy and converges this into a coherent stream of light. It is the collective convergence of energy that provides a laser with the strength to outperform other (apparently stronger) sources of energy. In the same way, service firms have to converge the energies of the organization to the specific goal of creating positive customer experience. If a company has customer focus of this sort, it possesses a powerful laser-like ability to dominate the market. It is this guiding idea of focus that has marked the transformation of service management from a sales-oriented task to a philosophical concept that directs a whole organization towards its goals. Thinking like customers, and anticipating the future needs of customers, are concepts at the leading edge of service management. From this, two activities that are fundamental to successful service organizations require further examination—internal marketing and relationship marketing.

'Internal' marketing

The service literature gives considerable importance to employees as being behind the success of service organizations (see Chapters 4 and 8). The conceptual thinking behind this notion is very different from the traditional idea of employees as a resource. In the manufacturing industry, marketing resources are devoted to developing effective product design, setting pricing, organizing promotion and distributing goods. *In the service business, however, the focus of marketing is very much on the service employees*, since they are the only people who can create and maintain relationships with external customers. Some of the most successful companies such as Starbucks, Disney, and Southwest Airlines recognize their employees as their greatest assets. For example, at Southwest the common mantra is, "customers come second . . . and still get great service." When organizations focus on value for their employees, those within the organization transform themselves into assets. By becoming valuable assets, employees are comparable to the firms' valued customers. Service management views employees as valued assets, or 'internal customers'. The basic idea of 'internal customers' is for the firm to recognize the value of employees and to create bonds with them. With this in mind, there has been a re-evaluation of the word 'customer' within service industries, along with the rise of the intriguing concept of the 'internal customer'—the firm's *employees*. Berry (1981) suggested that, in service organizations, jobs constitute 'internal products'. The concept has been endorsed by other writers who have observed that the needs of internal customers reflect those of external customers.

Employees, as internal customers, thus make or break most service organizations because employees create and maintain trusting relationships between a service firm and its external customers. And these external relationships are ultimately dependent on satisfactory internal attitudes and relationships. It is indeed the internal customers who live the brand and reflect its core values to the external customers (this will be further discussed in Chapter 8). Internal marketing therefore is primarily focused on the internal customers (employees) of the firm. The idea of internal marketing allows the firm to recognize the value of employees' contributions to the firm's success. Therefore internal marketing aims to create a trustful relationship with the employees. Service employees thus live the brand (through their customer-focused actions) since they share service values and vision with the firm. The service literature recognizes the importance of these internal relationships with employees as the primary precursor to successful external relationships with customers.

Service providers have the capacity, through their personal touch, to provide memorable positive experiences. For example, it is the human aspect of the service that truly differentiates one five-star hotel from another. Similar hotels might have comparable facilities and conveniences, but the human touch can make all the difference between these hotels. In the same way, similar shops might sell identical products, similar tourism attractions might offer similar attractions and similar airlines might use the same types of aircraft on the same routes, but the personnel who serve in these organizations can, from the customer's perspective, make one of these organizations quite different from another, despite their superficial similarities. In service industries today, it is the attitude, knowledge and skills of the workforce that provide a firm's competitive advantage, and progressive service organizations have to compete in the marketplace for appropriately talented employees. Attracting, developing, motivating and retaining service-minded employees is essentially achieved through the provision of jobs that satisfy their needs. If employees perceive that there is insufficient enthusiasm, teamwork, communication and training within the culture of the organization, this will be reflected in their own work, and will substantially reduce the quality of service offered to customers.

Many of the marketing processes applied to external relationships can be equally applied to internal relationships. The main aim of internal marketing must therefore be to

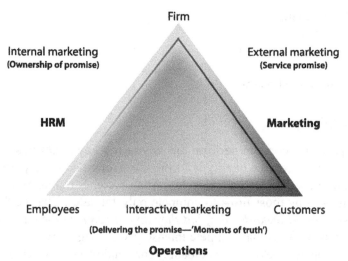

Figure 6.7
External, internal and interactive marketing
Adapted and modified from Grönroos (2000)

ensure that employees share an understanding of the overall objectives of the organization and the service position that it seeks to adopt with regard to its *external customers* (Unzicker, Clow and Babakus, 2000). The emphasis is thus on turning the well-honed communication techniques of marketing inwards—such that they are directed towards the firms' employees (see Figure 6.7).

Internal marketing ensures that all employees at all levels of the organization understand and experience the business activities that support a customer-oriented approach (Grönroos, 1990a), and ensures that all employees are motivated to act in a service-oriented manner. But these things do not happen without managerial planning and commitment. The concept of internal marketing redirects the focus of management to approach all activities in a strategic and systematic manner with a view to creating such a service culture within the organization (see Chapter 8). Internal marketing aims for an ongoing active engagement of employees.

The overall objectives of internal marketing are thus twofold:

► to ensure that the employees are motivated towards customer-oriented and service-minded performance, and thus towards fulfilling their roles as 'part-time marketers' during the service interface; and

► to attract and retain service-minded employees.

To enhance the effectiveness of internal marketing in an organization, Berry (1995) proposed that the firms should:

- ▶ compete for talent;
- ▶ offer a vision; and
- ▶ prepare people to perform.

Each of these is considered below.

Compete for talent

Hiring the best possible people to perform the service is a key factor in service. One of the principal causes of poor service quality is hiring the wrong people to perform the service. Many firms fail to think and act like marketers when it comes to human resource issues.

Marketing is used by most firms to compete only for sales. That is, they compete for *customer market share in seeking sales, but they do not compete for talent market share in seeking staff.* The same firms that compete intensely and imaginatively for customers seem to be content to compete meekly and mundanely for employees. The service firms that turn their marketing powers to the labor market will fare best in the 'talent wars' that lie ahead.

Offer a vision

A paycheck might keep a person on the job physically, but a paycheck alone is not sufficient to keep a person on the job emotionally. Great hospitality and tourism companies stand for something worthwhile, and they communicate this vision to employees with passion. The key is to add dignity to work. A good example is the Credo of Ritz-Carlton Hotels, which emphasizes that both its employees and its guests are ladies and gentlemen. The contribution that each employee makes to the satisfaction of the end customer must be emphasized, and re-emphasized. Employees work better when they understand the value of their contribution. The personal involvement of senior managers in such a vision is essential to preserving the company's culture (see Chapter 5 for more on service vision).

Prepare people to perform

Attract, develop, motivate and retain service-minded employees. In doing this, remember that employees first require knowledge on 'why', before they require knowledge on 'how'.

Therefore, learning should be an ongoing process, not a one-off event. Learning is a confidence-builder, a motivating force and a source of self-esteem. For this, better teachers should be promoted into middle management, and front-line service courses should first be offered to such middle managers, who can then pass this training onto front-line employees.

A firm's relationship with its customers is instigated, established and maintained by the service personnel who interact with the customers day in and day out. It is the service personnel's commitment to seamless, consistent and superior service that enables a firm to create lasting, loyal relationships with customers in which personal interaction assumes center stage. Direct personal contact with customers enables employees to develop an emotional connection through which they are able to appreciate the needs of their customers, and even anticipate the unexpressed desires of those customers. The concept of relationship marketing therefore extends to internal relationships with employees. Indeed, it is difficult to see how a firm can hope to form meaningful relationships with its external customers if it is not prepared to first form such relationships with its internal customers—its own employees.

Relationship and experience marketing

Why are relationships important in service organizations?

An examination of the service management literature has clearly brought a new understanding of the business philosophy, indicating the benefits of moving the focus from the firm to the customer and subsequently the realignment to a long-term perspective. This new business thinking recognizes the long-term advantages of the collaborative synthesis of various business relationships, enabling hospitality and tourism firms to harness resources both within and outside the organization through mutually beneficial relationships. This chapter therefore identifies the firm's secondary resource network and highlights the need to manage relationships both inside and outside the firm with a focus on long-term prosperity, growth and leadership.

This shift in focus manifests acknowledgment of the *lifetime value* of a customer, as opposed to the one-time sale. Organizations have realized that it is five times more expensive to attract a new customer than it is to retain an existing one. Additionally, researchers have identified some important benefits of using a relationship-focused business philosophy: increased purchases, reduced costs, free advertising through word-of-mouth, employee retention and the lifetime value of a customer.

© Stephen Van Horn/Shutterstock.com

Relationship marketing is all about securing and retaining the trust and loyalty of people inside and outside the organization. The challenge for hospitality and tourism organizations today is not merely to be successful, but to maintain their success. To achieve this, the primary focus of a successful service firm should go beyond merely attracting customers. It should seek to obtain their loyalty and their ongoing patronage for the long term. Such loyalty is not easily obtained. It is the end result of ongoing relationships based on an organization's ability to maintain and extend its service to its customers.

History of relationship marketing

From an historical perspective, before the industrial revolution and the subsequent mass production of goods and services, business was characterized by personal service and direct contact with the providers of goods and services. A local store-owner, for example, was a true 'relationship marketer' who nurtured customers as individuals and tried to fulfill their needs. In practice, merchants have had an interest in establishing close personal relationships with their customers for many centuries. In the past, a successful merchant was one who had a friend in every town. The 'friend' in this context refers to the customers and third parties associated with the merchant in his or her various transactions. In the context of modern trade, a firm's 'friends' involve an even wider circle, and includes customers, employees, suppliers, retailers and shareholders.

With the onset of the industrial revolution, firms were capable of increased production capacity, and subsequently sold many things to many customers; in effect they ended up distancing themselves from their customers and other associates. This produced a substantial reduction in collaborative networks as they had traditionally been forged for mutual benefit among merchants, employees, suppliers, retailers and customers. Rather, firms intensified their focus on the selling of their products and services. However, focus on present sales does not necessarily produce future sales. In fact, a focus on present sales transactions essentially inhibits a firm's long-term orientation—because it does not provide for the laying of a foundation for future sales. It traps a firm in the present. A foundation for future sales is essential if a firm is to succeed in a changing global marketplace in which competition has produced a surplus of products, services, employees, suppliers and retailers in so many different fields.

The advent of technology in every field of business has further exacerbated these problems. Modern technology plays a vital role in assisting firms with the development of innovative offerings—effectively rendering products and services obsolete in a short time, and presenting customers with an abundance of products and services. It has thus become increasingly difficult for firms to maintain distinctive product and service differentiation over long periods, and to retain the ongoing patronage of customers over long periods. This reduction in customer base has a significant impact on the profitability of firms—because customer acquisition is substantially more expensive than customer retention.

Although merchants have nurtured relationships with customers for many centuries, hospitality and tourism firms of today nurture and manage a greater variety of value-creating relationships with a much larger pool of stakeholders. These various business-to-customer (B2C) and business-to-business (B2B) relationships are crucial to the day-to-day operations of many hospitality and tourism firms. The focus therefore has shifted from winning new customers to maintaining loyal customers. In this regard, the seminal research contributions of Reichheld and Sasser (1990) and Reichheld (1996) demonstrated that a 5 percent increase in customer retention resulted in an increase in average customer lifetime value of 35–95 percent, thus producing an exponential increase in profitability. It has therefore become imperative for hospitality and tourism firms to devise means by which they can nurture and sustain their one-on-one loyal relationships with all stakeholders: customers, employees, suppliers, retailers and shareholders.

The conceptual thinking behind customer loyalty has therefore been widely accepted as central to hospitality and tourism firms' success by both practitioners and theoreticians. Furthermore, firms have realized that, given the changes in the marketplace, passive loyalty of the customer has limited advantages. They have realized that the firm can benefit considerably more if loyal customers exhibit attachment and commitment to engage with the company. Customer engagement and their positive feedback through word-of-mouth are of greater value to the hospitality firm than passive loyalty of the customer. Evidence indicates that customers' word-of-mouth acts as one of the most important influences on other customers for their purchase decision. Given the plethora of market-generated communications generated by the firm, customers consider word-of-mouth information from other customers as a more trustworthy source of information. The extensive use and adoption of technology, Internet and social media by customers today have given rise to the popularity of the online environment as a social phenomenon for customers to access online information. For example, the Internet allows customers to communicate to a larger number of people about positive and negative experience with a firm. In addition, the popularity of social media is enabling both the firm and customers to reach a larger, global audience which traditional media were unable to achieve. Social media is known to have notable impacts on both the transmitters' and receivers' behaviors. Customers engage in online word-of-mouth through writing reviews, blogging, and online recommendations. In addition, extensive use of social networking Web sites, including Facebook, Twitter, YouTube and TripAdvisor, have enabled customers to engage and voice their opinions about the product or service. Thus online access to communication dissemination has put more power in the hands of the customers.

Through engagement behavior, customers create value not only for themselves, but also for other customers. For example, those online platforms provided by the firm (Web sites or online booking engines) that allow customers to post their statements about the firm's products and service not only act as a cocreation tool for customers themselves, but also provide an important information source to other customers as well. Through posting, customers themselves may feel proud about being able to provide a valuable information source to others. This way, customers are able to share their opinions, preferences or experiences with others about the firm, products and service.

The extensive adoption of technology and various online communication channels, such as social media and customer communities, provide customers with a new role, and bring online communication and communities to life. Many customers today take up an active role not only as coproducer of value, but also the more important function of co-owner of the brand and its potential success. The strategic focus, beyond mere customer loyalty, is to achieve active engagement of customers as co-owners and cocreators of value as they act as brand missionaries, disseminating the marketing message among their contacts. Companies thus seek strategies to enhance customers' active engagement with the firm and ways to serve the customers as brand ambassadors (James, 2013).

Service innovation through customer engagement

Given the competitive nature of the hospitality and tourism industries, academics and practitioners have recognized the importance of innovation to sustain leadership in the market not only to attract customers but more importantly to provide them with a unique experience. Technology has changed the customers and thus the industry considerably, its widespread adoption and extensive use in society have led to considerable changes in people's social lifestyle. These changes in the society have compelled firms to adopt innovative business models to engage with customers and to gain a competitive position in the marketplace. Online co-innovation communities are one such innovative business model that has been used by firms to connect with customers through social networks (Pantano and Pietro, 2013). Chapter 4 has provided a more detailed overview of various online platforms and their role in better understanding and engaging the customers. This section aims to continue this discussion but rather from the perspective of building long-term relationships.

Firms have realized that customers today are in perpetual connectivity through multiple digital devices and mobile technologies. Given this digital connectivity, engaging and enticing customers to partner with the firm to cocreate value has been discussed in literature by Prahalad and Ramaswamy (2000, 2002, 2004a, and 2004b). Moreover, engaging customers in the process of innovation on an on-going basis has numerous advantages for companies. For example, Starbucks invested and built its own online co-innovation community platform *MyStarbucksIdea.com* in order to engage its customers and to participate actively in the community. Starbucks enticed the tech savvy community members with various incentives to share, vote, discuss and see the ideas in themed categories. As a result, a total of 196,730 ideas to date have been generated on *MyStarbucksIdea.com* and 1,024 ideas have been put in action for the improvement of Starbucks products and services, while at the same time enhancing customer experience and involvement. Other widely cited online co-innovation communities include *Heineken Ideas Brewery*, *Lego Cuusoo*, *Dell Ideastorm*, *Best Buy IdeaX*, and *McDonald's Mein Burger*, to name a few. Through the effective use of online co-innovation communities, these firms were able to successfully engage their customers to cocreate and co-innovate products and services.

Almost all business interactions can be understood as relationships between a firm and its customers, and maintaining these long-term relationships is the true indicator of a firm's success. However, in most business situations, it is not common to see truly long-term relationships between service providers and customers. Most of these relationships tend to be surprisingly short term in nature. On the assumption that they will lose many of their customers, firms strive to attract more customers than those with whom they realistically expect to forge a relationship. The marketing emphasis in the past was more focused on outreach, rather than retention. In a sense, firms thus consciously establish a system which ensures that only a proportion of their customers receive service commensurate with their expectations, while the remainder become dissatisfied. These subsequently leave, and the self-defeating cycle of attempting to attract new customers continues.

All relationships and experiences matter

The above discussion leads naturally to a consideration of the fact that *all* relationships matter. All service organizations have four major partners—customers, employees, suppliers and shareholders. The growth and prosperity of a service organization is dependent on the harmonious growth of relationships among all of these partners. The primary relationship is the firm's relationship with its customer—as facilitated through its employees or retailers. This primary relationship is the basic function and goal of the firm. However, the effectiveness of the firm's primary relationship is also affected by the strength of its secondary relationships. These secondary relationships involve other stakeholders in the success of the firm—including suppliers and shareholders. These other stakeholders must be considered when a firm is assessing its attitude to relationship marketing. A firm needs to go beyond its 'core relationship' to encompass a more 'holistic' view of relationships in which *all* stakeholders are involved (see Figure 6.8).

The inclusion of these other stakeholders is important in developing a corporate sense of commitment to the concept of relationship and to provide positive experiences for all stakeholders. It is this '*holistic relationship*' which makes a firm's offering distinctive in the marketplace. Although various other stakeholders could be included in the network of relationships, the above five partners (firm, customer, employee, supplier, shareholder) constitute those participants who are essential if a firm is truly to embrace relationship marketing.

Relationship and experience marketing thus involves all stakeholders in the success of the firm. If proactive strategies are developed to nurture relationships and manage experiences on an ongoing basis among all such stakeholders, the value of the firm's service

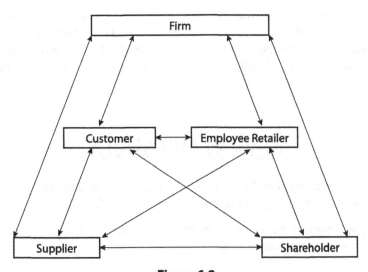

Figure 6.8
Secondary service relationship

offered in the marketplace will inevitably stay at the forefront in the market. This is particularly true of firms operating within industries in which service differentiation is difficult to achieve—such as hospitality and tourism, professional services, high-tech industries, the healthcare industry and so on. The whole organization must be committed to enhancing the relationships and experiences for all stakeholders.

Summary

Marketing has long been recognized as critical to the success of business organizations and, over the years, various marketing perspectives, theories and practices have been developed. Although the traditional marketing mix of the '4Ps' has long been useful to managers in planning and implementing their strategies, it is insufficient for many business firms, especially service firms, to compete successfully in today's marketplace.

As discussed in previous chapters, the increasing economic importance of the service sector, and the unique characteristics of service products, have highlighted the need for a different approach to marketing. This has led to the development of a new body of knowledge that aims to improve the competitive ability of service firms. The primary focus of service marketing is on value enhancement through relationship building during the production and consumption of service. To address this new perspective of service marketing three additional 'Ps' have thus been introduced as service marketers have attempted to create more appropriate marketing models for the service industry.

This chapter stresses the importance of building relationships and managing experiences on an ongoing basis with all stakeholders, both within and outside the company. The particular focus though lies on the external service implications of service marketing. Therefore, various concepts such as the critical 'moments of truth', word-of-mouth, and pre-, during- and post-consumption experience are specific to the service context and present service marketers with valuable insight into methods of improving their marketing effectiveness.

Review Questions

1. Briefly describe all four 'traditional' Ps. Explain how and why the three 'new' Ps can be seen as more appropriate marketing models for the service industry.

2. Once you remembered all the '7Ps' for service marketing, give an example of each 'P' within the restaurant setting.

3. Discuss and give examples of the implications for hospitality managers of the various 'new' marketing concepts designed especially for services. (For example, identify the 'moments of truth' in a hotel check-out situation.)

4. What place does service marketing take within the production-consumption process? Explain the role of customer experience and the critical importance of 'moments of truth'.

5. Explain why operations, marketing and human resources functions cannot be separated within the service sector. Link each to the concepts of external marketing, internal marketing and interactive marketing.

6. Explain the concept of the lifetime value of a customer. What role does relationship marketing play here?

7. Think of an example of service innovation driven by the purpose of engaging customers. Explain why service companies are interested in keeping their customers engaged.

8. Explain the importance of managing the 'holistic relationship' as opposed to the 'core relationship' within the marketing context. Which one can be represented as a service encounter triad?

Suggested Readings

This is a list of suggested further reading on topics covered in this chapter. For a separate list of full reference citations quoted in the chapter, see 'References', Chapter 6, page 329.

Coviello, N., Winklhofer, H., and Hamilton, K. (2006). Marketing practices and performance of small service firms. *Journal of Service Research*, 9(1), 38–58.

Dev, C. S., Buschman, J. D., and Bowen, J. T. (2010). Hospitality marketing: A retrospective analysis (1960–2010) and predications (2010–2020). *Cornell Hospitality Quarterly*, 51(4), 459–469.

Dev, C. S., and Olsen, M. D. (2000). Marketing challenges for the next decade. *Cornell Hotel and Restaurant Administration Quarterly*, February, 41–47.

Gilmore, J. H., and Pine II, B. J. (2002). Differentiating hospitality operations via experiences. *Cornell Hospitality Quarterly*, 43(3), 87–96.

LaTour, K. A., and Carbone, L. P. (2014). Sticktion: Assessing memory for the customer experience. *Cornell Hospitality Quarterly*, 55, 221–227.

Line, N. D., and Runyan, R. C. (2012). Hospitality marketing research: Recent trends and future directions. *International Journal of Hospitality Marketing*, 31, 477–488.

Lovelock, C., and Gummesson, E. (2004). Whither services marketing? In search of a new paradigm and fresh perspectives. *Journal of Service Research*, 7(1), 20–41.

Lovelock, C., Wirtz, J., and Chew, P. (2009). *Essentials of Services Marketing*. Singapore: Prentice Hall.

Melián-González, S., Bulchand-Gidumal, J., and López-Valcárcel, B. G. (2013). Online customer reviews of hotels: As participation increases, better evaluation is obtained. *Cornell Hospitality Quarterly*, 54(3), 274–283.

Pine, J., and Gilmore, J. H. (1998). Welcome to the experience economy. *Harvard Business Review,* July–August, 97–105.

Xie, K. L., Zhang, Z., and Zhang, Z. (2014). The business value of online consumer reviews and management response to hotel performance. *International Journal of Hospitality Management*, 43, 1–12.

Zeithaml, V., Bitner, M. J., and Gremler, D. D. (2009). *Services marketing: Integrating Customer Focus Across the Firm*. New York: McGraw-Hill/Irwin.

CHAPTER 7

Service Guarantees, Service Failure and Service Recovery

Study Objectives

Having completed this chapter, readers should be able to:

1. Understand the challenges of marketing service quality to potential and existing customers;
2. Understand the benefits and challenges of service empowerment, service guarantees and service recovery;
3. Appreciate the interrelationship of these strategies; and
4. Apply the proposed service system in a hospitality and tourism context.

Outline

- ▶ Introduction
- ▶ Service superiority: the basis for a competitive advantage
  - ▶ Reliability as the core of service quality
  - ▶ Perceptions of value
  - ▶ The two-way nature of 'loyalty'
  - ▶ Empowering employees to 'break the rules' to do the right thing
- ▶ Service failure
  - ▶ Types of service failures
  - ▶ Recognizing service failures
- ▶ Strategies for a competitive advantage
  - ▶ Service guarantees
    - ▪ Perceptions of risk
    - ▪ What is a service guarantee?

- Assurance of reliable service
- Guarantees and mutual trust
- Effective service guarantees
- Guarantees, service delivery and organizational feedback
- Marketing benefits from service guarantees
- Wider benefits of service guarantees
- The dual role of service guarantees
- Are guarantees always appropriate?
  - ▶ Service recovery
    - Retaining old customers or gaining new ones?
    - What is service recovery?
    - Service recovery is not just complaint handling
    - 'Doing it right the second time'
    - The forgiving customer
    - The 'Service Recovery Paradox'
    - Justice and Fairness Theory
    - Types of service recovery options
  - ▶ Learning from the experience
  - ▶ The importance of complementary strategies: guarantees, empowerment and recovery
- ▶ Coordinating the strategies for a competitive advantage
  - ▶ Step 1: Identifying 'fail points'
  - ▶ Step 2: Establishing and guaranteeing service standards
  - ▶ Step 3: Ensuring employee skills
  - ▶ Step 4: Developing a recovery strategy
  - ▶ Step 5: Obtaining feedback
- ▶ Summary
- ▶ Review Questions
- ▶ Suggested Readings

Key Words

Auto-alignment system	Employee recovery
Core offering	Functional offering
Customer feedback	Interactional justice
Customer loyalty	Justice / Fairness Theory
Customer perception	Mutual trust
Distributive justice	Pre-purchase guarantees
Employee empowerment	Procedural justice

Process recovery
Recovery strategies
Reliability / reliable service
Risk perception
Service failure
Service guarantee
Service loyalty
Service outcome

Service process
Service promise
Service recovery
Service system
Silent masses
Technical offering
Unconditional (service) guarantee
Value perception / perception of value

Introduction

To maintain their position in a competitive marketplace, leading organizations must continuously improve their service offerings and communicate the superiority of these offerings to various stakeholders. However, because service is generally intangible, quality is difficult to quantify. And with nothing tangible to assure them of promised quality, service customers understandably perceive a risk in purchasing services.

In addressing this problem, many service organizations offer *service guarantees*—thus communicating their commitment to service quality. However, from an operational perspective, the characteristics of service products present significant challenges to the control and standardization of service quality, and hence to the delivery of an effective service guarantee. The high level of human involvement in both the production and consumption of service products means that mistakes, or service failures, are unavoidable. For these reasons, service companies benefit from putting into place a service guarantee that puts pressure on the organization to fulfill their service promise, but they also establish effective *service recovery strategies* to back-up the system in the event of failures occurring.

This chapter proposes a systematic approach to gaining a sustainable competitive advantage by combining these two service strategies—service *guarantees*

© Photocammie/Shutterstock.com

and service *recovery*—to form a system that facilitates superior service quality and simultaneously reduces customer perceptions of risk and the chances of service duplication by competitors.

Why bother with guarantees and recovery?

The management strategies of service guarantees and service recovery can be combined with other practices in this text to form a system that facilitates superior service quality, reduces customer perceptions of risk and reduces the chances of service duplication by competitors.

Service superiority: the basis for a competitive advantage

Reliability as the core of service quality

The consensus of the literature on management theory is that a firm's competitive advantage can be attributed to organizational factors—primarily the firm's capability or core competencies (exceptional recruitment practices for example). However, with service firms, it is common that these very core competencies can still fail to meet customers' expectations. As we have noted in this book several times, research has shown that breaking the service promise is the single most important way in which service companies fail their customers. From the customer's point of view, a service firm's capacity to deliver the core competencies is inextricably linked to reliability—that is, the ability to offer service without failure.

© squarelogo/Shutterstock.com

Recall from Chapter 3 that research into service quality shows that service reliability lies at the heart of meeting customers' expectations for excellent service; it constitutes the single most important factor and is, in many ways, the *core* quality sought by most customers. Service reliability thus constitutes the foundation on which a reputation for outstanding service quality is built.

Perceptions of value

The success of leading hospitality and tourism organizations can be attributed to their ability to deliver their basic service promise. From a customer's perspective, it is the service promise and delivery of quality service which effectively determines the value of an organization's offering. Because service is intangible, value perceptions generally accumulate based on many factors, including the quality of the 'core' good or service as well as perceptions of the entire experience. Customers then equate what they received and make an assessment against the price paid to form a perception of value. *Value perceptions are important as customer loyalty is strongly associated with value (see example "in practice" below).*

Lexus = Omotenashi

A good example of the way value perceptions form is Lexus. When Toyota decided to enter the luxury car market, they knew that they would have to do more than just make a quality vehicle. Since the original Lexus 'covenant' emphasized the way customers would be treated (as guests in their home), the company has built a reputation for doing more than building cars. Lexus dealerships offer the expected technical service, but also offer a wide range of extras (peripherals), such as custom waiting lounges, Lexus loaner vehicles, complimentary car washes with free pickup and delivery, concierge services and office areas for customers to conduct business.

For instance, in Australia, the company offers the Lexus "Encore" program, which is automatic membership into a scheme which gives Lexus (new and used) drivers that something extra, including free loaner cars, airport pickup, access to shows and sporting events, a special magazine and 24-hour drive care protection which offers breakdown assistance similar to many automobile club programs (AAA in the USA). Indeed, Lexus loyalists value the entire package of owning a Lexus as much as they do the actual 'good' (car) itself.

The Japanese word for hospitality is *omotenashi*. It implies an insightful understanding of customer wants and needs, thoughtful caring about each customer's well-being and treating people as true individuals. Customer care is so important to Lexus that they blend the automobile and the caring for the customer at the very heart of their brand. This combination of attentive customer care and world-class automobiles is what Lexus believes creates a true luxury experience. Lexus uses the spirit of omotenashi to help them recognize that each guest has different needs and that their goal is to anticipate and personalize solutions to exceed expectations (Lexus, n.d., Online).

The two-way nature of 'loyalty'

Loyalty is a key concept in service management. Service organizations aim to gain the loyalty of customers, and customers seek the loyalty of an organization through an assurance

© Igor Shikov/Shutterstock.com

of a commitment to consistent and superior quality of service. Such a commitment on the part of a service provider can be termed 'service loyalty'.

In a competitive market, such *service loyalty* is a prerequisite if *customer loyalty* is to be achieved. It is imperative that service organizations convince their customers of their commitment to superior quality of service—now, and in the future. Success in the hospitality and tourism industry is determined by an organization's ability to offer *loyalty*—a loyalty to quality which will fulfill their customers' present needs, anticipate their prospective needs and facilitate and enhance ongoing relationships (see Chapters 3 and 6 for further discussion about the concept of customer loyalty).

Empowering employees to 'break the rules' to do the right thing

Personal interaction between the customer and the service provider is at the heart of virtually all service experiences and it is the responsibility of management to assist service personnel to offer exceptional service. Service managers thus need to adopt innovative strategies and design procedures that facilitate service personnel to go beyond their immediate job descriptions and to cross functional boundaries.

For customers, the most satisfying experiences are often those that occur when employees are empowered to 'break the rules' to respond quickly and flexibly to a particular service need. Much of what this chapter is about inherently relies on service employees and their knowledge, skills and authority to act on behalf of the customer. Although empowerment is used in this chapter as a basis for effective guarantees and service recovery strategies, we will discuss the concept of employee empowerment, and its wider value to service organizations, in further detail in Chapter 8.

Service failure

For service organizations where so much of the service offering is intangible and delivered by and to people, breakdowns, or service 'failures', are inevitable. The service might not fail in the eye of the service provider, but if it does not meet the customer's expectations then it has failed from their point of view. And of course service organizations must be customer-centric (see Chapter 3), so customer *perception* is a service firm's *reality*! Remember too that it only takes *one service failure* in *one step* of a service process to make a cus-

tomer dissatisfied (see Chapter 5 on the service encounter)! While excellent service organizations do not aspire to service failures, they do aspire to hear about them through easy and ongoing communication with customers. Great service organizations ensure that there are clear pathways for customers to provide feedback—good and bad—with every piece of feedback being an opportunity to learn and improve. We have already spoken of some of these examples in Chapter 4, such as Disney's 'customer listening posts'.

© mtkang/Shutterstock.com

Types of service failures

Service failures can be perceived differently by the various stakeholders involved in the service process and can occur for many different reasons; however, from a customer's perspective, especially if he or she is upset, what caused the failure might not matter. It is important for service managers to be clear about the typology of failure so that appropriate responses can be considered. There are literally dozens of ways to categorize a service failure. For example, failure can occur related to the service *process* (something went wrong with the way a service was delivered) or related to the service *outcome* (a customer was simply not satisfied overall). The four types of service failures below represent a synopsis of past research that provides a basic understanding about the different types and causes of service failure.

1. *The service itself.* In this case, the 'core' offering (or 'technical' offer) was perceived by the customer to be incorrect. For example, a reservation for a hotel room was not found by the person at the front desk, the room type reserved was not available or the wrong menu item was brought to the table or it was cold or incorrectly cooked. These are all failures related to the primary service offering.

2. *The service provider.* This type of service failure is primarily caused by the way in which the service was delivered (functional). For example, in the case above of the hotel room not being found in the system by the front-desk employee, the employee may have had a strongly negative attitude towards the customers (e.g., looking at the customers as if they were lying). There is much evidence to suggest that it is an uncaring or rude attitude of a service employee which causes the majority of dissatisfaction with a service.

3. *Things outside of the control of the service provider.* In some cases, service failure can occur but be outside of the direct control of the service firm. For example, air travel can be delayed by weather or mechanical problems, comfort in a hotel could be impacted by a power outage in the area or a person's cellular service could be impacted by the telephone itself rather than by the cellular service provider.

4. *The customer(s).* Also outside of the direct control of the service provider are the actions of customers themselves. In Chapter 5 we introduced some of the challenges firms face in managing the service encounter, one being deviant or difficult customers. The simple fact is that customers themselves can be complicit in causing a service failure. For example coming excessively late for a reservation only to find that the restaurant has given away the table can cause a customer to feel dissatisfied and therefore result in a service failure. Additionally, customers in the establishment, for instance who are loud or intoxicated, can lead to service failure from the perspective of other customers whose experience is impacted as a result.

© PathDoc/Shutterstock.com

Recognizing service failures

As suggested above, despite everyone's best efforts, service failure is inevitable. In a perfect world customers would feel compelled to proactively communicate with the service firm about signs of failure and dissatisfaction. However, the challenge for service managers is that the significant majority of people (some research suggests 90%) never complain! Although most of the research on service failure has been on service *recovery*, linked to those people who do complain, there is some research which examines that very important group of customers who do not complain. One notable research project (Voorhees, Brady, and Horowitz, 2006) labeled this group of dissatisfied customers who do not complain as "The Silent Masses". These researchers attribute the lack of complaining to a multitude of reasons broken into six major themes:

1. Time and effort (not worth the time or didn't have time to complain).
2. Service provider's responsiveness (nobody to complain to or didn't think anyone would take any corrective action "in one ear, out the other…").
3. Personality factors (customer assertiveness, mood, empathy towards service workers).
4. Organization-initiated recovery (before the customer could complain the firm proactively dealt with the service failure).
5. Miscellaneous (did not realize failure until too late, customer loyal regardless, failure is rare, etc.).
6. Alternative action (simply switched service providers rather than saying anything).

Service managers benefit from first understanding that unhappy customers or those who have experienced a service failure do not necessarily complain, and second from proactively putting measures into place which address the themes presented above. The reason being is that service failures can have various negative consequences, including a decline in customer confidence, customer defections and negative word-of-mouth. It is thus important that service failures are recognized and result in a satisfactory recovery for the customer. Service recovery strategies will be addressed later in this chapter.

Strategies for a competitive advantage

Creating competitive advantage requires service organizations to have outstanding organizational practices built into the fabric of the business. Many of these great companies utilize a variety of non-traditional strategies to gain and maintain a competitive advantage in the marketplace. It is often these organizational strategies that are the most difficult aspect of a business to copy. It is easy to build a nice hotel or a modern attraction, but operating it with skill and precision is far more difficult. There are many challenges that managers face when managing service organizations, yet the best service organizations find a way to excel by first understanding the nature of the service sector, and then by engaging a range of management principles and practices in order to achieve the highest levels of performance and success. This chapter focuses on two of these practices:

1. service guarantees; and
2. service recovery.

Before examining the strategies of *guarantees* and *recovery* in more detail, it is important to stress that these strategies should be seen as a cohesive system. Strategies such as innovative and service-focused people-management practices (Chapter 5), creating a workplace culture where front-line staff are empowered to make decisions (see Chapter 8), service guarantees and a proactive service recovery process are inherently complementary, and a successfully coordinated system of strategies will permeate the whole organizational culture, thus making it difficult for other organizations to emulate and therefore leading to a sustainable competitive advantage.

Service guarantees

Perceptions of risk

Every business transaction involves risk. And in every business encounter, one side of the transaction always assumes more of the risk than the other. This might occur explicitly or implicitly. Indeed, the participants might not always be consciously aware of the distribution of risk. However, in every business transaction, one party is always more at risk than the other, and some types of business transaction involve more risk than others.

When customers purchase a service, they usually take a relatively higher risk than when they purchase a physical object. In purchasing an intangible service for the first time they cannot pre-test the outcome, and there is, of course, no specific physical object to be examined before purchase. The purchase of hospitality and tourism service are perfect examples because the service cannot be reworked or returned. In effect, the customer makes a purchase in the *trust* and *expectation* of receiving a good result.

To encourage prospective customers to avail themselves of its offering, a service organization should therefore seek ways to reduce the perceived risk. Ideally, management should attempt to eliminate the perception of risk completely and thus create a risk-free transaction. In effect, management offers the customer a *guarantee of service (or a guarantee of the service promise)*.

Service is Risky!

In any kind of business transaction, one party takes more risk than the other.

With regard to service, customers are forced to take a relatively higher risk due to the fact that:

- ▶ A service cannot be pre-tested
- ▶ A service cannot be reworked
- ▶ A service cannot be returned

What is a service guarantee?

A 2009 review of 20 years of service guarantee research led to this definition: "A service guarantee is an explicit promise made by the service provider to (a) deliver a certain level of service to satisfy the customer and (b) remunerate the customer if the service is not sufficiently delivered" (Hogreve and Gremler, 2009, p. 324).

Assurance of reliable service

A guaranteed service transaction will be seen by the prospective customers of hospitality and tourism organizations as an added bonus—something that adds value to the offer by increasing the likelihood that they will achieve what they wish to achieve.

What can you promise?

Service guarantees should strive to be as 'unconditional' as possible, with a view to assuring the customer of service reliability. In essence, a service guarantee is a twofold vow:

▶ that service delivery will meet company promises; and, if it does not …
▶ that the company will promptly compensate the customer.

Service guarantees can be 'conditional' or 'unconditional'. Although the ideal objective is a completely risk-free offer, the reality is that no one can ever guarantee that mistakes will never be made. The best that can be done is a promise to make every effort to eliminate foreseeable and controllable error, together with an undertaking to make good any mistake that does occur—and to do so promptly. Service guarantees should thus strive to be as 'unconditional' as possible, with a view to assuring the customer of service reliability. In essence, a service guarantee is a vow that service delivery will meet company promises and, if it does not, that the company will promptly compensate the customer.

Pre-purchase guarantees are especially important in the case of service. Service, by its very nature, offers few cues to assist service customers with their pre-purchase decisions. Hospitality and tourism in particular are especially notable for not facilitating pre-purchase evaluation, and customers are thus commonly forced to rely on the post-purchase evaluation of others (word-of-mouth) in making assessments about a service. Past experience suggests that the value which drives the competitive advantage of service guarantees lies in *removing uncertainty and risk*, thus making the buying process of customers more convenient and less irritating.

Examples of service guarantees

▶ Crowne Plaza, Niagara Falls—promises complete satisfaction or the customer does not pay.

▶ American Airlines—offers the lowest guaranteed prices on their own website, and promises to match a lower price and give a $50 promotion code for future flight purchases.

▶ Brisbane Whale Watching—if a whale is not seen on the trip, guests will get to take another free trip.

▶ Merlo Coffee Company in Australia—offers a 200% satisfaction guarantee; they will replace a coffee if unsatisfactory, not charge the customer for it, and then give a voucher for a free coffee on the next visit.

▶ Hampton Inn Hotels—just celebrated 25 years of their 100% satisfaction unconditional guarantee.

In some cases, firms can even offer a 200% satisfaction guarantee. Dean Merlo's BarMerlo cafés in Brisbane, Australia, for example, have a policy whereby if a customer is unhappy with their coffee, it is remade, the customer is refunded and they receive a voucher for their next coffee. The commitment there is perfectly clear—satisfy the customer no matter what!

Guarantees and mutual trust

Above all, customers appreciate such guarantees for the commitment to service that they represent. A service guarantee is essentially a way of demonstrating an organization's *trust in its customers*—in the full knowledge that some customers will attempt to take unfair advantage of the offer (Bell, 1993).

GUARANTEED TO INSPIRE AND INFORM!**

** No Risk Guarantee - You have peace of mind knowing that if you are not delighted with the session(s), we will either –

(a) refund the difference between our fee and what you feel the program was worth, or

(b) refund the fee in full.

It's that simple. This guarantee is unconditional. YOU decide!

Figure 7.1
Example of a service guarantee—Shift Directions Consulting
(Reprinted by permission of author)

> ### Trust all around
>
> A service guarantee encourages mutual trust—mutual trust between a firm and its external customers, and mutual trust between a firm and its internal customers. The overall effect is a general increase in cooperation and commitment among all stakeholders, which is essential in service organizations that 'live or die' on the basis of enduring personal relationships.

Such trust makes customers feel valued. It communicates one half of a partnership reaching out to the other—thus facilitating a long-term relationship. The effect of this is that service guarantees create a commitment to the delivery of excellent service and reciprocal trust on both sides, resulting in an impressive customer retention rate.

Service guarantees create a customer-driven standard for service that defines the service promise of an organization to its internal and external customers simultaneously. That is, service guarantees not only set criteria by which customers can evaluate the quality of service they receive, but also establish the standard to which an organization needs to train its workers, so as to ensure that the staff are capable of delivering such quality service.

Effective service guarantees

It is not enough to offer a service guarantee as a public-relations exercise—cynically designed to attract attention and prospective customers—with no commitment to the concept of a *real* guarantee. An effective guarantee must be carefully designed and effectively organized as part of an overall commitment to a service-oriented culture.

Such a service-oriented guarantee should be:

- ▶ *unconditional*—when excuses are given, the customer feels cheated;
- ▶ *easy to understand and communicate*—specific and clear to both customers and employees;
- ▶ *meaningful to the customer*—promising something of real value if service is not delivered properly;
- ▶ *believable / credible*—promising something that could legitimately be delivered upon (if customers do not believe that they will receive what is promised, the level of risk is not reduced);
- ▶ *easy to invoke*—an unpleasant situation should not be exacerbated by a service guarantee that is difficult to invoke; and
- ▶ *easy to fulfill*—when a customer invokes a guarantee, the service provider should pay out immediately.

Incorporating these sorts of features into a service guarantee ensures that the guarantee is real and effective.

Real and effective service-oriented guarantees

Real and effective service oriented guarantees must be:

- ► unconditional;
- ► easy to understand and communicate;
- ► meaningful to the customer;
- ► believable / credible;
- ► easy to invoke and
- ► easy to fulfill.

Guarantees, service delivery and organizational feedback

Service guarantees have the capacity to change the entire service-delivery system of an organization, and will substantially improve operational efficiency. A risk-aversive philosophy tends to permeate all aspects of organizational life, extending well beyond the limits of mere financial risk implied by the word 'guarantee'.

The aim of service guarantees is to bring the customer loop right in to every employee in the company—the employees can literally hear the customer speaking to them through these guarantees. Bringing the voice of the customer into an organization in this way is a matter of great importance for service companies, and various authors have discussed the need for effective tools and approaches to achieve this (see Hogreve and Gremler, 2009). A service guarantee is one such effective strategy. It encourages customer feedback and offers an organization the opportunity to take immediate corrective action—one of the crucial factors in converting dissatisfied customers into satisfied customers.

Indeed, service guarantees can be a more effective strategy for gaining customer feedback than traditional customer feedback methods. For example, managers at Hampton Inn (a Promus Corporation hotel) adopted service guarantees, in association with rewards for employees for their commitment to such guarantees. These managers began to hear stories about their front-line staff members going out of their way to help and please customers. The service guarantee program at Hampton Inn thus assisted managers and staff to respond immediately when there was a need to improve the services on offer (Hilton Worldwide, 2014).

In the restaurant industry, one casual theme concept in the USA offered a "15 minutes or it's free" service guarantee at lunch, promising a free lunch to customers who are not served within 15 minutes of placing their order (from a limited menu). The company then becomes immediately aware of a service system breakdown based on the number of meals given away on any particular day and is then able to react immediately. The guarantee creates a 'real-time' barometer of the delivery of the service *promise* (fast lunch).

One of the important benefits of the service guarantee is, therefore, that it works as an effective conduit of feedback from customers. Such feedback enables employees to analyze situations and to take action to satisfy customers. Such a system thus enhances a firm's capacity to improve delivery systems continuously, while simultaneously providing an opportunity to transform dissatisfied customers into lifelong loyal customers.

In an effort to encourage both positive and negative feedback, the use of a reward system—directed at both customers and employees—can be very beneficial for the service organization. Such a reward system, by which customers are rewarded for their comments and by which employees are rewarded for solving problems, effectively compels the organization to respond to customer feedback. This is a great advantage to any firm according to research demonstrating that a powerful competitive advantage is available to any hospitality and tourism firm that is willing to offer a service guarantee and that proves capable of delivering on that promise.

Service guarantees thus offer benefits to the provider, as well as to the customer. For the provider, a service guarantee 'lifts the game' of the whole organization and implicitly improves the whole service delivery system.

Marketing benefits from service guarantees

From a marketing perspective, a service guarantee has the potential to influence customers to avail themselves of the services on offer. Hospitality and tourism organizations that offer service guarantees have been shown to command a substantially greater market share as compared with the competition, thus enabling them to set a premium price for their services. For example, Hampton Inn's '100% satisfaction guarantee' elevated it to the top of the consumer ratings.

A guarantee reinforces a company's service promise to its customers, effectively making the promise 'tangible'. This, in turn, attracts new customers, enhances repeat business, and retains customer patronage. Once established, service guarantees should constitute a permanent part of an organization's operating philosophy and be supported by an advertising campaign to reinforce the fact.

Wider benefits of service guarantees

Service guarantees also have benefits beyond the obvious—assuring reliability and thereby encouraging doubtful customers to try the service. These wider benefits permeate through the whole organization.

In summary, service guarantees have the following nine major benefits:

1. assuring reliability and encouraging sales;
2. clarifying expectations by indicating to *everyone* the level of expected service;
3. receiving immediate customer feedback;
4. improving service delivery systems;
5. identifying 'fail points' in the service system;
6. increasing customer satisfaction;
7. improving employee performance through training/education programs;
8. developing a general service-oriented culture in the business; and
9. maintaining competitiveness in the marketplace.

Taking these points together, a service guarantee policy serves as a service standard that cannot be compromised. This strategy effectively coordinates every system in the organization to become focused on better serving the customer. It can thus be considered to function as an internal 'auto-alignment' system.

Service guarantees are thus an effective and valuable management tool. All service organizations should embrace the strategy of a service guarantee because:

► it forces an organization to focus on the customer's definition of good service, rather than relying on management's assumptions of what constitutes such service;
► it sets clear performance standards;
► it generates reliable data on poor performance (through records of complaints and payouts);
► it forces an organization to examine its entire service delivery system for possible 'fail points';
► it builds customer loyalty and enhances positive word-of-mouth recommendation; and
► it encourages employees to show initiative and commitment to the firm and its customers.

The dual role of service guarantees

It is apparent from the above discussion that a service guarantee fulfills both an effective marketing function and an effective operational function. That is, it simultaneously enhances an organization's (internal and external) marketing effectiveness and its operating competency.

This dual role (marketing and operational) reflects the fact that *customer satisfaction* is the ultimate measure of both marketing effectiveness and operational competency in any service organization. Such a strategy also helps to establish a learning relationship with each and every customer—an important concept if an organization is to improve. Even if conceived essentially as a marketing strategy, a guarantee is able to nurture what might be termed an 'organizational learning process' as it focuses the whole organization on customer needs.

Are guarantees always appropriate?

As effective as service guarantees can be, there are cases where such a guarantee might not be appropriate. Examples include companies with strong reputations where an explicit guarantee may not fit their image, a new business where there is a period of organizational learning taking place and where a guarantee is likely to be counterproductive, firms where service and service quality are significantly hampered by external forces, such as weather / natural disasters (e.g., hot air ballooning), and in cases where consumers would see little financial, personal or physical risk and therefore no tangible value in invoking a guarantee.

Similarly, despite the obvious benefits of service guarantees, careful consideration should be given when putting in place a service guarantee to ensure that it is encouraging the right behavior and not putting the service quality, employees or customers in jeopardy. For example, an international pizza chain for many years offered free pizza if delivery was not made in 30 minutes. This guarantee sent the wrong message to employees (drivers were speeding and causing accidents) so the guarantee had to be removed. Therefore, it is important to keep in mind that not all guarantees will be effective in every situation.

Service recovery

Retaining old customers or gaining new ones?

Although it might sometimes seem that there is an unlimited pool of potential customers for any given service firm, the primary goal of an organization must be to focus on maintaining the loyalty of its existing customer base. This is because creating a new customer is always more costly than retaining an existing one. Indeed, it is not unusual to hear that it can cost over five times as much to attract a new customer as it does to retain an existing one. In addition, the restless searching for new customers can mean that present customers are treated less well, with resultant loss of customer satisfaction and corporate reputation.

Various researchers have indicated that the loyalty, retention and repurchase intentions of existing customers is inextricably linked to customer satisfaction. The main reason for customers leaving familiar service providers and seeking new ones has been repeatedly shown to be a failure in the core service of the firm. And dissatisfied customers not only defect but also trigger a chain of negative word-of-mouth comments. Jones and Sasser (1995) concluded that except in a few rare instances, complete customer satisfaction is the key to securing customer loyalty and generating long-term financial success.

Research findings suggest that:

▶ Many firms never hear from 96% of their unhappy customers. For every complaint received, on average there are 26 customers with problems, of which 6 are serious problems.

▶ Of the customers who register a complaint, between 54% and 70% will do business again with the organization if their complaint is resolved quickly.

▶ The average social media member has 243 friends and is 30% more likely to view an ad that has been liked or commented on by their friends.

▶ Customers who have complained to an organization and had their complaints satisfactorily resolved tell many people about the treatment they received.

What is service recovery?

Service recovery is a systematic process undertaken by an organization in an effort to return aggrieved customers to a state of satisfaction after a service has failed to live up to expectations. Michel et al (2009) suggest that service recovery is the set of actions a company takes to re-establish customer satisfaction and loyalty after a service failure (customer recovery), to ensure that failure incidents encourage learning and process improvements (process recovery) and to train and reward employees for this purpose (employee recovery).

In one of the earliest academic articles on service recovery, Hart and his colleagues (1990) wrote:

"Service companies must become gymnasts, able to regain their balance instantly after a slipup and continue their routines . . . Such grace is earned by focusing on customer satisfaction and a customer-focused attitude . . . " (Hart, Heskett, and Sasser Jr, 1990, p. 149).

Great service organizations respond not only to those problems which might be their fault, but also provide service recovery strategies linked to events which may not have been the company's fault! For example, Disney is known to have a special service in its parking facilities to cut keys for customers who have somehow misplaced their keys during their visit to one of the theme parks. Although not Disney's fault, the company managers know that a small gesture such as this can turn a potentially awful situation into a positive one.

Service recovery is not just complaint handling

An effective service recovery strategy involves not only reacting to complaints, but also being proactive in identifying failures even when a customer does not complain. As such, service recovery is not only about responding to complaints, but rather dealing with failures in advance of a complaint. This is the key difference between 'service recovery' and 'complaint handling'. As mentioned earlier in the chapter, the majority of customers never complain, so recovery strategies are very important to 'win back' the customer. For example, on a recent flight on Qantas Airways, the video system broke down and nobody was able to watch the in flight videos. Rather than waiting for customers to complain, Qantas sent letters to all of its Frequent Flyers who were on the flight, apologizing for the inconvenience and offering a small token of apology (a movie pass). This is truly a case of not waiting for a complaint—and a great way to keep loyal customers satisfied!

Virgin Atlantic Complaint Letter

Turning a critic into the biggest fan: one of the many success stories from Virgin Atlantic

A complaint made it to The Telegraph as the "world's best complaint letter" written by a passenger who was highly dissatisfied with his food on a Virgin Atlantic flight. Using witty remarks and attaching 7 photos of the meal in his letter, this complaint attracted lots of attention from the public . . . To address this issue, Sir Richard Branson personally called up the passenger and not only apologized but offered him a job to design a menu for future flights. Thus, the airline not only dealt maturely with the negative situation, but involved the customer into creating brand experiences, turning a critic into a fan and broadcasting a message that they take customer feedback seriously!

'Doing it right the second time'

A customer's intention to repurchase is obviously an indication of whether that customer will remain loyal to the firm or switch to a competitor and, in a competitive environment, customers choose to maintain their patronage on the basis of a firm's ability to exhibit superior service with flawless performance. Given the inevitability of error, as mentioned earlier in the chapter, the way in which a service organization responds to mistakes becomes a crucial factor in customer retention.

When mistakes do happen, a firm's true commitment to service quality is displayed to the customer by the manner in which it responds (Zemke and Bell, 1990). The title of Zemke and Bell's paper on this subject sums up the situation neatly:

© Ilin Sergey/Shutterstock.com

'Service Recovery: doing it right the second time'. It is imperative that a firm goes out of its way to satisfy customers after a service failure. In contrast, if the firm *fails* to ensure customer satisfaction following a service failure, the result will be a decline in customer confidence and an increase in negative word-of-mouth comments. An initial failure might be tolerated, but if the firm fails to recover from the initial service failure, it has effectively failed *twice*—thus magnifying negative customer perception. Bitner, Booms and Tetreault (1990) describe this as a 'double deviation' from expectation.

The forgiving customer

Most customers are sympathetic to unforeseen service failures. They understand that these things do occur despite a service provider's commitment to offer superior service. Customers are, in fact, seldom unhappy about inadvertent service mishaps. Rather, they are unhappy if the service organization is unwilling to accept responsibility for the mishap. More importantly, they are especially unhappy if the service provider is unable (or, worse, unwilling) to take immediate action to fix the situation.

Tax and Brown (1998; 2000) found that the majority of customers are dissatisfied with the way in which companies resolve their complaints. Kelley, Hoffman and Davis (1993) claimed that it is possible to recover from any failure—no matter what. They also found that, regardless of the type of failure experienced, customers will remain loyal to a service firm *provided that an effective recovery is executed.*

From a customer's perspective, recovering failed service demonstrates fulfillment of the firm's promise, and thereby confirms a firm's superior service.

Effective Service Recovery by using Standard Recovery Procedure (SRP)

▶ Service recovery is a proactive concept and hence the firm must pre-plan service recovery procedures for every operational activity.

▶ Service recovery therefore is the pre-planned procedure that supports every service operational activity.

▶ Therefore every Standard Operational Procedure (SOP) must be supported by a Standard Recovery Procedure (SRP).

The 'Service Recovery Paradox'

As noted above, firms are able to regain the trust and satisfaction of customers following a failure provided that a service recovery strategy is successfully executed. There is a peculiar irony evident in the service literature known as 'The Service Recovery Paradox'. The concept has been defined as a situation in which customer satisfaction can exceed prefailure satisfaction (McCollough and Bharadwaj, 1992). As Hart et al. (1990) stated, "a good recovery can turn angry, frustrated customers into loyal ones. It can, in fact, create more goodwill than if things had gone smoothly in the first place" (p.148). The lesson for service managers is that in service recovery situations, a customer who experiences a gracious and efficient handling of a complaint can become a company's best customer. Nevertheless, we are not advocating failure for the purpose of achieving the service recovery paradox!

Justice and Fairness Theory

In search of ways to understand the impacts of service recovery, researchers have adopted a number of conceptual and theoretical frameworks. One of the most frequently employed in the study of service recovery has been justice theory. The idea in using justice theory is that customers' levels of satisfaction and loyalty depend upon whether a customer feels as if they were treated fairly and that justice was done (in the eyes of the customer). According to justice theory, there are three different types of justice—distributive, procedural and interactional.

▶ *Distributive justice* is defined as what the customer *receives* as an outcome (for example a replacement meal or drink voucher). Judgments of distributive justice are seen to form from an often subconscious comparison with how a recovery attempt on one person compares to that of another person in a similar situation.

▶ *Procedural justice* is often not quite as easy to enact as a simple comparison, so the next level of justice is concerned with the process used to resolve a failure (e.g., formal policies are followed).

▶ *Interactional justice* relates to the manner in which the problem is dealt with by service employees and the specific interactions between the employee and customer (e.g., sensitivity, dignity, respect) (McColl-Kennedy and Sparks, 2003). Interactional justice has been shown to often be the strongest predictor of trust and overall satisfaction with a service recovery effort. This point highlights the importance of managing employee attitudes, covered in more detail in Chapter 9.

Types of service recovery options

Practically speaking, what can service managers do once a service failure has occurred? A number of service recovery strategies have been identified and studied over the years. These strategies include:

1. apology
2. correction
3. empathy
4. compensation
5. follow-up
6. acknowledgment
7. explanation

8. exceptional treatment
9. managerial intervention

Service managers are adept at knowing which strategy is the appropriate one for any circumstance. The list above generally follows a sequence, in that an apology and correction would be used in the first instance and in almost any service failure situation. Research into hotel sector service failures found that an apology and correcting the problem is often enough to satisfy customers. Yet this does not happen consistently enough—suggesting that service firms could enhance their competitive position by simply understanding that customers generally are not looking for anything unreasonable, but rather a simple acknowledgment of a mistake and some small effort to make a correction (depending on severity).

Recovering from a service failure—five steps to follow:

1. *Apologize*—apologize for the mistake, even if you were not involved.
2. *Take ownership*—let the customer know that you will assume full responsibility and will do everything possible to find a solution.
3. *Provide a timeframe*—inform the customer that you will get back to them in X number of minutes/hours/days.
4. *Involve the customer*—find out the customer's preferred solution.
5. *Offer the option to speak with a manager*—check whether the customer would like to discuss the incident with a manager.

Experience suggests that hospitality and tourism businesses should put into place some kind of easy-to-remember process for dealing with service failures. Many exemplary hospitality firms use some kind of acronym to help staff remember service recovery strategies. For example, Marriott employees practice the LEARN routine—Listen, Empathize, Apologize, React, Notify. Front-line employees of Marriott properties learn to listen to customers, empathize with whatever is upsetting them, apologize for the fact that they are unhappy, promise some kind of action and then very importantly to notify their manager or supervisor so that the problem is properly logged. Similarly, the Ritz-Carlton hotel chain trains its staff not to say a mere "sorry" but "please accept my apology" and gives them a significant budget to reimburse unhappy customers.

Learning from the experience

Although the primary purpose of service recovery is to return the aggrieved customer to a state of satisfaction, a firm can gain additional benefit for itself if it makes use of the information gained from the experience to prevent future failure. Every service failure and recovery experience should trigger a learning process across the whole organization—to prevent a recurrence of the mistake.

This concept of 'learning from failure' is crucial if an organization is to improve its people, its systems and its procedures. Modern service firms, taking advantage of technology, use databases to record, categorize and disseminate information to the entire organization to help everyone learn from the mistakes.

The importance of complementary strategies: guarantees, empowerment and recovery

Against this background, it is apparent that the establishment of the strategies of a *service guarantee* (discussed above) and *employee empowerment* (Chapter 8) are inextricably interwoven with the concept of *service recovery*. Effective service recovery involves a service guarantee to ensure an immediate response to failure, and employee empowerment to ensure effective corrective action to recover from that failure. If successfully executed, the combined strategies lead to enhanced perceptions of the firm's competence and a favorable image in terms of perceived quality and value (Zemke, 1995).

The literature on service recovery and service guarantees stresses that recovery is most effective if a firm's response is focused on each customer's individual needs, and if employees have highly developed interpersonal skills that enable them to react flexibly to each situation that they encounter. In fact, there is strong research evidence that when a firm has built up a strong relationship over time with a customer, that a customer will be far more tolerant of a service failure and more willing to accept an attempted service recovery (Robinson Jr., Neeley, and Williamson, 2011).

Because the responsibility for responding to a service failure often falls on front-line staff (to realize that there is a problem in the first place and then to do something about it), this is admittedly a potential area of concern for management, since it seems as if the firm might lose control of a situation and cede that control to more junior employees. Yet great service firms do an exemplary job in empowering employees to address service failures on the spot (more on this in Chapter 8). We know that if management utilizes the complementary strategy of a service guarantee (effectively running in parallel with a strategy of empowerment), this imbues employees with a sense of importance and urgency in their response.

Service guarantees and service recovery are thus complementary strategies that reinforce one another in practice. Management can have confidence in employees who have confidence in management. The complementary strategies of empowering front-line employees, an overt service guarantee and a clear service recovery process engender a spirit of mutual trust between management and employees—everyone is committed to the same goal of delivering quality service.

The service experience in its entirety thus progresses through various stages, with a service strategy applicable to each stage:

- ▶ pre-purchase communication (guarantee);
- ▶ service delivery (empowerment); and
- ▶ post-purchase relationship (recovery).

The integration of these complementary strategies (of empowerment, guarantee and recovery) within an organization results in an effective service culture which is not easily emulated by competitors, and thus constitutes a unique competitive advantage (see more on building a service culture in Chapter 8). But such a result is achievable only if the strategies are incorporated within a systemic infrastructure—a 'service system'. Such a system highlights the relationships of the respective strategies, and identifies the stages required in the delivery of superior service. We now turn to a consideration of such a coordinated service system.

Too important to be left to chance

The coordination of the vital strategies of *empowerment, service guarantee* and *service recovery* depends on an appropriate service system. Success in establishing this provides a service firm with a unique competitive advantage.

The establishment of such a system is thus too important a matter to be left to chance. It deserves and demands the full attention of committed management and staff.

Coordinating the strategies for a competitive advantage

There are five basic steps in the design and establishment of an effective and coordinated service system. They can be summarized as follows:

1. the identification of failure-prone areas;
2. the establishment of service standards;
3. ensuring that employees gain the requisite knowledge and skills;
4. the development of a service failure strategy; and
5. the obtaining of feedback.

Each of these is discussed below.

Step 1: Identifying 'fail points'

One of the first steps in the design of a superior service system involves the identification of failure-prone areas. In this regard, a service blueprint is a most effective resource in enabling managers to examine the entire service delivery process visually (Liang, Wang and Wu, 2013).

Using a blueprint (see Chapter 5), managers can identify the steps performed in view of (or in contact with) a customer. These steps represent critical points in the service delivery process at which quality must be assured.

The visual information contained in a blueprint, especially if employed during the design of a new service, will help managers to establish preventive support services as they are perceived to be likely to be required, and to offer special training for employees as appropriate.

Step 2: Establishing and guaranteeing service standards

The second step in setting up an effective service system is to establish (or update) service standards that reflect customer requirements, and to ensure these are communicated to customers by close coordination between operational and marketing departments. In this regard, service guarantees explicitly define a firm's promise to the customer—thus effectively marketing both capability and commitment.

Step 3: Ensuring employee skills

The third step in the design of a service system is to ensure that the firm's employees gain the requisite knowledge and skills to render services commensurate with the agreed service standards. In this regard, it is important to recognize that superior service often requires employees to go beyond their job tasks if they are to serve the special needs of customers (Schweikhart, Strasser and Kennedy, 1993). Adhering to structured job specifications and standards might not be sufficient in all situations.

In this regard, the strategy of empowerment is most useful. It allows employees the flexibility to be imaginative in finding alternative solutions for the myriad customer needs they encounter in their everyday jobs.

Step 4: Developing a recovery strategy

The fourth step in the setting up of a service system is the development of a service recovery strategy. This involves establishing procedures for employees to follow when service failure occurs—such as when customers register a complaint, or when a service guarantee is to be honored.

Recovery of service failure requires employees to possess special skills. It is at these moments that the touted service superiority of employees (and the whole organization) is most carefully scrutinized. It is imperative that every recovery of failed service is handled in a professional and courteous manner. This necessitates clearly established procedures to be followed by all employees, complemented by freedom to show initiative in special circumstances. Employees who can follow established procedures as required, but also show initiative in unusual circumstances, represent a valuable resource for any service firm. Their recruitment, training and retention must be a top priority for any firm that wishes to be successful.

Step 5: Obtaining feedback

The final step in designing a service system is the obtaining of feedback from customers. Service employees can also provide vital and reliable information about customers, especially with respect to customer needs and problems. It is essential that a firm establish a method to collect such customer feedback—both directly from customers, and indirectly via employees (for more information see Chapter 4).

In this regard, the use of service guarantees encourages customers to voice their dissatisfaction immediately. Moreover, if a guarantee is invoked, employees are required to recount and/or explain the incident to management. If this is complemented by an appropriate employee reward system, in which employees are acknowledged for their commitment and enthusiasm, managers will receive information on the positive experiences of customers also.

Such ongoing feedback is essential to the setting-up of an appropriate service system in the first place, and facilitates the review of any existing delivery processes.

Summary

Although the nature of service products means that a service organization is especially vulnerable to duplication of its offerings by competitors, a firm that can consistently maintain and enhance customer satisfaction and loyalty will be able to sustain a superior market position. To achieve and maintain a competitive edge, it is imperative that a firm systematically identify and manage the factors that influence service quality and customer satisfaction.

The intangible nature of service means that customer satisfaction depends, to a very large extent, on perceptions and personal judgments (rather than on predetermined standards set by management). And these perceptions and personal judgments are made throughout the entire service process—from pre-purchase (for example, communication with potential customers) to post-purchase (for example, after-sale communication and conflict-handling).

The service guarantee serves as a unique selling point that aims to promote the firm's customer orientation with real commitment. Such a service guarantee not only targets external customers, but also employees—who become acutely aware of the firm's service philosophy and service vision. The service guarantee thus establishes and communicates the firm's image and market position to its customers, competitors and employees. Ultimately, it will be reflected in customer satisfaction and loyalty.

To implement service recovery strategies successfully, a firm also needs to ensure coordination among guarantee, empowerment and recovery. These strategies should be seen as a cohesive system. Strategies such as innovative and service-focused people management practices (Chapter 5), creating a workplace culture where front-line staff are empowered to make decisions (see Chapter 8), service guarantees and a proactive service recovery process are inherently complementary, and a successfully coordinated system of strategies will permeate the whole organizational culture, thus making it difficult for other organizations to emulate and therefore lead to a sustainable competitive advantage.

Review Questions

1. Discuss the relationship between service loyalty and customer loyalty.
2. What are the types of service failure? Think of your own example for each type of failure within a tourism context.
3. What are the possible strategies for addressing service failures? Briefly explain why companies need to develop them.
4. Why is perception of risk different for purchasing services? What implication does it have for a service provider?
5. Explain the idea of service guarantee unconditionality. Why is mutual trust an important prerequisite here?
6. Why are service guarantees crucial from the service company perspective? Explain its 'dual' role for the company.
7. What are the important / necessary attributes of an *effective* service guarantee? Think of an example where guarantees might not be appropriate and rather harmful.
8. Why do effective service recovery strategies play an important role for the company? Briefly explain the differences among customer recovery, process recovery and employee recovery.
9. What are some service recovery strategies? What is the sequence of a service recovery process (use a hospitality or tourism context to give an example)?
10. Explain why service guarantees, empowerment and service recovery strategies are complementary and how they reinforce one another.
11. Discuss the implications of service empowerment, service guarantees and service recovery on internal marketing and relationship marketing.

12. What is the service system and which steps are essential to the setting-up of an effective service system?

13. It is possible that some customers might decide to take advantage of and abuse a service guarantee policy? Think of an example and the possible ways for service companies to prevent from this happening.

Suggested Readings

This is a list of suggested further reading on topics covered in this chapter. For a separate list of full reference citations quoted in the chapter, see 'References', Chapter 7, page 331.

Hogan, J., Lemon, K., and Barak, L. (2003). What is the true value of a lost customer? *Journal of Service Research,* 5(3), 196–209.

Kandampully, J. (2001). Service guarantee: An organization's blueprint for assisting the delivery of superior service. In Kandampully, J., Mok, C., and Sparks, B. (eds), *Service Quality Management in Hospitality Tourism and Leisure.* Binghampton, NY: Haworth Press, p. 239–253.

Kim, T., Yoo, J. J-E., and Lee, G. (2012). Post-recovery customer relationships and customer partnerships in a restaurant setting. *International Journal of Contemporary Hospitality Management,* 24(3), 381–401.

Levy, S. E., Duan, W., and Boo, S. (2013). An analysis of one-star online reviews and responses in the Washington, D.C., lodging market. *Cornell Hospitality Quarterly,* 54(1), 49–63.

Lewis, B. R., and McCann, P. (2004). Service failure and recovery: Evidence from the hotel industry. *International Journal of Contemporary Hospitality Management,* 16(1); 6–17.

Namkung, Y. and Jang, S. (2010). Service failures in restaurants: Which stage of service failure is most critical? *Cornell Hospitality Quarterly,* 51(3), 323–343.

Susskind, A., and Viccari, A. (2011). A look at the relationship between service failures, guest satisfaction, and repeat-patronage intentions of casual dining guests. *Cornell Hospitality Quarterly,* 52(4), 438–444.

Wirtz, J., Kum, D., and Lee, K. S. (2000). Should a firm with a reputation for outstanding service quality offer a service guarantee? *Journal of Services Marketing,* 14(6), 502–512.

Wirtz, J. and Kum, D. (2001). Designing service guarantees—is full satisfaction the best you can guarantee? *Journal of Services Marketing,* 15(4), 282–299.

Zoghbi-Manrique-de-Lara, P., Suárez-Acosta, M. A., and Aguiar-Quintana, T. (2014). Hotel guests' responses to service recovery: How loyalty influences guest behavior. *Cornell Hospitality Quarterly,* 55(2), 152–164.

CHAPTER 8

Managing and Engaging Employees in Service Organizations

Study Objectives

Having completed this chapter, readers should be able to:

1. Understand the role of 'people' in the service organization;
2. Be able to recognize the importance of human resource management and practices associated with it;
3. Understand the impact of internal service quality on external service quality and firms' key indicators; and
4. Be familiar with the benefits from having committed and engaged people in the company.

Outline

- ▶ Introduction
- ▶ Setting the benchmark
- ▶ Organizational psychology
- ▶ What is human resource management?
- ▶ HRM in a service context
- ▶ Why is HRM important?
  - ▶ Emotional labor
  - ▶ The internal work environment
    - ▪ Organizational culture and service culture
    - ▪ Organizational climate and service climate

- ▶ Effective HRM practices
  - ▶ Empowerment
    - Theory X and Theory Y
    - Empowerment in place/practice
- ▶ Benefits of effective HRM practices
  - ▶ Employee engagement
  - ▶ Organizational commitment
- ▶ Links between people, customers and firm performance
  - ▶ Service-profit chain
  - ▶ Internal service quality
- ▶ Summary
- ▶ Review Questions
- ▶ Suggested Readings

Key Words

Affective commitment	Organizational climate
Continuance commitment	Organizational commitment
Emotional dissonance	Organizational culture
Emotional labor	Organizational psychology
Employee attitude	People focus
Employee engagement	People management
Empowerment	Schein's model
Equation for empowerment	Service climate
Human resource management	Service culture
Human resource practices	Service-profit chain
Internal service quality	Theory X
Internal work environment	Theory Y
Normative commitment	

Introduction

Successful businesses require many interrelated parts working harmoniously to achieve business goals. Most businesses require investment in land, property, equipment, furnishings, fixtures and the like. But in service businesses, there is another important 'asset'—people! In many ways, people and people management practices are metaphorically what internal health means to humans—healthier blood and a healthy body allows a person to be in the best position to face the 'external' world. This is so important because the single most significant definer of the hospitality industry is the inherent focus on people-to-people transactions and the myriad of challenges associated with managing individuals (Grönroos, 2000; Lovelock and Wirtz, 2010; Schneider and White, 2004). People and their individual interactions are paramount to the provision of quality service outcomes (Bitner, Booms, and Mohr, 1994; Mattila and Enz, 2002). Because of the labor-intensive character of the industry, and the involvement of personal service in delivering the hospitality product, the hospitality industry is known as a 'people industry' requiring 'people skills' from its workers. In fact, hospitality workers are expected to be hospitable, exhibit positive attitudes toward the customer and work cohesively as a team.

It should be apparent now that people and service are inextricably linked. Employees in a service firm frequently represent the 'front-line' (see Chapter 5) in the relationship between the firm and the customer—and in many cases, the service production and consumption occurs simultaneously between the provider and customer, making the role of the employee, and therefore their attitude and suitability to the job, that much more important (see Chapter 2). Indeed, unlike a manufacturing organization, in service organizations, there are "flimsy and permeable" (Schneider and Bowen, 1993, p. 40) boundaries between the firm and their customers. This creates a circumstance where there is psychological and physical closeness between the firm and the customer—and one that brings on a range of challenges!

There are many analogies one can use to emphasize the importance of the front-line worker in service organizations. For example, in a battlefield, the difference between victory and defeat can often be attributable to the quality of the troops, how well they are trained, how motivated they are and how committed they are to the outcome. Although far less violent (hopefully), it is the people in a service organization (the right ones selected, and then trained, motivated, retained), combined with a sound strategy, standards, the right equipment and good leaders, which create a winning organization!

One of the challenges inherent in managing the tourism and hospitality workforce is that employment in these sectors is often characterized by absenteeism, high turnover of staff, low commitment levels, low job satisfaction and high job stress, thereby making the management of these organizations particularly challenging. Hospitality work is regarded as a low-status occupation, often a means to an end for some, or as an occupation that employs people with minimal education or training. Indeed, many students do not see hospitality as a career path, but rather convenient work they can undertake while they are studying towards their 'real job'. Long and irregular working hours, split shifts, seasonality, low wages, low industry image, the lack of career paths, and high 'casualization' (e.g., part-time workers) of the workforce are additional characteristics of this industry. It is ironic that these employees, working under the conditions referred to above, are expected to deliver high quality service encounters and excellent service to customers and colleagues.

Despite the challenges—it can be done! Great service organizations position people and people management processes central in their strategies and actions. In doing so, employees are likely to respond positively and be more inclined to deliver excellent service. If this is achieved, it gives the organization an immutable competitive advantage.

This chapter introduces many of the important concepts that service managers need to know and practice in order to bring out the best in the workforce. Engaged, committed, cared for workers do not just get that way by accident! The world's best service organizations know that, in order to maximize the firm's employees, an investment in time, effort and resources, focused on the worker, is critical. The difference can be stark and profound. The nicest hotel property, most amazing location for a restaurant, most comfortable airplane will mean next to nothing without committed workers.

Service managers and service organizations benefit from awareness and understanding of exceptional management of human resources. Employees, and how they are managed, can often define the difference between success and failure in a service organization. The purpose of this chapter is to provide an introduction to the critical issues related to managing the human element in service organizations, with a particular focus on hospitality and tourism organizations.

Setting the benchmark

Few industries provide a more appropriate and valuable context for the study of employee attitudes than the hospitality industry. In fact, past researchers have presented many practical and empirical lessons from hospitality organizations which could be used in other organizational contexts. One of the recurring themes of excellence in hospitality practices relates to the ways in which a firm focuses on its human resource management (HRM) practices. There are almost innumerable company proclamations about the importance of employees. Examples include Southwest Airlines' employee branding (where people are proclaimed as the single greatest strength and most enduring influence on long-term competitive advantage), and Marriott's "Marriott Way", ("take care of the associates, and they'll take good care of the guests, and the guests will come back"). It is not uncommon for most hospitality companies to have an explicit statement or motto that proudly displays the importance the company places on its workers. Unfortunately, many do not practice what they preach! Many internal (financial pressures leading to a devolution of HR functions from professionals to line-level staff) and external (demographic changes including younger and older workers) pressures put strain on organizations to genuinely practice what they preach in terms of people-focused HR practices (Solnet, Kralj, and Baum, 2014). Nonetheless, it is vital!

The role of managers in terms of managing people in a service organization is a much-debated topic both within practice and in academic literature. Given the inherent nature of service and the role of people within the service organizations, the traditional idea

---

Starbucks Coffee

*Starbucks claims that their focus is **people**, not the coffee, and that's what makes them successful.*

Figure 8.1
Starbucks is an example of the importance of people

of management is seldom proven sufficient in exemplar organizations. Great service managers are those who inspire, motivate, guide and support everyone around them. They gain the trust and confidence from everyone and know how to entice people to perform at their best. Unfortunately they are few and far between and are seldom created through training programs. Hence, we believe that it is not easy to emulate the success of a service organization by competing firms. It is the people and value-based culture they share and hold (this is discussed further later in this chapter) that lifts the organization to a higher level and that renders the all-important difference both inside the firm and in the marketplace. You will gain a better understanding of this by reviewing some of the exemplar cases we have included in Chapter 10.

Organizational psychology

Organizational psychology, closely connected to HRM, is the field of study and practice that investigates and seeks understanding about the impact that individuals, groups and structures have on behavior in the workplace (Robbins and Judge, 2009), and is very relevant and appropriate to the study of service management. The principal focus of organizational psychology is on how to improve organizational outcomes by way understanding the psychology of the workforce. This is achieved via a series of constructs and measures, such as motivation, absenteeism, organizational commitment, employee citizenship behavior, job satisfaction, teamwork and many others. Another instructive definition of organizational psychology dates back over 40 years—the application or extension of psychological facts and principles to the problems concerning human beings operating within the context of business and industry.

Organizational psychology has its roots in psychology—the study of the mind and human behavior. It transforms psychology at the *individual* level to the group and employee level in the study of workplace. Organizational psychologists are trained in human mental processes and the observation and interpretation of human behavior *in a workplace context*. They use these skills to solve problems related to work life quality, and study productivity, management, employee working styles, morale and other workplace-related issues by applying the principles of psychology to the workplace. A range of constructs have been developed over the years which help measure and then influence the right workplace attitudes and work environment, conducive to favorable organizational outcomes, which will be further discussed in this chapter.

What is human resource management (HRM)?

Human resource management—or 'HRM'—is concerned with the design of formal systems and continual proactive measures to ensure the effective and efficient use of a firm's people to accomplish organizational goals. In many organizations, finding ways to make efficient use of people is done haphazardly or not at all. However, great service organizations—and particularly those in the service-intensive hospitality industry—pay very close attention to their human 'assets', leaving little to chance.

© Roland Ijdema/Shutterstock.com

HRM is a term that is most often used to represent those parts of an organization's activities that are concerned with the sourcing, maintaining, management and development of its employees (Wall and Wood, 2005), and is often viewed as a 'bundle' of activities, designed to be of maximum value to enhance organizational performance (Barney, 2002).

HRM has often in the past been viewed as an administration function, tasked with recruitment, interviewing, performance reviews, managing employee personnel records and the like. However, today, a more strategic approach to HRM has been applied, in which employees are seen as valuable assets in the firm, to be 'invited in' and 'developed' rather than hired and trained. The mindset change has been viewing the workforce as an appreciable asset requiring investment and ongoing attention, rather than just as costs to be controlled. Most successful firms compete in the market to attract talented employees—the same way they compete to attract customers (see Chapter 6). In many high-performing hospitality firms today, the HRM function is now seen as part of the 'executive team'. The senior HR manager or executive is often involved in major decisions, thus ensuring that the topics reviewed in this chapter and drawn from international best practice are considered and applied in all management decision making. Many companies have changed the title of the HR manager to reflect this more strategic and important role of managing people in the organization. For example, Chief Talent Officer, Talent Director or People and Culture Manager.

This chapter does not attempt to present a comprehensive or technical review of the 'principles' of HRM, but rather a review of some of the critical subjects, concepts and measures known to be vital to successful service organizations. Much of the focus of this chapter has to do with workplace conditions, policies and practices which are conducive to motivating workers to be service-oriented. In fact, researchers across a number of disciplines, including organizational behavior, applied psychology, HRM and social psychology, for many years have been interested in gaining a better understanding of workplace conditions, polices and practices which impact employee attitudes and how employee attitudes link to important organizational outcomes.

HRM responsibilities can be seen to fit somewhere on a continuum from strategic to operational and administrative. In practice, those with HR 'manager' in their title tend to be tasked with broader strategic issues associated with an organization's employees, including planning for long-term staffing requirements linked to company growth forecasts, developing information systems to improve efficiencies across the organization, benchmarking practices against competitors, industrial bargaining, talent identification and management, succession planning and communicating with senior management to ensure that important decisions always take proper account of HR considerations. By contrast, the more operational tasks of the HR function include activities such as hiring, terminations, performance reviews, payroll and related and the like. In many organizations, line managers have found themselves playing the role of 'accidental' HR managers, as more and more of the core HR activities are being decentralized and handed down (Kulik, 2004).

© mypokcik/Shutterstock.com

HRM in a service context

Although much of the literature in the area of HRM does not delineate service organization HRM from non-service HRM, there are some important differences when managing service employees. Bowen and Ford (2002) offer the following five reasons for these differences (many of which are covered in various sections of this book):

1. **Coproduction.** Because many service employee tasks include customer interactions, the employees must not only produce the service, but also engage with it and involve customers into the process of service delivery through establishing trustworthy rapport and relationships with customers. This allows the employee to better understand the customers' wants and needs and to turn just satisfied customers into loyal ambassadors.

2. **Hiring for attitude.** The second difference is that employee selection and recruitment must focus on customer-relationship skills. While manufacturing organizations hire for technical skills and qualifications, service organizations hire for attitude first and can train for skills later. Therefore, service organizations must place more emphasis on personality, energy and attitude than on education, training and experience.

3. **Managing employee actions.** It is very difficult to manage every action an employee makes in a service organization. Rather, organizational norms and values are needed to guide behavior (see discussion later in this chapter on organizational

culture). A number of strategies are available to assist with managing the service employee, including the creation of a service climate and a service culture, which engenders an organizational-wide 'passion for service'.

4. **Emotional labor.** The next difference relates to emotional labor (see below)—the management of emotions to create observable facial and body displays to produce the intended impressions in the mind of others. The required emotions for different service positions can vary. For example, a fast food cashier would have a different requirement from a funeral director or a loan manager. The point is that service employees have to exert labor beyond just physical and mental labor.

5. **Part-time marketers.** As discussed in Chapter 2, service employees are expected to perform a marketing function. Because they coproduce the service experience, service employees are often expected to explain details about new products and services, and to attempt to get customers enthusiastic about the company and its products.

Why is HRM important?

Emotional labor

Service employees perform many different types of tasks, including *physical* tasks, such as carrying trays, cleaning rooms, polishing cutlery and carrying luggage, as well as *mental* tasks, such as problem solving, remembering names and adhering to service standards and expectations. But there is another important task that service employees perform—known as *emotional labor*. This is when an employee is required to demonstrate an emotion—such as care, enjoyment, concern and happiness. They are required to do so because, as we learned earlier (Chapter 3), customer perceptions of service quality rely on a number of important factors, including empathy (showing that you genuinely seem to care).

The term 'emotional labor' was coined by Hochschild (1983) and describes the work service employees perform that goes beyond physical or mental duties. Service employees, particularly those in a hospitality business where 'care' and 'genuine hospitality' are vital, must frequently present these demonstrative behaviors, for example, making eye contact, delivering smiles and showing genuine concern for guests' needs.

Despite its importance to hotel operations, emotional labor typically is difficult to manage, drawing as it does on front-line employees' feelings. Part of the challenge of emotional labor is

© Tashatuvango/Shutterstock.com

that employees must often conceal their real emotions and they must continue to 'act' in a positive and welcoming way regardless of how the guest might be interacting with them.

Emotional dissonance occurs when an employee is asked to display a set of emotions that conflict with their current real feeling. For example, a worker coming to work after a bad day at school or university (perhaps did not do well on an exam) or after a disagreement with a boyfriend or girlfriend has to then 'switch over' and become the warm, gracious, service-oriented host, with a genuine smile. This is not easy! Yet it is a requirement for service workers to come to work with their 'game faces' on.

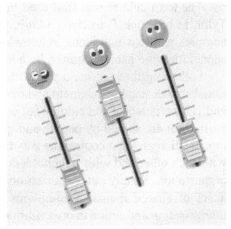

© tovovan/Shutterstock.com

The internal work environment

Organizational culture and service culture

Turning to key ideas about understanding the internal organizational environment, the study of climate and culture seeks to better understand how individuals behave, or are likely to behave, in an organization or business setting.

Every organization, whether intended or not, has a culture of some kind. Culture, from an organizational point of view, is often defined as the values and norms embedded into an organization. An organizational culture, particularly in a service business, has the ability to fill the gaps between:

1. what the organization can anticipate and train its people to deal with; and
2. the opportunities and problems that arise in daily encounters with customers (Ford and Heaton, 2001).

© Dusit/Shutterstock.com

Since managers cannot supervise every interaction which takes place between employees and customers, it is important for service organizations to develop a predominating norm of behavior which is customer-centric and focused on service quality. Such an approach minimizes the gaps which unforeseen circumstances might cause in service delivery and also works to motivate unsupervised employees.

The term culture was first used in a societal context by an anthropologist, Edward B. Tylor, in his book *Primitive Culture*, published in 1871. Tylor suggested that *culture* is a complex whole which includes knowledge, belief, art, law, morals, customs and any other capabilities and habits acquired by a human as a member of society.

Following these ideas, *organizational culture* was developed in the field of organizational studies and management and describes the psychology, attitudes, experiences, beliefs and values (personal and cultural) of an organization, or the specific collection of values and norms that are shared by people and groups in an organization and that control the way they interact with each other and with stakeholders outside the organization. Simply put, organizational culture is a set of shared mental assumptions that guide interpretation and action in organizations by defining appropriate behavior for various situations.

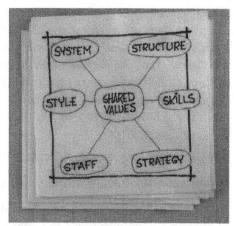

© marekuliasz/Shutterstock.com

Every organization has a culture—whether they like it or not! Successful businesses all have strong cultures, which give signals to employees about what is important to that organization. Following this logic, service organizations need to create and foster a strong *service culture* with a particular focus on customer satisfaction and outstanding service.

Edgar Schein (1990), one of the preeminent experts on organizational culture suggests that there are three basic levels of organizational culture. These levels refer to the degree to which culture is 'visible'.

1. **Artifacts and behaviors** are attributes that can be seen, felt and heard. This refers to the buildings, offices, furnishings, visible awards and recognition, the way that members dress and the like.

2. **Espoused values** are the professed culture of an organization's members. This includes company slogans, mission statements and other operational creeds that are often expressed. For example, mythical stories about the way a past employee or owner had done something extraordinary for a customer can become part of the company folklore. The Olive Garden Restaurant used to tell the story of a large customer who was uncomfortable in the regular chairs. So the CEO arranged for each restaurant to have a "Chair for Larry"—a slightly larger chair for any guest who might look too large to be comfortable in a regular-sized chair. The point here is not about large guests—but about the efforts the company is willing to go to in order to look after guests' needs.

3. **Shared assumptions** are at the deepest level and represent those attitudes and beliefs which are embedded, often tacit, unconscious assumptions. These are the

elements of culture that are unseen and not cognitively identified; the 'unspoken rules' that exist without the conscious knowledge of the membership or the *essence* of the organization. In service culture, the shared assumptions might include taking care of another human being or being helpful and generous and respectful to others.

The diagram below is a visual representation of organizational culture as described by Schein (1990) above. The size of each circle is representative of the level of managerial control over each element. In other words, service managers can easily affect the physical elements of a service environment and can, to some extent, influence the stories of success that circulate, whereas managers have limited direct access to the unconscious knowledge of the organization's employees.

A strong culture is said to exist where staff respond to stimuli because of their clear and non-ambiguous alignment to organizational values. Strong cultures help firms operate like well-oiled machines that may require only minor tweaking of existing procedures here and there. Conversely, in a weak culture there is little alignment with organizational values, and control must be exercised through extensive procedures and bureaucracy. A strong culture may be especially beneficial to firms operating in the service sector since members of these organizations are responsible for delivering the 'product' and often must be trusted to do the right thing even unsupervised.

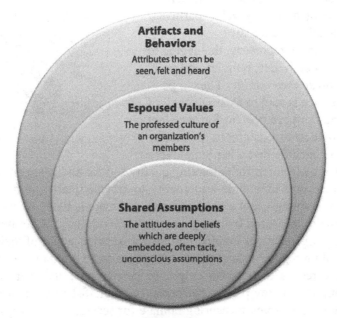

Figure 8.2
Levels of organizational culture
Source: Adapted from Schein 1990

There are many benefits from developing a strong culture, including:

► high employee motivation, engagement and loyalty;
► increased team cohesiveness among the company's various departments and divisions; and
► shaping employee behavior at work, enabling the organization to be more efficient.

Organizational climate and service climate

Organizational climate, similar to culture, is defined as *employee perceptions* of the practices and procedures in the organization (Denison, 1996). It differs from culture in that it represents an assessment of how employees perceive various aspects of an organization, whereas culture represents the values and norms, and often the aspirations, of management. Climate represents how well these aspirations are actually perceived by employees and those who come into contact with an organization. These aspirations are often communicated through artifacts, stories and myths.

An assessment of climate is normally obtained by measuring respondent perceptions of what goes on around them, in terms of organizational events, policies, practices, expectations and so on. Tagiuri (1968) defined climate as a relatively enduring quality of the total environment that is experienced by the participants in the organization, influences their behavior and can be described in terms of how they value particular sets of environmental characteristics.

A climate *for service* represents the degree to which all of a firm's activities, policies and practices are focused on *service quality*. Thus, a positive climate for service is said to exist when all of the aggregate conditions are present for excellent service to be provided to customers. Schneider and White (2004) conclude that when employees perceive that they are rewarded for delivering quality service and when employees perceive that management devotes their time and energy to service quality, and when employees receive appropriate training—that a positive service climate is likely to exist.

© Olivier Le Moal/Shutterstock.com

Climate is usually measured by using a survey methodology. Many best-practice tourism and hospitality organizations employ climate measures as a part of their organizational learning process. With regular measures of an organizational climate, progressive-thinking companies use the results to improve employee perceptions, and then utilize improved employee perceptions as a key part of performance. Table 8.1 presents a list of questions that would be asked in a survey measuring climate for service. It is always instructive and

Table 8.1
Service Climate Questions
(Global Service Climate from Schneider, White and Paul, 1998)

1. Rate the job knowledge and skills of employees in your business to deliver superior quality service?

2. Rate efforts to measure and track the quality of service in your business?

3. Rate the recognition and rewards employees receive for the delivery of superior service?

4. Rate the overall quality of service provided by your business?

5. Rate the leadership shown by management in your business in supporting the service quality effort?

6. Rate the effectiveness of our communications efforts to both employees and customers?

7. Rate the tools, technology and other resources provided to employees to support the delivery of superior quality service?

useful for service managers to ask these questions of their own organizations and how their own employees might answer them.

Organizational climate and organizational culture can be seen as a reflection of the HRM practices of management. From this perspective, in order to ensure high service quality and customer loyalty, service businesses need to recognize the necessity of nurturing service culture and service climate. The next section presents a vitally important strategy and managerial philosophy which encourages employees to be armed with the necessary information to make customer-focused decisions and not have to ask permission to do so! We also remind readers that Chapter 7 introduced the important interrelationship among service guarantees, service failure and service recovery—and the vital importance of empowered employees to make this management approach successful. The next section covers empowerment in more detail.

Effective HRM practices

Empowerment

Chapter 7 presented the need for a coordinated approach, blending service guarantees and service recovery into a cohesive approach in the management of service organizations. In that chapter, we advocated the importance of a service workforce that is empowered to read situations and act as necessary in order to meet or exceed customer expectations and also to address service failures on the spot so that an appropriate service recovery can commence as soon as possible. Empowerment—or an empowered workforce—is vital and a frequently found phenomenon in the world's great service organizations.

In the past, service organizations have tended to neglect a huge potential resource—the individual abilities of the employees. The rigid policies, structures and systems in many organizations have often presented barriers to the individual talent and imagination of those workers in front-line service situations. In other words, service organizations have been unable to reap the full potential of their human resources.

Traditional structures and work arrangements of many hospitality and tourism organizations often do the opposite to creating effectively empowered employees. Rather, they can engender a feeling of 'disempowerment' (Lashley, 1996). Successful service organizations that wish to instill a culture of empowerment must evolve systems and processes that do not restrict employees. For example, at some hotels, employees are encouraged to 'break the rules' of their traditional job description if those rules inhibit the likelihood of a satisfied customer.

The guiding philosophy of empowerment is non-bureaucratic and employee-oriented. Empowerment fosters an environment of commitment and ownership; an environment within which employees utilize information that they glean from their daily interactions with customers to improve service and contribute positively to the organization and to the customer's level of satisfaction. Ritz-Carlton, for example, uses the phrase "antennas up"— encouraging employees to listen and pay close attention to customer needs so that they can be met often before the customer has to ask. Empowered employees also feel more involved and have a sense of control, which can contribute not only to customer satisfaction but also to their own job satisfaction.

Employees should consistently be treated as equals, and should receive the same sort of respect as they are expected to offer to their customers. There is a clear and direct correlation between managers' relationships with their employees and the service behavior of those employees towards customers (Schneider, 1980). Such positive management-employee relationships can take various forms. For example, employees and managers at Marriott work together in identifying the specific needs of customers, and in seeking ways to satisfy those needs (Hubrecht and Teare, 1993).

Superior service does not result from employees undertaking systemized tasks according to set procedures with management adopting a training role. Rather, excellence in service comes from employees showing initiative in a trusting work environment in which management assumes a supporting role. Management must therefore ensure that it establishes appropriate strategies and systems whereby employees will be able to exercise trust.

An empowerment strategy provides benefits to management, employers and customers (see Table 8.2).

Table 8.2
Potential Benefits of Empowerment

Category	Benefits
Management	—creates good relationships with employees and customers
	—increased number of loyal customers
	—reduction in costs and employee turnover; increased productivity
	—increased market share, sales and profitability
	—opportunities for growth
	—ultimately results in a competitive advantage
Employees	—increased self-esteem and confidence, when given the authority to decide
	—increased job satisfaction in an informal and friendly environment
	—sense of ownership
	—increased motivation
	—personal autonomy in daily tasks
	—prevention of burnout
	—receive management support, as opposed to management control
	—'feel-good factor' of resolving customers' problems
Customers	—needs readily satisfied
	—feel valued and important when personal attention is given
	—receive more than what is expected
	—a good relationship with the organization
	—approachable employees
	—alleviation of stress and frustration in the long term
	—reduce time delay

The goal of empowerment is the 'best of all business worlds'—empowered employees confidently and capably addressing unique problems and opportunities as they occur. The concept of empowerment is best suited to organizations that embrace a creative philosophy that facilitates such best of all worlds. Such a firm is committed to:

▶ differentiating, customizing and personalizing service, thereby creating more value for customers;
▶ forming long-term relationships with customers (led by the face-to-face contact with service staff);
▶ being able to serve the complex, unpredictable and non-routine needs of customers;
▶ encouraging employees to make spontaneous decisions to assist customers; and
▶ attracting and retaining employees who have high aspirations, strong interpersonal skills and the ability to be self-motivated and self-managed.

Figure 8.3
How not to empower

If an organization can utilize its service personnel creatively to improve its service offerings, it has a critical competitive advantage. However, an empowerment strategy alone might not be sufficient to provide an organization with a competitive advantage. There are many internal organizational philosophies and considerations in relation to the 'state of mind' of the employees which great service organizations do well every day.

Theory X and Theory Y

In understanding empowerment and its effective implementation into an organization, it is helpful to have a basic understanding about management theory. One theory, known as Theory X and Y (developed in the 1960s), attempts to explain the way employers view employees.

In Theory X, management assumes employees are generally lazy and will avoid work if they can and that they inherently dislike work. As a result of this, management believes that workers need to be closely supervised and comprehensive systems of controls developed. Employees will show little ambition without very specific motivations and incentives. Managers who believe in this approach tend to create an atmosphere of mistrust and negativity. These managers feel the sole purpose of the employee's interest in the job is money and will rarely trust employees to act and behave appropriately without significant supervision.

On the other hand is Theory Y, a more positive view in which managers assume the best rather than the worst in workers. In this theory, management assumes employees may be ambitious and self-motivated and generally will work well. They possess the ability for problem solving, but their talents are often underused. A Theory Y manager believes that, given the right conditions, most people will want to do well at work and believe that the satisfaction of doing a good job is a strong motivation. Theory Y believes that employee development is a crucial aspect of any organization and will lead to even greater positive behavior from employees.

The reality is that most managers and leaders would fall somewhere in between these two extremes. But it is important to remember that to empower employees to act without the need to ask managers requires a significant change in philosophy for many leaders and managers who are brought up to generally distrust employees.

Empowerment in place/practice

Empowerment sounds sensible and logical, but creating a truly empowered workforce is far from simple! Employees simply do not suddenly feel or become empowered because a manager tells them they are or because the company issues a statement pronouncing that empowerment is now a policy (Bowen and Lawler III, 1995)! Indeed, it takes structures, practices, policies and consistency in order to send the message across the organization that employees are empowered to deal effectively with customers.

Empowerment is vital for hospitality businesses because they:

- ► have to differentiate, customize and personalize service
- ► aim to maintain long-term relationships with customers
- ► create value to their customers through personal service
- ► serve customers' complex, unpredictable and non-routine needs
- ► require employees to make spontaneous decisions to assist customers
- ► may have employees with high growth and social needs
- ► require employees to have strong interpersonal skills
- ► require employees to be self-motivated and self-managed

There are two significant benefits to empowered employees. First, problems can be handled on the spot because empowered employees can fix mistakes quickly. Second, empowered employees, armed with knowledge about the importance of highly satisfied customers, can be perfectly positioned to delight customers by exceeding their expectations. Ritz-Carlton has one of the most talked-about employee empowerment policies, in that every employee has $2,000 a day per guest to delight or make it right. The message is clear: "We trust our employees!" Of course, such a policy requires training and monitoring, but over the years, Ritz-Carton has been able to continue this policy, suggesting that it is used

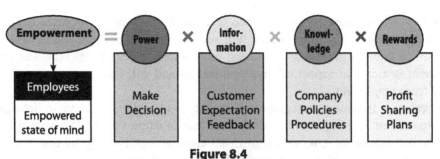

Figure 8.4
Composition of effective empowerment
(Adopted from Bowen and Lawler 1995)

wisely and effectively by its employees. In fact, Ritz-Carlton may indeed receive more benefits from this publicity than the actual implementation of it!

A useful equation for empowerment is illustrated in Figure 8.4. The equation states that empowerment equals power × information × knowledge × rewards. In this equation, *power* means that employees have the power to act and to do whatever it takes to please a customer. *Information* refers to the need for companies to disseminate information and share customer expectations and feedback across all employees. *Knowledge* refers to employees needing to know about the company goals and objectives and how their role fits into these. Finally, *rewards* must be given to employees to share in the company's successes and to reward those actions and behaviors which demonstrate empowerment activities. It is important to note the multiplication sign rather than a plus sign, indicating that if any of the elements are zero, empowerment cannot occur effectively (Bowen and Lawler III, 1995). We also caution those employing an empowerment approach that the 'knowledge' component in Figure 8.4 requires a firm to make it explicitly clear to employees (a) what the expectations are in terms of the firm's customer-service standards and (b) some rules or boundary conditions which must be followed in the carrying out of empowered acts. For example, a waitperson would know that there is a limit to the amount of food and beverage he/she can give away to a customer without permission—but that beyond that certain limit he/she must receive permission from a supervisor.

Benefits of effective HRM practices

Employee engagement

Employee engagement is currently a 'hot' topic for both practitioners and academics alike. Many hotel companies, for example, use iterations of engagement to measure internal service, and a range of empirical studies have found a positive link between employee engagement and key organizational outcomes such as customer satisfaction and loyalty, reduced employee turnover, return on assets and profitability (Schneider et al., 2009). Kahn (1990) is regarded as the scholar who first applied the concept of engagement at work via a qualitative study using grounded theory. His initial conceptualization was that the more employees feel they are able to express their preferred selves at work, the more they will invest in their work role and their organization. Since then, various scholars have built on Kahn's thesis and have suggested various ways to conceptualize and understand employee (or 'work') engagement.

Although Kahn is credited with the conceptual development of the engagement construct, he did not fully develop an operational definition which could lead to an effective and appropriate measure of engagement (Kim, Shin, and Swanger, 2009). Maslach and Leiter (1997) defined engagement in the context of job burnout, suggesting that engagement and burnout are situated at the opposite end of a continuum. Their view is that the state of engagement occurs when employees score low on exhaustion and cynicism, and high in professional efficacy. This continuum approach was countered by Bakker and Schaufeli (2008) who assert that engagement is an independent state of mind, thereby requiring a different operational definition and measure.

The claims about employee engagement being an important driver of organizational outcomes are supported by research. For example, engaged workers have been shown to be closely linked to a range of financial indices, including return on assets, profitability and shareholder value (Macey, et al., 2009). Engagement has been linked to economic prosperity, with the US Congress being advised to find ways to encourage individuals to invest more psychic energy in work as being a critical lever to improve productivity . . . ." (Erickson, 2005).

One of the challenges facing engagement researchers is the variation in definitions and levels of analysis. Simpson (2009) argues that over the past 15 years, four lines of related research have developed in a sequential manner, starting with personal engagement (when a person is inclined to be physically involved, cognitively vigilant and emotionally connected to work), burnout (the opposite of engagement—defined as exhaustion, cynicism and inefficacy), work engagement (a positive, fulfilling work-related state of mind) and employee engagement (an individual's involvement, satisfaction and enthusiasm for work). Each of these four constructs, although related, are defined and measured differently.

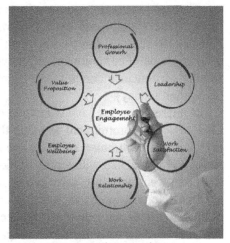

© arka38/Shutterstock.com

It is important to emphasize the distinction between the constructs of engagement and job satisfaction. A multitude of definitions of employee engagement exist on the websites of global HR firms, although many HR consultants and practitioners appear to employ measures of engagement that would be better described as measures of overall job satisfaction (Schneider et al., 2009). While job satisfaction is related to *what a company is doing for its employees* and involves employees' evaluations of such drivers as job security, benefits and opportunities for advancement, engagement is concerned with *the full utilization of an employee's skills and abilities* and a link between individual and organizational objectives (Schneider et al., 2009). In this light, an employee can be satisfied with their job, in that it pays well enough, is stable and offers future opportunities, yet still not be engaged in their work as the employee feels under-utilized and personally misaligned with organizational goals and values.

Further efforts have recently been made to clarify differences between engagement and other related measures. For example, organizational commitment has been differentiated from engagement in that commitment is purportedly an *attitude*; whereas engagement represents the degree to which an individual is *attentive and absorbed* in the performance of their roles. Differences between other related concepts such as job involvement have also been argued (May, Gilson, and Harter, 2004; Saks, 2006).

A number of studies have also shown that levels of employee engagement can predict turnover intentions, employee productivity, financial performance and customer satisfaction and as such engagement represents an important, new and emerging research area which has been surprisingly neglected until very recently.

Organizational commitment

Another aspiration for service managers—and a condition which leads to important service behaviors—is to build organizational commitment. *Organizational commitment* is an individual's psychological attachment to their employer (rather than to the job itself, for example). Organizational commitment is known to predict many other important work variables such as retention, citizenship behaviors and engagement.

There are many definitions of organizational commitment and numerous ways to measure it. One widely used conceptualization of organizational commitment is Meyer and Allen's (1991; 1990) three-component model (TCM), reflecting three psychological states or dimensions of commitment: affective commitment (emotional attachment to the organization), continuance commitment (perceived cost of leaving) and normative commitment (obligation to stay).

Numerous studies have examined commitment using these three dimensions and identified affective commitment as being the dimension most positively associated with favorable employee attitudes such as attendance, performance and citizenship behavior and negatively associated with stress, work-family conflict and quit intentions.

Employees with high affective commitment are more likely to engage in positive organizational actions—such as focusing on service excellence—because of their higher levels of shared values with their workplace. Affective commitment leads individuals to work harder toward the attainment of an organizational goal and to engage in behaviors that may not be explicitly specified to their job but which are beneficial to the organization. Thus, another interesting area is the links between people, customers and firm performance, which is discussed in the next section.

Links between people, customers and firm performance

Beyond the common sense behind sound people management practices in service organizations, there is a strong conceptual argument and empirical evidence that supports proactive and positive people management practices. The next section introduces a number of conceptual frameworks which help explain the important connection between creating positive employee attitudes and important organizational outcomes such as customer satisfaction, customer loyalty, increased revenues and profit.

Service-profit chain

The service-profit chain is a frequently cited conceptual framework developed in the mid 1990s. It was developed as the result of many years of research on and observation of the practices of successful service organizations. The authors (Heskett, Sasser, and Schlesinger, 1997) found that, in many successful service organizations, a chain of related organizational occurrences existed, effectively linking the internal functioning of an organization ('internal' service and the way employees feel) to employee loyalty and productivity, service value, customer satisfaction and finally to revenue growth and profitability (Heskett, Sasser, and Schlesinger, 1997).

The service-profit chain (Figure 8.5) proposes the following vital connections in a successful service organization:

1. Profitability and revenue growth is caused primarily by customer loyalty.
2. Customer loyalty comes from consistently satisfied customers.
3. Satisfied customers are those who perceive value in purchasing from a firm.
4. Value is created by satisfied, committed and productive employees.
5. Satisfied and productive employees are created by sound internal organizational practices (internal service quality).

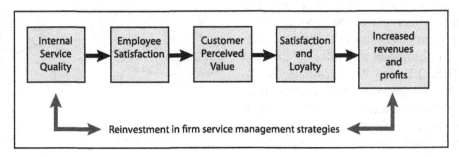

Figure 8.5
The service-profit chain
(adapted from Heskett et al. 1997)

So the service-profit chain (see Figure 8.5) proposes that successful service firms place predominant effort inside the organization—creating the right workplace conditions to engender caring, committed and engaged workers—rather than focusing directly on revenues and profits. This is not to say that service firms should not focus on the rest of the chain. Rather, that successful service firms realize that many of the aspects of this chain are caused by a chain reaction, all starting with the way they manage the firm's human resources.

More recently, Heskett and Sasser (2010) note the progression from the original premise of the service-profit chain on employee and customer satisfaction to customer and employee commitment, engagement and even 'ownership' as more effective predictors of profitability and organizational success. Despite including these additional factors, these authors contend that management interventions aimed at profit and revenue growth still must begin internally with actions aimed at creating the most effective workplace conditions for service employees.

Internal service quality

The service-profit chain advocates firm attention to internal service quality. Internal service quality is seen as the 'spark' that sets off a chain reaction, eventually creating increased revenue and profitability. Internal service quality is viewed as a multi-disciplinary concept drawing from marketing, operations, HRM and management (Berry, Parasuraman, and Zeithaml, 1994; Berry, Zeithaml, and Parasuraman, 1990; Zeithaml, Bitner, and Gremler, 2009) with a shared belief that in organizations where service quality is important, meeting the needs of those who service the customers (internal customers) is vital (see a more detailed discussion in Chapter 6). Hallowell, Schlesigner and Zornitzky's (1996) synopsis suggests that internal service quality consists of a combination of (depending on context and service type) tools, policies and procedures, teamwork, management support, goal alignment, training, communication and rewards and recognition. Another aspect of perceived internal service is the way in which a firm cares for the well-being of its staff. Employees who feel that their employer cares for them tend to go the extra mile. *Fortune Magazine* offers one of the more accepted lists of 'great places to work' in their "Hundred Best Companies to Work For" list each year (Great Place to Work Institute, 2014). From that list you can study various practices which companies use to attract, retain and motivate employees. The box on the following page provides one example of such a practice.

"What if, and I know this sounds kooky, we communicated with the employees."

© Cartoonresource/Shutterstock.com

> ### Starbucks to Help Employees Pay for Higher Education
>
> Any Starbucks employee who works a minimum of 20 hours per week can receive tuition reimbursement and financial aid to pay for an online degree. This benefit will be used by Starbucks as a way to retain employees, as up to 70% of them are either presently in college or planning to go to college.
>
> *The Wall Street Journal,* 6/16/14

Summary

Due to high market competition, service organizations must seek all the available points of differentiation. People who work for an organization represent a remarkable asset and can provide a company with a unique competitive edge that cannot be 'stolen' by rivals. Due to the nature of the service industry, service delivery and overall company performance is highly dependent on people. Therefore management should be interested in investing its time and resources to ensure that employees are engaged, passionate and committed. This chapter introduced a series of interrelated issues on people in service organizations and stresses the benefits of nurturing a service culture, service climate and employee empowerment. Finally, the service-profit chain was introduced to visualize and explain the algorithm of linking people to organizational performance.

Review Questions

1. Why are people management processes critical to the service industry? Can you think of any examples of successful service companies known for taking care of their staff?

2. Explain what HRM is and its role in an organization.

3. What does the HR function include? And why do some HR managers tend to change their title to Chief Talent Officer or Talent Director?

4. What are the core five differences in HRM for service organizations which were discussed in this chapter? Briefly explain each of them.

5. What does a strong service culture mean, and how can a service company benefit from it? Try to use Schein's model with some examples in your answer.

6. What is service climate and how can it be measured?

7. Why is a culture of empowerment crucial to service companies? Discuss the potential benefits of empowerment from the manager's perspective, employee's perspective and customer's perspective.

8. Explain the equation for empowerment and why it has a multiplication sign as opposed to a plus sign.

9. Define employee engagement and explain the distinction between the constructs of engagement and job satisfaction.

10. Briefly explain what organizational commitment is and describe three dimensions of commitment.

11. Use the service-profit chain model to explain the link between people, customers and firm performance.

Suggested Readings

This is a list of suggested further reading on topics covered in this chapter. For a separate list of full reference citations quoted in the chapter, see 'References', Chapter 8, page 332.

Ahmad, R., Solnet, D., and Scott, N. (2010). Human resource practices system differentiation: A hotel industry study. *Journal of hospitality and Tourism Management*, 17, 84–94.

Bernoff, J., and Schadler, T. (2010). Empowered. *Harvard Business Review*, July–Aug, 95–101.

Bouranta, N., Chitiris, L., and Paravantis, J. (2009). The relationship between internal and external service quality. *International Journal of Contemporary Hospitality Management*, 21(3), 275–293.

Davidson, M., McPhail, R., and Barry, S. (2011). Hospitality HRM: past, present and the future. *International Journal of Contemporary Hospitality Management,* 23(4), 498–516.

Evans, N. (2005). Assessing the balanced scorecard as a management tool for hotels. *International Journal of Contemporary Hospitality Management*, 17(5), 376–390.

Ford, R. C., Wilderom, C. P. M., and Caparella, J. (2008). Strategically crafting a customer-focused culture: an inductive case study. *Journal of Strategy and Management*, 1(2), 143–167.

Garlick, R. (2010). Do happy employees really mean happy customers? Or is there more to the equation? *Cornell hospitality quarterly*, 51(3), 304–307.

Gazzoll, G., Hancer, M., and Park, Y. (2010). The role and effect of job satisfaction and empowerment on customers' perception of service quality: A study in the restaurant industry. *Journal of Hospitality and Tourism Research*, 34(1), 56–77.

Heskett, J. L., Sasser, W. E., and Wheeler, J. (2008). *The Ownership Quotient*. Boston: Harvard Business Press.

Johanson, M. M., and Woods, R. H. (2008). Recognizing the emotional element in service excellence. *Cornell Hospitality Quarterly*, 49(3), 310–316.

Kaplan, R. S., and Norton, D. P. (1992). The balanced scorecard—measures that drive performance. *Harvard Business Review,* 70(1), 71–79.

Michel, J. W., Kavanagh, M. J., and Tracey, J. B. (2012). Got support? The impact of supportive work practices on the perceptions, motivation, and behavior of customer-contact employees. *Cornell Hospitality Quarterly*, 54(2), 161–173.

Phillips, P., and Louvieris, P. (2005). Performance measurement systems in tourism, hospitality, and leisure small medium-sized enterprises: A balanced scorecard perspective. *Journal of Travel Research*, 44 (November), 201–211.

Pugh, S. D., Dietz, J., Wiley, J. W., and Brooks, S. M. (2002). Driving service effectiveness through employee-customer linkages. *Academy of Management Executive*, 16(4) 73–84.

Raub, S., and Robert, C. (2012). Empowerment, organizational commitment, and voice behavior in the hospitality industry: Evidence from a multinational sample. *Cornell Hospitality Quarterly,* 54(2), 136–148.

Robinson, R. N. S., Kralj, A., Solnet, D., Goh, E., and Callan, V. (2014). Thinking job embeddedness not turnover: Towards a better understanding of frontline hotel worker retention. *International journal of Hospitality Management*, 36(0), 101–109.

Solnet, D. (2006). Introducing employee social identification to customer satisfaction research: A hotel industry study. *Managing Service Quality*, 16(6), 575–594.

Solnet, D., Kralj, A., and Baum, T. (2014). 360 degrees of pressure: The changing role of the HR professional in the hospitality industry. *Journal of Hospitality & Tourism Research*, in press.

CHAPTER 9

Leadership for Service Organizations

Study Objectives

Having completed this chapter, readers should be able to:

1. Identify the main differences between leadership and management;
2. Explain the differences among various leadership styles, including transactional, transformational and servant;
3. Understand the importance of emotional intelligence for the service leader;
4. Explain the value of a leader's characteristics such as ethical, authentic and an effective team-builder; and
5. Provide some examples of excellent leadership evident in a high-performance service organization and be able to explain why.

Outline

- ▶ Introduction
- ▶ Opening story
- ▶ Defining leadership
- ▶ The leader as more than a manager
- ▶ The leader who serves with style
  - ▶ Situational leadership
  - ▶ The transactional leader
  - ▶ The transformational leader
  - ▶ The servant leader

Contributed by Greg Latemore (Leadership Consultant, Educator, Executive Coach)

- ▶ The leader as an emotionally-intelligent person
  - ▶ Defining emotional intelligence
  - ▶ The importance of emotional intelligence
  - ▶ The history of emotional intelligence
  - ▶ The latest understanding of emotional intelligence
  - ▶ The links between emotional intelligence and leadership
    - ▪ Dimensions of emotional intelligence
    - ▪ Developing EQ
    - ▪ EQ and the leader
- ▶ The leader as an authentic person
- ▶ The leader as a team builder
  - ▶ Defining teams, team development and team leadership
  - ▶ Fostering team effectiveness
  - ▶ Diagnosing a team
  - ▶ Dysfunctions in a team
  - ▶ Team dynamics
  - ▶ Leading a high-performance team
  - ▶ A team charter
- ▶ The leader as an ethical exemplar and trust builder
  - ▶ Being ethical as a leader
  - ▶ Being trustworthy as a leader
    - ▪ The nature of trust
    - ▪ Trust management
- ▶ The leader as a change agent
  - ▶ Leading change
  - ▶ Being a transformational change agent
- ▶ The leader as a strategist and culture builder
- ▶ An integrating model of service leadership
- ▶ Conclusion
- ▶ Final story
- ▶ Summary
- ▶ Review Questions
- ▶ Suggested Readings

Key Words

Authentic person	Culture-builder
Aauthenticity	Dynamic capability
Change agent	Emotional intelligence (EQ or EI)
Change management	Ethical leader

Leader	Team development
Leadership	Team dynamics
Performance equation	Team effectiveness
Servant leader	Team leadership
Service excellence equation	Team-builder
Service leadership	Transactional leader
Situational leadership	Transformational leader
Team charter	Trust management

Introduction

"If you want something to do, be a manager;
If you want to do something, be a leader."

(Anonymous)

"Leadership is a series of behaviors rather than a role for heroes."

***Margaret Wheatley** (1941–)*
American social scientist, educator and author.

So far, this book has introduced readers to the world of service *management*. Many of the principles and applications learned in the book are tasked to managers (and in some cases marketers). But what about 'leaders' and 'leadership'? This chapter enters into the world of leadership as it pertains to service organizations and in particular to hospitality and tourism organizations. The importance of leadership in successful service organizations was underscored by Heskett and his colleagues (2008) in the 'service-profit chain' (see Chapter 8), when they insisted that great leadership underlies the success of the chain. So what is leadership and what kind of leadership is important for service organizations?

The word 'leadership' itself has many meanings and involves many levels and we do not intend to provide a full and comprehensive review of the vast leadership literature. However, it is important for young up-and-coming managers in service organizations to understand the difference between management and leadership and to have an understanding of the important role that leadership plays in successful service organizations. In this book we have given many examples of *companies* as leaders. This chapter turns to leadership at the *individual* level.

The purpose here is to give future leaders insights into leadership theory and practical tools in order to be result-oriented, responsible and reflective leaders. Areas covered in this chapter include the evolution of leadership theory, leaders as change agents, transformational vs. transaction leaders, leading teams, reflective and authentic leaders, servant leadership and the importance of being an ethical leader. It is important, throughout this chapter, that students reflect on the leadership theories presented and think, "how would this apply to me as a hospitality or tourism manager?" Clearly, some kinds of leadership styles, approaches and theories lend themselves to leading service organizations more than others.

Leadership researchers are forever searching to find better ways to understand and teach effective leadership. Inevitably though, is difficult or impossible to do so by way of specific personal attributes, particular roles or specific activities. Kim and Mauborgne (1992) offer a unique way to describe leadership's 'unseen space', and found that only through lessons and stories could leadership be truly understood. They turned to ancient stories from Oriental masters who taught about wisdom with the use of parables, or simple stories, offering a fresh understanding about what leadership is. They argued that parables have the power to show, with great simplicity, how great leaders hear the unspoken, act with great humility and see the world from many vantage points.

As an example, in one such parable from the third century, a king sends his son to a temple to study under a great master in order to be ready to succeed the king to the throne. When the prince arrives at the temple, the master sends him alone to the forest. After one year, the prince was to return to the temple to describe the sound of the forest. When recounting his experience, he recalled the sounds of the birds, the leaves, the wind and other similar sounds.

Dissatisfied with this, the master sends the prince back to the forest and instructs him to listen more deeply for other sounds. Suddenly, after some frustration, he indeed began to hear other sounds—very faint unheard sounds—like flowers opening and the sun warming the ground. When the prince returned home, the king explained to him that to be a great ruler, it is vital to listen closely to people's hearts, hear what they may *not* be saying, feel their needs and aspirations.

Of course one of the great lessons here is that great leaders must attend very deeply to those they lead! Other academics (e.g., Kaye, 1995; Solnet and Kandampully, 2008; O'Gorman and Gillespie, 2010) have used the power of stories and parables in discussing effective leadership—and we encourage students to use this chapter as a springboard to further learning and understanding about leadership in the context of service organizations.

Defining leadership

"People don't want to be managed. They want to be led."
(Bennis and Nanus, 1985, p. 22)

There are almost as many definitions of leadership as there are writers on the subject! There is no universal consensus. For our purpose, we like Northouse's (2013) definition, that "leadership is a process where an individual influences a group to achieve a common goal."(p. 3)

In other words, leadership is a *process*, not a trait or characteristic that necessarily exists in a leader; leadership involves *influence* and is concerned with how a leader affects followers. Leadership mostly occurs in the context of *groups*; leaders and followers have a shared *goal*, a mutual purpose to achieve something greater.

The leader as more than a manager

Before we progress, we cite Kotter (1990) in his efforts to make distinctions between leaders and managers. He says that management focuses on predictability, order and results, and uses a combination of management basics such as planning, budgeting, organizing, staffing, controlling and problem solving. Leadership, on the other hand, aims to produce change through vision setting, alignment of vision

© Rafal Olechowski/Shutterstock.com

to the organizational strategies and people, creating culture, thinking ahead and inspiring people to follow the stated direction. It is helpful to know that the word 'leadership' apparently comes from a Norse-Icelandic word that means 'furrow'. Therefore, leaders create a visible means for others to grow.

Zaleznik (1977) made an earlier distinction in that managers are often reactive, exercise unidirectional authority and have low emotional involvement in their followers; whereas leaders exercise multi-directional influence and are emotionally involved. More recently, Boyatzis and McKee (2005) even suggest that leadership is all about 'emotional contagion', where good leaders 'resonate' with their people to achieve great things (see also Tee et al. 2013 who argue that follower mood has a reciprocal effect upon leaders).

We also need to acknowledge here that leadership is distinct from but not better than management; both are important in building and maintaining a great organization. It is just that management deals with *complexity* while leadership deals with *change*—the two 'Cs"

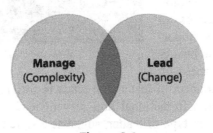

Figure 9.1
Management and leadership: Primary functions

(see Figure 9.1 above). Kotter (1990) famously states that management and leadership differ in terms of their primary function, where management creates and controls predictability and order whereas leadership produces change. He also argues that *both* are needed for organizations to prosper. We could add that management focuses mostly on systems, in addition to the present and the past, while leadership focuses on people, in addition to the present and the future.

The leader who serves with style

Situational leadership

Early studies at the Ohio State and Michigan State Universities in the USA discovered that there were two dimensions in leadership: production (task-oriented) and consideration (relationship-oriented). While Blake and Mouton (1964) postulated one best style (high task/high relationship), others espoused a more flexible, contingency approach. That is, the best style depends upon the context. The best-known version of this alternative approach is Hersey and Blanchard's (1969) situation leadership model, where good leaders employ a supportive (helpful, collaborative) or a directive (telling) style as the situation requires. What this highlights is that the leader's style should match the development level of followers: the more committed and competent the team, the more delegating the leader's style.

This type of leadership resonates in the service sector. In fact, Clark et al. (2009) found support for this in the hospitality industry where empowering leadership with mature teams produces commitment to shared values. There is compelling evidence that directive leadership is incompatible with a service environment.

With the rapidly progressing thought on leadership, the literature put forth the approaches which shifted the focus away from the leader-centered perspective towards the nexus created between the leaders and followers, and put more emphasis on the employees' behaviors. In this light, with the recognized importance of followers and their behaviors, more recent literature (especially

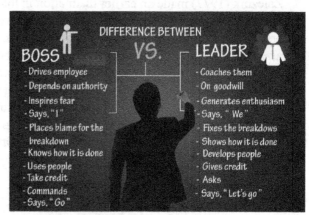

© Keepsmiling4u/Shutterstock.com

after 1970) reviewing the concept of leadership tends to differentiate three main styles of leadership—transactional, transformational and servant leadership. Transactional leadership, the more commonly seen type of leader, suggests a style that is premised upon compliance of his or her followers through various rewards and punishment mechanisms (Bass, 1985). The transformational style of leadership conversely assumes a more proactive framework where the role of charisma and strong relationships are introduced. In this sense, drawing on the ability of this type of leader to form strong and collaborative relationships via effective communication, team effort and resource-sharing, transformational leadership is distinguished as a more interpersonal and motivational form of leadership. Similarly, transformational leadership is noted to enhance the motivation and performance of followers and has been widely employed in a hospitality context.

Transformational leaders promote more self-assured and creative followers where the general level of commitment, effort, performance and job satisfaction remain higher in comparison to transactional leadership styles (Gill, Flaschner, and Shachar, 2006). The third style of leadership, servant leadership, is premised upon a leader type that acts through motivation to serve and empower his or her followers in which a more democratic leader-follower dynamic outflows. In this sense, this style of leadership is distinguished by a greater focus on employees and work ethics as well as continuous self-reflection and value-based problem-solving practices. As such, the transformational leaders tend to work towards enhancing the needs and goals of the organization whereas servant leaders are conceptualized as being more focused on employee development and empowerment (Brownell, 2010). These three styles will be discussed further below, followed by a number of other related leadership approaches, concepts and theories.

"Mohandas Gandhi is a classic example of the transformational leader
as he developed a relationship with his followers,
instilled the faith in freedom in them and drove them towards their goal"

(Sumi, 2014, p. 22)

The transactional leader

While there are substitutes for leadership, such as characteristics among followers (a high degree of professionalism) or the nature of the task itself (providing feedback without the need for a supervisor), leaders can and often do make a real difference to organizations and to the lives of their employees.

This difference can be merely transactional, where the leader simply offers an exchange relationship to their followers. In other words, "do what I ask, and I'll reward you". Transactional leadership, at least, helps followers identify what must be done to accomplish desired results, such as better quality output or reduced costs in service, in exchange for certain benefits such as a salary and bonuses—if you excel.

In a transactional approach, the leader merely relies on contingent reward and management by exception. Management by exception can take one of two forms: active, in which the leader monitors subordinates and intervenes before a problem occurs to prevent it from occurring; and passive, where the leader intervenes after a problem has been identified to rectify it and discipline the subordinate. In other words, if you achieve the goals, the leader, on behalf of the organization, will reward you; if you make a mistake, the leader will become more directive. If you do a good job, a transactional leader may never become visible or important to you!

The transformational leader

Leadership is transformational when it changes subordinates for the better and even changes the whole organization. Transformational leaders make a huge difference; these leaders want their people to do more than 'just their job'. Like servant leaders, transformational leaders are interested in follower potential and follower development, not just in what followers can do for their organizations as 'human resources'.

Transformational leadership is associated with inspiration, charisma, motivation (Castro et al., 2008), articulating a vision, promoting group goals and providing intellectual stimulation (Baek-Kyoo et al., 2012).

Researchers such as Bass (1985) and Avolio et al. (2009) have long examined the characteristics of transformational leadership. They suggest that such leaders display some four clusters of leadership behaviors:

- ▶ **Idealized influence**—behavioral charisma and attributed charisma. Behavioral charisma means that such leaders display high standards of ethical and moral conduct and become role models for their employees. These leaders are trusted and highly respected. Attributed charisma occurs where leaders are perceived by followers as displaying extraordinary capabilities. In fact, this is one of the outcomes of transformational leadership: higher levels of reported satisfaction with their leaders among followers.
- ▶ **Inspirational motivation**—motivating and inspiring people by providing meaning and challenge in relation to work. The leader's ability to define and communicate a clear vision encourages team spirit and 'esprit de corps' as members enthusiastically work towards achieving the goal to which they all aspire. This is commonly observed in crack military units or elite sporting teams, and even in top restaurants!
- ▶ **Intellectual stimulation**—challenging the team even when the team is doing well. Innovation and constant improvement is demonstrated by the leader and encouraged among followers. New approaches to problems are encouraged and different perspectives, from outside the team itself, are fostered. This is similar to what Belbin (1981) originally called the role of the 'plant', whose outside views are deliberately invited and considered by fellow team members.

▶ **Individualized consideration**—the leader is concerned for and has knowledge of what is important to followers as individuals, not just as employees. The leader fosters learning, growth and personalized support for them as human beings (Bass et al., 2003).

Transformational leaders facilitate the development of followers' competencies, awareness and individuality, thereby aiding the growth of themselves as leaders as well as the organization itself (Sumi, 2014). Transformational leaders motivate followers to exceed expectations, who then exercise what has been called 'discretionary effort' or, even, behaving as 'organizational citizens' perhaps with true psychological empowerment (Yao and Cui, 2010), where they operate well beyond what is simply required of them as employees.

With transformational leadership approaches, followers and leaders themselves can become better people as well as more productive and satisfied employees. This is surely a desirable outcome for both followers and leaders alike!

The servant leader

In tourism and hospitality businesses, arguably one of the best leadership styles and approaches is to embody and employ *servant* leadership behaviors. This does not mean being a 'slave' as a waiter, a chef, a porter, a hotel receptionist or as a tour operator! It is about being deeply concerned about the other person, beyond a mere service relationship. Specifically, servant leadership fosters follower development and growth.

Key servant leader behaviors are conceptualizing (thoroughly understanding the organization), emotionally healing, putting followers first, helping followers grow and succeed, behaving ethically, empowering and creating value for the community (Northouse, 2013, pp. 230–231). The outcomes of servant leadership are follower performance and growth, organizational performance and societal impact (see Walumbwa et al., 2010).

In the hospitality and tourism context there is strong support for this style of leadership, and the behaviors associated with it. Brownell (2010) agrees that developing cultures of trust and being ethical in the global workplace are desirable outcomes, which illustrates how servant leadership is "well-suited to guide today's service organizations into the future" (p. 368). Wong and Davey (2007) suggest five (5) best practices for businesses seeking to cultivate servant leadership characteristics:

1. Right identity—see oneself as a servant, and not entitled.
2. Right motivation—serve others rather than seek credit.
3. Right method—relate to others positively, listen, validate them.
4. Right impact—inspire others, model core values.
5. Right character—walk the talk, stand up for what you believe in.

The leader as an emotionally intelligent person

"We are all worms but I think I am a glow worm."
Winston Churchill *(1874–1965)*
Prime Minister of England 1940–1945, 1951–1955

Churchill certainly shows a degree of self-confidence which is important in a leader—before hubris (de Vries, 2006) or ego inflation sets in! Northouse (2013) agrees that self-confidence is one of the major traits of a leader, the others being: intelligence, determination, integrity and sociability.

Defining emotional intelligence

Emotional intelligence has been defined as the ability to perceive emotions, to access and generate emotions, to understand emotions and to be able to regulate emotions so as to promote emotional and intellectual growth (Mayer and Salovey, 1997). There are a number of related terms (See Table 9.1).

The importance of emotional intelligence

In the *Star Trek* television series and the ten movies, the dynamics on the flight deck between the various captains and science officers on the starships, all called *Enterprise*, are fascinating. The first series contrasted the emotionality of Captain James T. Kirk (a heart person) and the logic of the Vulcan Spock (a head person).

In the TV series *Star Trek: The Next Generation*, Captain Jean-Luc Picard is both a head and heart person, while his science officer is an android called Data (a head entity). Data has an emotion chip installed into his positronic robot brain. But when his emotions become too overwhelming in stressful battle situations, he has to turn it off. Maybe, we might like

Table 9.1
Related Meanings in the Field of Emotional Intelligence

Related Terms	Focus and Terms
Emotion	A positive or negative subjective experience
Mood	An emotional state that is more generalized
Feeling	A reaction to a specific event, sometimes physical
Temperament	A natural disposition or constitution

to have the same ability! Nonetheless, Data's desire to experience emotions is at the heart of his striving to become more human. Data gave his life to save the *Enterprise* and its crew, and in his eulogy, the captain praised him:

> "Data strived to be more than he was
> and in this he taught us what it meant to be human."

This is only a fictional example, but we believe that being and becoming more human is a worthy ambition in real life, and also in a leadership context.

The importance of emotional factors has only recently been understood. For example, Goleman (1995) believes that the vast majority of a person finding his or her place in society is determined not by standard intelligence (IQ), but rather other factors. While this percentage might be over-stated, scholars do agree that emotional aspects are still more important for success in life and work than IQ. Indeed, smart can be dumb, and cognition in human affairs is not enough (Goleman, 1995). As Goleman (2004) later reiterates, without EQ (emotional intelligence), all of the training, a highly analytical mind and smart ideas will not make a person an effective leader.

Overall, emotional intelligence is important for these reasons:

© arka38/Shutterstock.com

- ▶ to increase personal life satisfaction;
- ▶ to reduce interpersonal conflict;
- ▶ to help impulse control; and
- ▶ to enhance leaders to be more effective.

Emotional intelligence is repeatedly shown to be an important trait for leaders. But in industry sectors such as hospitality and tourism, it is even more important because of the nature of the industries, the reliance on people to serve others and the importance of the general attitudes of a firm's employees. An emotionally intelligent leader has a great ability to understand and empathize with and gain the trust of workers, which then influences the way the worker communicates with and serves customers. If you think about the service-profit chain (Chapter 8), emotionally intelligent leaders (i.e., those with high EQ's) have a greater likelihood of positively influencing the left side of the chain—the one that sets off the spark in the chain. So emotionally intelligent leaders can and do create a more powerful service-profit chain effect and this effect is magnified in 'people intensive' industries such as hospitality and tourism.

The history of emotional intelligence

The origins of emotional intelligence were in investigations into playground bullying and domestic violence. It is no secret that our jails are over-represented by young men who have lacked impulse control. Sadly, we see all too often that a husband and father has taken his family hostage and we see how young men in the USA take out their frustrations in mass shootings on campuses.

This is the sobering truth of being emotionally competent: if we can deal with our emotions, we can avoid dysfunctional behavior, and if we can even harness our emotions, we will have better relationships, families and communities. Emotions are an asset for good if we know how to access them. Otherwise, we will be swamped by our emotions and feel powerless and not be able to control ourselves.

The famous marshmallow test conducted on four year olds in the 1960s by Walter Mischel and his colleagues at Stanford University shows the difficulty and the importance of delaying gratification. In these studies, children were offered a choice between one small reward provided immediately, or two small rewards if he or she waited for about 15 minutes. The researchers determined through follow up studies that children who were able to wait longer for the greater rewards tended to have better life outcomes (test scores, education, careers, happiness). Clearly, self-discipline is one of the keys to success.

This issue is still hotly debated among academics. Practically, managers and leaders everywhere are interested in whether this stuff actually works in the real world—and the evidence is that it does and that it matters!

Table 9.2
A Brief History of Research into EQ

Years	Focus of Research	Researcher
1920s	Social intelligence	Thorndike
1950s	Affectivity and intelligence	Piaget
1980	Multiple intelligences	Gardner
1990s	Dimensions of EQ	Salovey and Mayer
1995	Popularizing the concept of EQ	Goleman
1997	First serious measure of EQ	Bar-On
2005	Questioning of the construct validity of EQ	Academy of Management
2011	Links between EQ and leadership	Academy of Management

The latest understanding of emotional intelligence

Walter et al. (2011) have examined emotional intelligence under three 'streams' of study:

▶ A set of interrelated emotional abilities—perceiving, using, understanding and managing emotions;

▶ Emotionally intelligent behaviors—same focus as above, but with self-assessment; and

▶ An array of dispositions and competencies—a broader definition with both self-assessment and 360-degree assessment.

Similarly, Ashkanasy and Humphrey (2011) have discovered five 'levels':

▶ Organization-wide—emotional climate, bounded emotionality;

▶ Groups and teams—emotional contagion, affective tone, leader member exchange, group EQ;

▶ Interpersonal—felt versus displayed emotion, emotional labor;

▶ Between persons—trait effect, EQ, leadership style; and

▶ Within person—mood, emotional states, impulsivity.

The links between emotional intelligence and leadership

Interestingly, most of us are used to critiquing and reframing our thoughts, "I am feeling angry with this client. I'd better not shout at her!" The power of EQ, and what is argued is actually 'intelligent' about emotions, is allowing our emotions to energize and reframe what we think, and then this impacts upon what we might do about our thoughts in action.

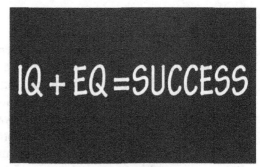

© woaiss/Shutterstock.com

For example, David Suzuki, the Canadian environmentalist, reportedly exclaimed, "If you are not angry with what we are doing to planet earth, our home, what are you going to get angry about?!" This is asking us to harness our emotions to challenge our thinking and then move to action.

Let us not forget that the word 'emotion' has the same Latin origin as 'motivation'—*motere* or "to move". Emotions move us; but thoughts do not necessarily lead to actions.

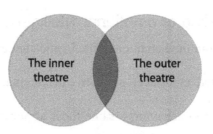

Figure 9.2
Two domains of EQ

Dimensions of emotional intelligence

Mayer and Salovey (1997) found there are some five basic dimensions in EQ:

1. Knowing one's own emotions
2. Managing one's own emotions
3. Motivating oneself
4. Recognizing emotions in others
5. Handling relationships with others

Two domains to the inner and outer world of emotional literacy have been described and are illustrated in Figure 9.2 (Callan and Latemore, 2008):

In other words, the 'inner theatre' of oneself consists of knowing and managing one's own emotions and motivating oneself. The 'outer theatre' involving others consists of recognizing emotions in others and handling relationships with others.

Developing EQ

It seems that EQ is not teachable, but, under the right circumstances, it is certainly 'learnable'. This is an important difference. If we are motivated and are sufficiently supported and challenged, we will learn to be more emotionally competent, if not more emotionally 'intelligent'. You cannot teach others to be emotionally competent without their commitment or their practicing the key behaviors of self-awareness and inter-personal relationships.

That is why feedback and perhaps undertaking a 360° review as a leader can be helpful to 'spark' the motivation to develop this important ability, which is just as important as self-awareness and interpersonal communication.

EQ and the leader

Mindfulness, compassion and hope are the hallmarks of being in tune with our people as 'resonant' leaders (Boyatzis and McKee, 2005). Effective leaders are:

▶ mindful—'look and listen' to what is happening around them, and do not get distracted by tunnel vision or too much multi-tasking!

- ► compassionate—show true empathy when needed, while not ignoring patterns of poor performance. It starts with listening.
- ► hopeful—appropriately positive and optimistic about the future and bring certainty where they can to their followers.

In conclusion, it is suggested that if EQ is learnable, then these additional strategies might help us:

- ► express, value and honor your feelings;
- ► maximize humanity and compassion at work;
- ► foster and reward emotionally-literate leadership;
- ► practice "tough-love" as a leader/coach; and
- ► spend time with emotionally literate people.

It is of particular importance for the hospitality and tourism industry to recognize the importance of EQ and learn how to embed it into the organizational culture. This is important due to human factors and a high involvement of people interactions, which by nature can be complex and irrational in decisions due to their emotions and moods. Therefore, it can be argued that EQ is just as vital for front-line service workers as for their leaders.

The leader as an authentic person

Authentic leadership is a relatively new and evolving view of leadership without consensus on a single definition or particular model. Northouse (2013) noted that it has been defined in three different ways. First, the intrapersonal perspective focuses on the personal characteristics of authentic leaders. From this perspective, authentic leaders:

© Gustavo Frazao/Shutterstock.com

- ► Exhibit genuine leadership.
- ► Lead from conviction.
- ► Are original, not copies.
- ► Base their actions on their personal values.

Second, the developmental perspective sees authentic leadership as something that can be nurtured over a lifetime, and is often triggered by major life events like a health crisis or losing one's job. This perspective emphasizes the importance of:

- Self-awareness—reflecting on one's "core values, identity, our emotions, motives and goals, and coming to grips with who you really are at the deepest level" (Northouse, 2013, p. 263).
- Internalized moral perspective—using one's own moral standards and values to guide behavior.
- Balanced processing—the ability to objectively analyze information and consider the opinions of others before coming to a decision.
- Relational transparency—being open and honest when presenting oneself and others—within reason.

Third, the interpersonal perspective highlights that authentic leadership occurs within the context of relationships where authentic leaders work with followers who identify with or accept the values held by the leader.

In recent years, there has been considerable interest in authentic leadership. This interest has been fueled by several high-profile examples of unethical leadership that have caused considerable harm in society and disillusionment with respect to leaders in positions of authority. Many believe that traditional models of leadership (e.g., transformational leadership, team leadership, charismatic leadership etc.) do not have a suitably strong ethical grounding. Authentic leadership aims to address this perceived failing.

© EugenioMarongiu/Shutterstock.com

There are several models of authentic leadership that reflect the three perspectives described above. For example, George (2003) adopts the intrapersonal perspective and has developed a model that describes some of the key personality traits and behaviors of authentic leaders. This model is shown in Figure 9.3, and highlights the following five authentic leadership attributes:

1. They understand their purpose.
2. They have strong values about the right thing to do.
3. They establish trusting relationships with others.
4. They demonstrate self-discipline and act on their values.
5. They are passionate about their mission.

Finally, Goffee and Jones (2005) present a model that urges leaders to combine honesty with skill, rather than being inept, mavericks or just robots. In other words, being inept is having no honesty and no real skill. Being a maverick is just being brutally honest without any people skills behind it, while being a robot is just being a role player with some trained skill but no real sincerity behind it. The best combination is for service leaders to display both inter-

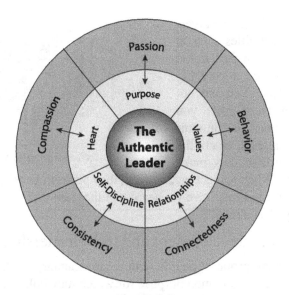

Figure 9.3
Authentic leadership attributes
(George, 2003 in Northouse 2013, p. 259)

personal skills and genuineness. With colleagues and clients, this means 'to speak the truth with finesse'.

There is a logical case to make that a leader of people in an industry or segment where the followers are expected to exhibit service-related characteristics and emotional labor of their own would benefit from being perceived by others as authentic. For leaders, it is always a challenge to blend authenticity with the kind of thinking and decision making that are needed. However, there is evidence that honesty and authenticity create more effective leaders, and that this type of leadership lends itself to the service sector, particularly in hospitality and tourism because people often will be more likely to connect and want to listen to a person whom they perceive is acting authentically.

The leader as a team builder

"A camel is a horse, designed by a committee"
*Attributed to **Alec Issigonis**, the engineer who designed the Mini car*

Do you share Issigonis's cynicism about committees and teams?! Or has your experience of working in or leading a team been more positive? Regardless, much of what we do in life—

whether it be in high school or university, work or even in activities such as sports—is done in teams. In fact, in the service industry, teams are a very big part of how things operate. You may not think if yourself as a 'team' when you are working in a restaurant, but in reality, the floor staff are a team, as are the kitchen staff, and, together, they make

up the restaurant team. When teams function well, they perform better than the whole of the parts (synergy). How many times have we heard that the team that won a championship did so because 'they played as a team'?

Defining teams, team development and team leadership

- ► A *team* is "a small group of people with complementary skills, who work together as a unit to achieve a common purpose for which they hold themselves collectively accountable" (Wood et al., 2010, p. 240).
- ► *Team development* refers to "the cohesiveness of the team, member satisfaction and the quality of member relationships" (Northouse, 2013, p. 299).
- ► *Team leadership* is a "team's capability to monitor its effectiveness and to take action where necessary" (Northouse, 2013, p. 291)

Fostering team effectiveness

Most tools developed to improve team leadership adopt what is known as the 'functional approach'. This approach believes that the key role of the team leader is "to do, or get done, whatever is not being adequately handled for group needs" (McGrath, 1962). Kogler-Hill (2013) provides a simple model of team leadership, whereby a team leader needs to first accurately diagnose the circumstances surrounding the team (that is, have an accurate mental model of the team's performance and environment). Next, he or she needs to monitor the team's performance and decide whether to take action or keep monitoring. If he or she decides to take action, there are some key leadership behaviors in three categories. The first is *task*-related (setting goals and clarifying roles), the second is *relationship*-focused (managing conflict and coaching), and the third is related to the

team's *environment* (buffering the team from unhelpful influences or seeking additional resources on behalf of the team).

Diagnosing a team

It is wise to diagnose the team's effectiveness and to involve the team in a workshop process when doing this. There are noteworthy features of high-performance teams (Kanaga and Browning, 2003), although it is important to determine which specific criteria your team would see as important. Some of the features include:

- ► They have a performance 'track record'.
- ► They have a clear purpose.
- ► They leverage the social roles people naturally prefer.
- ► They build and maintain productive external relationships.
- ► They receive strong organizational support.
- ► They are mutually accountable and develop as a team.
- ► They have positive internal relationships.

Dysfunctions in a team

Key dysfunctions of a team include an absence of trust, fear of conflict, inability to commit to the team's goals, a lack of accountability for team outcomes and an inattention to results (Lencioni, 2005).

Cohesion is good but 'groupthink' (Janis, 1972) occurs when too much cohesion exists and teams lose their critical, evaluative capabilities (Wood et al., 2010, p. 467). This can happen if team members like each other a lot and spend a lot of time together. Signs of groupthink include the illusion of control and unanimity, a sense of invulnerability, diffusion of responsibility and closed membership. The good news is there are ways of avoiding it, such as: client feedback, limits on the tenure of team membership and outsider input (Wood et al., 2010). This can also create a very negative service working environment where there is much gossip and ganging up on members of the team who might not be a part of this 'group'.

Other team dysfunctions or 'process losses' include:

- ► Social loafing (lazy team members get carried along by good team members. Fix it by holding all members accountable and reporting on each person's contribution or non-contribution).
- ► Risky shift (teams take more risks than do individuals as responsibility for poor decisions is shared or diffused. Fix it by ensuring all decisions are not made by consensus and being clear when the group has to make the decisions or the best 'local expert' does.)

Team dynamics

Teams typically, but not always, go through various stages in their development. Tuckman (1965) famously proposed that teams generally go through the following five stages:

1. Form   inclusion, time together and goal setting is vital
2. Storm   sort out early conflict, confusion and who is in charge
3. Norm   make the rules and expectations for the group very clear
4. Perform   clarify how the team delivers on task and relationships
5. Mourn/Adjourn   celebrate success and individual and team contributions.

Leading a high-performance team

Establishing agreed-upon norms or informal rules for the team is one way of ensuring team cohesiveness early on in the life of a team (Wood et al., 2010).

Team (or social) roles have long been recognized as being important in team functioning. Effective leaders encourage and employ 'distributed / shared leadership', where the leadership role in teams is undertaken by more than one person (Day et al., 2004). 'Boundary-spanning leadership' (Ernst and Chrobot-Mason, 2010) is relevant to leaders in the tourism and hospitality industry because there are so many ways and places that workers are unsupervised; however, when others feel a shared sense of purpose (e.g., culture), they are more likely to act in the best interests of the organization. Dogmatic and authoritarian leadership on the other hand is not effective; leaders need to do more than transact, they must at times transform. Team leaders can use this model to help diagnose what the team needs at a particular time and identify appropriate leadership behaviors to use as a team leader.

A team charter

If a team gets into trouble, another way of intervening is to involve them in diagnosing the issues, say in focus groups, and then 'workshopping' them to agree to solutions. Creating a 'team charter' is also a great way of encouraging accountability and fostering high-performance. To do this, the team agrees on their shared values (no more than six values), lists indicative behaviors (no more than three behaviors per value) and decides how to manage compliance or non-compliance with their agreed-upon values and behaviors (see Table 9.3).

This is particularly important for senior management teams, who must be given serious work and establish team norms—such as commitment, transparency, participation and integrity with each other (Wageman et al., 2008).

Table 9.3
A Team Charter (example)

Our Shared Values	Indicative Behaviors	How will we manage this?
Respect	Listen Don't criticize first Be polite in communication	Any team member can 'call' the behavior at any time. We report our team progress once a month.
Service excellence	Measure service delivery Seek client feedback Peer reviews	Report and debrief client feedback non-defensively once a week

The leader as an ethical exemplar and trust builder

This section explores two aspects of being a good leader—demonstrating ethical principles, and being able to build and restore the trust of staff and customers.

Being ethical as a leader

"Why be good?"
Socrates *(469–399 BCE)*
Greek philosopher

The importance of ethical behavior in the hospitality industry needs to be stressed. Unethical practices can include conflicts of interest, room theft, acceptance of cash or gifts and revealing trade. Sadly, some current management evaluation practices merely encourage 'short term-ism' which tempts managers to be less ethically oriented (Minnett et al., 2009).

Ethics can be defined as principles, norms and standards of conduct that guide actions and behaviors (Trevino and Nelson, 2007). In practical terms, ethical leaders are aware of, and care about, the needs and concerns of people who could be affected by their leadership activities.

© iQoncept/Shutterstock.com

Ethical leadership then must demonstrate appropriate conduct through personal actions and interpersonal relationships, and promote such conduct to followers through effective communication, rewarding of ethical behavior and disciplining those who do not behave ethically (Brown et al., 2005).

There has long been supporting evidence that top management support for ethical behavior tends to lead to a significant drop in unethical behavior. In a study of 324 middle managers in 30 different hotels across 8 different national and international brands, Kim and Brymer (2011) demonstrated that executives' ethical leadership is positively related to their middle managers' job satisfaction and their affective organizational commitment. In other words, ethical bosses have happier middle managers who want to stay. There is therefore clear support for the link between ethical behavior and positive organizational outcomes: it is not just 'nice to be good', it makes business sense! There are many opportunities in the workplace, particularly in the hospitality and tourism businesses, where unethical behavior can be tempting. Whether it is giving away drinks at the bar, skimming money from a tip jar, giving favors to friends in return for favors at their business—hospitality leaders, managers and employees are faced with literally hundreds of opportunities to act unethically. Ethical behavior in business starts with the leaders.

Freeman (2002) suggested that the ethical leader:

► Searches for outcomes that reflect the values and ethics of the leader, followers and society as a whole.
► Seeks to include others and avoids 'them and us thinking'.
► Tries to get the right things done the right way.
► Fosters an open and honest conversation about ethics and values in the organization.

Northouse (2013) summarizes five basic principles for ethical leaders:

► They respect others.
► They serve others.
► They are just.
► They are honest.
► They build communities.

© Tang Yan Song/Shutterstock.com

Guidelines on how to make ethical decisions have been presented by Preston (2001). These guidelines include the need to assess the situation (check facts); evaluate against shared values (eg. respect, fairness); aspirational character factors (is this the kind of firm, person we wish to be?); make a full assessment and determine priorities and finally, to make the decision (but be prepared to give an account of this decision publicly).

Being trustworthy as a leader

"When the trust account is high, communication is easy, instant and effective."
(Covey, 2004, p. 198)

The nature of trust

Trust is important—trusting each other and your leader are vitally important! Hilton hotels believes so strongly in trust that their annual employee survey (Team Member Engagement Survey) places great importance on the way Hilton employees trust the organization and their leadership. This is understandable, as Hilton has to rely on its employees to do the right thing, to be 'brand champions'—and to do so, it realizes that employees must trust them.

Trust is linked with moral courage, a substantive virtue that is especially required of leaders (Etter, 2012). Some scholars have defined trust as confident, positive expectations regarding a trustee's conduct, motives and intentions in situations involving risk (Lewicki and Bunker, 1996).

Another approach, and indeed the most commented-upon theoretical conception of trust (de Jong, 2011), is based on the work of Mayer et al. (1995) where trust refers to being vulnerable to a third party's behavior in a context of uncertainty, with the expectation that this behavior will not be operating on the basis of ill-will and irrespective of any monitoring or control mechanisms.

Dimensions of trust are classified under knowledge, or cognition-based trust, goodwill or affect-based trust and identification-based trust (McAllister et al., 2006). Knowledge-based trust is rooted in past performance and promise-keeping; goodwill-based trust is rooted in emotional involvement and caring and identification-based trust is rooted in a sense of shared values and fit.

Trust scholars suggest a multi-faceted approach which combines control and trust processes. Control is one vehicle to order the complex structure of social relationships and trust is the other (de Jong, 2011). Malhotra and Lumineau (2011) have highlighted that the coordination function of a contract might be more efficacious than the control function. They

© Sampien/Shutterstock.com

found that control provisions in a contract increase competence-based trust but reduce good-will-based trust, resulting in the diminished likelihood of continued collaboration.

Robbins et al. (2001) have outlined the dimensions of trust as including: integrity, competence, consistency, loyalty and openness. Other authors elaborate similar abilities in that the trustee needs to be competent, skilled, efficient, caring, loyal, principled and fair (Colquitt and Rodell, 2011). In terms of most trusted brands, customers look for consistency, delivery on promises and open communication (Gardner, 2009).

Trust management

Repairing trust seems to be closely linked with what also builds it, namely, a preparedness to show vulnerability. This vulnerability is exercised through four qualities: ability (technical competence which complies with the role's obligation, and which includes skills, efficiency and dedication), benevolence (a genuine concern for the other's well-being which includes 'doing good' and being caring and open), integrity (adherence to morally acceptable principles or shared values), and behavioral consistency or predictability in the relationship (Gillespie and Dietz, 2009).

The key generic trust-repair strategies that emerge from a review of the literature are: displaying vulnerability/openness, and then exhibiting integrity, competence/ability, benevolence and predictability.

An organization needs to make trust-repair interventions that both constrain any untrustworthy behavior, and also signal renewed trustworthiness (Gillespie and Dietz, 2009). Distrust regulation might include acknowledging the incident, expressing regret, announcing an investigation and committing resources to prevent a recurrence. Trustworthiness demonstration might include an apology and making reparations (Gillespie and Dietz, 2009; Latemore, 2012).

For a leader, this means that a leader in the service industry must be open, competent, caring and predictable. When things go wrong, then this can be managed by apologizing, taking steps to prevent it happening again and 'making it up' to affected staff or customers. Such a quality is even more critical to service businesses because of service failure—and the simple fact that failure is inevitable (see Chapter 7). We know great service organizations handle failure with grace and efficiency—a quality that starts with leadership.

The leader as a change agent

*"Do not repeat the tactics which have gained you one victory,
but let your methods be regulated by the infinite variety of circumstances."*

Sun Tzu *(544-496 BCE)*
Chinese military strategist and philosopher

Leading change

The vast majority of managers and leaders today adopt a planned approach to large-scale organizational change (Callan et al., 2004). Many managers and leaders find that in their particular circumstances, they can apply a linear, step-by-step process in planning and implementing major change.

There are many examples of such step models, including John Kotter (1996; Kotter and Cohen, 2002). His model is highly influential in Australia and elsewhere as demonstrated by the number of organizations that explicitly apply his framework. Kotter (1996) instructs managers to plan their change in the following order:

1. Create (increase) a sense of urgency.
2. Build the powerful guiding coalition.
3. Get the vision right.
4. Communicate for buy in.
5. Empower action.
6. Create short-term wins.
7. Do not let up.
8. Make change stick.

In further research (Callan et al., 2004), especially in large organizations, we have seen managers apply each of these steps to guide not only the change process, but also to provide a language that structures most conversations about change in their business ("how are we going in building the powerful guiding coalition?").

The following summary guidelines are suggested when leading and managing change (Callan et al., 2004):

1. Adopt a linear step-by-step view about change.
2. Realize that organizational change does not always occur in an orderly, predictable and linear manner.
3. Managers need to develop capabilities in themselves and in their employees to cope with the uncertainty and complexity of change.
4. Expect and plan for conflict, rivalry, distinctions about winners and losers during change, and in building important new identities.
5. Use multiple channels of communication to reflect the complexity of any change situation. Where it is possible, face-to-face communication should be the first choice in explaining the vision, purpose and timing of the change.
6. The leaders of change should brief and encourage their first-line supervisors to be the most visible communicators with employees. People trust communication from their immediate supervisor, before they will believe any communication from higher up.
7. Focus on the humanity of change, not just on the systems and structures for change.

8. When leaders do communicate, they need to speak with one voice.
9. Adopt a trusting and 'open book' approach with employees.
10. Tolerate ambiguity and allow messiness. Remember, while a swamp may be full of mud, decay and mosquitoes, it is still a sign of a healthy biosphere.

Being a transformational change agent

Adopting a transformational approach rather than a transactional one is better for sustained change. This means that you would move followers beyond your immediate self-interest while employing idealized influence (charisma), inspirational motivation, intellectual stimulation or individualized consideration (Bass, 1990). This is in contrast to a transactional approach where you would simply manage by exception and issue rewards that are contingent upon staff compliance with your instructions. It is a completely different approach to leadership and to being a leader!

© Rawpixel/Shutterstock.com

As Kouzes and Posner (2012) elaborate, being transformational in the change management process means that you would: challenge the process, enable others to act, inspire a shared vision, model the way and encourage the heart.

© Cartoonresource/Shutterstock.com

The leader as a strategist and culture builder

"You can take my factories, burn up my buildings, but give me my people
and I'll build the businesses right back again."
Henry Ford *(1863–1943)*
American industrialist, founder of Ford Motor Company
(cited in Hickman and Silva, 1984, p. 57)

Resources matter, but people are crucial—they can 'make or break' an organization, as
Henry Ford knew. Being an effective service leader is one thing; being an effective service
organization is another. This chapter now concludes with a consideration of the context
within which good leaders operate—their organizations.

We now propose, as did Hickman and Silva (1984), an equation for service excellence
(Figure 9.4):

Accordingly, what service leaders must strive to become and to do is craft the strategic
direction of their organizations (strategy) and build and bind their cultures to provide superior service (culture). As discussed previously in Chapters 5 and 8, for a service organization, the importance of commitment to a clear strategic purpose together with fostering a
sound culture cannot be over-stated. This is what effective service leaders must do—set
strategy and build culture. While 'excellence' and even 'effectiveness' might have fallen out
of favor among scholars (Cameron, 2010), superior and sustained organizational performance has not.

Interestingly, this equation in Figure 9.4 echoes another formula (Blumberg and Pringle,
1982), which is still being used in managing performance (Figure 9.5):

| Strategy | + | Culture | = | Service Excellence |

Figure 9.4
Service excellence equation
(Hickman and Silva, 1984)

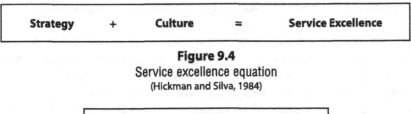

P = f (AMO)
where
P = performance
f = a function of
A = ability
M = motivation
O = opportunity to perform

Figure 9.5
Performance equation

In other words, service leaders need to harness the knowledge, skills and abilities of individual employees, engage them and provide opportunities for them to excel. The responsibility for good performance is not merely dependent upon the individual's own ability (A) or capacity to perform and motivation (M) or willingness to perform, but also whether there is an opportunity (O) to perform—are there resources, training and an enabling culture? This approach signals to the service manager that good performance is not just the responsibility of their staff, but also the organization itself, in partnership with their employees, must provide the tools and the environment which their employees need to perform and excel.

In a similar vein, Deming was known to say, "Don't blame the worker; look at his machine and the factory first".

In addition to individual knowledge, skills, attributes and other characteristics (KSAOs), the superior service organization needs policies, systems and managerial will to make high-performance happen. As Sull (2007) reminds us, execution is just as important as strategic sense-making and choice-making. Apart from individual competencies, organizations need capability. In fact, what is needed has been called 'strategic resources'.

Developing an organization's strategic resources occurs through core competencies, strategic assets and core processes (Hamel, 2000). These strategic resources help to provide a sustained competitive advantage in the marketplace. Service organizations are becoming increasingly sophisticated about what drives such superior, sustained performance—brand awareness, reputation and a systemic commitment to service quality. These days in the service industry, it is about being better, faster, closer to the customer and sometimes, but not always, cheaper than your competitor.

Of course, if you are smart, you can commit to a 'blue ocean' strategy, where in the deepest ocean there are few or no competitors—this is 'uncontested market space' (Kim and Mauborgne, 2005). *Cirque du Soleil* is an example of this, where in their entertainment sector they have few, if any, rivals. In effect, they have made the competition irrelevant in their space.

To enable all this to happen, superior organizations are committed to developing what has been called 'dynamic capability'; that is, being clever about not just what employees learn, but how they learn and how they keep on learning (Teece, 2007).

Interestingly, building a robust organizational culture is what really counts in high-performance organizations. Culture beats strategy every time! In other words, the pattern of basic assumptions, values and beliefs which are shared among employees (Schei, 1986) has a stronger effect upon performance than senior managers' crafting and communicating a brilliant strategy.

One way to build and bind a cohesive organizational culture is to help people come 'HOME' to the organization (Gross and Schichman, 1987):

History   ...   develop a sense of history and tell stories about the past
Oneness   ...   create a sense of 'family' and being 'one'
Membership ...   promote a sense of belonging
Exchange   ...   increase interactions among members.

Finally, research on the organizations which move from being 'good to great' (Collins, 2001) recognizes three strategic questions which help organizations to drive such commitment to sustained superior performance. These are: What are you passionate about? What drives your economic engine? and What can you be the best in the world at?

An integrating model of service leadership

Attempting to pull all this together, we suggest an integrating model for leaders in the tourism and hospitality industry. Authentic leaders need to demonstrate their soul, head, heart and hands.

Simply put, service leaders must establish an authentic and ethical base for themselves (*soul*), co-craft a sound strategic vision and direction for their organization within the service and hospitality industry (*head*), create empathy with their colleagues, suppliers and staff as they build a respectful and high-performance culture (*heart*) and make sure they

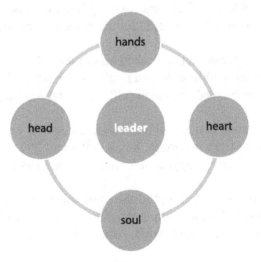

Figure 9.6
An integrating model of service leadership

execute this in practice as they provide quality service for their clients and other key stakeholders (*hands*).

Conclusion

"All our dreams can come true if we have the courage to pursue them."

***Walt Disney** (1901–1966)*
American entrepreneur, film director and producer, founder Walt Disney Company.

Walt Disney was right in that having a vision and courage are important to success. We would add that we also need respect and authenticity with our colleagues and our clients. In the end, what matters now are 'farmer values', that is, traditional respect for each other and ethical practice, where greed is neither extolled nor ignored and people create real value with honest sweat and hard work (Hamel, 2012).

Service leaders must display right conduct with their customers, their staff and each other—indeed, all their stakeholders. Developing and expressing authentic relationships with people is what is now expected of leaders—meaningful, professional relationships which transcend cynicism and tokenism.

Do you strive to provide genuine hospitality or just service? Loyal customers expect a sincere experience and deserve nothing less. Do you inspire, motivate and serve your people? Good employees expect good leaders, and they deserve nothing less.

Final story

Once upon a time, in old Korea, there was a young boy called Son Ki. At that time, Korea had the finest archers in the whole world. Son Ki wanted to be the best archer of all—the best of the best.

So he went to his village sensei and asked him to teach him how to be the world's best archer. "First, go and pluck a whisker from a lion's face" instructed his teacher. Son Ki knew about the fierce lions that roamed outside his village and he was very afraid. Still, he wanted to be the best archer.

So the next day, at dawn, Son Ki left his village and soon found a pride of lions. He saw one lion that was separate from the group. Son Ki sat about 200 meters away from this solitary lion, just watching. The lion appeared to glare at Son Ki as he crept away at the end of that first day.

The next day and the next, Son Ki did the same thing. He sat for hours, gazing at the lion. Soon his fear turned to admiration. After four weeks, Son Kin sat closer and closer, watching the lion with love and admiration. After three months, Son Ki was only a meter away.

Now, Son Ki was trembling with excitement and anticipation—up close, the lion was magnificent and gazed back at Son Ki. One day, Son Ki suddenly realized that his fear was gone.

After four months, Son Ki could touch the lion's paw. After six months, Son Ki gently plucked a whisker from the lion's face and then slowly, he walked away from the lion.

Son Ki ran back to his sensei with the whisker. He asked, "Now master, will you teach me to be a great archer?" "Yes", replied the sensei, "but now you must hold up the trunk of a tree and point it at the wild geese which fly over our village at sunset".

So, for the next month, Son Ki tried to hold up the trunk of a tree but it was too heavy. So, he started with a small branch and held it high as he focused on the flying geese.

After three months, his arms were no longer tired and he could hold a bigger branch for a longer and longer time. After six months, So Ki could hold still the trunk of a small tree in either arm and point it at the flying geese.

Then he went back to his sensei and showed him what he could do and asked him to begin teaching him to be a great archer.

"No, I don't need to", said the old man. "You are already a great archer. Pick up your bow, and fire your quiver of arrows at the furthest target in our village practice range".

Son Ki did as he was told and he was astonished when he hit the target in the center every time.

That is how Son Ki became the greatest archer of his time. He had faced his fears, he had learned patience, and he found strength and determination to pursue his goal.

Comment on Final Story: To become a true professional, whether as a warrior or a service provider, one needs to build one's capacity. This takes courage, time and patience. The character of leaders (Sarros et al., 2006), their courage, patience, strength and determination, is as important as are their technical skills.

Once again, as we see here, a good story, like a picture, is worth a thousand words …

Summary

This chapter was an ambitious one. We strived to canvas the rich theory about leadership. We began by distinguishing management from leadership. Both are important but leadership is vital if one wishes to create a high-performing service organization.

We then examined various aspects of leadership—various leadership styles and servant leadership in particular, emotional intelligence, being authentic and ethical as a leader, leading teams, leading a change program, setting strategy and building culture. All of this helped us to understand what it takes to create and sustain a great service organization, that is, great leaders, with a clear strategy and a solid culture.

In all this, a leader's authenticity needs to be maintained. To be effective in the long-term, in order to bring quality service to customers and sustainability to the community, leaders need to be genuine with people and 'speak the truth with finesse'.

Review Questions

1. What are the main differences between leadership and management?

2. How and why does leadership play such an important role in managing service organizations? Refer to the service-profit chain in your answer.

3. Briefly describe and explain the differences among transformational, transactional and servant leadership styles.
   a. Have you been led by leaders who seem to display servant leadership behaviors? What do you think of them as leaders? Did you feel empowered to exercise discretionary effort and did you report higher levels of satisfaction with them as leaders?

4. Define emotional intelligence.
   a. What are the key dimensions of emotional intelligence?
   b. Which role does it play within the organizational context?

5. What are the characteristics of being an ethical and authentic leader?

6. From a leader's point of view, how would you achieve a synergy and build a high-performing team?

7. How would you go about managing and leading a change initiative in your team / organization?

8. What are some effective ways of creating a high-performance service organization? (You might consider the service excellence equation and service leadership model.)

Suggested Readings

This is a short list of suggested further reading on topics covered in this chapter. For a separate list of full reference citations quoted in the chapter, see 'References', Chapter 9, page 335.

George, B., Sims, P., McLean, A., and Mayer, D. (2007). Discovering authentic leadership. *Harvard Business Review,* February, 129–138.

Greger, K. R., and Peterson, J. S. (2000). Leadership profiles for the new millennium. *Cornell Hotel and Restaurant Administration Quarterly*, 41, 16–29.

Hon, A. H. Y., and Chan, W. W. H. (2013). Team creative performance: The roles of empowering leadership, creative-related motivation, and task interdependence. *Cornell Hospitality Quarterly*, 54(2), 199–210.

Kara, D., Uysal, M., Sirgy, M. J., and Lee, G. (2013). The effects of leadership style on employee well-being in hospitality. *International Journal of Hospitality Management*, 34, 9–18.

Liao, H., and Chuang, A. (2007). Transforming service employees and climate: a multilevel, multisource examination of transformational leadership in building long-term service relationships. *The Journal of Applied Psychology*, 92(4), 1006–1019.

Michelli, J. A. (2008). *The New Gold Standard: Five Leadership Principles for Creating a Legendary Customer Experience, Courtesy of the Ritz-Carlton Hotel Company*. McGraw-Hill: New York.

Sessa, V. I., Kabacoff, R. I., Deal, J., and Brown, H. (2007). Generational differences in leader values and leadership behaviours. *The Psychologist-Manager Journal,* 10(1), 47–74.

Sipe, L. (2012). Service-leadership competencies for hospitality and tourism management. *International Journal of Hospitality Management*, 31(3), 648–658.

Suh, E., West, J. J., and Shin, J. (2012). Important competency requirements for managers in the hospitality industry. *Journal of Hospitality, Leisure, Sport & Tourism Education*, 11, 101–112.

Testa, M. R., and Sipe, L. (2011). Service-leadership competencies for hospitality and tourism management. *International Journal of Hospitality Management*, 31(3), 648–658.

CHAPTER 10

Bringing Service Management to Life! Case Studies of Best Practice

Outline

- ► Introduction
- ► Case studies from Australasia
  - ► 1. Long Beach Hotel, Mauritius
  - ► 2. Cactus Jack's Restaurants, Australia
  - ► 3. Emporium Hotel, Australia
  - ► 4. Spicers Retreats, Australia
  - ► 5. Haidilao, China
  - ► 6. Hotel ICON, Hong Kong
  - ► 7. Pun Pun Sustainable Living and Learning Centre, Thailand
- ► Case studies from Europe
  - ► 8. Bio-Hotel Stanglwirt, Austria
  - ► 9. Best Western Premier (BWP) Hotel Slon, Slovenia
  - ► 10. Strand Spa and Conference Hotel, Estonia
- ► Case studies from North America
  - ► 11. Starbucks, United States of America
  - ► 12. Four Seasons Hotels and Resorts, United States of America
  - ► 13. Cameron Mitchell Restaurants, United States of America
  - ► 14. The Greenbrier, United States of America
- ► Summary
- ► Suggested Readings

Introduction

The purpose of this chapter is to provide you with real life examples of firms that have effectively used various concepts that are discussed in this text. These cases will allow you to understand how hospitality firms can effectively utilize service concepts, theories and ideas to provide them with a competitive advantage in the market while at the same time gaining customers' and employees' loyalty. In developing this chapter of cases, our aim was to identify a diverse group of mainly hospitality businesses from different parts of the world that have become recognized leaders in their market by adopting service-focused strategies. There are of course hundreds of other great companies out there practicing service management principles brilliantly, and many of these have been mentioned as examples throughout the book. Our hope is that the cases presented in this chapter will help illuminate the key ideas from this book in a 'real-world' way and help the reader see how everyday businesses put service management principles into action.

The way we sourced these cases was through our networks around the world—trying to find cases from non-traditional places such as Thailand, Africa and Eastern Europe. We provided a brief to our industry associates about the cases, and we asked them, often with the support of an academic colleague locally, to follow a basic script we provided, basing their case on some work that we, the two authors of this text, did some years ago (Solnet and Kandampully, 2008). In that study, we analyzed many successful service firms—those who are in the service 'folklore' where we inevitably hear stories reported all of the time about great customer service. We analyzed these companies and identified a number of common attributes that these firms possessed. Some of the attributes we identified included:

1. Brand strength (how internal and external customers perceive the organization)
2. Commitment to customer orientation / customer obsession (how the business stays steadfastly customer focused)
3. Commitment to employees / employee obsession (clear processes and values which emphasize employee well-being, training etc.)
4. A focus on the 'process' of service, rather than the core offering (clearly stated service systems and processes that set standards to guide employees)
5. Effective use of non-financial metrics to evaluate success (such as customer and employee measures)
6. Leadership in innovation and use of technology (innovative integration of technology to improve the customer experience)
7. Adherence to standards (often made public via books or freely available online to share)
8. Frequent recipients of awards for excellence (celebrate success and frequent recipients of awards for excellence including best employers)
9. Effective leadership and direction from a single founder / entrepreneur (often driven by strong leader / founder / entrepreneur)

© Lightspring/Shutterstock.com

At the end of each case are some questions. We hope that you will read these cases through a service management lens, one which is able to learn further the applications of service management concepts and theories practiced effectively in the industry. What we ask you to do is to pause as you read, reflect on the prior nine chapters and relate back to the concepts and theories examined to what is being practiced in the industry. That is where, we believe, the true learning will take place in this chapter—connecting theory to practice. As students, these examples will help you to understand the application of service management in everyday life and in business. What you learn in this book will change forever the way you assess firms and it will impact the way you relate to your place of work and to the people around you.

Case studies from Australasia

1.   Long Beach Hotel, Mauritius

By Associate Professor Thanika Devi Juwaheer

Introduction to the business

With 30 years' experience in the tourism and hospitality industry, The Sun Resorts Limited owns and manages beach resorts on the islands of Mauritius and the Maldives. The newest of their properties is the Long Beach Hotel, a resort which balances an urban feel with a relaxed, natural vibe that complements the beach setting. The company's philosophy is based on excellence in all fields of service, offering luxurious accommodation, impeccable cuisine, and a wide choice of sporting, recreational and entertainment facilities. The Long Beach Hotel is a prime example of a great service organization as it has received numerous awards for excellence, demonstrates a strong commitment to both customers and employees, and promotes a strict adherence to standards in order to enhance the service experience.

Its story of service excellence

Frequent recipients of awards for excellence

The close collaboration among the hotel's directors, architects, builders, landscape gardeners and interior designers ensured that the Long Beach Hotel has been a hit with guests and tourism professionals alike. Its accolades since its grand opening in 2011 include being listed among the *Sunday Times Travel Magazine*'s 100 Best Hotels in the World, receiving Best Resort 2011 from the prestigious French magazine *Hotel & Lodge,* being awarded a 'Certificate of Excellence' by TripAdvisor in 2012, and being commended as Country Winner in the Luxury Family Hotel category at the 2013 World Luxury Hotel Awards held in Phuket, Thailand. The World Luxury Hotel Awards recognize the world's most sought after hotels, lodges and resorts and are positioned as the pinnacle of achievement for luxury hotels worldwide, with voting being conducted by international tour operators, travel agents and hotel guests and winners being judged primarily on service delivery and effective management.

Vladimir Scanu, General Manager of the Long Beach Hotel, acknowledges the valuable contribution of his team of hotel employees in winning the award: "We take pride in having been selected Best Luxury Family Hotel in Mauritius, a prime destination with numerous competitive high end properties and recognized luxury hotels brands. I am glad to associate the passionate and committed team of professionals of Long Beach to this award".

Nicolas de Chalain, Chief Sales Officer of Sun Resorts, and himself a former General Manager of the Long Beach Hotel, welcomes this award as an opportunity to showcase the hotel on the world stage: "Today's travelers look for excellent value, impeccable service and the highest standards of quality in making their travel choice. Winning a World Luxury Hotel Award will help Long Beach to position itself as a resort celebrating exclusivity and uniqueness; indicators that truly define a luxury hotel".

Customer and employee obsession

All members of the Long Beach Hotel team share a passion for outstanding service delivery and a determination to exceed guests' expectations by offering a one-of-a-kind experience. The hotel has successfully developed these passionate, committed employees by creating a work environment where all team members feel fully integrated, respected and recognized as individuals working towards the same goals.

The organization's goals and core values are centered on the motto "blow away the customer", and include:

- offering products and services that exceed guests' expectations,
- creating the element of surprise (the 'wow factor'); and
- delivering a unique, personalized experience to every guest during his or her stay to encourage return visits.

Hotel managers remain focused on their customers by regularly updating the guest satisfaction questionnaire, conducting focus group interviews and tracking customer opinions on Web sites such as TripAdvisor.com. These methods provide valuable feedback on the hotel's performance and to improve the service experience. By demonstrating a commitment to continuous learning and knowledge sharing, the hotel managers also remain focused on their employees and foster a strong sense of collaboration and team spirit.

Standards and compliance

The Long Beach Hotel has successfully achieved and implemented a range of certifications and international quality standards, such as the ISO 9001 Quality Management System and the ISO 22000 Food Safety Management System. Among the measures of control, testing of food samples is done on a regular basis and the choice of suppliers is based on a strict set criteria. Employee training in proper hygiene, food handling and safety control, coupled with ongoing communication regarding current regulations, equips the employees of the Long Beach Hotel with the knowledge required to assess each and every stage of the food flow system. The certification therefore ensures both the quality and safety of the food served and can be seen as another way in which the Long Beach Hotel affirms its commitment to service excellence.

Conclusion

The Long Beach Hotel demonstrates a commitment to excellence that is an evolving journey, having already achieved international recognition for their service delivery, yet still aiming to improve the service experience for both employees and customers. Managers of the hotel proudly recognize the notable achievements to date and continuously strive for excellence by maintaining quality standards at all times, fostering a strong team environment and encouraging employees to offer all guests one of the most extraordinary experiences of their lifetimes.

Review Questions

1. If you were an employee at the Long Beach Hotel in the housekeeping department, how could you enact the organization's motto and "blow away the customer"?
2. Research other properties that have been recognized through the World Luxury Hotel Awards and list some key attributes that they all have in common.
3. Using your knowledge of service management, identify the tools the property employs to ensure employee and customer obsession.
4. Explain how international certifications such as the ISO 22000 for Food Safety Management system can enhance the satisfaction of hotel guests during their hotel stay.

2.   Cactus Jack's Restaurants, Australia

By Associate Professor David Solnet, in consultation with Jon Van Grinsven and Trent Van Grinsven, owners of the Pierre Restaurant Group and the Cactus Jack's Restaurant Group

Introduction to the business

Cactus Jack's is a small chain of casual theme restaurants based in Townsville, North Queensland, Australia. The restaurant company is based on the "Tex Mex" (Texas-Mexican) concept popular in the USA. The firm consists of eight full-service restaurants in Queensland and has been in business for over twenty years. The growth of the company has been driven by demand; when one restaurant in a market is unable to meet the demand from diners, they open up another one not too far away to ease the demand. The company's expansion across Queensland is testament to how busy and successful Cactus Jack's is.

The driving principle behind the restaurant chain is that eating out should be a complete experience and that the customer must have fun! Everything from the menu to the décor has been designed to enhance the sights, sounds, smells and tastes that customers experience when they visit.

Jon van Grinsven, Founder of Cactus Jack's, stated that his main aim was "to create a place where as soon as you step in, you feel like you are transported to another world and where the daily pressures and stresses could be left outside the door for a while." This has been achieved, in part, by instilling the right attitude in their staff, which enhances the feeling of escaping to 'Margaritaville'. Further reasons behind Cactus Jack's success will be outlined in the following sections.

Its story of service excellence

Customer obsession

Although there are many factors that have led to the success of the company, it is probably the singular and unbreakable focus on creating a particular customer experience that has kept the company so successful for so long.

The mission statement at Cactus Jack's is, "To serve inexpensive, high quality food in a uniquely designed atmosphere". However, it is the clear company philosophies, fully based on **"THE CUSTOMER IS KING"** principle, that have driven nearly all of the company decisions. Every employee in the company has the following values impressed upon them from day one:

1. Providing great value for money is vital to customer loyalty.
2. We must always treat guests as if they are always right even when they are wrong.
3. We care for all our clients (Ourselves. Our Team. & Our Customers).
4. We believe that if we look after our guests they will come back for more.
5. We will always try to seek a better way of doing things.

6. Work should be fun and challenging.
7. Standard systems will be the basis of our success . . . There is only one best way to operate and we want everyone operating that way (until we identify another best way).

Effective use of non-financial metrics to evaluate success

As the company began to grow from one to eight restaurants, keeping that steadfast customer focus became more challenging. With a strong vision for Cactus Jack's, combined with the challenges of growing and opening more restaurants further away from Townsville, the owner learned about balanced scorecards as applied to hospitality businesses via a 2006 magazine article written by one of the authors of this textbook.

The benefits of implementing a balanced scorecard type of system were highlighted in the article and seemed to align with his own (and his father's) basic business principles. In order to 'systemize' these ideals, the company embarked on the following mission:

1. Identify the important drivers of success (customers, employees);
2. Clarify and document detailed standards of customer experiences;
3. Determine a way to measure the non-financial performance of the business; and
4. Create staff and management bonus systems based on these non-financial metrics.

Over the course of the first 12 months, work was undertaken in consultation with management and staff to create a diagnostic system which would effectively measure the key strategic drivers listed above. This was designed to help the owner identify and gauge the long-term performance of the business.

The summary below provides further information about the way in which the balanced scorecard was set up for Cactus Jack's and highlights some of the key issues related to each area.

1. **Financial performance.** A matrix was created which was modeled on the company budgets for sales and profits. Weightings were then allocated to each criterion based on the importance given to that area by the owner and the company leadership team.
2. **Customer perceptions.** A detailed and complex customized Customer Experience Evaluation Program (similar to what is often called a mystery shopper program) was created. The first step in this process was a detailed mapping of the customer experience standards for the business (one of the benefits of this type of program is that it forces the business to clarify these standards in great detail). Once the standards were created, and some pilot tests run on the questionnaire, a regular series of visits were undertaken during every six-month period by highly trained evaluators. The results of each key service criterion were then tabulated and scored, with detailed reports which outline opportunities and provide scores for each aspect of each visit. Each report and the corresponding scores were e-mailed to the corporate

office and the respective management teams for review. This information was used to (a) improve the business, (b) let the corporate office gain an in-depth perspective about satisfaction and standards adherence and (c) inform the management remuneration program.

3. **Employee perceptions.** A customized organizational engagement survey was developed, which integrated service climate factors coupled with other related measures such as staff turnover intentions, internal service quality, employee engagement, perceptions of owner commitment to excellence and, finally, to provide a gauge of how well the company was 'practicing what it preaches' in terms of its philosophies. The survey is administered every six months with scores continually assessed for areas of improvement and areas where there are opportunities to improve. Managers meet in teams to strategize ways to improve various aspects of the survey results to ensure continuous work is done to improve the way employees perceive their workplace.

All of the measured items were weighted for importance with weightings varying from one year to the next, depending upon which areas the owner believes need particular focus for that year. All full-time staff and management are given specific goals whereby bonuses are paid provided certain targets are achieved.

Conclusion

As a result of the successful implementation of a balanced scorecard approach, major changes have occurred in the company. The entire team began to rally around the exact performance measures which the owner identified as important drivers for success. By focusing on customers, employees, training and individual performance ("What gets measured gets managed!"), sales and profits naturally flowed. The team has been able to share in small wins, work more closely in teams trying to make their targets and feel as though they could share in the successes of the business.

Rather than seeking success through financial measures only, the balanced scorecard measurement system has altered the focus to the important drivers of success and has helped take Cactus Jack's to a higher plane and protect its long-term viability.

Review Questions

1. Cactus Jack's has a clear mission statement that effectively conveys to both employees and customers why the company exists. Based on its mission and core philosophies, write a vision statement for the restaurant chain.

2. The managers of Cactus Jack's have defined 'one best way' of operating to guide employees in their practical service delivery. What are the three key elements that need to be taken into account to understand a service process properly?

3. If you were a service management consultant assisting a SME to improve their service offering, pitch a case as to why they should apply a balanced scorecard measurement system. Outline the potential challenges but also the ultimate benefits that the business could enjoy as a result.
4. Why is it important to understand the balance between service quality and costs?

3. Emporium Hotel, Australia

By Maria Golubovskaya, a former employee of the Emporium Hotel and Research Assistant to Associate Professor David Solnet

Introduction to the business

Emporium Hotel Brisbane is an independently owned and operated hotel, well-known for its luxury facilities and outstanding service. The property features 102 guest suites, a cocktail bar, pool, gym, sauna, patisserie and a conference center. The Emporium Hotel also benefits from its prime location in Fortitude Valley and proximity to restaurants, retail and entertainment options. The hotel is committed to superior service quality and delivering a memorable experience, promising an exquisite stay for every guest.

Emporium has a strong reputation in Australia and has triumphed against major brands in the market by consistently taking the title of Australia's Best Luxury Accommodation and Best Boutique Hotel (awarded at Queensland Tourism Awards 2014, 2013, 2012, 2009 and 2008; HM Awards 2013; Qantas Australian Tourism Awards 2013 and 2012). This case study will reveal the hotel's service attributes and the strategies that underpin its success.

Its story of service excellence

Brand strength

By virtue of winning a host of major industry awards over the years, the Emporium brand is well-recognized on a national scale as an outstanding luxury hotel. Opened in 2007, Emporium Hotel has already gained a strong reputation and is a powerful competitor to international five-star hotel chains. Emporium markets itself as a boutique, service-focused hotel that creates 'exquisite stays' for its guests. The hotel offers relaxation, luxury and indulgence, with the quality amenities, fixtures and overall design of the property supporting this image.

Due to the strength of its brand, the hotel enjoys a high level of customer loyalty. Emporium excels at retaining its existing customers and building its base of loyal clientele by providing seamless, personalized service and professional, hospitable staff that ensure a positive guest experience. The hotel also attracts new customers through various communication mediums, including printed and broadcast advertising, by promising a magical and memorable stay.

Customer and employee obsession

A key factor of the hotel's success is a steadfast focus on both its customers and employees. Emporium's philosophy, "We recognize that our guests are the reason we are here," sends a clear message to employees regarding the hotel's expectations for customer service (from the interview with HR manager and Marketing Director). This creates a unique service-oriented organizational culture where employees are trained, rewarded and encouraged to prioritize the guests and their needs to ensure a flawless experience. The hotel provides regular training sessions to encourage employees to go the extra mile for the guest, be sensible and empathetic, and to have a keen eye for detail. By providing the freedom and space for employees to do so, the hotel is well recognized for its personalized, outstanding service and liberal empowerment policy. Furthermore, the hotel holds staff award ceremonies on a quarterly basis where staff are recognized for service excellence and a customer-oriented approach. The winners are presented their awards by the General Manager and are posted on the staff noticeboard and the hotel's Facebook page. This reinforces a service climate in the organization and reminds all staff about the hotel's core values.

Further demonstrating Emporium's customer focus is the customer feedback system that is taken very seriously by management. All customer feedback is systematically tracked and reviewed on a daily basis and addressed by the General Manager himself. Any compliment, complaint or comment is given a personal response and recognized as an opportunity to improve the guest experience.

With regard to gaining employee commitment, the hotel adopts a strategic view of HRM that sees its employees as a valuable resource and long-term investment. Such powerful loyalty enables the hotel to create a competitive advantage and makes it difficult for competitors to replicate. The hotel offers a supportive and positive working environment that encourages open communication and stimulates a team spirit. Employees feel they can rely on and learn from each other, have the freedom to voice their ideas and feel empowered to provide service that goes above and beyond their job descriptions.

Emporium also provides customized training programs that assist staff to develop 'skills for life' (i.e., developing a proactive approach, building self-esteem and problem-solving skills). Every employee, from department heads to front-line staff, will participate in an average of four full days of training per year, where staff can share their experiences and exchange useful tips on how to handle different situations and how to better cope with the pressures they are exposed to in the workplace. Every new employee also attends an orientation day and induction training session to learn about the company and brand standards. In addition, monthly meetings are held within each department, providing opportunities to build strong social bonds between employees. To further develop employee cohesion, the hotel runs a number of staff social events during the year, such as 'Taste of Harmony' lunches, family day with BBQ, and the annual Christmas party, which encourages employees to interact and build connections across all hotel departments (from the interview with HR Manager and Marketing Director). All these HR initiatives encourage employees to stay engaged and committed to the hotel, as well as to better understand the hotel's culture of customer service.

Driven by a strong leader

To a great extent, the company owes its success to its General Manager, without whom the level of service excellence achieved would not be possible. Firstly, by adopting an open door management style, the Emporium General Manager cultivates an organizational climate that emphasizes values such as trust and empowerment, and demonstrates an openness to suggestions and feedback. Secondly, the GM's consultative/coaching management style contributes to the employees' well-being and happiness, which in turn translates into superior customer service. And last but not least, the Emporium General Manager advocates the hotel's adoption of non-financial metrics to evaluate employees' performance based on customer satisfaction, highlighting a commitment to continuous improvement in guest experiences. Thus, as the hotel's leader, the Emporium General Manager has successfully established a competitive business and fostered an environment that ensures both guests and employees are delighted, satisfied and happy.

Conclusion

Overall, Emporium Hotel's success is primarily attributable to its strong leader and the unwavering customer-focused approach he instills, which is supported by strategies including empowering employees, encouraging collaboration and cooperation across all departments and recognizing service excellence through employee awards. Such a strong service culture in turn creates memorable guest experiences that build customer loyalty and positive word-of-mouth and, consequently, enhances the strength of Emporium's brand in the market.

Review Questions

1. As an independent hotel, the Emporium enjoys a high level of brand strength and customer loyalty. What attributes of the hotel do you think primarily contribute to such positive value perceptions and how easy would these be for competitors to emulate?
2. List some of the non-financial benefits that the Emporium Hotel will enjoy from developing a strong organizational culture.
3. What makes the Emporium General Manager a 'leader' rather than just a 'manager'?

4. Spicers Retreats, Australia

By Siobhán Freyne, Research Assistant to Associate Professor David Solnet, in consultation with Mr David Assef, Managing Director of the Spicers Retreats

Introduction to the business

The Spicers Retreats are a collection of seven luxury boutique hotels and lodges located in South East Queensland and the Hunter Valley in New South Wales, Australia. Guests are promised "an escape from the everyday into a world of luxury, personalized service and attention to detail" (Spicers Retreats, n.d., online). Whether it is amongst the vineyards, on a mountaintop, surrounded by the rainforest or accompanied by a working cattle farm, each property is unique and is designed to epitomize 'relaxed luxury'.

The key to Spicers' success is that they have focused their efforts on providing an exceptional *experience* based on a collection of elements including food and beverage, spa treatments, a friendly yet unobtrusive guest service team and the natural environment. They note that "it's not solely about a comfortable bed, quality furnishings, personalized service and great food, it's just as much about the feeling of being renewed and reinvigorated by the land itself" (Spicers Retreats, Online, n.d.), which showcases the beauty and richness of flora, fauna and history that delivers another level—an adventure or experience with substance. The Spicers management team successfully enhances the service encounter and ensures that every 'moment of truth' is maximized by remaining steadfastly focused on both their customers and employees, and by integrating technology into their service processes to improve the customer experience. Through the combined effect of these attributes, Spicers has established a reputation for service excellence both within Australia and internationally.

Its story of service excellence

Customer obsession

Mr. David Assef, Managing Director of the Spicers Retreats, states that the creation of quality guest experiences is essentially driven by the philosophy of "people over profit", which encapsulates the organization's strong customer focus. Personalization is a key feature of Spicers' service processes. From the reservation system to the arrival and farewell gifts, each guest's experience is customized to suit their preferences and the occasion. To better meet their customers' needs and also evaluate success, Spicers utilizes guest feedback surveys and regularly monitors and analyzes online rating websites such as TripAdvisor and Dimmi. Importantly, the managers at Spicers have recognized the importance of a well-trained guest service team in achieving the organization's goal of delivering an exceptional experience. This strong focus on their employees complements their customer- centric approach.

Employee obsession

An unwavering employee orientation is demonstrated by the organization's human resource management strategies. When recruiting, the key attributes managers look for in potential employees are strong communication skills, a 'can do' attitude, natural warmth and smile, drive and determination, and prior experience in the industry. Above all, however, employees must have a customer- and team-centric approach, to ensure that they are always focused on enhancing the guest experience. The induction process is also clearly defined and includes an orientation program, on-the-job mentoring and a buddy system, all of which contribute to the development of a strong service culture within the organization.

To foster employee well-being, the management team at Spicers utilizes a variety of tools and techniques. For instance, consideration is given to the benefits of an aesthetically pleasing work environment, and monthly 'one on ones' between managers and front-line employees are scheduled to provide an opportunity for every voice to be heard. Empowerment is also a key HRM strategy within the organization. Team members are empowered to contribute to change and are also held accountable for quality standards, which engenders a feeling of commitment towards shared goals and results. Furthermore, a unique feature of Spicers' HRM strategy is their 'Brightness of Future' (BOF) program, which, according to David Assef, is about "ensuring that should an employee wish to grow, improve and be promoted within then we like to set a path and work with them to achieve this". The opportunity is provided to employees to move between departments or properties to broaden their experience and also engage in further development relevant to their career with external education providers. Ultimately, this program enhances team motivation, increases earning capacity and improves retention rates. Finally, an annual awards night is organized where both financial achievements and service excellence are recognized. While improving employees' motivation and job satisfaction, the combination of these techniques also reinforces the organization's constant customer focus.

Leadership in innovation and use of technology

The Spicers Retreats offer a prime example of how widespread and easily accessible technologies can be harnessed to improve the guest experience. For instance, e-mail represents a simple yet powerful tool for providing personalized service. At the conclusion of their stay, guests of Spicers receive a 'welcome home' e-mail that gives them the chance to provide feedback directly to the property or via TripAdvisor and, six months later, a follow-up e-mail is sent to invite guests back with a special offer. Monthly e-newsletters are also sent to keep customers abreast of any changes and notify them of current specials and packages, which builds Spicers' brand community. In addition, a cloud-based reservation system is used to allow each property to check reservations across the organization so that guests do not have to make multiple inquires. The reservation system tracks multiple stays as well as guests' individual likes, dislikes and dietary requirements, enabling employees to provide a personalized service experience regardless of which Spicers Retreat the customer returns to.

Conclusion

As a result of their commitment to customers' and employees' well-being, and by effectively utilizing technologies in their service processes, the Spicers Retreats have established a multi-award-winning brand within the luxury accommodation market. The key factor that differentiates a Spicers property from another accommodation property is the unique *experience* on offer, generated by a collection of elements including outstanding service, gourmet food, finely appointed furnishings and spectacular natural settings, which work together to leave a lasting impression. While it may be easy for competitors to reproduce the tangible elements, it is the strong service culture and unwavering commitment to service excellence that are fostered within the organization and that would be hard to emulate.

Review Questions

1. A key factor in Spicers' success is the way the service system has been specifically designed to ensure superior service. What are the three fundamental principles that form the basis of a well-planned and executed service system and how does the way Spicers operate reflect these?
2. As outlined in this case study, the Spicers team strives to maximize the 'moments of truth' to ensure a positive customer experience. Outline the key challenges associated with managing the critical encounters and how service organizations can overcome these.
3. If you were an employee at Spicers, what additional activities would you suggest to assist the organization to better meet or exceed every customer's expectations and also reinforce the existing brand promise of 'relaxed luxury'?

5.   Haidilao, China

By Jun Luo, Martin J. Liu and Alain Yee-Loong Chong

Introduction to the business

Hot-pot, also known as 'steamboat', is a traditional Asian food that is eaten by placing a metal pot in the middle of a dining table and adding vegetables, meat and flavorings to a simmering soup base. Due to this standardized cooking style, restaurants in the hot-pot industry are not easily differentiated. However, Haidilao, a 19-year-old hot-pot restaurant chain in mainland China, regularly exceeds its competition by ranking first on the rating website Dianping—the Chinese version of Yelp. According to customers' feedback and the founder Zhang Yong's self-reflection, the secret for Haidilao's success lies in its excellent service and its operational philosophy—service first, customer first.

Demonstrating its popularity, Haidilao has won some of the most influential awards in the catering industry in China and has experienced rapid expansion. The company's growth has increased from six branches in the first six years to around 50 branches opening in the following six years, amounting to more than 90 branches in total. Subsequently, Haidilao has become an international restaurant chain, having launched new branches in Singapore and the United States of America.

Its story of service excellence

A focus on the 'process' of service

Haidilao's ultimate goal is to offer comprehensive and considerate service to satisfy customers' needs. To achieve that goal, Haidilao has standardized procedures, because the operational flow of the service encounter and procedures will influence customers' satisfaction. While standardized service procedures are necessary to meet customers' expectations, in order to exceed expectations some customized service procedures are also highly advocated. Ultimately, Haidilao strives to provide detailed, caring and customized services for their customers.

The care shown for customers is evident throughout the whole service experience. For instance, attendants are available in the car park to assist with parking, customers are greeted at the entrance by a waitress, and, even after going to Haidilao just two or three times, the employees will usually remember the names and even dining preferences of customers. These small but personal gestures often make positive impressions on customers and contribute to the overall service experience. Furthermore, due to the popularity of Haidilao, customers may need to wait for a few hours to get a table; however, to alleviate the stress of waiting customers are provided with a series of amusements or activities to keep them entertained. For instance, drinks and snacks are offered, along with books, magazines, games of poker and chess, as well as origami paper. Customers who can create more than 30 paper cranes while waiting will be served a starter free of charge later on. Each Haidilao also has a designated space for children to play in, and, while waiting, women can get their nails done while men can have their shoes polished. All of these activities not only minimize potential dissatisfaction that could be caused by the long waiting time, but also create a unique dining experience.

Throughout the service process, Haidilao employees are passionate and attentive, show initiative to creatively satisfy customers' needs, and constantly try to predict what customers may want and then provide it before being asked. Efficiency is also key, so when customers enter the dining areas, waitresses will give each guest a towel to freshen up, take drink orders and provide free fruit as soon as they sit down. In order to make the dining experience more comfortable, customers are also given aprons and a small plastic bag for keeping clothes and phones safe from any spills from the hot pot, as well as a cloth to clean glasses and headbands for women with long hair. Special care is also provided for seniors and children, who are offered soft food such as steamed eggs, soft tofu and porridge. There are even employees available to help with childcare and feeding. Such thoughtful support mechanisms offered by Haidilao motivates its employees to continuously think of creative ways to enhance service and to exceed customers' expectations and the success of this strategy is evident in the Haidilao's high retention rate, with 85% being repeat customers.

Effective use of non-financial metrics

Haidilao does not assess its performance based on profit because this would have a negative impact on employees' initiative, which, in turn, would have a negative effect on customer satisfaction. For instance, employees in Haidilao do not 'force' customers to purchase higher priced food and would even suggest half portions if they perceived that customers had ordered too much. Additionally, Haidilao's employees would not suggest any alcohol consumption unless consumers make a specific request, despite the potential profits this could make for the company.

Employee obsession

Haidilao greatly acknowledges the value of their employees as the key points of contact for the customers. The company's managers believe that only when employees are satisfied, their efficiency and productivity can be enhanced and, in turn, high customer satisfaction (the ultimate goal) can be reached. As such, Haidilao treats each of their employees as family members and offers them the following package of benefits. Apartments are rented for employees in upmarket residential areas that are typically a 20-minute walk from the restaurant, to minimize the commute to work. To ensure their comfort, amenities such as air conditioners, heating systems and Internet service are provided, along with housekeepers to clean. Furthermore, Haidilao provides higher salaries relative to other restaurants, health insurance for both employees and their parents and assistance finding schools for their children. Haidilao believes that if the employees have better living conditions, they are likely to have fewer burdens or worries and will thus be able to fully focus their attention on serving their customers. Subsequently, Haidilao has a low staff turnover rate and, most importantly, its employees' appreciation, which means that in return they work wholeheartedly, creatively and efficiently to provide service back to their company.

Additionally, Haidilao provides a series of training sessions for their employees. Unlike other organizations, the training extends beyond 'on the job' requirements to include practical 'survival skills' that could benefit employees outside their life within the organization, for instance, typing, IT skills, accounting and driving. Haidilao also adopts the tutor-tutee system. The tutors are responsible for training both the basic serving skills and the organizational philosophy—'customers first'. After being appropriately trained, Haidilao employees are empowered to make prompt decisions to satisfy customers, such as offering discounts or providing free meals to customers. This ensures that when service failures occur, service providers can make immediate recovery efforts to improve the customer's experience. The empowerment strategy also indicates respect and trust in employees, which improves their enthusiasm, creativity and efficiency. For these employees, Haidilao is not just a job, but also their own family business. They are not just one of many employees, but rather members of an extended family. According to an old Chinese saying, "gentlemen die for those who appreciate them".

Conclusion

Haidilao is an outstanding service organization that has established a reputation for excellent customer service and built a loyal customer base by taking a keen interest in employee well-being. The management approach of measuring success based on non-financial metrics contributes to customers' and employees' satisfaction, while the focus that is placed on the service process, rather than the core food and beverage offering, has enabled the restaurant chain to develop a unique advantage in a highly competitive market. Haidilao enjoys positive word-of-mouth from its regular customers with one customer commenting online that "there is no human being who could stop Haidilao's caring services". This encapsulates the organization's unwavering commitment to customer service and highlights the superior nature of the service experience at Haidilao.

Review Questions

1. Considering Haidilao's growing number of branches across multiple countries, outline the pros and cons behind standardizing versus customizing the service experience.
2. How could Haidilao's strategies of balancing supply and demand be applied in other service contexts such as hotels?
3. Describe some of the ways in which Haidilao could understand its customers' expectations better in the new markets that the company is trying to enter.

6.   Hotel ICON, Hong Kong

By Professor Kaye Chon and Dr. Sam Kim

Introduction to the business

Hotel ICON was officially opened on the 21st of September 2011 with a special purpose: to offer a learning environment in which the aspirations of future hoteliers come to life. The hotel is part of the School of Hotel and Tourism Management (SHTM) at the Hong Kong Polytechnic University and is under the academic leadership of its Dean, Professor Kaye Chon. In this hotel, students, teachers and seasoned hospitality professionals come together united by one goal: "to make your stay utterly memorable and pleasurable."

There are two key facets to the complex—the hotel itself, which consists of 262 accommodation rooms, restaurants, a swimming pool, spa and conference rooms, and the SHTM side, which includes the faculty and staff offices, classrooms, laboratories, a training restaurant and a resources center. The hotel is managed by a team of professionals hired by the university with about 500 students under training throughout the year. Despite being independently owned and managed by the university without any affiliation with a renowned brand or company, Hotel ICON has been highly successful. This was evident in its second year of operation, with the hotel running at an average occupancy rate of 85% or higher and with an average daily room rate of more than US$250. Furthermore, TripAdvisor has consistently ranked Hotel ICON among the top three hotels in Hong Kong.

Its story of service excellence

Customer obsession

The service experience at Hotel ICON is shaped by research conducted at the SHTM, which continuously explores customers' preferences and trends. By better understanding its customers, Hotel ICON can improve its service offering and, ultimately, its guests' experiences. The research also provides solutions for some of the hotel's management challenges, such as guests' willingness to pay more for luxury room amenities, the effectiveness of internships, green management strategies, competition and financial forecasting.

Hotel ICON puts theory into practice and demonstrates its strong customer focus through its service design and processes. For instance, lounge facilities are provided for guests who arrive earlier than check-in time and all items in the room minibar are complimentary to minimize potential disagreements between guests and front-office staff. Hotel ICON also offers membership in the Wine and Dine program, which provides customers with invitations to attend special dinners prepared by world-renowned chefs and wine-pairing dinners with industry experts. Looking beyond its paying customers, Hotel ICON also serves the community in which it operates by donating food to an organization that provides meals for local families in need.

Employee obsession

Being built for the SHTM, Hotel ICON operates under a clear mandate to benefit the local hotel industry through experimentation, research and, importantly, training of the future workforce. As such, employees' well-being and development are emphasized. When joining Hotel ICON, employees undertake an intensive orientation conducted by the General Manager and division heads, as well as an induction program that ensures employees are well versed in the relevant skills required to serve guests. A wide range of professional classes are also offered to encourage employees to further extend themselves, and employee-driven social and recreational activities are organized to engender strong working relationships.

In line with its education-oriented approach to hotel management, internships for undergraduate classes of the SHTM are offered to ensure that all interested students are given the opportunity to participate. Since its opening, about 150 student interns have worked at Hotel ICON on customized training programs, which involve one trainer mentor per three trainees. Some of the interns who successfully complete the program are then selected as employees. In addition, the hotel provides scholarships to students who are potential future employees. Therefore, the purpose behind Hotel ICON and its links to the university ensures that employees remain top-of-mind and training is seen as a key corporate priority.

Leadership in innovation and use of technology

The focus on teaching and research assists Hotel ICON to be at the forefront of innovation and utilization of technology and setting new standards in hotel management. For instance, the SHTM has a dedicated facility, the Samsung Digital Lab for Hospitality Technology, which is equipped with state-of-the-art technology. Reserved for use by students and researchers, each computer has a variety of software packages available including specialized hospitality and tourism programs, business applications and advanced data analysis systems.

Another example of leadership in innovation is the SHTM's global competition that challenged hotel suppliers in design, technology and well-being to create 'Tomorrow's Guestrooms'. Entries included an energy efficient and eco-friendly minibar, a wireless locking system that allows cell phones to open access-controlled doors and a television that allows the guest service agent to communicate visually with guests by uploading hotel and city information in real-time to the screen. Winners were rewarded by having their products and services implemented within three dedicated guestrooms at Hotel ICON for six months, to test and explore customers' responses. With a view to shaping the future of hotel rooms, the project showcased new products, designs and business concepts and highlighted the importance of the hotel, university and industry all working in partnership. By conducting research of this type and by constantly encouraging innovation, the hotel demonstrates its support of the industry and future hoteliers, and also further improves and drives excellence in the hospitality industry.

With regard to 'green' considerations and sustainability, Hotel ICON also utilizes new innovations and technologies to improve the customer experience. For example, the hotel has been designed with a vertical garden in the lobby, which has 8,603 plants of 71 species, a green roof and a landscaped garden, to stimulate the release of oxygen and thereby provide clean, fresh air for guests. Furthermore, Hotel ICON's check-in process is paperless, which saved 2.39 tons of paper (or 40 trees) in 2012, a recycling system is in place for hotel waste and the "We Care" program allows guests to choose when they want linen and towels to be replaced. To save energy without impacting guests' comfort, the hotel tries to maximize the use of natural ventilation and lighting, lamps are installed with high-efficiency LED lights and, if a space is not being used, electronic sensors switch off all lights and other electric functions. As a result of the hotel's energy-saving practices, it was awarded the Carbon-Care® Label by Carbon Care Asia Ltd, which recognizes an achievement in carbon footprint reduction.

Conclusion

Hotel ICON is a unique service organization due to its function as a teaching and learning facility for future hoteliers. While there is an intense focus on the well-being of its students and employees, there is equally strong attention paid to the customer. Being linked to the university, Hotel ICON applies research outcomes to working practices for higher quality customer service and more efficient management. The hotel also applies the latest technologies and innovations with the aim of improving the guest experience and for research purposes. Each element of the hotel's design and processes are fashioned with stakeholder interests in mind, from nurturing future service providers, ensuring a seamless and comfortable stay for guests, contributing to society through energy saving and food donations and partnering with industry operators in order to drive innovation and excellence in hospitality service provision. All of these factors combined highlight how Hotel ICON is a customer-centric organization that is setting new standards in service excellence.

Review Questions

1. To what extent do you think sustainable management practices contribute to Hotel ICON's profitability and guest satisfaction?
2. You have been offered the opportunity to enter Hotel ICON's competition to shape the future of hotel rooms—pitch a new and innovative hotel product, design or business concept that you believe should be in 'Tomorrow's Guestrooms'.
3. Hotel ICON is committed to supporting not only their employees and immediate customers, but also the broader local community where potential customers live—a philosophy which can be applied across all service contexts. Provide examples of how other service organizations, such as airlines and restaurants, can give back to the communities in which they operate and describe how such a strategy can create a competitive advantage.

7. Pun Pun Sustainable Living and Learning Centre, Thailand

By Dr. Benjamin Piers William Ellway

Introduction to the business

Pun Pun is a sustainable living and learning center situated on an organic farm in the northern province of Chiang Mai, Thailand. On average, between 15 and 20 community members live and work at Pun Pun. Pun Pun's key service activity is holding monthly on-site workshops, longer courses and internships on self-reliance practices, which include growing organic food, building natural adobe homes and experimenting with low-tech appropriate technologies. The Centre also welcomes daily casual visitors and is active in delivering off-site workshops, conducting outreach projects, selling a range of products made on-site and in collaboration with local villagers and operating two organic vegetarian restaurants in Chiang Mai City. In addition, an on-site seed center collects and propagates indigenous and rare varieties, and shares and exchanges these with individuals across Thailand. Demonstrating its success, Pun Pun celebrated its tenth anniversary in 2013, its courses are often fully booked, and a new restaurant is currently being built that is due to open in 2014.

Its story of service excellence

Brand strength

One of the critical drivers for the success of Pun Pun has been its brand strength, which has developed largely as a result of the attention that its activities have drawn. For example, Pun Pun has been featured on a number of Thai TV shows, including a full-length documentary. Its founder, Jon Jandai, is regularly invited to give talks across Thailand and has published a number of books that focus on his life, Pun Pun and seed saving. Furthermore, Pun Pun is reaching a larger audience due to the popularity of Jon's TEDx talk called "Life is Easy", which as of August 2014 had attracted over 360,000 views. Internationally, Pun Pun's brand is also well-known in the sustainable living community. This is a result of Pun Pun's involvement in community networks that span countries across the globe. The local and international strength of Pun Pun's brand is demonstrated in the popularity of its various training sessions and workshops, which are attended by both Thai nationals and participants from a vast number of countries.

Customer obsession

It is important to clarify precisely who Pun Pun's customers are. They include participants in its on-site training courses, but also represent a more diverse group. For example, Pun Pun regularly leads or contributes to outreach activities, such as a homebuilding project for Karen hill-tribes and a yearly women's building workshop that attracts international participants. By co-producing and selling locally made products and running two restaurants, they broaden their customer base further.

Given its diverse range of services and products, how does Pun Pun orientate its activities to its customers? The answer is through its focus on well-being, which is both a central value that guides its philosophy and also a key aspect of value that its customers can receive and develop. For example, all the food and beverages in both restaurants are made using locally sourced organic vegetables, fruit and herbs, which result in healthy meals that in many cases have medicinal benefits. This focus on improving the well-being of its customers is also reflected in the products it sells on-site, as well as its courses and outreach activities. For instance, the practical skill-based training is immediately followed by an experience-sharing session, through which the trainers and community members at Pun Pun provide an emotionally safe and open environment to provide participants with the opportunity to share their experiences, fears, concerns or hopes. It is clear that while customers benefit greatly from practical engagement in specialized activities, they also value the experience of being able to discuss and listen in these sessions, which are a source of inspiration and increased confidence.

Employee obsession

Commitment to employees' well-being, who are more commonly referred to as 'community members', is at the core of what Pun Pun does, since the very notion of sustainable self-reliant living is centered on the values of physical, mental and spiritual health. While each person at Pun Pun receives a very modest monthly salary, it is the safe, clean and relaxing natural work environment that they value. Openness and tolerance towards others, in terms of gender, race, age, religion and sexuality, is practiced at the site and is explained at the introductory training session for all courses. Pun Pun is not driven by profit; however, there is a central fund that, when available, is shared in the form of travel grants for its community members to participate in training elsewhere or for knowledge transfer to other communities. Finally, Pun Pun encourages its members to grow and experiment. Anyone can propose or start a new project or initiative and there are great opportunities for each person to learn new skills and develop knowledge either on-site or elsewhere. Structured meetings are infrequent, yet everybody is approachable and people talk informally, which creates a relaxed but respectful work environment.

Leadership in innovation and use of technology

The absence of cutting-edge gadgets or the latest mainstream innovations does not stop Pun Pun from leading in the use of technology and placing it at the center of the customer experience. For instance, all accommodation is built using natural building techniques that automatically cool rooms through excellent heat absorption and retention, while solar panels heat water in the cooler season so everyone can enjoy a hot shower. Another important innovation is the year-round fresh drinking water that is available straight from any tap in the community (a luxury that not even the most exclusive of hotels in Thailand can boast), which is enabled by a low-tech filtration system. Innovative use of technology is also evident in the rice that customers eat, which is grown on-site and prepared using a special process that emerged from experimentation with the semi-separation of the husk from the grain. The process is based on a special milling technique only applicable to small-scale production and involves the subsequent steaming of the rice to prepare it for consumption. The result? A deliciously fragrant variety of rice which customers are unlikely to experience elsewhere. Since Pun Pun grows most of its food organically with support from local networks, both casual visitors, workshop participants and interns experience the community's passion to experiment with low technology.

Driven by a strong leader

The success of Pun Pun can be firmly placed at the feet of its founder, Jon, a humble and wise man who built the center together with his wife Peggy and a tight-knit group of friends.

Starting from a piece of land that upon moving onto it was barren and lifeless, the group worked tirelessly to develop it into a thriving natural environment that provides food and shelter. The community members at Pun Pun hold a deeply felt sense of respect and reverence for Jon. Despite his lack of a formal higher education (he dropped out of university) and his disinterest in business, Jon instills confidence, calm and hope in all those around him and who visit Pun Pun. Through his gentle style of interaction with others, his openness to new ideas and his desire to let everybody find their own path, Jon exhibits a unique style of leadership that makes members and visitors understand that he respects all, judges none, and shows others, through his own work, what is possible.

Conclusion

Pun Pun and its members are not your average service business. In fact, if asked, they would probably not even consider themselves to be a business or a service provider. There is little formal structure, limited planning and meetings are infrequent. There is no career path for members and they receive a very small monthly salary. But community members are happy, and this shines through in the quality and authenticity of all its service offerings. Similarly, despite limited formal service design in structuring their courses, customers enjoy the training and in many instances it has a lasting impact, changing what they do and how they live their lives. Its restaurants attract tourists but also have a large base of regular customers who are happy to wait for its self-labeled 'slow-food' that might take a little longer and vary in its ingredients each time, yet is always based upon the best quality produce and prepared with care. With ongoing interest from and exposure in the media, and regular interaction and network building within the community, Pun Pun will continue to be an exemplar of service excellence in the field of sustainable living, organic farming and food and self-reliance.

Review Questions

1. Despite its informal and unstructured approach, list three key service management practices or principles that are evident in the way Pun Pun operates.
2. If Pun Pun decides to grow its business, what challenges do you think it will face and how would you recommend it addresses these challenges? In particular, think of how they will balance supply and demand.
3. If you were a start-up business in the service industry, what lessons could you learn from Pun Pun and how would you integrate them into your own way of operating?

Case studies from Europe

8.   Bio-Hotel Stanglwirt, Austria

By Christina Zhang, Research Assistant to Professor Jay Kandampully

Introduction to the business

The Bio-Hotel Stanglwirt, located in Going (near Kitzbühel), Tyrol, Austria, is one of the oldest hotels in Europe, with a history dating back to 1609. The hotel boasts 270 employees, accommodates more than 110,000 overnight stays and serves in excess of 100,000 guests per year, making it an important economic engine in Austria. However, it is not its size that makes Stanglwirt outstanding in such a competitive hospitality industry, but rather it is the exceptional service that enables Stanglwirt to maintain its position over 400 years and successfully connect its customers to the brand.

Its story of service excellence

Customer obsession

Service orientation is the norm in Stanglwirt. Buzzwords such as tradition, sustainability and hospitality fuel the well-defined philosophy of service at Stanglwirt: "400 years of hospitality, at home, at the Stanglwirt" (Stanglwirt, 2014, online). As this statement suggests, the hotel strives to make every guest feel like he or she is at home, which encourages a customer-centric culture to permeate the organization. According to the Stanglwirt marketing team, they implement a customer-focused service philosophy by seeking every opportunity to manage guests' expectations—"everybody should get the right view, nothing exaggerated, nothing dishonest. We mean what we promise." This ensures that the guests' actual experiences at least match their expectations, which will in turn increase perceptions of service quality and customer satisfaction. Therefore, service orientation and customer obsession can be seen as the essence of the Stanglwirt's competitiveness. This is endorsed by the numerous awards it has won, including the TripAdvisor Travellers Choice Award in 2013, and being recognized as one of the best hotels worldwide no less than 12 times, as rated by their guests.

Employee obsession

The Stanglwirt is 'home' not just to the guests, but also to the employees. It is one of the largest employers in the Austrian hotel industry and there is a genuine understanding within the organization that its employees play a key role in achieving high-quality service. It is a challenge to achieve high levels of satisfaction among such a large number of employees, especially the young staff members, apprentices and trainees who are generally more difficult to handle because it is often their first stay away from their family home (Stanglwirt, 2014). However, recognizing their value, Stanglwirt is very creative and focused on their young employees. For instance, an effective and unique project was created by Stanglwirt for its apprentices and trainees, being the Lehrlingsprojekt 2012. It was an event organized only by young staff members and included a gala dinner for their parents, various department managers and experienced staff members. The event was a success and provided an opportunity for the young staff members to learn from more experienced staff members and establish stronger relationships with the management team in the hotel.

Conclusion

The Bio-Hotel Stanglwirt has maintained its reputation for over 400 years because it provides an experience that guests and employees can connect with. "At home at the Stanglwirt" encapsulates the well-defined service strategy of ensuring the comfort of both their external and internal customers and the goal of creating an atmosphere where everybody gets exceptional hospitality. Overall, the Stanglwirt successfully positions itself to be the perfect place to stay for guests and the ideal working environment for employees.

Review Questions

1. If employees of the Stanglwirt live on-site at the hotel, discuss the implications of this with regard to managing supply and demand.
2. The Lehrlingsprojekt 2012 was a simple yet effective way of enhancing employee satisfaction and building team morale. If you were the HR Manager at the Stanglwirt, suggest other activities or strategies that you could implement to ensure employees feel at 'home'.
3. Explain the logic behind the Stanglwirt's marketing strategy with reference to the 'Gaps' Model.

9. Best Western Premier (BWP) Hotel Slon, Slovenia

By Maja Uran Maravic

Introduction to the business

The Best Western is the largest global hotel brand, connecting almost 4,078 independently owned and managed hotels in 98 countries. As a member of this chain, the Best Western Premier (BWP) Hotel Slon is a 4-star business hotel in the historic center of Slovenia's capital, Ljubljana. The BWP Hotel Slon is among the most financially successful hotels in Slovenia, with one of the highest annual room occupancy rates despite its relatively high accommodation price. The ability to charge higher prices does not stem from the hotel's favorable location but rather from its excellent service, given that there are other hotels nearby that enjoy the same location but have lower room rates. During the slow growth times from 2007 to 2012 while other hotels were cutting costs, BWP Hotel Slon instead improved the variety and quality of services offered to guests and kept prices consistent.

Subsequently, the hotel increased its income by 25%, its REVPAR (revenue per available room) by 17%, its occupancy rates by 10% and the salaries of its employees by 37%. This customer-focused approach to management is thus an ideal example of how service managers can remain competitive despite external challenges.

Its story of service excellence

Brand strength

In Slovenia, there are only two international hotel chains (Best Western and Kempinski Hotels) with four properties altogether, which stand alongside several hotels that are owned by a few local companies. The manager of BWP Hotel Slon sees many advantages of being a member of an international hotel chain, including brand awareness, quality assurance, a rewards program, additional promotion at trade shows, global corporate contracts, an employee benefits program and a knowledge network.

Customer obsession

As aforementioned, while other hotels in the region were concentrating on reducing costs, BWP Hotel Slon chose a different business strategy that demonstrated their unwavering customer focus. They defined a service strategy that focused on three areas that were thought to be the most important to their guests: location, bed concept and breakfast. The hotel's main service strategy was, and remains to be, providing the best rooms and breakfast in town at the best location. Managers thoroughly studied the guest's value chain and prepared a plan of critical investments, including a soft refurbishment. In recent years, the hotel has changed the bed concept, improved the breakfast provided, replaced the towels, bath robes, textiles and air conditioning system and renovated the function rooms, spa and fitness center. Despite the costs involved, these upgrades were made in order to improve the customer experience, which highlights the hotel's customer-centric approach.

Employee obsession

The BWP Hotel Slon is led by a young and professionally qualified manager who is focused on setting a good example to all employees and ensuring their well-being. The low turnover rate is testament to the positive organizational culture that exists. Recognizing that salary is an important motivational tool, especially given that wages in the hospitality industry can be uncompetitive compared to other employment opportunities, employees at BWP Hotel Slon receive salaries that are 20% higher than the industry average. Managers use different motivational tools for different employee groups, such as in-house education and training programs, teambuilding activities, supporting employees' attendance at national competitions, bonuses, paid lunch breaks and a company telephone. Managers nurture a strong service culture by delivering feedback for improvement to employees in a constructive way with the aim of helping them to improve their service skills and empowering employees to quickly resolve guests' concerns. This encourages employee commitment and improves their performance, which in effect enhances the customer experience.

Effective use of non-financial metrics and frequent recipients of awards for excellence

In line with the hotel's customer-centric approach, the General Manager monitors the results of surveys and rating websites such as TripAdvisor on a daily basis to understand guests' level of satisfaction and measure the hotel's success. An analysis of the hotel's ratings on TripAdvisor and Medallia shows that the BWP Hotel Slon has a higher rating than the chain's average and has increased its guest satisfaction level from 2007 to 2012, demonstrating a return on investment on the hotel's aforementioned upgrades and renovations. Accordingly, the hotel received a Certificate of Excellence from TripAdvisor in 2012 for winning top quality hotel in Ljubljana. In the same year, the hotel also received an overall score of 4.5 out of 5 on the website Expedia, with 97% of guests providing a positive recommendation.

Among the hotel's other accolades are being a regular recipient of the BW Quality Award, meaning that it was awarded at least 975 out of a possible 1,000 points at the annual review, being awarded the Ljubljana Quality Award by Ljubljana Tourism in 2012, and the hotel's à la carte restaurant winning second place in its category and ninth overall among all the restaurants in the city. In addition to the hotel's success, its employees take part in the annual Slovene hospitality meeting, where they have consistently won various awards. To recognize its employees' achievements, the hotel provides bonus payments and displays the awards in the hotel so that guests are aware of the high service standard.

Leadership in innovation and use of technology

The hotel has successfully integrated new technologies with the aim of improving the customer experience. In particular, a Wi-Fi-based e-concierge service enables guests to access all of the hotel's important information and services from their tablet, telephone or computer, including ordering spa treatments, room service and selecting from the pillow menu, to name a few. The BWP Hotel Slon has also implemented a new customer relationship management (CRM) system that enables the recognition of a returning guest and his or her needs, thereby allowing hotel staff to provide a more personalized experience.

Effective leadership and direction from a single founder/entrepreneur

In most organizations the secret to success lies in the leader who creates the vision, culture and climate to motivate the workforce. The philosophy of the BWP Hotel Slon's General Manager, Mr. Jamnik, is to always strive for improvement to ensure the satisfaction of guests and employees. He has a friendly management style, a keen attention to detail and sets high standards for himself and his co-workers. Accordingly, Mr. Jamnik has established a well-organized and positive working environment. Importantly, the hotel's General Manager also displays a passion for the hospitality industry and has a 'hands-on' approach. Mr. Jamnik maintains regular contact with guests to build loyalty, is personally involved in the service recovery system and checks the quality of the hotel's products and services daily, including the hotel rooms and food in the restaurant.

Conclusion

The way in which BWP Hotel Slon remained committed to providing excellent service in the face of low economic growth and their subsequent success highlights how an unwavering focus on customers and employees is a valuable management strategy. By offering customers a greater variety of services and amenities for the same price and providing salaries that are above industry average, the hotel clearly indicates its loyalty to its guests and employees and highlights how investment in internal and external customers can be more valuable in the long-term than cost-cutting strategies that would provide short-term financial gains. Additional factors that contributed to the hotel's story of success include the strength of the Best Western international brand, the use of non-financial metrics to measure success, introducing new technologies to provide a more personalized experience and, most importantly, effective leadership and direction from the hotel's General Manager. Ultimately, the BWP Hotel Slon is a prime example of how applying key service management principles in practice can result in organizational success.

Review Questions

1. The manager of BWP Hotel Slon sees many advantages of being a member of an international hotel chain. From a theoretical perspective, describe the link between branding, customer loyalty and competitive advantage.

2. In addition to the existing non-financial metrics that BWP Hotel Slon managers use, outline two key performance measurement scales that could be utilized to evaluate service quality.

3. According to the hotel manager, the key to improving BWP Hotel Slon's service offering lies in a complete renovation of the property. From a service design perspective, what factors should be taken into consideration and how could this enhance the customer experience?

10. Strand Spa and Conference Hotel, Estonia

By Heli Tooman and Aime Vilgas

Introduction to the business

Each company has its own unique story of the decisions made and their journey leading to the present day. The Strand SPA and Conference Hotel originates from an era when 'competition' and 'hospitality' were concepts hardly known to Estonian hoteliers. Built in 1985 in Pärnu, an Estonian seaside resort town, the building was accessible to only a select group—journalists of the Soviet news agency Novosti. It operated as a boarding house until Estonia regained independence in 1991, after which time it was privatized and relaunched as a hotel in 1992. Today, the Strand has expanded into a 4-star hotel with 187 rooms. The Strand's facilities are unparalleled in Estonia, with a 500-seat conference hall and numerous smaller meeting rooms, a night club, spa and private saunas, wellness center, restaurant and lobby bar and even an indoor mini golf course. This case study will outline the Strand's journey from a small, three-star hotel to the successful facility it has become, and how the quality of service has been vastly improved through a clear commitment to the training and development of its employees.

Its story of service excellence

Employee obsession

A critical report of the Strand's first 100 days of operation, compiled for the owners by the Managing Director, points out many deficiencies, making it clear that even the Managing Director himself disapproved of the hotel's standards. For instance, a shortage of skilled employees and the inadequate food and beverage offerings were noted in the following statements: "Planned learning has stalled, the training company's invoice has not been paid and thus we cannot continue negotiations with it," and, "Restaurant dishes are beyond criticism, the bar lacks everything one needs for its normal operation; it is a complete shambles." Furthermore, a mere 36 rooms out of 60 were suitable for selling, yet heating them was problematic due to technical issues, and lack of money discouraged any advertising. Nevertheless, management was full of enthusiasm and sought financing for renovations, which was eventually obtained and three stars were awarded to the hotel in 2003. Service quality and hospitality were now the center of attention and action.

In the early days, however, the critical role of employees was underestimated. The number of job applicants often far exceeded the jobs available and selection was based primarily on professional qualifications and job experience. There is no evidence in the hotel's records that values, personal characteristics and attitudes carried any weight. Managers' main concern lay with their poor financial situation and employee training and development was not seen as a solution to this.

Today, staff are regarded as the key to success. Great attention is paid to management strategies, which are based around the values of inclusion, empowerment of staff and ongoing training, to ultimately create a positive service culture and encourage continuous improvement of service quality. The tools being utilized to ensure service quality include written service standards, an induction program for new employees and training courses. Feedback from guests is highly valued and is a key factor when delivering staff training and making service quality improvements. In an attempt to minimize staff turnover, a large proportion of the managers' daily work is focused on personal development of employees and a motivation program is also in place that recognizes the best front- and back-office staff and awards them with incentive holidays in other hotels. There are employees who have been working for the company since its early years and whose attitudes and actions have dramatically changed to become more customer-centric. This shift has come about as a result of the realization that it is the people who make sales, not the rooms or fabric of the building.

Highlighting the hotel's success in developing its employees and improving the quality of service is the story of Kaarel, a receptionist at the Strand. It was a rainy day and Kaarel was serving a woman who was checking out. It had been raining for several days and when she was fumbling for the car key in her handbag Kaarel noticed a car sitting in the middle of a puddle in the car park. He asked if it was hers and when she replied yes, he asked her to give him the car key, rolled his trousers up and waded through the puddle. He then drove the car to the front door, returned the key to the owner and wished her a safe journey home. Kaarel then took off his wet socks and shoes, called home to ask for a dry pair, and continued work as usual.

Conclusion

Since its humble beginnings, the Strand has come a long way and demonstrates the journey a service organization can take to improve both its financial stability and its customers' experiences. A strong commitment to training and developing its employees has allowed the hotel to overcome its initial poor service quality standards and has strengthened its service culture. The Strand continues to follow its service management journey and fulfill its mission to help every guest enjoy every moment of his or her stay.

Review Questions

1. How does the Strand's approach to service management reflect the service-profit chain? Describe each link in the chain.
2. In addition to those mentioned in the case study, what other tools could the hotel managers utilize to ensure service quality?
3. How does the story of Kaarel strengthen the hotel's service culture and which element of service culture is it an example of?

Case Studies from North America

11. Starbucks, United States of America

By Tingting (Christina) Zhang, PhD student, The Ohio State University, USA

Introduction to the business

In 1971, the Starbucks coffee house chain was founded in Seattle, Washington, USA. Starbucks has now expanded to 20,863 retail stores across 65 countries, employing over 300,000 full-time staff and attracting more than 65 million weekly visitors. Starbucks has incorporated many service management principles in building to this success. This case focuses on the extraordinary obsession with its customer-focused experience by way of the successful adoption of social media.

Its story of service excellence

Customer obsession and leadership in innovation and use of technology

The ability to provide a customer-focused service experience cannot be achieved without a clear understanding of customers' needs, expectations and habits. To gain this clear understanding, it is appropriate and often necessary to involve them in the process of developing, improving and delivering the products and services. Starbucks has been using various online and social media channels, including My Starbucks Idea, Starbucks Digital Networks, Facebook, Twitter and YouTube, not only to reach out to its customers, but more importantly to engage them in the service development and improvement process. Responsive customers are encouraged and rewarded for sharing their suggestions and opinions about Starbucks' services and products.

Starbucks currently engages in 12 types of social media, both maintained by the firm itself (for example, My Starbucks Idea) and third-party services (for example, Facebook, Twitter, YouTube and Foursquare), in order to better understand the needs of its customers and actively engage with them to ultimately enhance the service experience. The openness and participation properties of social media entwine users and content, rendering it ideal for the dynamic, customer-focused strategies of Starbucks.

One of the key online channels that focuses on gaining *customers' feedback* to improve Starbucks' position in the market is My Starbucks Idea. It works as an *online community* for all Starbucks customers to share their ideas and experiences—both positive and negative. Customers give opinions on things such as products, services, layout, advertising, corporate social responsibility, in-store music and so on. Customers can contact Starbucks representatives through multiple forums on its social network, which enables the company to increase interaction with its customers, respond directly to customer feedback and conduct polls to gauge customer satisfaction. Starbucks features and rewards the most active users and implements many of the ideas received from customers. It is estimated that more than 50,000 ideas that customers have suggested via MyStarbucksIdea.com have been implemented in-store (Hesham, 2012), which has brought the company huge success in the improvement and development of their products and services. This practice also benefits the customers as it empowers them to voice their needs and wants for innovations and improvements, which enhance their overall experience with Starbucks.

Starbucks' ultimate goal in building its digital and social media presence is to ensure customers have a delightful experience with the organization and, in turn, develop a strong relationship with the company. To this end, Starbucks has tried various ways to increase the *delightful interactions* with its customers. For example, in 2006, Starbucks conducted a campaign called "Espresso Dating Guide" with the Yahoo! Personals dating site, offering advice from a "dating and relationship expert". Starbucks has also collaborated extensively with Apple Inc., distributing weekly iTunes songs, offering a customized Starbucks iTunes channel and integrating in-store music to display a Starbucks button in iTunes for further sampling and purchase. Through iPhone apps, Starbucks customers can check multiple things about Starbucks, such as store menus, nutrition information, store locators, card management and even payment facilities. Such a variety of customer interactions collectively enhances the service experience, which contributes to the positive customer relationship.

Starbucks does not treat social media services as isolated applications. The services generally complement one another to *mutually reinforce* their overall impact on the customer experience with the organization (West, 2012). For instance, Starbucks issued a 60-second advertisement prior to the 2008 presidential election in the USA, promising a free cup of brewed coffee to every voter. Posting the commercial in a video sharing website, Starbucks jointly used Facebook and Twitter to stimulate its viewership and amplify its effect. Till the day of the election, the video was viewed 419,000 times. In Facebook, it attracted over 400,000 comments while customers were found tweeting on Starbucks every eight seconds (Miller, 2009). Such an integrated approach of linking various social media services has helped the organization maximize its reach and interaction with its customers and enhance the image of customer-focused Starbucks by promoting the notion "We care about every aspect of our customers' life".

Conclusion

Starbucks' strong customer-focused strategy is demonstrated through their social media activities, which have been successful in enhancing the service experience. This case study highlights how the company has utilized social media to maximize their opportunities to engage with customers and how they have embraced user-generated content as a way of building deeper understanding and relationships with existing and potential guests. This case thus provides valuable insights for other service organizations and future service managers in how new technologies can be successfully utilized to enhance the customer's experience and set new standards in providing excellent service.

Review Questions

1. As a customer, how does your role as a 'coproducer' in the service experience differ from when you visit your local, independent coffee store compared to when you interact with Starbucks?
2. Discuss the pros and cons of using feedback from social media and other online communities to learn about customers' satisfaction, interests and trends, versus more traditional methods of customer-perception research such as focus-groups, in-depth interviews with individuals and statistical customer surveys.
3. In addition to collaborating with Apple Inc., what other strategic partnerships could Starbucks pursue in order to build deeper customer relationships and improve the service experience?

12.   Four Seasons Hotels and Resorts, United States of America

By Tingting (Christina) Zhang, PhD student, The Ohio State University, USA

Introduction to the business

Four Seasons Hotels and Resorts (hereinafter referred to as Four Seasons) is an exquisite hotel group that strives to provide unparalleled luxury and impeccable personal service in the hospitality industry. As an internationally recognized brand, Four Seasons has grown from a single hotel in Toronto, built in 1961, into a global hotel management firm with 92 properties in 38 countries employing over 37,000 employees worldwide (Four Seasons Hotels Limited, 2014). Rather than a builder of hotels, Four Seasons focuses on high-end hotel management and is headed by founder and CEO, Isadore (Issy) Sharp. His goal to establish "medium size hotels of exceptional quality and try to be the best" (Hughes, 2009, online) is part of the simple, yet enduring philosophy that has ushered the company into the 21st century.

Its story of service excellence

Employee obsession and effective leadership and direction from
a single founder/entrepreneur

What has made Four Seasons excellent is what has made it unique: creating world-class customer service through world-class service to employees. This particular hotel management strategy is well known as The Golden Rule in Four Seasons. By focusing on The Golden Rule in every aspect of their business—from corporate to front-of-house—Four Seasons has been able to create a reputation of unmatched service quality in the luxury hotel market.

Isadore believes that a company needs to talk about what is important to its employees before talking about what is important to the company. The hotel chain recognizes the importance of pleasing its employees just as much as its guests, because ultimately they are responsible for creating a positive interaction and providing excellent service to the guests. The understanding of employee orientation is key to guaranteeing sustainable superior customer service, and this concept is deeply rooted in the service culture engendered by Four Seasons.

Four Seasons emphasizes the essential role of empowered employees in improving exceptional customer service. Isadore Sharp is known to regularly state that not a single manager could ensure good service in the hospitality industry; rather, good service depends on the front-line employees—doormen, bellmen, waiters and maids—yet the lowest-paid people are often, in most companies, the least motivated. Therefore, hoteliers need to acknowledge that these front-line staff are indeed their product to the customers. Consequently, Four Seasons gives front-line workers the authority to make most decisions they feel necessary to satisfy guests. For instance, when a tsunami struck the Four Seasons in the Maldives in 2004, Four Seasons employees chartered a plane within 24 hours to fly every guest to safety. Indeed, empowered employees do make the difference at Four Seasons.

The prerequisite of empowering employees is to select the right person who shares the same value system with the corporate culture. Four Seasons only hires individuals who have been tested and qualified through their rigorous interview process. They hire employees with qualities like genuine caring and regard for other people, a desire to help and be service-oriented and an ability to get along with all people. These are soft skills that cannot be taught, but rather are usually part of the general personality and character of a person. Four Seasons uses standards to train employees in specific job duties; employees are then empowered to make decisions during 'moments of truth' with customers. Training in standards gives them a framework in which to operate so that customers' experiences of their stay at Four Seasons, especially the 'moments of truth' such as check-in/out, room service, room reservation etc. are consistent. Additionally, Four Seasons recognizes the diversity of customers and allows the flexibility to tailor service and interactions with each customer. Knowing that they are a trusted and valued part of a team, Four Seasons employees feel a sense of pride in themselves and the organization. In fact, most applicants prior to applying for jobs at Four Seasons will have already been exposed to the brand and will likely have been attracted to its mission of service and reputation for excellence (Talbott, 2006).

Conclusion

As a result of their strong employee-oriented strategy, Four Seasons has been recognized as a workplace of choice in the hospitality industry and, most notably, has been listed among *Fortune Magazine*'s 100 Best Companies to Work For since 1998 (ranked #91 in 2014). Accordingly, Four Seasons hotels have many employees who stay with the company for 15+ years and, as Four Seasons stated in their announcement of Employer of Choice, they acknowledge that their most valuable partners on their path toward phenomenal growth continue to be their employees. With strong leadership from the hotel's founder and CEO, Isadore Sharp, who continues to advocate The Golden Rule, Four Seasons enjoys a solid relationship with its employees that, in turn, has led to high levels of customer satisfaction and loyalty year after year. It is the combination of effective leadership and an intense employee focus that will allow Four Seasons to continue to provide an unparalleled service experience and maintain a sustainable competitive advantage.

Review Questions

1. List some of the potential benefits that the Four Seasons managers, employees and customers will enjoy as a result of the organization adopting an empowerment strategy.
2. In addition to empowering employees, if you were a manager at a Four Seasons, how would you try to shape a customer-focused organizational culture? Provide an example at each level of organizational culture.
3. If you were the HR manager at a Four Seasons, how you would measure the organization's service climate?

13.   Cameron Mitchell Restaurants, United States of America

By Tingting (Christina) Zhang, PhD student, The Ohio State University, USA

Introduction to the business

Founded in 1993, Cameron Mitchell Restaurants consists of a diverse portfolio of dining concepts, ranging from multi-location, upscale destinations to single, 'neighborhood favorites'. Cameron Mitchell Restaurants started in Columbus, Ohio, and have expanded to various states across the US. Due to its high-quality, made-from-scratch food and exceptional guest service, Cameron Mitchell Restaurants has won the recognition of being a great collection of 'Tasty Restaurants'. "Yes is the answer, what is the question" best defines the service culture and philosophies Cameron Mitchell Restaurants hold themselves to on a daily basis. Because of the superb service that guests receive and the successful achievement of their goal of making "raving fans" out of all those who come in contact with the restaurants, the company has enjoyed financial success and received multiple Readers Choice Awards over the years.

Its story of service excellence

Effective leadership and direction from a single founder/entrepreneur

Cameron Mitchell is the president and founder of Cameron Mitchell Restaurants. The core values of this successful restaurant group are very present in the company and are seen through the culture that everyone involved with Cameron Mitchell Restaurants adopts:

- ▶ What do we want to be? An extraordinary restaurant company.
- ▶ Who are we? Great people delivering genuine hospitality.
- ▶ What is our role? To make raving fans of our associates, guests, purveyors and communities.
- ▶ What is our mission? To continue to thrive, driven by our culture and fiscal responsibilities.

▶ What is our goal? To be better today than we were yesterday and better tomorrow than we are today.

In line with this hospitality-centric culture, Cameron Mitchell encourages communication between all 'associates' within the company. From the Vice President to the hourly 'associates', he encourages and nurtures the feeling that all 'associates' have a stake in the company. "Cameron's very much an open book," says Vice President Chuck Davis. "That leaves very little confusion about what the status of the company is. He (Cameron Mitchell) says [to 'associates'], 'tell me what's going on in your restaurant. Don't pull any punches. Give me the good, the bad and the ugly.'" (Ravneburg, 2006, online). This open communication style and empowerment of his associates is part of what makes Cameron Mitchell and his company such a success in one of the most competitive industries.

Customer obsession

Cameron Mitchell Restaurants uphold a service philosophy that is 'guest obsessed' by always saying "yes" to guests and actively catering to guests' needs. Every 'associate' in Cameron Mitchell Restaurants walks this walk and talks this talk throughout the organization, which creates a strong guest-oriented service culture. Cameron Mitchell Restaurants strives to outdo its competition to exceed guests' expectations (DiJulius, 2006), to ensure customer satisfaction and to win market share. Simply meeting a guest's needs is not sufficient; 'associates' are taught to continually strive to exceed guest expectations. This eagerness to impress the guests and the belief that it is the guests who make a successful business guarantees that Cameron Mitchell Restaurants will always be raising the service bar.

Employee obsession

Cameron Mitchell Restaurants put their 'associates' first, as they are seen as the foundation of the organization, and by doing so they have achieved spectacular results. Based on the belief that superior service comes from the heart, Cameron Mitchell Restaurants realizes that their guests will have a wonderful experience only when their 'associates' are truly happy (Brefere, Drummond and Barnes, 2008). Demonstrating the value they recognize in their 'associates', the company has a Future Leaders Program, which identifies and encourages hourly 'associates' who have the goal of becoming a manager. Through the Future Leaders Program, 'associates' have access to opportunities for professional development, such as learning managerial skills and undertaking culinary training. This 'associate'-oriented philosophy led to Cameron Mitchell Restaurants receiving the 2006 runner-up award for The Best Place to Work from Columbus Business First.

Conclusion

Cameron Mitchell Restaurants provides an exceptional dining experience for guests by implementing and remaining steadfastly guest and 'associate' obsessed. Their success is also attributable to the entrepreneurial spirit of its founder, Cameron Mitchell, who creates a pleasant working environment through open communication and empowerment of the company's 'associates'. With strong service management practices and principles guiding it, Cameron Mitchell Restaurants has succeeded in its goal of presenting every dish with superior service, excellent quality and a unique flair.

Review Questions

1. Which leadership style do you think Cameron Mitchell best reflects and why?
2. Explain the success that Cameron Mitchell Restaurants has enjoyed by using the 'Performance Equation' discussed in Chapter 9.
3. The 12 restaurants within Cameron Mitchell's company operate under various names, such as Hudson 29, Cap City and The Barn, to name a few. Discuss the implications of this from a branding perspective, with particular consideration of brand associations, brand trust and brand communities.

14. The Greenbrier, United States of America

By Tingting (Christina) Zhang, PhD student, The Ohio State University, USA

Introduction to the business

The Greenbrier is a four-star luxury resort located just outside the town of White Sulphur Springs in Greenbrier County, West Virginia, United States. Founded in 1778, The Greenbrier is considered to be one of the top luxury hotels in the world and has won numerous honors and recognitions due to its exceptional service. The Greenbrier is also famous for its special historical significance, being the only resort where a total of 26 US presidents have stayed on various occasions. Also on its guest list are many Hollywood stars and prominent figures, which supports its reputation for luxury and royalty. The Greenbrier's vision statement is: "where experiences are timeless and memories last forever, The Greenbrier will be the leader of luxury resorts around the world." The secret to The Greenbrier's success, and the reason why it has maintained its position as a top luxurious resort for over 200 years, lies in its strong focus on both its guests and employees.

Its story of service excellence

Customer obsession

The philosophy of guest obsession is implemented throughout The Greenbrier resort, from its décor design and amenities provision to its range of activities on offer. For instance, Dorothy Draper, the first interior designer at The Greenbrier resort, indicated that the rooms were designed as if they were Hollywood sets, which shows her devotion to make every guest at The Greenbrier resort feel like he or she is a celebrity. In addition, The Greenbrier provides a variety of amenities that cater to its guests' individual needs, which contributes to its excellent customer-oriented service.

The Greenbrier resort is focused on delivering exceptional service, starting from the very beginning of its guests' stay to the end. The resort consists of 710 rooms and 10,000 acres, which cater to a wide variety of activities. According to the resort's brochure, horseback riding, swimming, kayaking, hiking, bowling and tennis are just starters; guests can also be taken on a guided tour of the resort to bask in the historic architecture, renowned interior design, myriad of antiques and priceless art. For guests who are golf enthusiasts, The Greenbrier also offers five championship golf courses to choose from. Customer satisfaction is held with the highest regard at The Greenbrier and, by offering a range of amenities and activities that can be tailored to suit individual needs, the resort fulfills its vision of being a place "where experiences are timeless and memories last forever."

Employee obsession

"Legendary experiences begin with an exceptional spirit to serve" (LinkedIn, 2014, online). This epitomizes the way The Greenbrier operates when it comes to their employees. One key attribute about The Greenbrier that separates them from other resorts is its exceptional employees, who are considered as an integral part of the "dazzling decor". Their employees are said to be the heart and soul of the experience at The Greenbrier. Accordingly, the company is dedicated to taking care of its employees and considers them to be their 'guests'. To enhance employee satisfaction, The Greenbrier offers competitive salaries, excellent benefits and numerous training opportunities. In addition to full-time and part-time employment, the company provides ongoing advancement and internal growth opportunities in a wide variety of areas. By promoting from within, The Greenbrier aims to produce hard-working and loyal staff members throughout the entire organization. The Greenbrier focuses on making its employees comfortable and ensuring their time at the resort is just as enjoyable as it is for their customers. By exhibiting such a strong staff focus, The Greenbrier attracts the best individuals to become members of their staff. With flexible working hours, staff discounts for rooms and a strong emphasis on a friendly work environment, The Greenbrier successfully creates a unique employee-oriented workplace.

As further evidence of their employee obsession, The Greenbrier shows immense loyalty towards its employees and fosters diversity, which filters from the top down. For example, in 2009 when bankruptcy threatened the resort's future, employees were let go. However, once Jim Justice, the present owner of The Greenbrier, bought the resort, he rehired all the employees who had lost their jobs. This demonstrates the dedication Jim Justice has for his employees and his recognition of the value that employees have to the business. Such strong devotion exhibited by the organization enhances employees' loyalty and encourages them to perform at their highest degree of excellence. In line with an employee focus, loyalty holds equal importance to diversity in The Greenbrier model. As the resort's website states: "creating an environment of inclusion for our employees, guests and suppliers isn't just the right thing to do; it is the very core of our business." (The Greenbrier, 2013, online). This strong unity between the employer and employees allows for the ultimate sense of loyalty and security for all. Importantly, employees see themselves as a part of the business, which translates into the best service being provided.

Conclusion

The Greenbrier has a history of prominence that continues today due to a strong commitment to upholding the highest service standards. From personalized amenities to an expanding multitude of activities, each aspect of the resort works together to create a memorable stay for every guest. Furthermore, The Greenbrier understands that without its staff, the resort is simply unable to provide any of its distinguished services. With that understanding, employees are treated with the same consideration that is regularly afforded to guests. Ultimately, The Greenbrier has maintained its reputation for luxury and exceptional service for over two hundred years because it provides an experience unlike any other.

Review Questions

1. How has The Greenbrier designed it service environment in an experience-centric way?
2. When Jim Justice re-hired employees who had been let go during hard financial times, he demonstrated recognition that service quality is the key to a sustainable competitive advantage. Describe the positive economic impacts of quality, as outlined in Chapter 3, that The Greenbrier is able to enjoy.
3. If you were a manager at The Greenbrier, which technologies or social networking applications would you suggest the company adopt to enhance customer engagement and loyalty?

Summary

This chapter brings together 14 case studies of service companies from all over the world: Europe, Australasia and the USA. This chapter aims to demonstrate the way all these companies achieved service excellence and serves as a bridge between the theory discussed in all nine chapters prior to this one and the 'real world' businesses. These 14 cases demonstrate that putting service management principles into action allows firms to achieve a significant competitive edge as well as to gain a strong reputation and loyalty among both customers and employees.

Even though we recognize that there are many other successful examples which were not covered by this chapter, the reader might have already noticed that all these great companies have common intrinsic attributes which are supported and resonate with service management theories presented in prior chapters. We hope that by connecting theory to practice we took the learning curve to another level, while making this book more practical and 'realistic'. We also encourage our readers to practice applying a service management lens (and knowledge they gained from this book) at their workplace . . . We promise the results will exceed your expectations!

Suggested Readings

This is a list of suggested further reading on topics covered in this chapter. For a separate list of full reference citations quoted in the chapter, see 'References', Chapter 10, page 339.

Delighted, returning customers: Service the Ritz-Carlton way: Gold star advice from the leaders in service excellence. (2004). *Strategic Direction*, 20(11), 7–9.

Dube, L., Enz, C. A., Renaghan, L. M., and Siguaw, J. A. (2000). Managing for excellence. *Cornell Hotel and Restaurant Administration Quarterly*, 41(5), 30–39.

Enz, C., and Siguaw, J. A. (2000). Best practices in service quality. *Cornell Hotel and Restaurant Administration Quarterly*, 41(5), 20–29.

Ford, R. C., Heaton, C. P., and Brown, S. W. (2001). Delivering excellent service: Lessons from the best firms. *California Management Review*, 44(1), 39–56.

Four Seasons Hotel. (2000), "2000 Annual Report–Four Seasons Hotels and Resorts", *Docstoc.com*, available at: http://www.docstoc.com/docs/83500213/2000-Annual-Report—Four-Seasons-Hotels-and-Resorts (accessed 15 November 2014).

Heracleous, L., and Wirtz, J. (2010). Singapore Airlines' balancing act. *Harvard Business Review*, 145–149.

Michelli, J. A. (2008). *The New Gold Standard: Five Leadership Principles for Creating a Legendary Customer Experience, Courtesy of the Ritz-Carlton Hotel Company*. New York: McGraw-Hill.

Solnet, D., Kandampully, J., and Kralj, A. (2010). Legends of hospitality service excellence: The habits of seven highly effective companies. *Journal of Hospitality Marketing and Management*, 19(8), 889–908.

Stanford. (2010, May11), "Empowered Employees Make the Difference, Says Four Seasons CEO Isadore Sharp | Stanford Knowledgebase", available at: http://web.stanford.edu/group/knowledgebase/cgi-bin/2010/03/11/empowered-employees-make-the-difference-says-four-seasons-ceo-isadore-sharp/ (accessed 15 November 2014).

Wirtz, J., and Johnston, R. (2003). Singapore Airlines: What it takes to sustain service excellence—a senior management perspective. *Managing Service Quality*, 13(1), 10–19.

Wirtz, J., Heracleous, L., and Pangarkar, N. (2008). Managing human resources for service excellence and cost effectiveness at Singapore Airlines. *Managing Service Quality*, 18(1), 4–19.

References

Chapter 1   Introduction: The Metamorphosis of Service

Albrecht, K. (1988). *At America's service: How your company can join the customer service revolution*. New York: Warner Books.

Booms, B. H., and Bitner, M. J. (1981). *Marketing Strategies and Organizational Structures for Service Firms*. Chicago: American Marketing Association.

Central Intelligence Agency. (2011). Field Listing: GDP—Composition, by sector of origin. *The World Factbook*, https://www.cia.gov/library/publications/the-world-factbook/fields/2012.html, (visited October 2013).

Edvardsson, B., and Gustavsson, B. 1992, *Problem Detection in Service Management Systems: A Consistency Approach to Quality Improvement*, QUIS-2, Business Research Institute at St John's University, New York, 231–50.

Engel, E. (1857). 'Die Production—und Consumptionsverhaltnisse des Konigreichs Sachsen', in *Zeitschrift der Statistischen Bureaus des Koniglich Sachsischen Ministerium des Inneren*.

Grönroos, C. (1993). From scientific management to service management. *International Journal of Service Industry Management*, 5(1), 5–20.

Jääskelä, J., and Windsor, C. (2011). Insights from the Household Expenditure Survey. *Reserve Bank of Australia*, http://www.rba.gov.au/publications/bulletin/2011/dec/1.html, (visited October 2013).

Kandampully, J. (2007). Services management: The new paradigm in hospitality. Upper Saddle River, N.J: Prentice-Hall.

McCarthy, E. J. (1960). *Basic Marketing*. Homewood, Ilinois: Irwin.

Rafiq, M., and Ahmed, P. K. (1995). Using the 7Ps as a generic marketing mix: An exploratory survey of UK and European marketing academics. *Marketing Intelligence and Planning*, 13(9), 4–15.

Schneider, B. (2004). Research briefs: Welcome to the world of services management. *Academy of Management Executive,* 18(2), 144–150.

United Nations World Tourism Organisation. (2012). *UNWTO Tourism Highlights: 2012 Edition.* http://mkt.unwto.org/sites/all/files/docpdf/unwtohighlights12enhr.pdf, (visited October 2013).

Vandermerwe, S., and Rada, J. (1988). Servitization of business: Adding value by adding services. *European Management Journal,* 6(4), 314–324.

Vargo, S. L., and Akaka, M. A. (2009). Service-dominant logic as a foundation for service science: Clarifications. *Service Science,* 1(1), 32–41.

World Travel and Tourism Council. (2012). Our rapidly changing world. Presented at the *WTTC 12th Global Summit,* Tokyo, http://www.wttc.org/events/tokyosendai-2012/global-summit-coverage/day-two/session-2/, (visited October 2013).

Chapter 2   The Nature of Service

Berry, L., Wall, E., and Carbone, L. (2006). Service clues and customer assessment of the service experience. *Academy of Management Perspectives,* 20(2), 43–57.

Bowen, J., and Ford, R. C. (2002). Managing service organizations: Does having a "thing" make a difference? *Journal of Management,* 28(3), 447–469.

Fisk, R. (2009). A customer liberation manifesto. *Service Science,* 1(3), 135–141.

Grönroos, C. (2011). Value co-creation in service logic: A critical analysis. *Marketing Theory,* 11(3), 279–301.

Heinonen, K., Strandvik, T., Mickelsson, K-J., Edvardsson, B., Sundström, E., and Andersson, P. (2010). A customer-dominant logic of service. *Journal of Service Management,* 21(4), 531–548.

Lovelock, C. H., Patterson, P. G., and Walker, R. H. (2001). *Services Marketing: an Asia–Pacific Perspective,* 2nd ed. Pearson Education Australia, Sydney.

Maister, D. (1985). The Psychology of Waiting Lines. In J. A. Czepiel, M. R. Solomon, and C. F. Surprenant (Eds.), *The service encounter: Managing employee/customer interaction in service businesses.* Lexington, MA: D.C. Heath and Company, Lexington Books.

Prahalad, C. K., and Ramaswamy, V. (2000) "Co-opting customer competence," *Harvard Business Review,* January–February, 79–87.

Shah, D., Rust, R. T., Parasuraman, A., Staelin, R., and Day, G. S. (2006). The path to customer centricity. *Journal of Service Research,* 9(2), 113–124.

Shemwell, D. J., and Cronin, J. J. (1994). Services marketing strategies for coping with demand/supply imbalances. *Journal of Services Marketing,* 8(4), 14–24.

Shostack, G. L. (1977). Breaking Free from Product Marketing. *Journal of Marketing,* 41, April, 73–80.

Surowiecki, J. 2005. *The Wisdom of Crowds.* New York: Anchor Books.

Tapscott, D., Williams A. D., 2006. *Wikinomics: How Mass Collaboration Changes Everything.* New York: Portfolio.

Vargo, S. L., and Lusch, R. F. (2004). The four service marketing myths—Remnants of a goods-based, manufacturing model. *Journal of Service Research,* 6(4), 324–335.

Wind, Jerry, and Rangaswamy Arvind, (2000). "Customerization: The Next Revolution in Mass Customization," MSI Report No. 00–108,

Marketing Science Institute, Cambridge, MA.

Chapter 3   Service Quality

Brady, M. K., and Cronin, J. J. (2001). Some New Thoughts on Conceptualizing Perceived Service Quality: A Hierarchical Approach. *Journal of Marketing,* vol. 65 (July 2001), 34–49.

Cronin, J. J., and Taylor, S. A. (1992). Measuring Service Quality: A Reexamination. *Journal of Marketing,* 56, (July), 55–68.

Crosby, P. B. (1979). *Quality is Free,* McGraw-Hill, New York.

Crosby, P. B. (1984). *Quality without fears: the art of hassle-free management,* McGraw-Hill, New York.

Crotts, J. C., and Ford, R. C. (2008). Achieving service excellence by design: The organizational alignment audit. *Business Communication Quarterly*, June, 233–240.

Dabholkar, P. C., Thorpe, D. I., and Rentz, J. O. (1996). A Measure of Service Quality for Retail Stores. *Journal of the Academy of Marketing Science,* 24 (Winter), 3–16.

"Delighted, returning customers: Service the Ritz-Carlton way: Gold star advice from the leaders in service excellence." (2004). *Strategic Direction,* 20(11), 7–9.

Deming, W. E. 1982, *Out of the Crisis,* MIT Press, Cambridge, MA, USA.

Dixon, M., Freeman, K., and Toman, N. (2010). Stop trying to delight your customers, *Harvard Business Review,* July–August, 116–122.

Feigenbaum, A. V. (1956). Total Quality Control. *Harvard Business Review,* 34: 93–101.

Grönroos, C. (1982a). *A Service Quality Model and Its Managerial Implications,* Working paper presented at the Workshop of Research into the Management of Service Business, London Business School, January 1982.

Grönroos, C. (1982b). *Seven Key Areas of Research: According to the Nordic School of Service Marketing, Emerging Perspectives on Services Marketing,* Berry, L. L, Shostack, G. L., and Upah, G. D. (eds), AMA Services Marketing Conference Proceedings.

Grönroos, C. (1991). The Marketing Strategy Continuum: Towards a Marketing Concept for the 1990s. *Management Decision,* 29(1), 7–13.

Grove, S. J. and Fisk, R. P. (1982). The Dramaturgy of Service Exchange: An Analytical Framework for Services Marketing, in Berry, L. L., Shostack, G. L., and Upah,, G. D. (eds), *Emerging Perspective on Services Marketing,* AMA Services Marketing Conference Proceedings.

Gupta, S., McLaughlin, E., and Gomez, M. (2007). Guest satisfaction and restaurant performance. *Cornell Hotel and Restaurant Administration Quarterly,* 48(3), 284–298.

Johnston, R. (2004). Towards a better understanding of service excellence. *Managing Service Quality*, 14(2/3), 129–133.

Jones, T. O., and Sasser Jr, W. E. (1995). Why satisfied customers defect. *Harvard Business Review*, Nov–Dec, 88–99.

Kiechel, W. (1981). Three (or Four or More) Ways to Win. *Fortune*, 19 October, 181–8.

Lehtinen, J. R. (1983). 'Customer Oriented Service System,' Service Management Institute Working Paper, Helsinki, Finland.

Lehtinen, U., and Lehtinen, J. R. (1983). 'Service Quality: A Study of Quality Dimensions,' unpublished working paper, Service Management Institute, Helsinki, Finland.

Oliver, R. L. (1980). A cognitive model of the antecedents and consequences of satisfaction decisions. *Journal of Marketing Research*, 17 (November), 460–469.

Oliver, R. L. (1999). Whence customer loyalty? *Journal of Marketing*, 63, 33–44.

Parasuraman, A., Berry, L. L., and Zeithaml, V. A. (1991). Understanding, Measuring, Improving Service Quality Findings from a Multiphase Research Program. *Service Quality: Multidisciplinary and Multinational Perspectives,* Brown, S., Gummesson, E., Edvardsson, B., and Gustavsson, B. (eds), Lexington Books, Lexington, Mass.

Parasuraman, A., Zeithaml, V. A., and Berry, L. L. (1985). A Conceptual Model of Service Quality and Its Implications for Future Research. *Journal of Marketing,* vol. 49, Fall 1985, 41–50.

Parasuraman, A., Zeithaml, V. A. and Berry, L. L. (1988). SERVQUAL: A Multi Item Scale for Measuring Consumer Perception of Service Quality. *Journal of Retailing,* 64(1), 12–40.

Parasuraman, A., Zeithaml, V. A., and Malhotra, A. (2005). E-S-Qual: a multiple-item scale for assessing electronic service quality. *Journal of Service Research*, 7(3), 213–233.

Pine, J., and Gilmore, J. (1998). Welcome to the experience economy. *Harvard Business Review*, July–August, 97–106.

Porter, M. E. (1985). *Competitive Advantage: Creating and sustaining superior performance,* Free Press, New York.

Rust, R. T., and Oliver, R. L. (1994). Service Quality: Insights and Managerial Implications from the Frontier, in Rust, R. T. and Oliver R. L. (eds), *Service Quality: New Directions in Theory and Practice,* Sage Publications, Thousand Oaks, California, USA, 1–19.

Rust, R., and Oliver, R. (2000). Should we delight the customer? *Journal of Academy of Marketing Science*, 28(1), 86–94.

Sasser, W. E., Olsen, R. P., and Wyckoff, D. D. (1978). *Management of Service Operations,* Text and Cases, Allyn and Bacon, Boston.

Chapter 4   Understanding and Engaging Customers

Camilo, A. A., Connolly, J. D., and Woo, G. K. (2008). Success and failure in northern Carolina: Critical success factors for independent restaurants. *Cornell Hotel and Restaurant Administration Quarterly,* 49(4), 364-80.

Deming, W. E. (1982). *Quality, Productivity, and Competitive Position,* Massachusetts Institute of Technology Center for Advanced Engineering Study, Cambridge, Massachusetts.

Denzin, N. K., and Lincoln, Y. S. (Eds.). (2008). *Collecting and interpreting qualitative materials* (3rd ed.). Thousand Oaks, CA: Sage.

Dev, C. S., Buschman, J. D., and Bowen, J. T. (2010). Hospitality Marketing: A Retrospective Analysis (1960–2010) and Predications (2010–2020). *Cornell Hospitality Quarterly*, 51(4), 459–469.

Dietz, J., Pugh, S. D., and Wiley, J. W. (2004). Service climate effects on customer attitudes: An examination of boundary conditions. *Academy of Management Journal*, 47(1), 81–92.

Disney. (n.d.). *The Walt Disney Company*, http://thewaltdisneycompany.com/, (visited July 2014).

Drucker, P. F. (1973). *Management*. Harper and Row: New York.

Drucker, P. F. (1954). *The Practice of Management*. HarperCollins: New York.

Ford, R. C., Latham, G. P., and Lennox, G. (2011). Mystery shoppers: A new tool for coaching employee performance improvement. *Organizational Dynamics*, 40(3), 157–164.

Heskett, J. L., Sasser, W. E., and Schlesinger, L. A. (1997). *The service profit chain: How leading companies link profit and growth to loyalty, satisfaction and value*. Free Press, New York.

Kaplan, A. M., and Haenlein, M. (2012). Social media: back to the roots and back to the future. *Journal of Systems and Information Technology*, 14(2), 101–104.

Levitt, T. (1981). Marketing intangible products and product intangibles. *Harvard Business Review*, 59(3), 94–102.

Marriott, J. W. (Jnr) (1988). Foreword. In Albrecht, K., *At America's Service*, Dow Jones, Irwin, NY.

Pantelidis, I. S. (2010). Electronic Meal Experience: A Content Analysis of Online Restaurant Comments, *Cornell Hospitality Quarterly*, 51(4), 483–491.

Reichheld, F. F. (2003). The One Number You Need to Grow. *Harvard Business Review*, December, 46–54.

Schneider, B., Macey, W. H., Lee, W. C., and Young, S. A. (2009). Organizational service climate drivers of the American Customer Satisfaction Index (ACSI) and financial and market performance. *Journal of Service Research*, 12(1), 3–14.

Shah, D., Rust, R., Parasuraman, A., Staelin, R., and Day, G. (2006). The path to customer centricity. *Journal of Service Research*, 9(2), 113–124.

Chapter 5   Service Vision, Service Design and the Service Encounter

Berry L. L. (1995). *On Great Service: A Framework for Action*, FreePress, New York.

Brownell, J. (2008). *Building Managers' Skills to Create Listening Environments*. Ithaca: Cornell University.

Cactus Jack's Restaurants, Interviews with owner Jon Van Grinsven, 2014.

Carlzon, J. (1987). *Moments of Truth*, Ballinger Publishing Company, Cambridge, Mass, USA.

Chang, E. (1998). Dispositional optimism and primary and secondary appraisal of a stressor: Controlling for confounding influences and relations to coping and psychological and physical adjustment. *Journal of Personality and Social Psychology*, 74, 1109–1120.

Chase, R. B. (2004). It's time to get to first principles in service design, *Managing Service Quality*, 14(2/3), 126–128.

Collins, J. C., and Porras, J. (1996). Building your company's vision. *Harvard Business Review*, September, 65–75.

Cook, L. S., Bowen, D.E., Chase, R. B., Dasu, S., Stewart, D. M., and Tansik, D. A. (2002). Human issues in service design. *Journal of Operations Management*, 20, 159–174.

Covey, S. (2004). *The 7 Habits of Highly Effective People: Powerful Lessons in Personal Change*, 25th Anniversary edition, New York: Simon and Schuster.

Crosno, J. L., Rinaldo, S. B., Black, H. G., and Kelley, S. W. (2009). Half full or half empty: The role of optimism in boundary-spanning positions. *Journal of Service Research,* 11(3), 295–309.

Crotts, J. C., Dickson, D. R., and Ford, R. C. (2005). Aligning Organizational Processes with Mission: The Case of Service Excellence. *The Academy of Management Executive*, 54–68.

Deming, W. E. (1982). *Quality, Productivity, and Competitive Position,* Massachusetts Institute of Technology Center for Advanced Engineering Study, Cambridge, Massachusetts.

Dreamworld. (n.d.a). *Dreamworld History.* http://www.dreamworld.com.au/schools/pdf/dw-schools-history.pdf, (visited September 2014).

Dreamworld. (n.d.b). *Our Vision, Mission & Values.* http://about.dreamworld.com.au/Employment/Our-Vision--Values/Our-Vision--Values.aspx?tileid=6339407422216345930, (visited September 2014).

Ellett, J. (2012). Holiday Inn Turns 60, Refines Brand Strategy. *Forbes*, http://www.forbes.com/sites/johnellett/2012/11/05/holiday-inn-turns-60-refines-brand-strategy/, (visited July 2014).

The Fat Duck. (2014). *The Menus.* http://www.thefatduck.co.uk/The-Menus/, (visited October 2013).

Fisk, R., Grove, S., Harris, L. C., Keeffe, D. A., and Reynolds, K. L. D. (2010). Customers behaving badly: a state of the art review, research agenda and implications for practitioners. *Journal of Services Marketing,* 24(6), 417–429.

Frei, F. X. (2008). Four Things a Service Business Must Get Right, *Harvard Business Review*, April, 70–80.

Grandey, A. A., Fisk, G. M., Mattila, A. S., Jansen, K. J., and Sideman, L. A. (2005). Is "service with a smile" enough? Authenticity of positive displays during service encounters. *Organizational Behavior and Human Decision Processes,* 96, 38–55.

Grönroos, C. (1993). From scientific management to service management. *International Journal of Service Industry Management,* 5(1), 5–20.

Harris, L. C. and Reynolds, K. L. (2003). The consequences of dysfunctional customer behavior. *Journal of Service Research*, 6(2), 144–161.

Harvard Business School Press (Ed.). (2005). *Strategy: Create and Implement the Best Strategy for Your Business*. Harvard Business School Publishing, Massachusetts.

Hosick, W. M. (1989). The Use of Blueprinting to Achieve Quality in Service. *Service Excellence: Marketing's Impact on Performance,* Proceedings of the AMA 8th Services Marketing Conference.

House, R. J., and Rizzo, J. R. (1972). Toward a measurement of organizational practices: Scale development and validation. *Journal of Applied Psychology*, 56(5), 388–396.

IHG. (2014). Holiday Inn. http://www.ihg.com/holidayinn/hotels/us/en/reservation, (visited July 2014).

Ishikawa, K. (1985). *What is Total Quality Control?—The Japanese Way*, translated by Lu, David J., Prentice Hall Inc., Englewood Cliffs, NJ.

Jimmy John's Franchise. (2014). Company History. *Jimmy John's Gourmet Sandwiches*, https://www.jimmyjohns.com/company/, (visited July 2014).

Kim, E., and Yoon, D. J. (2012). Why does service with a smile make employees happy? A social interaction model. *The Journal of applied psychology*, 97(5), 1059–1067.

Kingman-Brundage, J. (1989). The ABCs of service system blueprinting. In Bitner, M. J. and Crosby, L. A., *Designing a Winning Service Strategy*, American Marketing Association, Chicago.

Lehtinen, J. R. (1983). Customer Oriented Service System. Service Management Institute Working Paper, Helsinki, Finland.

Lovelock, C. H. (1996). *Services Marketing*, 3rd ed., Prentice Hall: Upper Saddle River.

Lovelock, C. H., Patterson, P. G., and Walker, R. H. (2001). *Services Marketing: An Asia–Pacific Perspective*, 2nd ed., Pearson Education Australia: Sydney.

McDonald's. (2010). *Mission and Values*. http://www.aboutmcdonalds.com/mcd/our_company/mission_and_values.html, (visited October 2013).

McKechnie, D. S., Grant, J., and Bagaria, V. (2007). Observation of listening behaviors in retail service encounters. *Managing Service Quality*, 17(2), 116–133.

Meyer, D. (2006). *Setting the Table: The Transforming Power of Hospitality in Business*. New York: Harper Collins.

Michelli, J. A. (2008). *The New Gold Standard: Five Leadership Principles for Creating a Legendary Customer Experience, Courtesy of the Ritz-Carlton Hotel Company*. New York: McGraw-Hill.

Parasuraman, A., Berry, L. L., and Zeithaml, V. A. (1991). Understanding, Measuring, Improving Service Quality Findings from a Multiphase Research Program. *Service Quality: Multidisciplinary and Multinational Perspectives*, Brown, S., Gummesson, E., Edvardsson, B., and Gustavsson, B. (eds), Lexington Books: Lexington, Mass.

The Pod Hotel. (2014). Our Story. http://www.thepodhotel.com/about-pod-hotels, (visited July 2014).

Porter, M. E. (1996). What Is Strategy? *Harvard Business Review*, 74(6), 61–78.

The Ritz-Carlton Hotel Company. (2014). Gold Standards. http://corporate.ritzcarlton.com/en/About/GoldStandards.htm, (visited July 2014).

Segal-Horn, S. (2003). Strategy in Service Organizations. In *The Oxford Handbook of Strategy. Volume 1: A Strategy Overview*, Oxford University Press: New York, USA, 467–500.

Senior, M. and Akehurst, G. (1990). *Perceptual Blueprinting in the United Kingdom*, QUIS-2, Business Research Institute, St John's University: USA.

Shostack, G. L. (1981). *How to Design a Service,* in Donnelly, J. and George, W. (eds), *Marketing of Services,* Chicago American Marketing Association, 221–9. (also appeared in *European Journal of Marketing,* 1982, 16, 1).

Shostack, G. L. (1983). Service design in the operating environment. In George, W. R. and Marshall, C. (eds), *Developing New Services,* American Marketing Association: Chicago, 27–43.

Shostack, G. L. (1984a). Designing Services that Deliver. *Harvard Business Review,* 62, January–February, 133–9.

Shostack, G. L. (1984b). Service Design in the Operating Environment. In George, William R. and Marshall, Claudia E. (eds), *Developing New Services,* American Marketing Association: Chicago, 27–43.

Shostack, G. L. (1985). Planning the Service Encounter. In Czepiel, Solomon and Surprenant (eds), *The Service Encounter,* Lexington Books: Lexington, Mass.

Shostack, G. L. (1987). Service Positioning through Structural Change. *Journal of Marketing,* 51, January, 34–43.

Shostack, G. L. (1990a). Why Do Service Firms Lack Design? Paper presented at the Quality in Services Conference, QUIS-2: St John's University, USA, 133–46.

Shostack G. L. (1990b). Service Blueprint's Help to Iron Out System Design Flaws Before Front Liners Take the Fall. *The Service Edge,* July–August, 8.

Southwest Airlines Co. (2014). About Southwest. *Southwest,* http://www.southwest.com/html/about-southwest/index.html?clk=GFOOTER-ABOUT-ABOUT, (visited July 2014).

Victorino, L., Verma, R., and Wardell, D. G. (2008). *Service scripting: A customer's perspective of quality and performance.* Ithaca: Cornell.

Chapter 6   Service Marketing: Managing Customer Experiences and Relationships

Berry, L. L. (1981). The employee as customer. *Journal of Retail Banking,* 3(1), 33–40.

Berry, L. L. (1995). *On great service: A framework for action.* Free Press: New York, NY.

Bitner, M. J., and Zeithaml, V. A. (1987). Fundamentals in services marketing; Add value to your service. Surprenant, C. (ed.), AMA Services Marketing Conference Proceedings: Chicago, USA.

Booms, B. H., and Bitner, M. J. (1981). Marketing strategies and organization structures for service firms. In Donnelly, J. H. and George, W. R. (eds), *Marketing of Services,* American Marketing Association: Chicago, 47–51.

Carlzon, J. (1987). *Moments of Truth,* Ballinger Publishing Company, Cambridge, Mass, USA.

Gentile, C., Spiller, N., and Noci, G. (2007). How to sustain the customer experience: An overview of experience components that co-create value with the customer. *European Management Journal,* 25(5), 395–410.

Grönroos, C. (1990). *Service Management and Marketing: Managing the Moments of Truth in Service Competition.* Lexington Books: Lexington, Massachusetts.

Grönroos, C. (2000). *Services management and marketing: A Customer Relationship Management Approach.* 2nd ed., Wiley: West Sussex, England.

James, J. (2013). The heart makes the mouse: Disney's approach to brand loyalty. *Journal of Brand Strategy*, 2(1), 16–20.

Kumar, V., Petersen, J. A., and Leone, R. P. (2010). Driving Profitability by Encouraging Customer Referrals: Who, When, and How. *Journal of Marketing*, 74(5), 1–17.

Kwon, J. M., Bae, J-I., and Blum, S. C. (2013). Mobile applications in the hospitality industry. *Journal of Hospitality and Tourism Technology*, 4(1), 81–92.

Meyer, C., and Schwager, A. (2007). Understanding customer experience. *Harvard Business Review*, February, 117–126.

Michelli, J. A. (2008). *The new gold standard: 5 leadership principles for creating a legendary customer experience courtesy of the Ritz-Carlton hotel company.* New York: McGraw-Hill.

Normann, R. (2000). *Service Management* (3rd ed.). West Sussex: John Wiley and Sons Ltd.

Ostrom, A. L., Bitner, M. J., Brown, S. W., Burkhard, K. A., Goul, M., Smith-Daniels, V., Demirkan, H., and Rabinovich, E. (2010). Moving forward and making a difference: Research priorities for the science of service. *Journal of Service Research*, 13(1), 4–36.

Pantano, E., and Di Pietro, L. (2013). From e-tourism to f-tourism: Emerging issues from negative tourists' online reviews. *Journal of Hospitality and Tourism Technology*, 4(3), 211–227.

Pine, J., and Gilmore, J. H., (1999). *The Experience Economy: Work is theatre & every business a stage.* Harvard Business School Press: Boston, Massachusetts.

Prahalad, C. K., and Ramaswamy, V. (2000). Co-opting customer competence. *Harvard Business Review*, January–February, 79–87.

Prahalad, C. K., and Ramaswamy, V. (2002). The co-creation connection. *Strategy and Business*, 50–61.

Prahalad, C. K., and Ramaswamy, V. (2004a). Co-creation experiences: The next practice in value creation. *Journal of Interactive Marketing*, 18(3), 5–14.

Prahalad, C. K., and Ramaswamy, V. (2004b). Co-creating unique value with customers. *Strategy & Leadership*, 32(3), 4–9.

Reichheld, F. F. (1996). Learning from Customer Defections. *Harvard Business Review*, March–April, 56–69.

Reichheld, F. F., and Sasser, W. E. (1990). Zero defections: quality comes to services. *Harvard Business Review*, September–October, 105–11.

Unzicker, D., Clow, K. E., and Babakus, E. (2000). The role of organizational communications on employee perceptions of a firm. *Journal of Professional Services Marketing*, 21(2), 87–103.

Chapter 7 Service Guarantees, Service Failure and Service Recovery

American Airlines. (n.d.). Why book on AA.com? http://www.jennycraig.com.au/weight-loss-programs/diet-plan/our-guarantee, (visited October 2013).

Bell, C. R. (1993). In Customers We Trust. *Executive Excellence,* 10(8), August, 13–14.

Bitner, M. J, Booms, B. H., and Tetreault, M. S. (1990). The service encounter: Diagnosing favorable and unfavorable incidents. *Journal of Marketing,* 54, January, 71–84.

Brisbane Whale Watching. (2014). Frequently Asked Questions. http://www.brisbanewhale watching.com.au/faq/, (visited October 2013).

Crowne Plaza Niagra Falls Hotel. (2014). Crown Plaza Hotel Service Guarantee. http://www.niagarafallshotels.com/crowne/service.php, (visited July 2014).

Hart, C. W. L., Heskett, J. L., and Sasser, W. E. (1990). The Profitable Art of Service Recovery. *Harvard Business Review,* 68(4), July–August, 148–56.

Hilton Worldwide. (2014). 100% Hampton Guarantee. http://hamptoninn3.hilton.com/en/about/satisfaction.html, (visited July 2014).

Hogreve, J., and Gremler, D. (2009). Twenty years of service guarantee research. *Journal of service research,* 11(4), 322–343.

Jones, T. O., and Sasser Jr, W. E. (1995). Why satisfied customers defect. *Harvard Business Review*, Nov–Dec, 88–99.

Kelley, S. W., Hoffman, D. K., and Davis, M. A. (1993). A Typology of Retail Failures and Recoveries. *Journal of Retailing,* 69(4), Winter, 429–52.

Lexus. (n.d.). *Our Story: Unsurpassed Customer Care.* http://www.lexus-int.com/our-story/customer-care.html, (visited December 2013).

Liang, T-P., Wang, Y-W., and Wu, P-J. (2013). A system for service blueprint design. Paper presented at the *2013 Fifth International Conference on Service Science and Innovation,* Taiwan, 252–253.

Merlo Coffee Company, Brisbane Australia.

McColl-Kennedy, J. R., and Sparks, B. A. (2003). Application of Fairness Theory to Service Failures and Service Recovery. *Journal of Service Research,* 5(3), 251–266.

McCollough, M. A., and Bharadwaj, S. G. (1992). The recovery paradox: An examination of customer satisfaction in relation to disconfirmation, service quality, and attribution based theories. In *Marketing Theory and Allications*, Allen, C. T. (Ed.). American Marketing Association: Chicago.

Michel, S., Bowen, D. E., and Johnston, R. (2009). Why service recovery fails. *Journal of Service Management,* 20(3), 253–273.

Robinson Jr, L. R., Neeley, S. E., and Williamson, K. (2011). Implementing service recovery through customer relationship management: identifying the antecedents. *Journal of Services Marketing,* 25(2), 90–100.

Schweikhart, S., Strasser, S., and Kennedy, M. (1993). Service Recovery in Health Service Organisations. *Hospital and Health Service Administration,* 38(1).

Tax, S. S., and Brown, S. W. (1998). Recovering and Learning from Service Failure. *Sloan Management Review,* Fall, 75–88.

Tax, S. S., and Brown, S. W. (2000). Service recovery: Research insights and practice. In Swartz, T. A. and Iacobucci, D. (eds), *Handbook of Services Marketing and Management,* Sage Publications: Thousand Oaks, California.

Voorhees, C. M., Brady, M. K., and Horowitz, D. M. (2006). A voice from the silent masses: An exploratory and comparative analysis of noncomplainers. *Journal of the Academy of Marketing Science,* 34(4), 514–527.

Zemke, R. (1995). *Service Recovery: Fixing Broken Customers.* Productivity Press: Portland, USA.

Zemke, R., and Bell, C. (1990). Service Recovery: doing it right the second time. *Training,* June, 42–8.

Chapter 8   Managing and Motivating Employees in Service Organizations

Bakker, A. B., and Schaufeli, W. B. (2008). Positive organizational behavior: engaged employees in flourishing organizations. *Journal of Organizational Behavior,* 29(2), 147–154.

Barney, J. B. (2002). Strategic management: From informed conversation to academic discipline. *Academy of Management Executive,* 16(2), 53–57.

Berry, L. L., Zeithaml, V., and Parasuraman, A. (1990). Five Imperatives for Improving Service Quality. *Sloan Management Review, Summer,* 29–38.

Berry, L., Parasuraman, A., and Zeithaml, V. (1994). Improving service quality in America: Lessons learned. *Academy of Management Executive,* 8(2), 32–52.

Bitner, M. J., Booms, B. H., and Mohr, L. A. (1994). Critical service encounters: The employee's view. *Journal of Marketing,* 58(October), 95–106.

Bowen, D. E., and Lawler III, E. E. (1995). Empowering service employees. *MIT Sloan Management Review,* 36(4), 73–84.

Bowen, J., and Ford, R. C. (2002). Managing service organizations: Does having a "thing" make a difference? *Journal of Management,* 28(3), 447–469.

Denison, D. (1996). What is the difference between organizational culture and organizational climate? A native's point of view on a decade of paradigm wars. *Academy of Management Review.* 21(3) 619–654.

Erickson, T. J. (2005). *Employee Engagement.* Washington, DC: US Senate Committee on Health, Education, Labour and Pensions.

Ford, R. C., and Heaton, C. P. (2001). Lessons from hospitality that can serve anyone. *Organizational Dynamics,* 30(1), 30–47.

Great Place to Work Institute. (2014). Celebrating Great Workplace Cultures: 2014 FORTUNE's 100 Best Companies to Work for. *Great Place to Work.* http://www.greatplacetowork.com/best-companies/100-best-companies-to-work-for, (visited August 2014).

Grönroos, C. (2000). *Service management and marketing: A customer relationship management approach,* (2nd ed.). West Sussex: John Wiley and Sons, Ltd.

Hallowell, R., Schlesinger, L., and Zornitsky, J. (1996). Internal service quality, customer and job satisfaction: Linkages and implications for management. *Human Resource Planning,* 19(2), 20–32.

Heskett, J. L., and Sasser, W. E., Jr. (2010). The Service Profit Chain. In P. P. Maglio, C. A. Kieliszewski and J. C. Spohrer (Eds.), *Handbook of Service Science,* Springer US, 19–29.

Heskett, J. L., Sasser, W. E., and Schlesinger, L. A. (1997). *The Service-profit chain.* New York: Free Press.

Hochschild, A. (1983). *The Managed Heart.* University of California Press: Berkeley and Los Angeles, California.

Hubrecht, J., and Teare, R. (1993). A Strategy for partnership in total quality service. *International Journal of Contemporary Hospitality Management,* 5(3).

Kahn, W. A. (1990). Psychological conditions of personal engagement and disengagement at work. *Academy of Management Journal,* 33, 692–724.

Kim, H., Shin, K., and Swanger, N. (2009). Burnout and engagement: A comparative analysis using the Big Five personality dimensions. *International journal of Hospitality Management,* 28(1), 96–104.

Kulik, C. T. (2004). *Human resources for the non-HR manager.* Mahwah: Lawrence Erlbaum Associates.

Lashley, C. (1996). 'Research issues for employee empowerment in hospitality organisations,' *International Journal of Hospitality Management,* 15(4), 333–46.

Lovelock, C., and Wirtz, J. (2010). *Services Marketing: People, Technology, Strategy* (Seventh ed.). Upper Saddle River, NJ: Pearson/Prentice Hall.

Macey, W. H., Schneider, B., Barbera, K. M., and Young, S. A. (2009). *Employee Engagement: Tools for Analysis, Practice and Competitive Advantage.* West Sussex: Blackwell Publishing.

Maslach, C., and Leiter, M. P. (1997). *The truth about burnout: How organizations cause personal stress and what to do about it.* San Francisco, CA: Josses-Bass.

Mattila, A., S., and Enz, C., A. (2002). The role of emotions in service encounters. *Journal of Service Research,* 4(4), 268–277.

May, D. R., Gilson, R. L., and Harter, L. M. (2004). The psychological conditions of meaningfulness, safety and availability and the engagement of the human spirit at work. *Journal of Occupational and Organizational Psychology,* 77, 11–37.

Meyer, J. P., and Allen, N. J. (1991). A three-component conceptualization of organizational commitment. *Human Resource Management Review,* 11, 299–326.

Michelli, J. A. (2007). *The Starbucks experience: 5 prinicples for turning ordinary into extraordinary.* New York: McGraw-Hill.

Robbins, S. P., and Judge, T. A. (2009). *Organizational behavior.* Upper Saddle River, NJ: Pearson Prentice Hall.

Saks, A. M. (2006). Antecedents and consequences of employee engagement. *Journal of managerial psychology,* 21(7), 600–619.

Schein, E. (1990). Organizational culture. *American Psychologist,* 45, 109–118.

Schneider, B. (1980). The Service Organisation: Climate is Crucial. *Organizational Dynamics,* 9, Autumn, 52–65.

Schneider, B., and Bowen, D. E. (1993). The service organization: Human resources management is crucial. *Organizational Dynamics,* 21(4), 39–43.

Schneider, B., Macey, W. H., Lee, W. C., and Young, S. A. (2009). Organizational service climate drivers of the American Customer Satisfaction Index (ACSI) and financial and market performance. *Journal of Service Research,* 12(1), 3–14.

Schneider, B., and White, S. (2004). *Service Quality Research Perspectives.* Thousand Oaks, CA: Sage.

Schneider, B., White, S., and Paul, M. (1998). Linking service climate and customer perceptions of service quality: Test of a causal model. *Journal of Applied Psychology,* 83(2), 150–163.

Simpson, M. R. (2009). Engagement at work: A review of the literature. *International journal of Nursing Studies,* 46, 1012–1024.

Solnet, D., Kralj, A., and Baum, T. (2014). 360 degrees of pressure: The changing role of the HR professional in the hospitality industry. *Journal of Hospitality & Tourism Research, in press.*

Tagiuri, R. (1968). The concept of organizational climate. In *Organizational climate: Exploration of a concept.* Tagiuri, R., and Litwin, G. H. (Eds.). Boston: Harvard University Press.

Tylor, E. B. (1871). *Primitive Culture: Researches into the Development of Mythology, Philosophy, Religion, Art and Custom.* Bradbury, Evans, and Co., Printers, Whitefriars: London.

Wall, T. D., and Wood, S. J. (2005). The romance of human resource management and business performance, and the case for big science. *Human Relations,* 58(4), 429–462.

Zeithaml, V., Bitner, M. J., and Gremler, D. D. (2009). *Services Marketing: Integrating Customer Focus Across the Firm* (Fifth ed.). New York: McGraw-Hill/Irwin.

Chapter 9 Leadership for Service Organizations

Ashkanasy, N., and Humphrey, R. (2011). Current emotion research in organizational behavior, *Emotion Review,* 3(2), 214–224.

Avolio, B., Walumbwa, F., and Weber, T. (2009). Leadership: Current theories, research and future directions. *Annual Review of Psychology,* 60, 421–449.

Baek-Kyoo, J., Yoon, H., and Jeung, C. (2012). The effects of core self-evaluations and transformational leadership on organizational commitment. *Leadership & Organization Development Journal,* 33(6), 564–582.

Bass, B. (1985). *Leadership and Performance Beyond Expectations,* New York: Free Press.

Bass, B. (1990). From transactional to transformational leadership: Learning to share the vision, *Organizational Dynamics,* 18, 19–31.

Bass, B. M., Avolio, N. J., Jung, D. I., and Berson, Y. (2003). Predicting unit performance by assessing transformational and transactional leadership. *Journal of Applied Psychology,* 88(2), 207–218.

Belbin, R. M. (1981). *Management Teams: Why They Succeed or Fail*, London: Heinemann.

Bennis, W., and Nanus, B. (1985). *Leaders: The Strategies for Taking Charge*, New York: Harper & Row Publishers.

Blake, R., and Mouton, J. (1964). *The Managerial Grid*, Houston, TX: Gulf Publishing Company

Blumberg, M., and Pringle, C. (1982). The missing opportunity in organizational research: some implications for a theory of work performance, *Academy of Management Review*, 7, 560–569.

Boyatzis, R., and McKee, A. (2005). *Resonant Leadership: Renewing Yourself and Connecting with Others through Mindfulness, Hope, and Compassion,* Boston: Harvard Business School Press.

Brown, M., Trevino, L., Harrison, D. (2005). Ethical leadership: A social learning perspective for construct development and testing, *Organizational Behavior and Human Decision Processes*, 97, 117–134.

Brownell, J. (2010). Leadership in the service of hospitality. *Cornell Hospitality Quarterly*, 51, 363–378.

Callan, V. J., and Latemore, G. (2008). All the world's a stage. *Monash Business Review*, 4(2), 38–39.

Callan, V., Latemore, G., and Paulsen, N. (2004). The best laid plans: Uncertainty, complexity and large-scale organizational change, *Mt Eliza Business Review*, Winter–Spring, 10–17.

Cameron, K. [ed.] (2010). *Organizational Effectiveness,* Cheltenham, UK: Edward Elgar Publishing Limited.

Castro, C., Villegas, P., and Bueno, J. (2008). Transformational leadership and followers' attitudes: the mediating role of psychological empowerment. *The International Journal of Human Resource Management*, 19(10), 1842–1863.

Clark, R., Hartline, M., and Jones, K. (2009). The effects of leadership style on hotel employees' commitment to service quality, *Cornell Hospitality Quarterly,* May, 50(2), 209–231.

Collins, J. (2001). *Good to Great: Why Some Companies Make the Leap and Others Don't,* Sydney: Random House.

Colquitt, J., and Rodell, J. (2011). Justice, trust and trustworthiness: A longitudinal analysis integrating three theoretical perspectives, *Academy of Management Journal,* 54(6), 1183–1206.

Covey, S. (2004). *The 7 Habits of Highly Effective People: Powerful Lessons in Personal Change,* 25th Anniversary edition, New York: Simon & Schuster.

Day, D., Gronn, P., and Salas, E. (2004). Leadership capacity in teams, *The Leadership Quarterly,* 15, 857–880.

De Jong, F. (2011). *The Role of Rumour in Chilean Organisational Culture,* Unpublished Master of Communication thesis, The University of Queensland, Brisbane, Australia.

de Vries, M. K. (2006). *The Leadership Mystique: An Owner's Manual,* 2nd ed., London: Prentice Hall.

Ernst, C., and Chrobot-Mason, D. (2010). *Boundary-spanning Leadership: Six Practices for Solving Problems, Driving Innovation, and Transforming Organizations,* New York: McGraw Hill.

Etter, Z. C. (2012). Future now: operation agility—conference report on the SLA Leadership Summit. *Library Hi Tech News*, 29(2), 1–3.

Freeman, W. (2002). Ethical Leadership in Turbulent Times, Presentation to the Darden School of Business, May, PowerPoint slides cited at www.authorstream.com/Presentation/aSGuest8516-129524-ethical-leadership-turbulent-times-spiritual-inspirational-ppt-powerpoint/, viewed 1st March 2014.

Gardner, P. (2009). Eye on Australia: Commentary on Grey & Sweeney's research report, http://walteradamson.com/2009/10/trust-gfc-australia-most-trusted-brands.html, viewed 2nd March 2014.

George, B. (2003). *Authentic Leadership: Rediscovering the Secrets to Creating Lasting Value*, San Francisco: Jossey-Bass.

Gill, A. S., Flaschner, A. B., and Schachar, M. (2006). Mitigating stress and burnout by implementing transformational-leadership. *International Journal of Contemporary Hospitality Management*. 18(6), 469–481.

Gillespie, N., and Dietz, G. (2009). Trust repair after an organization-level failure, *Academy of Management Review*, 34(1), 127–145.

Goffee, R., and Jones, G. (2005). Why Should Anyone Be Led By You? *Harvard Business Review*, September–October, 63–70.

Goleman, D. (1995). *Emotional Intelligence: Why it can Matter More than IQ*, London: Bloomsbury.

Goleman, D. (2004). What makes a leader? *Harvard Business Review*, [Cited in 'Best of HBR' 1998], January, 1–10.

Gross, W., and Schichman, S. (1987). How to grow an organizational culture, *Personnel*, September, 52–56.

Hamel, G. (2000). *Leading the Revolution*, Boston: Harvard Business School Press.

Hamel, G. (2012). *What Matters Now: How to Win in a World of Relentless Change, Ferocious Competition and Unstoppable Innovation*, San Francisco: Jossey-Bass.

Hersey, P., and Blanchard, K. (1969). Life-cycle theory of leadership, *Training and Development Journal*, 23, 26–34.

Heskett, J. L., Sasser, W. E., and Wheeler, J. (2008). *The Ownership Quotient*. Boston: Harvard Business Press.

Hickman, C., and Silva, M. (1984). *Creating Excellence: Managing Corporate Culture, Strategy and Change in the New Age*, Boston: George Allen & Unwin.

Janis, I. (1972). *Victims of Groupthink: a Psychological Study of Foreign-Policy Decisions and Fiascoes*, Boston: Houghton Mifflin.

Kanaga, M., and Browning, H. (2003). *Managing Team Performance: An Ideas into Action Guidebook*, Greensborough, North Carolina: Centre for Creative Leadership.

Kaye, M. (1995). *Myth-Makers and Story-Tellers*, Chatswood: Business & Professional Publishing.

Kim, W., and Brymer, R. (2011). The effects of ethical leadership on manager job satisfaction, commitment, behavioral outcomes and firm performance, *International Journal of Hospitality Management*, 30, 1020–1026.

Kim, Chan, W., and Mauborgne, R. (1992). Parables of leadership, *Harvard Business Review*, July–August, 70(4), 123.

Kim, Chan, W., and Mauborgne, R. (2005). *Blue Ocean Strategy: How to Create Uncontested Market Space and Make the Competition Irrelevant*, Boston: Harvard Business School Press.

Kogler-Hill, S. (2013). Team leadership. In Northouse, P., *Leadership: Theory and Practice*, 6e, London UK: Sage. 287–318.

Kotter, J. (1990). *A Force for Change: How Leadership Differs from Management*, New York: Free Press.

Kotter, J. (1996). Leading Change: Why Transformation Efforts Fails, *Harvard Business Review*, March-April, 59–67.

Kotter, J., and Cohen, D. (2002). *The Heart of Change: Real-Life Stories of how People Change their Organizations*, Boston: Harvard Business School Press.

Kouzes, J., and Posner, B. (2012). *The Leadership Challenge*, 5e, San Francisco: Jossey-Bass.

Latemore, G. (2012). Restoring trust in two Australian Organizations: The cases of Herron and Qantas, in W. Amann and A. Stachowicz-Stanush [eds.], *Integrity in Organizations: Building the Foundation for Humanistic Management*, Houndmills UK: Palgrave Macmillan.

Lencioni, P. (2005). *The Five Dysfunctions of a Team: A Field Guide for Leaders, Managers and Facilitators*, San Francisco: Jossey-Bass.

Lewicki, R., and Bunker, B. (1996). Developing and maintain trust in workplace relationships, in R. M. Kramer and T. R. Tyler [eds.] *Trust in Organizations: Frontiers of Theory and Research*, Thousand Oaks: Sage, 114–130.

Malhotra, D., and Lumineau, F. (2011). Trust and collaboration in the aftermath of conflict: The effects of contract structure, *Academy of Management Journal*, 54(5), 981–998.

Mayer, R., Davis, J., and Schoorman, F. (1995). An integrative model of organizational trust, *Academy of Management Review*, 20, 709–734.

Mayer, J., and P. Salovey, P. (1997). What is emotional intelligence? in P. Salovey and D. Sluyter (eds.) *Emotional Development & Emotional Intelligence: Implications for Educators*, New York: Basic Books, 3–31.

McAllister, D., Lewicki, R., and Charturvedi, S. (2006). Trust in developing relationships: From theory to measurement, in K. M. Weaver [ed.] *AOM Best Paper Proceedings*.

McGrath, J. E. (1962). Critical leadership functions. In R. Hackman and R. Walton (1986), P.s. Goodman and Associates [eds.] *Designing Effective Work Groups*, San Francisco: Jossey-Bass, 96.

Minnett, D., Yaman, H., and Denizci, B. (2009). Leadership styles and ethical decision-making in hospitality management, *International Journal of Hospitality Management*, 28(4), 486–493.

Northouse, P. (2013). *Leadership: Theory and Practice*, 6e, Los Angeles: Sage.

O'Gorman, K., and Gillespie, C. (2010). The mythological power of hospitality leaders? A hermeneutical investigation of their relevance on storytelling, *International Journal of Contemporary Hospitality Management*, 22(5), 659–680.

Preston, N. (2001). *Understanding Ethics*, 2e, Riverwood: The Federation Press.

Robbins, S. Millett, B., Cacioppe, R., and Waters-March T. (2001). *Organisational behavior: Leading and Managing in Australia and New Zealand,* 3e, Frenchs Forest: Prentice Hall.

Sarros, J., Cooper, B., Hartican, A., and Barker, C. (2006) *The Character of Leadership: What Works for Australian Managers—Making it Work for You,* Milton QLD: John Wiley.

Schein, E. (1986). *Organizational Culture and Leadership: A Dynamic View,* San Francisco: Jossey-Bass.

Solnet, D., and Kandampully, J. (2008). How some service firms become part of 'service excellence' folklore—An exploratory study, *Managing Service Quality,* 18(2), 179–193.

Sull, D. (2007). Closing the gap between strategy and execution, *MIT Sloan Management Review,* 48(4), 30–38.

Sumi, J. (2014). Transformational leadership and psychological empowerment: Determinants of organizational citizenship behavior, *South Asian Journal of Global Business Research,* 3(1), 18–35.

Tee, E., Ashkanasy, N., and Paulsen, N. (2013). The influence of follower mood on leader mood and task performance: An affective, follower-centric perspective of leadership, *The Leadership Quarterly,* 24, 496–515.

Teece, D. (2007). Explicating dynamic capabilities: The nature and micro-foundations of (sustainable) enterprise performance, *Strategic Management Journal,* August, 28(13), 1319–1350.

Trevino, L., and Nelson, K. (2007). *Managing Business Ethics: Straight Talk about How to Do It Right,* 4e, Hoboken: Wiley.

Tuckman, B. (1965). Development sequence in small groups, *Psychological Bulletin,* 63, 384–399.

Wageman, R., Nunes, D., Burruss, J., and Hackman, J. (2008). *Senior Leadership Teams: What it Takes to Make Them Great,* Boston: Harvard Business School Press.

Walter, F., Cole, M., and Humphrey, R. (2011). Emotional intelligence: Sine qua non of leadership or folderol? *Academy of Management Perspectives,* February, 45–59.

Walumbwa, F., Hartnell, C., and Oke, A. (2010). Servant leadership, procedural justice climate, service climate, employee attitudes, and organizational citizenship behavior: A cross-level investigation, *Journal of Applied Psychology,* 95, 517–529.

Wood, J., Zeffane, R., Fromholtz, M., Wiesner, R., Creed, A., Schermerhorn, J., Hunt, J., and Osborn, R. (2010). *Organisational Behaviour: Core Concepts and Applications,* 2nd Australasian edition, Milton QLD: John Wiley & Sons Australia.

Wong, P., and Davey, D. (2007). *Best Practices in Servant Leadership,* Paper presented at the Servant Leadership Research Roundtable, Regent University, Virginia Beach, VA.

Yao, K., and Cui, X. (2010). Study on the moderating effect of the employee psychological empowerment on the enterprise employee turnover tendency: taking small and middle enterprises in Jinan as the example. *International Business Research,* 3(3), 107–128.

Zalaznik, A. (1977). Managers and leaders: Are they different? *Harvard Business Review,* May–June, 67–78.

Chapter 10   Bringing Service Management to Life!
Case Studies of Best Practice

Assef, D. (2014). Managing Director, Spicers Retreats, Australia, Interview.

Brefere, L., Drummon, K., and Barnes, B. (2008). *Interview: Cameron Mitchell, Owner, Cameron Mitchell Restaurants.* http://www.globalgourmet.com/food/cookbook/2008/chef/ cameronmitchell.html#axzz1ddkzlPrW, visited July 2014.

Cactus Jack's. (2014). *Cactus Jack's Employee Toolkit.* Brisbane.

Cameron Mitchell Restaurants. (2014a). *Great People Delivering Genuine Hospitality.* http://www. cameronmitchell.com, visited July 2014.

Cameron Mitchell Restaurants. (2014b). *Who Is Cameron Mitchell?* http://cameronmitchell.com/ cameronsbio.cfm, visited July 2014.

de Chalain, N. (2013). Chief Sales Officer, Long Beach Hotel, Mauritius, Interview.

DiJulius, J. (2006). *What's the Secret?* http://www.hotelfandb.com/biol/march-april2006-dijulius. asp, visited July 2014.

Emporium Hotel, Interview with Senior Managers in 2014.

Espresso Dating Guide. (n.d.) http://advision.webevents.yahoo.com/personals/espressodating/ espresso_dating_guide.htm, visited August 2014.

Four Seasons Hotel. (2000). "2000 Annual Report—Four Seasons Hotels and Resorts", Docstoc. com, available at: http://www.docstoc.com/docs/83500213/2000-Annual-Report---Four- Seasons-Hotels-and-Resorts (accessed 15 November 2014).

Four Seasons Hotels Limited. (2014). *Four Seasons Hotels and Resorts: About Us.* http://www. fourseasons.com/about_four_seasons/, visited May 2014.

The Greenbrier. (2013). *About The Greenbrier: Employment.* http://www.greenbrier.com/Top- Navigation-Pages/About-Us/Employment.aspx, visited July 2014.

Hesham, N. (2012). *My Starbucks Idea.* http://nehalhesham.com/2012/03/18/my-starbucks-idea/, visited August 2014.

Hotel ICON. (2014). *Hotel ICON.* http://www.hotel-icon.com, visited April 2014.

Hughes, L. (2009). Leaders in Luxury: Isadore Sharp. *Elite Traveler,* http://www.elitetraveler.com/ leaders_detail.html?lid=86, visited May 2014.

Jandai, J. (2014). Founder, Pun Pun Sustainable Living & Learning Centre, Thailand, Interview.

Khadaroo, S. (2013). Hygiene and Safety Manager, Long Beach Hotel, Mauritius, Interview.

LinkedIn. (2014). *The Greenbrier: About this company.* http://www.linkedin.com/jobs2/ view/13020261, visited July 2014.

Michelli, J.A. (2007). *The Starbucks Experience: Five Principles for Turning Ordinary into Extraordinary.* McGraw-Hill: New York.

Miller, C. C. (2009). New Starbucks ads seek to recruit online fans. *The New York Times,* www. nytimes.com/2009/05/19/business/media/19starbux.html, visited August 2014.

Pun Pun. (2011). *Pun Pun: Center for Self Reliance.* http://www.punpunthailand.org/, visited July 2014.

Ravneburg, C. (2006). *Cameron Mitchell Restaurants: entrepreneur goes from 'dish room to boardroom' to realize dream of growing multiconcept company into Midwestern restaurant empire.* http://business.highbeam.com/409700/article-1G1-141800943/cameron-mitchell-restaurants-entrepreneur-goes-dish, visited July 2014.

Scanu, V. (2013). General Manager, Long Beach Hotel, Mauritius, Interview.

Solnet and Kandampully. (2008). How some service firms have become part of "service excellence" folklore: An exploratory study. *Managing Service Quality,* 18(2), 179–193.

Spicers Retreats. (n.d.). *Spicers Retreats: Relaxed Luxury.* http://spicersretreats.com/, visited July 2014.

Stanford. (2010 May11). "Empowered Employees Make the Difference, Says Four Seasons CEO Isadore Sharp|Stanford Knowledgebase," available at: http://web.stanford.edu/group/knowledgebase/cgi-bin/2010/03/11/empowered-employees-make-the-difference-says-four-seasons-ceo-isadore-sharp/ (accessed 15 November 2014).

Stanglwirt. (2014). *Bio Hotel Stanglwirt,* http://www.stanglwirt.com/en/about-us.html, visited July 2014.

Statistic Brain. (2014). *Starbucks Company Statistics.* http://www.statisticbrain.com/starbucks-company-statistics/, visited August 2014.

Talbott, B. M. (2006). The Power of Personal Service: Why It Matters, What Makes It Possible, How It Creates Competitive Advantage. *CHR Industry Perspectives*, 1, http://www.fourseasons.com/cgi-bin/pdf-we.exe//pdfs/about_us/service_culture/PersonalService.pdf, visited May 2014.

TedX Talks. (2011). *TEDxDoiSuthep—Jon Jandai—Life is easy. Why do we make it so hard?* https://www.youtube.com/watch?v=21j_OCNLuYg, visited July 2014.

TripAdvisor LLC. (2010). *Cameron Mitchell Restaurants.* http://www.tripadvisor.com/Restaurant_Review-g50226-d403314-Reviews-Cameron_Mitchell_Restaurants-Columbus_Ohio.html, visited July 2014.

West, T. (2012). Starbucks tops social engagement study: what can your biz learn? *Birmingham Business Journal*, www.bizjournals.com/albuquerque/blog/socialmadness/2012/04/starbucks-tops-social-engagement.html, visited August 2014.

Index

4 Ps of marketing mix, 13, 158, 159
7 Ps of marketing, 13, 168, 168–179

A

Access, 77
Accommodation, as hospitality component, 10, 11
Advocates, 109–110
Alignment, 127–128
Appraisal costs, 57
Assef, David, 294
Assessment tool, 100
Assurance, 78
Attributed charisma, 256
Authentic leadership, 263–265
    attributes, 264, 265

B

Back-of-house functions, 148
Back-stage, 148
Balanced processing, 264
Behavioral charisma, 256
Best Western Premier (BWP) Hotel Slon, Slovenia, 307–310
Bio-Hotel Stanglwirt, Austria, 306–307
Blog, 105

Blueprint within a blueprint, 150
Blumenthal, Heston, 135
Bundles, 14–15
    two general types of, 14
Business-to-business (B2B), 188
Business-to-customer (B2C), 188

C

Cactus Jack's, 135, 136, 288–291
Cameron Mitchell Restaurants, 317–319
Capacity, 45–47
Carlzon, Jan, 140, 182–183
Case studies, 284–321
Category, of customer, 91–108
    external, 92–105
    internal, 106–108
Chat room, 105
Chon, Kaye, 299
Cocreation, 32
Combination of services, 3, 14
Commercial hospitality, 11
Communication, 77
Competence, 77
Competitive advantage, 13–14, 88, 198, 215–216
    strategies for, 203–220

Competitors' customers, 91
Conditional service guarantee, 205
Confirmation, 67
Confirmation/disconfirmation paradigm, 67
Consumer behavior, 62
Consumption, 63, 163–166
Continuum of tangibility and intangibility, 25
Controllable variables of marketing, 159
Coordinated benefits, 14–16
Coproducer (customer as), 141
Coproduction, 229
Core services, 16–17
    and differentiation between peripheral, 17
Corporate image, 73
Cost of exceeding customer requirements, 57
Cost of lost opportunities, 57
Cost of quality, 56, 57
Courtesy, 77
Covey, Steven, 115
Creative thinking, 133–134
Credibility, 77
Critical-incident technique (CIT), 99
Crosby, Philip, 57, 59–60
Crosby's four absolutes, 60
Cross-functional service system, 15
Culture, 231–235
Current external customer, 91
Customer, 62, 87, 141
Customer advocates, 109–110
Customer, categories of, 91
Customer-centric, 89–90, 201
Customer centricity, 89
Customer-centric processes, 178
Customer delight, 65
Customer deviance, 142
Customer experience, 163
Customer Experience Evaluation (CEE), 100
Customer focus, 121–122
Customerization, 28
Customer lifetime value (CLV), 64
Customer loyalty, 63–64, 200
Customer management system, 130
Customer needs, and design of offer, 16
Customer research, 93–105

critical-incident/complaint analysis, 99
customer-to-customer communication,
    103–105
focus groups, 95–96
in-house customer satisfaction surveys,
    97–99
interviews, 94–95
market surveys, 96–97
mystery shopper, 99–103
Customer satisfaction, 62–63
    cost, 129
Customer-to-customer communication,
    103–104, 103–105
Customer-to-customer interactions (C2C), 104
Customer, understanding, 87–88
Customer variability, 142
Customization, 28
Customized service processes, 179

D
De Chalain, Nicolas, 286
Demand, 41–45
Deming Prize, 55
Deming's chain reaction, 58
Deming, W. Edwards, 55, 57, 58–59,
    109, 276
Demographics, and tourism, 8
Digital revolution, 8
Disconfirmation, 67
Disney, 90, 91, 167
The Disney Way, 90
Distance, and marketing, 161
Distributive justice, 215
"Do it right first time," 59
Donovan, Carter, 68
Dreamworld, 137, 139
Drucker, Peter, 89
During-consumption marketing, 164–165

E
Economic development, 7
Economic growth, and hospitality, 9
Economic impact of quality, 56
Electronic (web) service quality, 81

Ellway, Benjamin Piers William, 302
Emotional dissonance, 231
Emotional intelligence (EQ)
   defined, 258
   developing, 262
   dimensions of, 262
   history of, 260
   importance of, 258–259
   latest understanding of, 261
   and leadership, 261–263
Emotional labor, 230, 230–231
Emotions, 142
Empathy, 78
Employee
   as customer advocate, 109–110
   management, 224
Employee deviance, 142
Employee management system, 130
Employee research, 108
Employee stress, 141–142
Emporium Hotel, Australia, 291–293
Empowerment, 235–240
   benefits of, 237, 239
   effective, 240
   goal of, 237
Encounter points, 149
Engel, Ernest, 5
Engel's model, 5
Entertainment, as hospitality component, 10, 11
E-service quality, 81
E-S-QUAL, 81
Essence of service, 125–126
Ethical leadership, 269–270
E-word-of-mouth, 166
Ex-customers, 91
Expanded Nordic model, 74
Expectation, 66–69, 86–87
Expenditure, on services, 4–5
Experience, 3, 18
Extended Marketing Mix, 13, 168, 168–179
External customer, 87, 92–105
customer-perception research, 93–105
   importance of customer information, 92

External failure costs, 57
External marketing, 185

F
Facebook, 166
Face-to-face interaction, 146
Face-to-face research, 91
Facilities, quality of, 70
Fail points, 149, 219
Failure, of service, 201. *see also* Service failure
The Fat Duck, 135, 136
Feedback, 97, 98, 99, 133, 220
Feigenbaum, Armand V., 55, 60
Fishbone diagram, 132
Focus group, 95–96
Food and beverage, as hospitality component, 10, 11
Four Seasons Hotels and Resorts, 315–317
FreeOnlineSurveys.com, 96
Frenzel, Michael, 8
Freyne, Siobhán, 294
Front-of-house functions, 148
Front-stage, 148
Functional approach, to team leadership, 266
Functional quality, 71–72
Funding mechanism, 130

G
Gap model, 71, 76–77
GDP. *see* Gross domestic product (GDP)
Global tourism, 7
Golubovskaya, Maria, 291
The Greenbrier, 319–321
Gross domestic product (GDP), 5, 6, 8
Groupthink, 267
Guarantee, 203–204, 204–211
Guest communications, 91
Guestology, 90–91

H
Haidilao, China, 296–299
Heterogeneity, 26–28
   levels of, 26
   management challenges of, 39–40

High participation, 141
High-performance team, 268
High-tech interaction, 27
High-touch interaction, 27
Holiday Inn, 137, 138
Holistic relationship, 191
HOME, 277
Hospitality
    basic components of, 10–11
    changing patterns of, 9
    defined, 10
    growth in, 9
    as service industry, 9–10
Hotel ICON, Hong Kong, 299–302
In-house customer satisfaction survey, 97–99
Household expenditure, 4
Human resource management (HRM), 12, 144,
        161, 167, 226
    benefits of, 240–242
    defined, 227–228
    effective practices of, 235–240
    employee engagement, 240–242
    importance of, 230–235
    in service context, 229–230

I

Idealized influence, 256
IHIP, 23–34
    management implications for, 35–47
Image, 173–174
Impression management, 144
Inbuilt flaws, 130–132
Incident-based measurement, 99
Income, family, 4, 5
Individualized consideration, 257
Information, 240
Inseparability, 28–32, 108–109
    and marketing, 29–30
    and multiple consumption, 31–32
    during production, 29
    and quality, 30–31
    and value cocreation, 32
Inspirational motivation, 256

Intangibility
    and customer's perspective, 36–37
    defined, 24
    importance of, 24–26
    and manager's perspective, 37–39
Integrating model of service leadership,
        277–278
Intellectual stimulation, 256
Interactional justice, 215
Interaction quality, 80
Interactive marketing, 185
Interdependency, of service provision, 14–17
Interdependent services, 107
Internal customer, 87, 91, 106–108
Internal failure costs, 57
Internalized moral perspective, 264
Internal marketing, 183–187, 185
    objectives of, 185
Internet, 81
Interviews, 94–95
Ishikawa diagram, 132
Ishikawa, Kaoru, 132
ISO 9001 Quality Management System, 287
ISO 22000 Food Safety management System,
        287

J

Japan
    management approach, 110
    and quality, 55–59
Jimmy John's Gourmet Sandwiches, 116
Jun Luo, 296
Juran, Joseph, 55, 57, 59
Justice theory, 215
Juwaheer, Thanika Devi, 285

K

Kandampully, Jay, 306
Kim, Sam, 299
Knowledge, 240
Knowledge, pricing, 172
Kotter, John, 273

L

Laval, Bruce, 90
Leader
    as authentic person, 263–265
    as change agent, 272–275
    and emotional intelligence, 258–263,
        262–263
    vs. manager, 253–254
    servant leader, 257
    as strategist, 275–277
    as team builder, 265–269
    transformational, 256–257
    transactual, 255–256
    trustworthy and ethical, 269–272
Leadership, 249–278
    as change agent, 272–274
    defined, 252–253
    functions of, 253–254
    integrated model of, 277–278
    situational, 254–255
    styles, 254–257
LEARN routine, 216
Leisure tourism, 137, 139
Lexus, 199
Lifestyle, and tourism, 8
Line of visibility, 147–148
Listening skills, 145
Liu, Martin J., 296
Long Beach Hotel, Mauritius, 285–287
Lost value, 35
Low participation, 141
Loyalty, 199–200

M

Management, 3, 7
Maravic, Maja Uran, 307
Marketing, 7
    controllable variables of, 159
    primary function of, 159
    and separability, 29–30
Marketing mix, 159
Marketing Mix 7 Ps, 13
Marketing paradigm, 159

Market segment, 122
Market share, 56
Market survey, 96–97
Marriott, J. W., 108
Materials, quality of, 70
McDonald's, 135, 136
Measurement, of online services, 81
Merlo, Dean, 206
Mobile app, 105
Moderate participation, 141
'Moment of truth,' 146, 149, 152, 180–182
Moments of Truth (MsOT), 140
Multiple consumption, 31–32, 38, 68–69
Mystery shopper, 99–103
Mystery shopper questionnaire, 101, 103

N

Negative disconfirmation, 67
Net Promoter Score (NPS), 99
Nordic quality model, 70, 71
    expanded, 74

O

Online community, 105
Operations, 161, 167
Optimism, 144–145
Organizational climate, 234
Organizational commitment, 242
Organizational culture
    artifacts and behavior, 232, 233
    defined, 231
    espoused values, 232, 233
    shared assumptions, 232–233, 233
Organizational psychology, 227
Outcome, of service, 17, 126
Outcome quality, 80
Output quality, 75–77
Overall cost leadership, 56
Ownership and control, of a service, 34–35

P

Pareto chart, 131
Pareto principle, 131

Pareto, Vilfredo, 131
Part-time marketer, 230
People, in marketing mix, 13, 159, 168, 175–176
Perceived service quality, 80
Performance equation, 275
Performance, service, 62
Peripheral services, 16–17
Perishability, 32–35, 40
Personal experience, 170
Personalization, *vs* customerization, 28
Personnel, 70
Pessimism, 145
Phantom Guest, 99
Philosophy of quality, 61
Physical environment, 80
Physical Evidence, in marketing mix, 13, 159, 168, 176–177
Place, in marketing mix, 13, 158, 168, 174–175
Plan-do-check-act cycle, 55, 58
Planned reduction of variation, 58
Pod hotels, 136, 138
Porter, Michael, 123
Positive disconfirmation, 67
Positive image, 173
Post-consumption marketing, 165–166
Potential future customers, 91
Power, 240
Pre-consumption marketing, 164
Pre-purchase guarantee, 205
Prevention costs, 57
Price, 13, 158, 168, 170–172
Price discrimination, 171
Primitive Culture, 232
Prior expectations of performance, 66
Procedural justice, 215
Process description, 170
Process, in marketing mix, 13, 159, 168, 178–179
Process quality, 73–75, 126–127
Product, 13, 158, 168, 170
Product-centric approach, 89
Product differentiation, 56

Product management, 12
    to service management, 12–13
Profitability, 56
Profit impact of market share (PIMS), 56
Progression of economic value, 73
Promotion, 13, 158, 168, 172–174
    of image, 173
    of production skills in service, 172–173
    traditional role of, 172
Pun Pun Sustainable Living and Learning Centre, Thailand, 302–305

Q
Qualitative research, 93
Quality, 53
    economic impact of, 56
    history of, 54–55
    outcomes of, 62–65
Quality control, 54–55
    shortcoming of methods, 59
Quality Control Handbook, 55
Quality "gurus," 57–60
Quality, history
    1920s, 54–55
    WWII developments, 55
Quality is Free, 59
Quality movement, in goods manufacturing, 61
Quality, service, cleanliness and value (QSC&V), 135
Quality theory, 61–62, 66–69. *see also* Service quality theory
Quality without Fears, 59
Qualtrics, 96
Quantitative research, 93
Questionnaire, 97

R
Recovery, 203–204, 211–218
Recovery strategy, 219–220
Relational transparency, 264
Relationship building, 180
Relationship marketing, 187–192
    history of, 188–189
    importance of, 187

Reliability, 77, 78, 198
Reliability, and timing, 33
Repeat business, 63, 64
Research, 94–105. *see also* Customer research
Responsiveness, 77, 78
Retention, 211
Return on investment (ROI), 160
Review Analyst, 105
Rewards, 240
Risk perceptions, 204
Risky shift, 267
Ritz-Carlton, 65, 137, 138, 236
Role ambiguity, 142
Role conflict, 142

S

Satisfaction, and loyalty, 64–65
    non-linear relationship between, 64
Scandinavian Airlines System (SAS), 182
Scanu, Vladimir, 286
Schein, Edgar, 232
Schneider, Ben, 11
Scripting, 145
Scripts, 145
Secret Shopper, 99
Security, 77
Segal-Horn, Susan, 125
Self-awareness, 264
Servant leader, 257
Service, defined, 3
Service advantage, 13
Service blueprint
    defined, 147
    line of visibility in, 148
    of overnight hotel stay, 151
Service blueprinting, 146–152
Service bundling, 14
Service characteristics, 24–35
    heterogeneity, 26–28
    inseparability, 28–32
    intangibility, 24–26
    perishability, 32–35
Service climate, 234
Service concept, 116

Service culture, 231, 232
Service economy, 4–5
Service encounters, 3, 138–146
Service encounter triad, 139–140
Service enhancement, 169
Service excellence equation, 275
Service expenditure, 4
Service failure, 201–203
    recognizing, 202–203
    recovery steps for, 216
    types of, 201–202
Service guarantee, 204–211
    appropriateness of, 211
    benefits of, 209–210
    defined, 205
    dual role of, 210–211
    effective, 207, 208
    examples of, 206
    and mutual trust, 206–207
    mutual trust, 206–207
    perceptions of risk, 204
    reliability, 205–206
Service image, 122
Service interrelationship, 15–16
Service loyalty, 200
Service management, 3, 7, 53
    defined, 11
    evolution of, 12–14
    multidisciplinary nature of, 11, 12
    origins of framework in, 11–12
Service management overlap, 12
Service management theory, 17–18
Service marketing, 7, 160–161
Service model, 117
Service performance, dimensions of, 70
Service process, 118, 122, 124–127
    analysis, 125
Service products, *vs* tangible products, 23
Service-profit chain, 243–244
Service provision, 3
    interdependency of, 14–17
Service quality factors, 77
Service quality measurement, 69–80
Service quality models, 71

Service quality theory, 66–69
  confirmation and disconfirmation of
    expectations, 66–67
  exceeding expectations, 68
  expectation and performance, 66
  meeting expectations, 67–68
  multiple consumption, 68–69
Service recovery, 211–218
  defined, 212
  justice and fairness theory, 215
  types of options in, 215–216
Service recovery paradox, 214–215
Services, defined, 3
Servicescape, 176–177
Service sector growth, 5, 6
Service strategy, 118, 123–124
Service superiority, 198–201
Service system, 126
Service system design, 118, 128–134
  key elements in, 130
  process, 132–133
Service vision, 116, 119–122
  components of, 122
  defined, 120
  vision statement vs. mission statement, 119
Servitization, 13–14
SERVPERF, 71, 80
SERVQUAL, 71, 77, 127
The Seven Habits of Highly Effective
    People, 115
Shewhart, Walter, 55
Shostack, Lynn, 24, 26, 146, 149
"The Silent Masses," 203
Simultaneous production and consumption, 29
Situational leadership, 254–255
SMS (short messaging service), 97
Social loafing, 267
Social media, 8, 91, 93, 103–105, 105, 106
Solnet, David, 288, 291
Southwest Airlines, 124
Specialization, 11
Spicers Retreat, Australia, 294–296
Standard Intelligence (IQ), 259
Standard Operational Procedure (SOP), 214

Standard Recovery Procedure (SRP), 214
Starbucks, 94, 190, 226, 245, 313–315
Starwood Hotels and Resorts Worldwide, 8
Statistical control, 58
Strand Spa and Conference Hotel, Estonia,
    311–312
Strategy, 123
Supply, 45–47
Supply and demand, 33
  service, 40–47
Survey Gizmo, 96
SurveyMonkey, 96, 97

T
Tangibles, 77, 78
Team, 266
Team builder, 265–268
Team charter, 268, 269
Team development, 266
Team dynamics, 268
Team dysfunction, 267
Team effectiveness, 266
Team leadership, 266
Technical quality, 71, 72
Technological innovations, 13
Technology
  and heterogeneity, 27
  and product development, 13
  and tourism, 8
Theory X, 238
Theory Y, 238–239
Three-component model (TCM), 242
Timing and speed, 174–175
Tooman, Heli, 311
Total experience, 3
Total quality management (TQM), 60
Tourism
  changing patterns of, 8
  digital shift in growth of, 8
  growing importance of, 7–8
  and hospitality, 7–11
  service components in, 15
  as service industry, 9–10
  as system, 15

Tourist, change in social habits of, 8
Training tool, 100
Transactional leader, 255–256
Transformational change agent, 274
Transformational leader, 256–257
TripAdvisor.com, 104
Trust, 271–272
Trust management, 272
Two-dimensional quality model, 73–77
Two-way communication, 109
Tylor, Edward B., 232

U
Unconditional service guarantee, 205
Understanding/knowing customer, 77, 87–88
Uniformity of service, 28
Union of Japanese Scientists and Engineers (JUSE), 55
United Nations World Tourism Organization (UNWTO), 7
User-generated content (UGC), 166

V
Value, 3
Value cocreation, 18, 32

Value perceptions, 198–199
Van Grinsven, Jon, 288
Van Grinsven, Trent, 288
Van Paasschen, Frits, 8
Vilgas, Aime, 311
Virgin Atlantic, 213
Vision, 119–122. *see also* Service vision
    defined, 119
Vision statement, *vs.* mission statement, 119

W
Web sites, 91
Word-of-mouth (WOM), 104, 164, 166
World Travel and Tourism Council (WTTC), 8

Y
Yee-Loong Chong, Alain, 296
YouTube, 166

Z
Zero defects, 59
Zhang, Christina, 306, 313, 315, 317, 319
Zone of tolerance, 79